Group Politics
and
Public Policy

A. PAUL PROSS
Director, School of Public Administration
Dalhousie University

Toronto OXFORD UNIVERSITY PRESS

FOR CATHERINE

CANADIAN CATALOGUING IN PUBLICATION DATA

Pross, A. Paul, 1939–
Group politics and public policy

Includes bibliographical references and index.
ISBN 0-19-540542-0

1. Pressure groups—Canada. 2. Pressure groups—
Canada—History. 3. Canada—Politics and government. I. Title.

JL148.5.P76 1986   322.4'3'0971   C86-94148-5

Copyright © Oxford University Press Canada 1986
OXFORD is a trademark of Oxford University Press
2 3 4—9 8
Printed in Canada by Webcom Limited

Contents

Figures and Tables   viii
Preface   ix

CHAPTER 1   Introduction: Groups and Politics   1
What are Pressure Groups?   3
Analysing Pressure Groups   13
The Pattern of the Book   16

Part I: The Evolution of a Policy Actor
CHAPTER 2   Beginnings: Space versus Sector   20
Colonial Interests and Local Development   24
Centralizing Trends   35
The First Stages of Bureaucratic Influence:
Handmaiden to the Handmaiden   39

CHAPTER 3   'To Have a Say You Need a Voice'   46
The Age of the Technostructure   46
Group Politics During the Regime of the Mandarins   53
Power Diffused, Power Confused   62
(i) The Growth of Government   63
(ii) The Diffusion of Power   66
(iii) The Search for Legitimating Institutions   71
The Evolution of a Policy Actor   79

**Part II: The Analysis of Pressure Groups:
What They Do and How They Work**
CHAPTER 4   Function: The Context of Pressure Group Life   84
Interest Promotion   87
The Systemic Functions   88
(i) Communications   88
(ii) Legitimation   92
(iii) Regulation and administration   93
Conclusion: The Functions of Pressure Groups   95
Pressure Groups in the Policy Process: The Role of Policy
Communities   96

CHAPTER 5   Types of Groups   108
Power, Adaptation, and Bureaucratic Organization   108
An Institutional Typology   114
Institutional groups   114
Issue-oriented groups   117
Institutionalization of issue-oriented groups   119
Categorizing Pressure Groups   127

CHAPTER 6   Groups in Action: Influencing the Policy Community   130
(i) The executive   134
(ii) The lead agency   137
(iii) The sub-government   145⁻
(iv) The attentive public   149

CHAPTER 7   Beyond the Policy Community:
Strategies for Working in the Broader Environment   155
Influencing Public Opinion   156
Variations on a Theme: Adaptations in Pressure Group Tactics   165
(i) Influencing intergovernmental negotiations   165
(ii) Domestic/external influences   168
(iii) Using the courts   170
Conclusions   173

CHAPTER 8   The Interior Life of Groups   176
The Bases of Support   176
Group Types and the Availability of Resources   185
(i) Knowledge   185
(ii) Mandate   191
(iii) Wealth   194
Organization and Management   201

Part III: Group Politics and Democratic Government
CHAPTER 9   Models of Interest Representation: Corporatism   208
What is Corporatism?   211
Corporatist Trends in Canada   216

CHAPTER 10   Models of Interest Representation:
Pluralism and Post-Pluralism   227
Pluralists and Anti-pluralists   228
The Post-pluralists   234
Applying Post-pluralism to Canada   238

CHAPTER 11   Space, Sector, and Legitimacy:
Addressing the Dilemmas of Representation   248
The Representation of Space and Sector   249
Pressure Groups and the Revival of Parliament   256
Towards Equality in Representation   261
(i) Regulation   262
(ii) Resources   266
(iii) Processes   270
Group Politics and Public Policy   272

Notes   274
Bibliography: Canadian Pressure Group Studies   321
Index   334

Figures and Tables

FIGURE 1-1: A Funnel of Mobilization   6

TABLE 2-1: Historical Development of Canadian Policy Institutions   22–3

TABLE 3-1: The Stages of Legislative Development in Canada During the 1950s and 1960s   57

TABLE 3-2: Interest Group Interaction with Legislators   58–9

FIGURE 4-1: The Policy Community   100

FIGURE 4-2: The Canadian Farm and Food Policy Community   101

TABLE 5-1: The Continuum Framework   120–1

TABLE 8-1: Reasons for Joining Interest Associations   179

TABLE 8-2: Maintenance of Membership in Interest Associations   180

Preface

This book has three objectives: to expand the university audience for Canadian pressure group studies; to develop an analytical approach to the study of pressure groups; and to contribute to an important public debate.

The Canadian political science curriculum has been slow to accord pressure group studies the attention it pays to other major policy institutions. This is partly because pressure groups were not until quite recently prominent actors in the policy process, and tended not to attract the attention of scholars. In the last twenty years pressure groups have become increasingly active in public debate and more and more research has been conducted into their behaviour, structure, and role in policy-making. Readers who compare the bibliography in this book with the one I prepared for *Pressure Group Behaviour in Canadian Politics* (1975) will be impressed by the growth in our literature generated by this research. For the most part, however, this literature is discussed in the graduate seminar. The time has come to push pressure group studies out of that specialized forum and into the lecture hall, where students with no long-term involvement in political science, but a life-long stake in understanding the policy process, may be brought to appreciate the significance of pressure group politics in this country. Consequently the book introduces the reader to the variety of groups active in Canada; compares them with their counterparts elsewhere; traces their origins; and, above all, explores their role in our political system. It seeks to draw together the literature that now discusses Canadian pressure groups and to consider it in the light of internationally recognized theories. By taking this broad approach I hope both to encourage further interest in the study of the field and to extend awareness and understanding of the role of pressure groups in Canadian political life.

Pressure group studies have not kept pace with the changes we have seen in pressure group politics in recent decades, nor with the development of public debate. This is the case everywhere, but particularly in Canada—partly, I believe, because we have not developed the necessary analytical tools for a proper understanding of pressure group behaviour. As long as pressure groups are examined primarily through case studies and newspaper clippings, we will not grasp their real significance in political life, and students of politics will look elsewhere for stimulating research questions. Accordingly I have attempted in this book to put forward and apply an analytical framework that relates pressure group politics to the influence of the state in the political system. To some extent this aspect of the book is secondary to its other two objectives, but if it brings some coherence to the study of Canadian pressure groups it will not only assist the undergraduate student but will contribute to public debate.

Public debate is important because the growing influence of pressure groups in policy-making worries many Canadians. Though I cannot agree with those who argue that pressure group politics is inherently undemocratic, I am aware that 'sectoral representation' can subvert the representative institutions we have built over the last four centuries. It is not easy to harness pressure group politics to democratic institutions, but by striving to understand why pressure groups are necessary in modern industrialized democracies we may be able to avoid flagrant errors of repression and to fashion policies that strengthen other political institutions while taking advantage of the benefits of pressure groups. The perspective put forward here is not definitive, and the suggestions developed for regulating—and democratizing—pressure group politics do not address all the problems we can identify, but I hope they will contribute to a necessary discussion.

In a sense this book's three objectives are not readily intertwined. Since I have felt compelled to address all three in a single book, I have given first consideration to the need to speak to the general undergraduate audience. Rather than follow a conventional structure and introduce the student first to the theoretical and analytical concepts that political science has evolved to explain pressure group politics, I have begun by reviewing the evolution of pressure groups in Canada and the development of their relationship to the state. This approach reflects my own experience, which has taught me that students are more comfortable with theory and analysis if it is preceded by description. For similar reasons the normative discussion of the book is confined to the concluding chapters.

I began writing this book in the summer of 1982. The idea of putting together a book that examined pressure group behaviour in the context of the policy process was encouraged by the many opportunities I have been given to observe life in and around pressure groups; by discussions with group members and representatives, politicians, and officials; and by debating my observations with colleagues and students. These encounters have put me in the debt of dozens of individuals, only a few of whom can be formally acknowledged here. Some of them—particularly Peter Aucoin, Herman Bakvis, Paul Brown, Joe Jabbra, and Vince Wilson—contributed because they enjoy the lively discussion academics look for in their colleagues. I should also like to acknowledge with thanks the permission of William Coleman and Henry Jacek to draw more than once on their excellent 1981 paper, 'The Political Organization of the Chemical Industry in Canada'. Others to whom I am indebted were students, especially those in my 1985 class in 'Pressure Group Politics' who gamely accepted my decision to use a draft of the manuscript as their text. Their response to it helped me greatly to appreciate and deal with problems of style, content, and approach. I am extremely grateful to them, as I am to a class at Acadia University under Greg Pyrcz, who himself made useful suggestions for the text and debated with me some of the normative problems pressure groups pose for modern democracies. Three students—Steve Pinter, Chris Parke, and David Mac-Donald—helped me at various times with the research for the book. I am grateful to them all, but particularly to David MacDonald for his painstaking, and often ingenious, checking of my footnotes.

Several colleagues have read all or part of the manuscript and have given me valuable advice and suggestions: Tran Quang Ba, Alan C. Cairns, William D. Coleman, A. Grant Jordan, Terry Morley, Jeremy Richardson, and Mildred A. Schwartz. While I have not always followed their advice— sometimes because I preferred my own view but at other times because data or time or space were not available—it was in each case considered and always valued. The flaws in the work are mine alone.

A Social Science and Humanities Research Council of Canada Leave Fellowship made it possible for me to spend time in France and Britain in order to add a European perspective to the understanding I had earlier acquired of Canadian and American pressure groups. I prized the opportunity highly and can only regret that the recent cancellation of the Leave Fellowship program will deny other academics similar occasions for reflective scholarship. In Europe I appreciated the hospitality of both Jean Tournon and his associates at the Centre des Etudes Canadiennes, Université de Grenoble II, Grenoble, and Michael Rush and his colleagues at the University of Exeter.

As the book progressed to publication William Toye, Editorial Director of Oxford Canada, and his colleague, Patricia Sillers, gave me a good deal of the kind of guidance that every author needs but seldom immediately appreciates. I wish to express my gratitude not only for the thoroughness with which they tackled the manuscript and the problems of publication, but for the interest they have shown in the project.

Finally, I thank my family for their fortitude and tolerance as my struggles with the cycle of research, composition, and publication had their effect on the tenor of life at home. From time to time my wife's assistance was invaluable and her own observations of the life of one particular pressure group helped me understand why and how many of our groups act as they do in this country. I hope this book will be of use to her.

CHAPTER 1

Introduction: Groups and Politics

'It is one thing', Robert Stanfield declared in 1977, 'for individuals to pursue their own interests as they always have: it becomes a qualitatively different kind of society when individuals organize to pursue their individual interests collectively. National life has become a struggle for advantage among large and powerful organizations—not simply trade unions and corporations. Organized pressure groups abound'.[1]

Thirty years before this speech was made, pressure groups were of so little moment in Canadian politics that R. MacGregor Dawson did not mention them in his pioneering and highly respected text, *The Government of Canada*.[2] They were a minor feature of federal and provincial politics, insignificant in comparison with such major policy actors as political parties, members of various élites, senior public servants, provincial leaders and, above all, members of the federal Cabinet. By 1977, however, Robert Stanfield's concern lest pressure groups harm democratic government was shared by many who were familiar with the way policy is made in the federal and provincial capitals.

They were worried by the declining influence of political parties; the diminished role of Parliament; the growing power of the Prime Minister and his isolation from traditional influences in the Cabinet and the country; and by the extent to which policy-making authority was being delegated to the public service. In the shadowed areas of politics, where these changes were taking place, observers could make out more and more prominently the influence of pressure groups. As early as 1965 John Meisel had linked their rise to the decline of political parties:

> Pressure groups are often unwilling to permit their interests to be expressed and transmitted only by parties, but wish to participate directly in making their voices heard and their influence felt. . . Their numbers and means permit them to become rivals of political parties. These rapidly proliferating groups and institutions can gain access to the decision-making process without having recourse to parties which thus become by-passed in the vital area of mediation between individual and group interests and the state.[3]

A series of academic publications in the early 1970s helped delineate the activities of pressure groups and seemed to confirm the worst fears of

1

observers.[4] Thus Robert Stanfield's 1977 speech crystallized a growing concern. Between 1969 and 1985 private members proposed to the House of Commons no less than 19 bills providing for the registration and regulation of lobbies.[5] In September 1985 the Mulroney government announced that it would introduce a government bill to achieve these objectives.[6] Politicians and journalists criticized retired civil servants who had taken positions with consulting firms and other representatives of special interests.[7] To many this recent trend smacked of 'influence peddling'. Another eminent observer, J.A. Corry, warned that Canada was well on the way to becoming a 'special interest state'.[8] The Globe and Mail, which had published Stanfield's speech in its entirety, ran a series of articles highlighting similar concerns in the United States. Significantly, the series was entitled 'The special-interest disease' and it emphasized U.S. politicians' fear of ' "lobbyists" growing power'.[9] Inevitably, too, various institutes and groups sponsored conferences and research reports on the problem. The title of one of these expressed in a nutshell the growing debate: *Lobbying: A Right? A Necessity? A Danger?*[10]

These questions express not only the widespread fear that the activities of pressure groups threaten democratic government, but they also raise other fundamental questions. Why do we have them? What developments in the last two decades of Canadian politics have made them so prominent? Are they now essential institutions? If so, why? Again, if they are necessary, is it sufficient to point to the dangers they pose for Canadian democracy, or should we go further and try to devise ways in which they can be safely absorbed into our political system? This book addresses these questions.

We will argue that pressure groups are essential in any modern state, and that Canada is no exception to this rule. Furthermore, we will argue that the capacity of pressure groups for channelling information to and from policy makers can work to the advantage of society without jeopardizing traditional democratic institutions. We will even suggest that the recent proliferation of pressure groups has enhanced Canadian democracy, not undermined it.

This argument is not easy to make. Anyone who has studied the policy process in industrialized states knows that while it is a simple matter to demonstrate the functional importance of interest groups, it is much harder to show how they can live in harmony with the institutions of representative government. Nevertheless we believe that with an understanding of why pressure groups exist in the modern state, how they work and what they do, how they relate to other political institutions, and why—the problems they create can be addressed optimistically.

Two parts of this book are especially concerned with these questions. In the following three chapters we asssess our experience with pressure groups. We look at their historic origins and at how their roles have developed as those of other institutions have changed. Pressure groups are seen as 'adaptive' instruments of political communication, equipped with sensitive antennae for locating power. As other political institutions—political parties, cabinets, Parliament, and bureaucratic agencies—have gained and lost power and influence, pressure groups have adjusted their relations with them, expanding their contacts on occasion or letting them dry up. As Robert Stanfield and others have done, we will find they have indeed proliferated and their influence has swollen. Our historical survey will develop an explanation for their expansion that will be used in the last chapters of the book to give us insight into the measures that have been proposed, and occasionally implemented, to harness pressure groups' political power.

WHAT ARE PRESSURE GROUPS?

Pressure groups are *organizations whose members act together to influence public policy in order to promote their common interest.*

The chief characteristic of the pressure group is the fact that it tries to persuade governments to pursue the policies it advocates. Persuasion takes many forms, nearly all of them intended to exert political pressure on government. Most groups hope that the force of logical and well-prepared argument will be sufficient to convince reluctant ministers and skeptical bureaucrats that their proposals should be adopted. Failing that, many groups will look to an aroused public to persuade government of the error of its ways, as pensioners did when the 1985 budget proposed reducing their incomes. They may imitate the response of the unions to the Trudeau government's wage and price controls and withdraw from advisory boards and other joint activities, actions that can not only embarrass government but deny it access to information. They may threaten economic sanctions. When Indian organizations threatened to boycott Expo '86 as a means of forcing the British Columbia government to discuss Haida land claims, the tactic was considered by some to be more effective than the demonstrations that had marked the first part of the campaign. In theory, the choice of tactics of persuasion is as extensive as the relationship between government and the society it serves.

Persuasion depends on organization. Modern governments are not easily convinced. Persistence; extensive knowledge of substantive issues and policy processes; and the financial resources necessary to communicate with the public as well as with government, are all essential ingredients in a lobbying campaign. Common objectives must be identified, strategies worked out, modes of procedure adopted, responsibilities assigned, and consistent positions formulated if a group is to persuade government to take specific action and if it is to watch over the development and implementation of supporting policies. Above all, pressure-group activity must have continuity if it is to have lasting effect. These activities require organization, and it is the quality of organization that distinguishes the pressure group from the mob on the one hand and the movement on the other. The mob is an ephemeral thing, a product of chance. It may win clearly stated and immediately realizable goals. It cannot provide for the future because it cannot provide for its own continued existence. It lacks organizational capacity. In contrast, movements do exist over time, but they represent generalized progressions of public opinion. Organized groups participate in the progression, but the movement as a whole consists of too many distinct elements to be described as a coherent unit such as a pressure group. For this reason nationalist movements, for example, are not treated by most writers as pressure group activities, though we recognize that pressure groups take part in them.[11] Organization—the association of individuals within a formal structure—is, then, the second defining characteristic of pressure groups.

Organizational capacity facilitates a third characteristic: the articulation and aggregation of common interests. Formal structures and constitutional procedures enable group members to identify the demands they wish to make on government and to explore the conflicts that arise when the objectives of some members clash with those of others. Debate, though it may entail disaffection and secession, brings these demands together and eventually achieves agreement and support.

Other groups besides pressure groups possess formal organization, the ability to articulate and aggregate common interests, and a willingness to act in the political system. Political parties are notable examples. The fourth characteristic of pressure groups—the desire to influence those who hold power rather than to exercise the responsibility of government—distinguishes them from these other organizations. Pressure groups focus on the special interests of a few and avoid trying to engage the support of the mass public, a restricted role that permits them to complement rather than to rival political parties in the process of political communication.[12] The power they do exert is delegated to them by government and is narrowly defined. By delegating to professional associations the power to regulate their members, for example, the state acknowledges 'the political need to afford a measure of autonomy to those whose activities have been brought within the scope of the law', and admits that the state lacks the administrative capacity to 'fine tune' the relations between a professional group and the public.[13] Even so, the state can always change the powers delegated or even withdraw them.

Having defined what pressure groups are, we must draw distinctions between some of the terms commonly associated with pressure group activity. For example, the terms 'pressure groups' and 'interest groups' are often used interchangeably. The term 'interest groups' conveys a sense of the general, non-political activities of these groups. It, more than the term 'pressure groups', helps us remember that for most of these organizations political activity—activity carried on in relation to the political system—is often a minor and unwelcome addition to the concerns that have brought the group together. Unfortunately the term's frequent use in referring to aspects of political life that do not really involve pressure groups tends to confuse the study of such groups. Observers of élite behaviour may speak of governments' responding to pressure from 'the interests', without meaning to suggest that these interests have engaged in the type of organized behaviour under study here. Even though pressure group politics may have been a part of the activity to which these observers refer, the more important part probably has been an unorchestrated but compelling expression of individual opinion and the exertion of personal political power by those who stand to gain or lose through changes in government policy. Sometimes these 'groups' are categorized, or grouped together, by the observer because they behave in a certain way or share a common interest, not because they have developed the organizational structures we associate with formal pressure groups. Simply because consumers are said to want a particular policy, we should not assume that consumers' associations have lobbied for that policy. Again, organizations that claim to speak for specific interests may take positions quite different from those adopted by the interests themselves. Our terminology has to be precise enough to enable us to recognize such distinctions. Consequently, faced with a choice between using the inclusive term 'interest group', which is apt to be used imprecisely, and 'pressure group', this author prefers the latter, even though it focuses on a narrow aspect of the behaviour we are concerned with, and despite the fact that some feel it emphasizes a part of the relationship between groups and government that they find distasteful.[14]

Nevertheless the literature refers so frequently to 'interest groups' that we must find a way to distinguish among the various uses made of the term. We do this by dividing the entire spectrum of interests associated with any given public policy into three categories: formal interest groups, solidary groups, and latent interests.[15] We prefer to call formal interest groups 'pressure groups' and in general will continue to do so. A solidary group is 'made up of individuals with common characteristics who also share some sense of identity'.[16] What these individuals have in common may be sufficient to encourage them to vote for one another, or in one another's interest. It may foster enough group feeling to elicit a common reaction to public events, which may register in individual interventions in public debate (letters to politicians, for example) or in a clustering of group opinion in the polls. But in a solidary group the recognition of common interest does not extend far enough to bring about a formal organization that can consciously mobilize group effort to achieve policy goals. Thus the composition of the group usually remains vaguely defined and its political power and influence indeterminate.

Latent interests are even harder to define—both theoretically and in actual political life—than solidary groups. As the word 'latent' suggests, these interests have not yet been mobilized to recognize shared interests, much less act upon them. Nevertheless they have political significance. Policy-makers are aware that such interests are potentially able to achieve self-consciousness and eventual mobilization, and that once those processes are set in motion their political impact may be incalculable. Consequently politicians and civil servants are often anxious to identify the attitudes of those they judge to be latent interests. Opinion surveys are carried out, experts consulted, and media reports analysed so that policies are developed that are sensitive to the needs of latent interests.

These categories of interests can be related to one another in a funnel of mobilization:

Figure 1-1: A Funnel of Mobilization

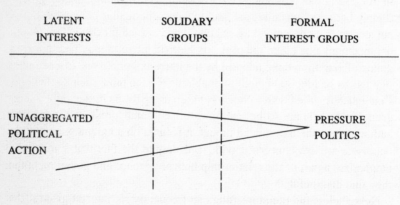

Latent interests are comprised of individuals and corporations with interests in common but with no sense of solidarity with one another. They may be extremely active in protecting their individual interests, but do not feel the need to recognize their mutual interest and register a collective voice in order to promote it. In the centre are solidary groups, which are inspired to a heightened awareness of themselves as groups and have moved, informally, to support one another. Their sense of political power is thereby increased, but it has not yet inspired them to establish formal associations to take political action. This occurs in the last stage when interest groups are formed and actually carry out campaigns designed to 'promote their common interest'. We should not assume, however, that because some people with shared interests have been mobilized into pressure groups, the entire interest community—all those who share, or are likely to share a specific interest—is equally alert and prepared to engage in pressure politics. Many people never recognize their shared interest, others are indifferent, some oppose the use of pressure tactics, and a few would rather act individually than join the particular interest groups that have established themselves. The variety and indefiniteness of individuals' concern for their own interests challenges both pressure group leaders and policy-makers. Group leaders cannot be sure that their members are either fully committed to a particular cause or represent significant portions of the interest community. Policy-makers want to know whether the group truly reflects the views of a significant proportion of the public and must assess whether the commitment of group members will enable it to take actions that demand a policy response.

Recent history has given us many examples of interests passing through the mobilization experience. Indians, while clearly a solidary group, for many years paid scant attention to their potential power. Since the Second World War, however, their awareness has grown apace and in the last two decades it has given birth to various Indian pressure groups, and their loose confederation in the National Indian Brotherhood and the Assembly of First Nations.[17] Ronald Manzer's account of the 1960s debate over bilingualism and biculturalism illustrates the way in which native groups, along with other language and cultural groups, became more and more conscious of their political interests and the need to articulate them:

> During the 1960s two rival perceptions of Canada became the subject of political debate. These were 'The Two Nations Theory' and the 'Mosaic Theory'. The first was expressed most frequently by French Canadians who saw Canada as a partnership between two relatively monolithic language groups. The second prevailed outside French Canada (and especially outside Quebec) and saw Canada as the home of peoples of many different origins working to form a new nation.
>
> Articulation of these perspectives during the 1960s debate over Confederation, and particularly during the hearings of the Royal Commission on Bilingualism and Biculturalism aroused the concern of two other segments of the Canadian community: the aboriginal peoples and Canadians who were neither of native origin nor English, nor French Canadian. The Indians asked 'Why is the Indian always forgotten? This was the first culture and this was the first language in Canada.' As for others: 'the Royal Commission found that the idea of Canada having a dual culture aroused particular fears among members of European and Asian ethnic groups. They saw themselves and their part in the development of Canada being forgotten in a dialogue defined as being between Canadians of French and British origin, and wanted more emphasis on the multi-cultural character or 'mosaic' of Canadian society. For them, "in the complex ethnic situation existing in Canada, the only kind of unity which can reasonably be striven for and achieved is unity in diversity: the harmonious cooperation of all ethnic groups in the Canadian country as a whole." '[18]

The major middle-class social movements of the 1970s—the women's movement, consumerism, and environmentalism—went through similar processes of mobilization, with vanguard groups, like the Consumers' Association of Canada and the Canadian Wildlife Federation, anticipating the change and doing much to bring it about.[19] Sometimes mobilization has occurred within unsuspected latent interests. The Rusty Ford Owners' Association came into being because one disgruntled owner of a rusty Ford was angry enough, energetic enough, and sufficiently persevering to identify a latent interest, whip it into self-consciousness, and organize it into legal and political action.[20] This group made legal history and initiated improvements in consumer protection for automobile owners. Another latent interest that has mobilized recently is the English-speaking population of Quebec. Perhaps because English Quebecers had for many years held a recognized place in provincial politics, only after their traditional economic and cultural position had been significantly eroded by legislation intended to enhance that of the French-Canadian community did they slowly develop a well-defined sense of solidarity and give substantial support to pressure groups that aspired to speak for them.[21] Property owners constitute another interest whose mobilization has been sporadic and, until recently, dependent on local conditions. Ratepayers' associations were a part of local politics in some cities for many years, but were virtually unknown in others. The trend towards city planning and the intrusion of large apartment buildings into areas dominated by single-family homes accelerated the formation of such groups, just as the introduction of rent controls and rental commissions fostered a sense of solidarity among landlords and prompted the creation of organizations designed to promote their interests.[22] As a result of the mobilization of these latent and solidary interests, political life in Canadian cities has become increasingly vibrant and dynamic.

Because the chief concern of this book is the behaviour of formally organized groups as they work within the political system, latent interests and solidary groups will not be discussed at length. Nevertheless we should keep them in mind, for the essence of pressure group influence is the sense (it cannot be more definite than that) in the minds of both group representatives and policy-makers that pressure groups speak for a significant part of the public, a part that can be mobilized into political action should its interests not be reasonably accommodated in public policy. This is at the heart of pressure group influence in the modern state; and, as we shall see, it explains why governments try to gauge the legitimacy of specific pressure groups and the strength of their mandates. Such assessments are not only useful in group-government bargaining, but also serve to protect governments from adopting policies that lack real public support.

We have separated pressure groups (as analytical units) from some of the other elements in the communications network that links government to the community at large, distinguishing them from social movements and from political parties, and showing how pressure groups are related to latent interests and solidary groups. We must now distinguish pressure groups from government itself.

As governments have expanded their activities and have come into contact with wider, more diverse segments of the public, they have developed a warm regard for the communications skills of pressure groups. Many of their responsibilities could not be met if these organizations did not exist. Consequently governments have not only encouraged many groups, they have often created so-called 'pressure groups' and bodies that some observers consider to be interest groups. This raises a difficult question: When is an apparent pressure group really a government agency?

We have already used our definition of a pressure group to differentiate among political parties, groups, and rather loosely defined social groupings. Now, in order to distinguish between genuine pressure groups and government agencies, we shall build on three other concepts incorporated in the definition: the concepts of membership, collective action, and promotion of common interest.

Membership—the willingness of supporters to list themselves as dues-paying participants in an organization—is central to the legitimacy of any pressure group. An association derives legitimacy from membership by showing that it speaks for all those it purports to represent.[23] Ideally groups aspire to include as members everyone in the relevant interest community. Trade unions and inclusive associations, such as the provincial colleges of physicians and surgeons, derive a good deal of their authority from the fact that they can realize this aspiration. Less fortunate are groups whose potential membership lacks equivalent economic and legal incentive to join. They must be content with some form of voluntary association—either self-selection on the part of would-be members, as is usually the case, or invitational membership emanating from those who are already members, as is the case in a few academic associations—and many seek to ensure that the group encompasses as great a proportion of its potential membership as possible, and to demonstrate that the group's actions have the support of the larger interest community. To demonstrate such support groups often take out newspaper advertisements that urge like-minded citizens to send postcards, telegrams, and prepared coupons to MPs and cabinet ministers. Policy-makers particularly dislike this form of pressure politics and claim that it makes no impression on them. Nevertheless its repeated use suggests that group leaders believe that a heavy volume of mail does convince officials that the group *does* represent the views of a much larger public. In summary, then, a legitimate pressure group must be able to show that it speaks for an entire interest community or that it can elicit the support of a significant part of that community. Membership statistics are an important aspect of its claim.

Government-affiliated groups, such as advisory boards like the Economic Council of Canada, cannot readily meet these conditions since they are frequently appointive bodies. If membership is neither inclusive nor voluntary, the group leadership cannot plausibly claim to have a mandate from the interest community. Consequently, on the score of membership the legitimacy of a government-affiliated group is in doubt.

Collective action also presents criteria that cannot readily be met by government-affiliated groups. Here we are concerned with the ability of the group, and particularly of its leadership, to act autonomously in the use of its resources. We cannot expect any group to be entirely free to deploy its resources in a completely independent fashion. Most have some patron or revenue source whose sensitivities must be consulted. Nevertheless a genuine pressure group should be expected to have a substantial degree of autonomy in choosing methods for promoting its goals. The resource-allocation decisions of a true pressure group cannot be overruled independently by an outside actor. Government affiliated groups—especially those supported by annual grants from departmental budgets—frequently do not meet this condition, since funding may be tied to specific activities, or may be withheld if certain types of pressure politics are pursued.

Group decisions relating to the use of non-financial resources may also denote the existence of a genuine pressure group. For most groups the quality of the staff available to them, and the manner of their deployment, are critical factors. In many cases groups with extremely limited financial resources have been able to make a disproportionate impression on public policy simply because their employees and their members have possessed great ability and exceptional dedication. It is therefore important for the group membership, and particularly its leadership, to have complete freedom to hire, fire, and manage its employees. Many government-affiliated groups lack this freedom. Because the resources generated by their members are insufficient to employ the quality of staff such groups need, experts are frequently seconded from the public service. Often outstanding in their field, these people make excellent employees, but because their careers are oriented towards success in government service, not towards achievement in the particular group for which they have agreed to work for a year or two, they cannot be expected to be as whole-heartedly committed to the organization or to identifying with its aims as employees of more independent groups often are. Again, the Economic Council of Canada offers an example. Its administrative leaders and employees are appointed from the public service of Canada. Even the chair of the Council has been held by individuals who came from, or went to, deputy ministers' positions elsewhere in the service. Many of its research staff have been associated with various economic ministries of the federal government, such as the erstwhile Departments of Regional Economic Expansion, or Industry, Trade and Commerce. It would be naïve to expect such people to criticize very vigorously policies they helped to develop, or agencies with which they might hope to be associated. Yet these are the people from whom the members of the ECC itself must receive the studies that will help it tender 'independent' advice to the Government of Canada. [24] For these reasons, we cannot call the ECC a true pressure group.

Our last criterion for distinguishing a pressure group from a government agency is that of 'common interest'. We must ask: 'Who determines the common interest of the group—the membership or some external agency?' If some external agency determines the group's common interest—and by this we mean not only the day-to-day determination of the group's common needs and goals, but its basic, long-term goal—then we cannot consider that group a true pressure group. Only if its goals are established by the membership—or can only be changed at the instigation and with the concurrence of the membership—can we classify a group as a genuine pressure group.

We have defined a pressure group as 'an organization whose members act together to influence public policy in order to promote their common interest'. Further, in the interests of systematic inquiry and practical politics, we devised a method for using this definition to distinguish pressure groups from some of the other elements in the political system—latent interests, solidary groups, social movements, political parties and government-affiliated groups—that at times act like pressure groups and may sometimes be confused with them. Taken together, these individual tests give us the following formula for determining whether any specific group is a full-fledged pressure group:

TEST	CRITERION
ORGANIZATION: Does the group possess a formal organization?	A FULL-FLEDGED PRESSURE GROUP WILL: possess a formal organization;
POWER: Does the group seek power or simply influence?	seek only influence;
MEMBERSHIP: Is membership inclusive of the interest community; self-elected from that community; or selected from that community by the existing membership?	derive its membership in one of these ways;
COMMON INTEREST: Is the common interest determined internally?	determine its own common interest and its own long-term goals;
RESOURCE USE: Is the group free to deploy and manage its resources as its members see fit?	substantially determine its use of resources autonomously.

We are likely to encounter some groups in the political system that cannot be said categorically to be either a true pressure group or a government-affiliated group. For example, Canadian Parents for French, an organization dedicated to promoting French language education in anglophone schools, might be one of these. It has received considerable assistance from the federal government, but at the same time possesses an extensive and dedicated membership. By applying the tests we have devised we should be able to confine these anomalies to a reasonably small number.

There are two important reasons for making this distinction. First, as people engaged in political life we must be able to determine the source of policy advice and weigh that information against our sense of the public interest. The legitimacy of policy advice depends on its source, or its quality, or both. The legitimacy of pressure group advice derives first from its source, only secondarily from its quality. A group that is known to speak for its interest community is listened to by government, regardless of the quality of the advice it tenders. Good advice may come from a group that is totally a creature of government, but in such cases it is the quality of the advice that gives it legitimacy, not its source. Such advice, however sound, is not useful if it fails to win the support either of the interest community or the public at large. A government that fails to appreciate the difference is at best running the risk of misunderstanding public opinion, and at worst trying to manipulate that opinion.

A second reason for clarifying the status of pressure groups stems from our need as social scientists to strive for clarity of analysis. In this case, a clear understanding of the relationship between pressure groups and governments has important implications for political theory and political philosophy. Some scholars have remarked on the blurred distinctions between agencies and groups, suggesting that because groups may exercise power on behalf of government or come close to exercising a veto over government policy, they in effect share power with government. Others point to the fact that government financial assistance and positional politics allow the state to manage groups and blur the distinction between groups and governments.[25] These scholars believe that groups and the state work together in a 'corporatist' system by sharing the power and responsibility of government. Their arguments will be discussed in a later chapter. Their approach is not adopted here, although we recognize that it is often extremely difficult to disentangle the respective roles of groups and agencies. This study assumes that ultimately the state alone has the authority to impose its will on the interest community. It may delegate that authority, but does not alienate it. Pressure groups may exercise delegated authority and they may be extremely influential, but their power and influence is held on sufferance from the state, which may withdraw it at any time.

ANALYSING PRESSURE GROUPS

A great deal has been written about pressure groups. Some of these writings have helped to create the philosophical underpinnings of modern American ideology; Bentley's *The Process of Government* and Truman's *The Governmental Process*, for example, articulated an understanding of pluralism that is still potent, despite being subjected to vigorous criticism.[26] Case studies also abound. Yet very few studies of pressure groups systematically and rigorously apply existing theoretical perspectives to the experiences described in the case studies. As one writer puts it, the student of pressure groups has 'a temperamental disinclination to define' and, not coincidentally, 'is less likely to start with a conspectus of political theory, than with a file of press clippings'.[27]

Canadian pressure group studies have shared this poverty-stricken analytical approach. There have been two basic difficulties: with a few important exceptions scholars did not until the early 1970s move beyond descriptive, historically oriented case studies, and they have not worked within the context of a conceptual framework for the analysis of the Canadian policy process as a whole. A third problem stems from the early uncritical adoption of the pluralist analytical perceptions of American scholars. While the majority of studies explain how Canadian interest groups carry on their activities, very few explain why pressure groups exist in Canadian politics or why some methods of organization are functional in this setting, but others are not. Only in the last few years have Canadian scholars, goaded by concerned politicians like Robert Stanfield, tackled important theoretical issues. In short, there has been little probing analysis of the roots and consequences of pressure group behaviour.

By the early 1970s only two attempts had been made to tackle the analytical problem. Engelmann and Schwartz, studying party/pressure group relations, approached their analysis from a communications and organization perspective: 'The aim of interest articulation is to affect government outputs. Any interest system must, therefore, be oriented toward the maximization of access to governmental structure and, therefore, be adapted to this structure.'[28] Their brief review concluded with the significant observation that there was 'a tendency among organized interest groups to transmit their demands directly to the governmental structure, and not to parties'.[29] In other words, the form of pressure group adaptation in Canada had tended to exclude the political party from the pressure groups' area of interest. Schwartz and Engelmann thus gave an early indication of Canada's susceptibility to the problems that concerned Robert Stanfield.

In 1973 and 1974 Robert Presthus published an important comparative study of élite accommodation in Canada and the United States.[30] Since Presthus defined élites in terms of the leadership of organized interest groups, this research shed a great deal of light on the activities of such groups in their interactions with the federal government and three provincial regimes. Presthus confirmed suppositions suggested by earlier work—notably the strength of the relationship between highly organized groups and administrative agencies—and challenged the widely held view that pressure group interaction with Parliament is limited and relatively insignificant. His was, however, a partial discussion of pressure group behaviour in Canada since it dealt only with élite groups and not with the many lesser groups whose influence, though individually minuscule, is collectively as significant. These aspects were tackled by the present writer in a series of papers whose argument will be expanded here.[31] Several later studies and papers also pursued these issues; and in a pioneering systematic study a team of scholars at McMaster University, in conjunction with a European group, have conducted an elaborate and exhaustive compilation of data about Canadian business interest groups with a view to estimating the extent to which this country has developed the corporatist state-group relationships widely noted in Europe.[32] Our study contributes to this growing body of systematic observation by building a conceptual framework for understanding relationships between Canadian pressure groups and the political system.

In order to do this, we must ask four basic questions: Who, or rather, what, are pressure groups? What do they do? Why do they do it? How, when, and where do they do it? These questions revolve around a central one: What roles do pressure groups play in the Canadian political system? To answer that, we must first decide how to describe pressure groups. There are many actors in the political system, most of them skilled in using 'pressure tactics' to gain power and influence. It is not easy to distinguish one from another, but it is important to do so, for their behaviour grows out of different capacities and roles whose differences must be understood if groups are to be channelled into directions that are in the public interest. Definition, then—the first concern of the scholar—should also be the first concern of the activist and policy-maker. In fact it is. For some years federal politicians have debated the registration and regulation of lobbyists, but have been stymied by their inability to define the term 'lobbyist'.[33]

Clear definitions are also needed to sort out the roles groups play. Our first impression of pressure groups is that they play communications roles in politics. They transmit demands from sectoral constituencies to public authorities and they carry messages, including demands, from the authorities to their members. Close examination reveals that they fill other roles as well. They help build public support for programs and policies. They even administer some programs for government, and they often engage in regulatory activities. This is not all, however. Critics of pressure group studies point out that because most writers in the field are interested in the political influence of groups, they forget that few groups participate in policy formation out of an altruistic desire to shape the goals of the community at large.[34] Rather, their activity is demanded by the interests of members: their first concern—their primary role—is to serve their members' needs, only some of which have anything to do with public policy. Canoeists form clubs so that they can share their sport with others. By working together they can arrange ambitious canoeing trips and learn from one another. They can also obtain discounts from suppliers. Organized involvement in public policy is not likely to be one of their objectives. Participation lurks in waiting, as it does for every voluntary organization—perhaps taking the relatively passive form of signing petitions for new public parks, or even lobbying vigorously to preserve or extend amenities—but it is seldom welcomed by members. Analysts, preoccupied with the influence of groups on public policy, often forget that the particular concerns of the member-ship figure more prominently than public policy in the lives of most groups. But it is essential to bear that in mind because it helps us understand the variability of the effort that individual groups will make to influence public policies. To meet the primary demands of members many groups ration the energies they devote to policy causes. Their role in policy formation is consequently diminished and that of groups single-mindedly concerned with policy issues is enhanced.

Once pressure groups and their roles are defined as precisely as possible we can tackle the questions of how, when, and where they play these roles and, most significantly, why they play them. The fact that most groups play public roles to promote their members' interests does not explain why the political system grants them participation. We need to understand the reciprocal benefits involved in order to discover why some groups are so much more influential than others; why policy-makers accommodate some groups but not others. By studying how, when, and where groups exert pressure on the system, we learn a great deal not only about groups, but about the system as well. Case studies teach us, for example, that the policy process is highly bureaucratic and that the most successful groups are those that know whom to talk to—and when—and are able to communicate in a bureaucratic fashion, with briefs, working papers, and professional consul-tations, rather than with placards and demonstrations. By classifying the information of case studies, we discover that different types of groups tend to follow predictable behaviour patterns that can be related first to what the political system expects of groups, and second to the resources that groups bring to the process. Case studies, then, help us classify; typologies help us find out why groups play the roles they do. By applying the analysis thus achieved to historical data, we can see how the roles of Canadian groups have changed over time and observe trends that are currently at work. We can also learn a good deal about our own system, and we gain valuable practical information as well, by comparing group politics in other countries. Concern that our pressure groups are becoming Americanized has brought much discussion and some inappropriate policies.[35] Comparison not only helps us understand that Canadian behaviour similar to that of American groups has different, indigenous, roots, but also suggests more temperate and constructive methods of containing and utilizing the immense energies generated by pressure group politics.

Once we understand that governments encourage pressure groups because they provide policy-makers with essential information, we stop calling for the elimination of pressure groups because they compete with political parties and begin asking how more representative institutions—our legislatures, in particular—might play a larger role in the communications process. We realize, in effect, that group/party competition is a symptom of a decline in the policy role of political parties and of our elected representatives, and not the problem itself. These and other examples will help us to see how a systematic, as opposed to an anecdotal, approach to the study of Canadian pressure groups will help us address the criticisms of them raised by Robert Stanfield and others.

THE PATTERN OF THE BOOK

We will be asking two types of questions: clinical and normative. Clinical questions are purely factual; they look for explanations of events and try to fit many different observations into a coherent pattern. Normative questions ask whether certain types of pressure group behaviour should be permitted, whether they promote or undermine democratic institutions. The book is divided into three parts, the first two clinical in orientation, and the third normative.

In the first two parts we investigate the environment in which pressure groups flourish. We explore the reasons for their developing in one way in some settings and differently in others. We review the part groups play in policy formation and look at some of the trends suggested by pressure group development. These discussions try to establish the facts about Canadian pressure groups: how they work; what functions they perform; who joins them; who runs them; how they differ from one another; how these differences lead them to behave differently in the political system; and so on. In the chapters following we will be concerned with the evolution of pressure groups in the Canadian polity. Our account will be descriptive, showing how early groups developed, the forces that influenced them, and their gradual assumption of a significant voice in politics. Though largely historical and descriptive, these discussions will lead us to make several more theoretical observations that will become pertinent when we deal with both conceptual and normative issues in the later chapters. We will be especially interested in the tension that has always existed in Canadian politics between its territorial dimensions (the need to represent geographic communities) and its concerns for the representation of specialized, or sectoral, interests. This tension is one of the most difficult problems facing all representative industrialized democracies, but it is particularly compelling for Canadians.

Part II will focus on the groups themselves rather than on the larger system that houses, feeds, and uses them. In the course of this discussion we will define the functions of pressure groups; develop an analytical framework; and build a typology of interest groups on the basis of their functional relationships to their members and to the policy systems in which they find themselves. Thus we will move towards the global picture we are seeking of the relationship between group politics and public policy. This discussion will not be exclusively theoretical, however. It will look at the practical problems faced by pressure groups and those who organize them, especially the problems of 'groups in action' and those associated with the internal operations of groups. A prominent pressure group leader has said that good management is the key to pressure group success. Much of our discussion will demonstrate the importance of his observation, though we will also point out some other significant ingredients. Part II will also elaborate further our functional typology, demonstrating how groups of different types vary their internal behaviour as they adapt to their specific resources and to their opportunities to relate to the political system.

In asking why pressure groups develop here, are retarded there, and why they do this or that, we expect that determining the dependent relationships between groups and their environment will guide us to a better understanding of the advantages and disadvantages they bring to democratic political systems. In this way our clinical investigation will help us respond to the weighty value-laden questions about the impact of pressure group politics on democratic government that are taken up in the last portion of the book. There we look at pressure groups from the perspective of the policy system as a whole: What do pressure groups contribute to policy formation? Are they necessary to the modern industrialized state? How are they related to other elements in the political system, such as political parties, the media, and administrative agencies that are also involved in policy communication? We conclude that they are necessary because in an era of highly diffused power the political system depends on special publics—we call them policy communities—to articulate, implement, and monitor the general will. Pressure groups contribute vitally to the life of policy communities. They perform functions that other institutions cannot perform. They are necessary. At the same time, they create a major problem in democratic representation, threatening to substitute sectoral representation for the geographically based representation upon which our legislative system depends. These two systems of representation can co-exist, but not as equals. History has determined that in Canada the state's legitimacy depends on maintaining legislative representation that is geographically based. Consequently sectoral representation, through presssure groups, must take second place to the representation of territory that is organized through political parties and manifested in our legislatures. Pressure groups must therefore be contained, and other institutions strengthened. In the final chapters we explore some of the available means of accomplishing this. Our dilemma, however, remains. We must contain and channel the energies of pressure groups without destroying the vitality and creativity they contribute to modern democracy.

Part I

The Evolution of a Policy Actor

CHAPTER 2

Beginnings:
Space versus Sector

Pressure groups have never been strangers to Canadian politics. In colonial days it was common for groups to lobby authorities in the mother country— whether France or England—for public policy concessions that would promote their interests.[1] A typical venture of this sort was launched in 1804 when a group of Nova Scotia merchants organized themselves into a committee to lobby for the maintenance of protective measures against American competitors in the West-Indies trade. For several years the committee focused its attention on the Governor and Council, but by 1811 it had decided to take its appeals directly to London. There the group's members encountered 'very great difficulties in promoting their applications . . . , the same being frequently neglected or misrepresented by persons interested in opposing them'. They soon learned the business of lobbying, however. Informed that 'the West India Planters were accustomed on particular occasions, to employ Special Agents in London to solicit their interests—being Gentlemen intimately conversant in the object of their immediate pursuit', the Halifax committee followed suit and was soon able to report, with satisfaction, that 'their success has . . . been answerable to their expectations'.[2] As long as dominion status fell short of complete independence, a number of groups continued to make the trek to Westminister. Presumably the intensive lobbying of British parliamentarians before the patriation of the constitution in 1982 was the extravagant finale to this custom.[3] For the most part, though, in the first half-century following confederation these delegations turned to Ottawa and the provincial capitals, rather than to London.

By the end of the First World War pressure groups were becoming numerous. The Canadian Manufacturers' Association (CMA) was by then well established and others, like the Canadian Construction Association, were being encouraged by government.[4] In 1932, when federal trade negotiators were preparing for that year's Ottawa conference of Commonwealth leaders, pressure groups were clearly a part of the policy process, as this comment by one of the officials demonstrates:

If it can weather this summer's meeting I think we can say that the Commonwealth has come thro' its most critical stage. I'm not sure it will but prospects
are more propitious than some months ago: . . . Bennett to do him justice is
as ready to bully the CMA as any other organization—and has already read
them the riot act. They have not taken his orders with very good grace but
have at least abandoned their first . . . impertinence of asking for further
all-round increases on the (tariffs applied against British goods) as a preparatory
'bargaining measure' for the coming Conference. The export industries—
notably lumber and mining—have organized their own influential lobbies
and are busy looking for concessions on manufactured goods to be offered in
return for preferences in the British market.[5]

Despite the patronizing tone of these remarks, they indicate that interest
groups had established a bridgehead in some aspects of policy-making at
least and that their views—though unwelcome—carried some weight. The
expanded role of interest groups following the Second World War, particularly during the 1960s and 1970s, has often been described in terms as
dramatic as those used by Kayyam Z. Paltiel:

The 1960s were characterized by an explosion of self-awareness among
consumers, students, women and native groups and in Canada by Quebecois
nationalism and ethnic group self-consciousness. These social movements
were accompanied by a bursting forth of clientelist groups created in response to
the elaboration of the welfare state during the same period. In turn, the
emergence of these new formations galvanized established institutional groups
into renewed action to protect themselves against the demands of the newly
conscious and to restore a shattered equilibrium which had previously operated in their favour.[6]

It was this proliferation of activity and accession of influence that prompted
Robert Stanfield and others to worry publicly about the effects of pressure
groups on the operation of democratic institutions. Although it is interesting
to note the extent to which Canadian groups have sought to influence public
affairs for many generations, it is more important here to appreciate how
much the development of interest groups has mirrored the evolution of the
Canadian state, and particularly the evolution of its policy systems. This
relationship will be the focal point of the present chapter as we trace the
historic development of pressure groups and present a factual base for later
analytical discussions. We will consider some of the underlying factors
influencing the evolution of the policy process and precipitating specific
pressure-group adaptations. The most influential of these factors are associated with the impact of economic development on political life, particularly
on the roles of key institutions such as Parliament, parties, Cabinet, and
bureaucracy. We will find that the evolution of pressure group behaviour
reflects the shift of power among these institutions. As an aid to understanding
these complex inter-relationships, Table 2-1 presents a summary of the historical processes to be discussed in this chapter and the next.

Table 2-1. Historical Development of Canadian Policy Institutions

PERIOD	ECONOMIC STRUCTURE	CABINET	PARLIAMENT
Confederation 1867	Interdependent but decentralized	Principle of ministerial responsibility established. Cabinet dominance developing unevenly across country.	MPs have considerable personal influence. In some provinces 'parties' are analogous to late 18th-century British factions, but party system developing.
Late 1800s to Depression ('Executive dominance')	Development of joint stock company ushers in process of corporate and economic concentration.	Cabinet dominance established. PM and key ministers in turn dominate cabinet and bureaucracy.	Party discipline tightens. Pork-barrel politics becomes a major preoccupation. Role in policy formation is more and more limited.
Mid-1930s to early 1960s ('Age of the Mandarins')	Considerable concentration. The 'planning system' (Galbraith's term) becomes central as multinationals develop.	Political leadership continues to dominate cabinet and Parliament, but control of civil service only secured through close co-operation of senior civil service.	Debates banal. Parliament is increasingly seen as ineffectual.
Mid-1960s to present. ('Diffusion of Power')	Concentration in economy increasingly seen as threatening, though necessary.	Cabinet and mandarin control broken. Cabinet re-organization (a) through committees, and (b) through inner cabinet & envelope budgetting seeks to re-establish co-ordinative control, but not fully successful.	Reform of committee system, recent creation of Parliamentary 'task forces' gives MPs opportunities to develop sector knowledge, encourages group attention to Parliament. Diffusion of power undermines legitimacy of cabinet and bureaucracy but benefits Parliament.

BUREAUCRACY	INTERGOVERNMENTAL RELATIONS	PARTY SYSTEM	PRESSURE GROUPS
Plays almost no policy role.	No institutionalized co-ordination between governments. Ottawa seeks to regulate provinces through disallowance, guidance of Lt.Gov.. Period of constitutional challenge in courts.	Decentralized. Local party organization competent to transmit sectoral and spatial concerns to centre.	Little institutionalization. Chiefly voluntary groups. Only a few (e.g. WCTU) effective nationally.
Develops expertise, but decision-making is still centred in political leadership. Decision-making tends to be *ad hoc*.	Some specialized intergovernmental agreements. Meetings of leaders becoming institutionalized by end of period.	Power shifts to leadership. Loss of local influence. Grass roots organization becomes primarily a 'fighting machine' for elections; dispenses petty patronage	Begin to develop institutionalized structure (e.g. CMA) but still predominantly local in orientation. Lobbyists prominent.
Run by the 'mandarins'. A small group of senior officials and key ministers has extensive control.	Responses to Depression and WW II accentuate growing federal role. Co-operative federal major feature of '50s and '60s. Provinces become concerned at diminution of sovereignty. Intergovernmental conferences (executive federalism) a growing part of policy process.	Party has virtually no policy influence. Below cabinet and senior levels main function is to dispense petty patronage, win elections.	More influential, but in tutelary relationship with bureaucracy. Some publicity-conscious issue-oriented groups, but most group influence exercised privately through sub-governments, contained government agencies, and institutionalized groups.
Bureaucratic pluralism—centre and line agencies tussle over policy dominance via policy communities, corporate structures. Lessened legitimacy forces more attentive relationship to Parliament.	Major policy increasingly made through intergovernmental conferences, which—as growing disputes suggest—may have reached limits of effectiveness. Relations beset by much tension as federal and provincial governments each seek key role in demand and supply management.	Attempts to revive policy role make little headway.	Increasingly active and numerous. Considerably freer of agency tutelage. Tendency to form policy communities. More publicity-conscious and more attentive to Parliament.

The table divides our time-frame into four epochs; each is distinguished from its predecessor and its successor by a major shift in the relations between the central institutions of public policy-making and those governing the economy. On paper these distinctions seem to be clear-cut, but in actuality they merged into one another. Across the table brief characterizations of the policy institutions convey their principal features during these development epochs. By making comparisons across the table and between epochs, the reader can obtain a synoptic view of a complex pattern of development.

We will identify the historic trends that have marked Canadian pressure group development. We will also examine the intervention of pressure groups in public policy-making from the colonial period to the present. A good part of this historical overview will be concerned with such issues as the contribution pressure groups have made to the declining policy role of political parties, the rise of bureaucratic influence, and the diffusion of power—which is one of the most important difficulties currently facing Canadian governments. A feature of the evolution of Canadian groups that will be pointed out here but explored more fully in a later chapter, is the tension between the sectoral representation of interests through pressure groups and the spatial representation of interests through legislatures and political parties.[7] Our legislatures are organized around the selection of representatives from geographically defined constituencies. Neither they, nor the party system upon which they depend, are effective vehicles for considering the needs of those whose interests cut across geographic barriers. These, whether they be hand-loom weavers or bankers, electricians or academics, have found it necessary to express their needs through pressure groups concerned solely with their special or sectoral interests. So easily and naturally do these groups ally themselves with the bureaucracies that advise the political executive that many public agencies have come to treat the pressure groups they deal with as a functional constituency equally significant—and often as influential—as the constituencies represented in the legislatures. Inevitably, as the representatives of territory and the representatives of sector struggle to gain their respective objectives, a tension develops that excites the criticism of pressure groups cited earlier. Because this tension is of great importance to the Canadian government, it is a central concern of the last three chapters of the book. This chapter and the next, which focus on the evolution of pressure groups, permit us to see when, and to some extent how, this problem developed.

COLONIAL INTERESTS AND LOCAL DEVELOPMENT

A colony may possess institutions needed for full statehood—legislatures, executives, and judicial systems—but in the final analysis the power to make key political decisions resides elsewhere. Early pressure group activity in Canada reflected this reality. In the most settled regions groups pivoted around issues of colonialism: trading relations between the colonies, the powers of colonial officials, and so on. Such issues mobilized colonial élites that—as the history of the Family Compact, the Chateau Clique, and similar groups suggests—were by no means unsophisticated in the use of influence. Because the British imperial system made no provision for the parliamentary representation of colonial territory, these élites turned to sectoral representation and became adept at sending delegations to London. While much of this lobbying activity promoted personal interests, some petitions did come from groups we could call formal interest groups, even though they were seldom more than convenient extensions of colonial élites. The Halifax delegation, which sought to maintain the navigation laws, was clearly an interest group of this sort. It and many similar bodies were issue-oriented groups. They developed from the constant need of local interests to petition authorities in the mother country about specific sectoral issues.

Colonial ties brought attitudes and institutions that encouraged pressure-group development. Robert Presthus attributes to our British heritage the fact that 'the activities of such groups are so deeply integrated into the policy-making system that no question of their legitimacy has arisen among observers'.[8] While we may not entirely accept this view, there is no doubt that during the years when our political institutions were forming and were most susceptible to outside influence Britain was herself experiencing a vigorous and lively flowering of interest groups. The crusade against the slave trade, the long and tortuous struggle to reform working conditions, the campaigns to improve public health, to give the poor access to education, to promote free trade, and to reform Parliament and public administration were all spearheaded by pressure groups. The leaders of the Committee for the Abolition of the Slave Trade, the Chartists, the Anti-Corn Law League and many other associations believed that it was necessary to 'raise an agitation through the length and breadth of the land' in order to influence Parliament.[9] Their activities were watched with interest by colonial politicians, and, though their concerns were often different, their example was followed in a variety of ways.[10] Robert Gourley, for example, whose campaign for reform riveted Upper Canada in 1818 and influenced the rebellion of 1837, was a British immigrant who began 'his plague of petitions against the tyranny of the poor laws' as early as 1815, two years before he immigrated to Canada.[11]

Less dramatic imitations of the British tendency to form associations could be found in every town and village across British North America. Intellectual concerns and governmental reform excited some groups, but the majority were created to meet more prosaic needs. In Kingston, Ontario, which for several decades witnessed the trek to the frontier of destitute, weary, and disease-ridden emigrants from the British Isles, the need for 'philanthropy' was ever present. Initially individuals and churches did what they could, but the tide engulfed them and in 1817 the Kingston Compassionate Society was formed to provide for 'the relief of the sick poor in their own homes and to forward destitute emigrants to their place of destination. . .'[12] This society in turn evolved into the Female Benevolent Society, which by 1829 found its work so extensive that it turned to government for help, securing a small grant in that year and £3,000 a few years later to assist in the building of a new hospital.[13] These were the first of many grants to charitable organizations, thus preparing the way for state support of health and social-welfare institutions.[14]

Today business interest groups are considered to be the most sophisticated of pressure groups, but in the first half of the nineteenth century they were probably far less well developed than charitable organizations like the Kingston Female Benevolent Society or the reading and discussion circles, such as the Canadian Institute, that were beginning to influence intellectual and political life in many centres by the 1850s.[15] The political impact of the latter groups was two-fold: they provided a forum for the discussion and dissemination of politically relevant ideas and promoted policies that would further the interests of at least some of their members. Between 1857 and 1860, for example, the Institut Canadien de Longueuil devoted more than a third of its meetings to issues in provincial administration, commerce, and the problem of emigration from Canada to the United States. Another third were taken up with local issues, particularly road improvement. In Drummond County between 1856 and 1868, and between 1879 and 1898, the Drummond County Mechanics' Institute and Library Association devoted twenty-seven meetings to subjects such as the repeal of the union of Upper and Lower Canada, confederation, defence, the Intercolonial Railway, and so on—but approximately a dozen sessions were spent on local matters. Since these groups counted local political notables among their active members and since prominent politicians were sometimes invited to attend special meetings—the member of the assembly for Richmond County attended the discussion of defence and a visiting Duke of Wellington was treated to a debate on confederation—we can assume that these groups played a part in disseminating ideas about the political issues of the day and in the creation of local consensus. In other words they were concerned with a *mélange* of spatial (or geographical) and sectoral matters.

In major centres it is likely that the chief political function of such groups was the development of opinion and the encouragement of political institutions. In smaller communities they performed another function, one more clearly akin to modern pressure group activity, one that reflected the need for state institutions capable of providing services that could not be administered directly from London or even from the colonial capitals: the active promotion of specific policies and programs. In Longueuil, for example, an interest in local affairs—especially local road works—clearly reflected the particular interests of members, some of whom were merchants, as well as the fact that nearly a fifth of the members held civic office. In Drummond County the educational goals of the Mechanics' Institute were much to the fore in its early years. Soon after erecting a permanent home the group rented part of the building to the local public school commission:

> The Institute having taken into consideration the difficult position in which the School Commissions are placed in [sic] for the want [sic] of a School House—and have no place to keep the school in operation—and the Institute being desirous of promoting the course of education that the following proposal be offered to the School Commissions by the president: that the Institute will finish the basement or understory of the Institute for the use of a School room to be left at the disposal of the School Commissions, paying to the Institute the sum of thirty pounds. . .[16]

As public education became widespread and as other forms of recreation overtook reading and conversation in popularity, these groups lost their vitality and died out. In their prime, however, they performed several functions still associated with interest group activity. By providing a forum for discussing public policy and a base for influencing policy—as in agitating for better roads and promoting education—they helped their members to understand the possibilities and responsibilities of citizenship. These activities also helped develop local institutions of government, for their meetings enabled local representatives to test community opinion, which often helped to build consensus and thus gave moral support to civic leaders seeking concessions from distant officials. Moral support of this sort translated into enhanced legitimacy not only for local government officials, but for the municipal institutions they represented. Thus we can see even at this early stage of pressure group politics a tendency for interest groups to develop a supportive relationship with the institution—in this case local government—with which they are most closely associated. We can also see the first indications that the political community was looking for ways to express sectoral interests—as in the Drummond County Mechanics' Institute's offer of a schoolroom to the public school authorities. For the most part, however, these expressions were latent or indistinct. These groups had not striven to develop a voice for themselves in any particular sphere of public policy; in general, they seem to have assumed that their range of concerns coincided with those of the community.

Other organizations did have more clearly defined and lasting public-policy objectives. Among them were the fraternal associations that came to social and political prominence during the industrialization and urbanization of the later Victorian period. The policy goals of some of these groups seem curiously mixed to modern eyes. On the one hand they promoted the ascendancy of either the Catholic or the Protestant faith, often violently; on the other, one of their important reasons for existing—and a source of their political strength—was mutual assistance. The most notorious of these, the Orange Lodge, which at times claimed 100,000 adherents in Ontario alone, attracted a good deal of middle-class, professional support that saw in it a vehicle for meeting. . .

> . . . a need for the kind of welfarism which was, in other instances, provided by Catholic Hibernian societies and 'sick and death benefit' societies organized by socialists in continental Europe. Orangemen had always been under the obligation to help one another. In some instances, this had meant joining in donnybrooks or helping guilty Orangemen evade justice, but it also meant finding work for a brother Orangeman, caring for indigent Orange families and, above all, providing decent burial for the deceased Orangemen.[17]

The Orange Lodge, along with other fraternal organizations and charitable associations, 'provided for social needs which could not be supplied easily by other agencies'.[18] As the state expanded its role in delivering social programs, theirs declined but was not abandoned. John Woodburn Langmuir, Inspector of Prisons and Asylums in Ontario from 1868-82, shared the general belief that social programs could only succeed if they were assisted by private individuals and associations. Taking his cue from British and American experience, he encouraged the formation of prisoners' aid societies and secured for them financial support from the public treasury.[19] Similarly the Ontario Royal Commission on the Prison and Reformatory System, which was concerned with the plight of destitute children, in 1890 recommended the formation of an association 'having local boards in every important centre of the Province who shall take upon themselves the important but delicate duty of looking after and caring for these children'.[20] Like Langmuir, the Commission recommended that the government should defray 'actual expenses incurred' by the association, which, as the Ontario Children's Aid Society, continues to carry out the function proposed for it nearly a century ago.

Businessmen also formed groups to petition governments for measures that would promote trade, or protect it. As the nineteenth century progressed, informal groups and *ad hoc* committees gave way to more permanent organizations. Boards of Trade, as they generally called themselves, coalesced in every important town, by turns advocating expansionary and protective policies. The Toronto Board of Trade was probably typical. It received its charter in 1844, though it had been in existence for some years before that, and it represented the newer merchant class in the rapidly expanding town. Its concerns during the 1840s and 1850s were those of a frontier business community:

First, it favoured 'development' of all sorts. Second, it sought 'freer' trade, an end to various restrictions and burdens which were seen to exist. Third, it desired greater ordering and structuring of trade, in the interests of clarity and security. These objectives were not closely and precisely defined; they were not always logically reconcilable; they were often not even achievable. Above all, the board desired further development, and it supported all projects which it thought would add to Toronto's hinterland and tighten its control over it. It welcomed government involvement in the achievement of these ends but preferred local control over such projects. During the [1850s] its horizons gradually broadened and shifted as the economy boomed and its ambitions grew.[21]

To achieve these ends it established close ties with Toronto members of the legislature, several of whom were members of the Board. On occasion it would organize meetings to drum up wider support for its views and would present resolutions to the Legislature, but 'it preferred to reinforce such pressure by sending representatives to call on members and ministers'.[22] This was a style of lobbying that Canadian business-interest associations pursued for many years.

Although the promise of the frontier and the development of Canada's resources—usually described as 'boundless'—excited extravagant visions in which railways, immigration, and burgeoning industry figured largely, and which could generally be brought about only through government action, business groups also wanted to protect their members from the rapacious behaviour unleashed by the ideology of free enterprise. Like the merchants of Halifax, who were anxious to perpetuate the protection offered by the navigation laws, countless merchants in Ontario's villages and towns sought to protect their businesses by establishing laws that would prevent some shopkeepers from undercutting their rivals by staying open late or on the sabbath.[23] The most adept protectionists, however, were professional men. Dentists, in particular, became very successful in securing legislative monopolies for their work and, according to one historian, by the 1870s had 'won a legitimacy in . . . Ontario [they] had not yet achieved anywhere else in the world'.[24]

The groups active in pre-Confederation Canada were first and foremost local institutions. Boards of Trade, which were being organized as vigorously and optimistically in tiny hamlets as in major centres, shared a name and had similar ambitions but were essentially oriented to specific communities. This is not to say that they were unaware of, or uninterested in, wider circles of like-minded people or sister organizations. A number, the Boards of Trade and the Mechanics' Institutes among them, were established in imitation of groups in Britain, the United States, and perhaps other parts of British North America. Their members corresponded with and visited their counterparts elsewhere, but beyond the local level organization was difficult and generally limited. There were four reasons for this. First, travel and communications were extremely difficult in the sparsely populated colonies. As the British novelist Anthony Trollope put it in 1862, Canadians and Maritimers 'seldom see each other'.[25] Second, the groups were voluntary associations in the fullest sense. They employed no specialized staff to carry out organizational chores or to forge links with related groups. To the extent that these things were accomplished they were achieved by individual members who devoted their own time and resources to the group's interest. Third, local loyalties often precluded co-operation between groups in rival centres. The Toronto Board of Trade claimed, at times, to speak for the interests of Upper Canada, but its members came exclusively from Toronto[26] and, during the 1850s at least, co-operation between Boards of Trade was the exception rather than the rule. On the one occasion, in 1852, when a convention of Boards of Trade was held, a squabble over tariff policy brought it to an untimely end.[27] Finally, pressure group politics could be decentralized and locally oriented because the greatest part of public policy was concerned with local issues and was administered in a decentralized fashion. The role of the state was limited. The great social programs that exist today were unheard of then and their precedecessors were entrusted to local charitable and fraternal associations. Economic and development policy, which frequently did have imperial and colony-wide dimensions, could not be addressed readily by locally-oriented business groups that lacked the cohesion needed to maintain a continuing lobby in London or the colonial capital. Even if that capacity had existed, it is doubtful whether it could have been effective in a legislative system where every member was a 'loose fish' uninfluenced by party discipline and bound to obtain for his constituency, and particularly his supporters, whatever patronage his vote would buy.[28]

As the nineteenth century passed the mid-point these conditions changed, and pressure groups changed with them. Communications improved, and local rivalries, though still burning across the country, paled in the stronger light of the ambitions aroused by Confederation. Confederation itself brought new national and political configurations. The state began its inexorable extension into the daily lives of citizens and its agencies started developing into complex bureaucratic structures. The trend towards sectoral representation in British North America quickened as latent interests became solidary interests and solidary interests perceived the advantages of organization.

The impact of improved communications is perhaps seen most dramatically in the national and international conventions that consolidated and inspired interest in a variety of causes during the closing decades of the century. In 1887, according to Richard Splane, a conference in Toronto of Prisoner's Aid Associations, presided over by Rutherford B. Hayes, former President of the United States, drew delegates from across the continent for a week of meetings that

> . . . gave currency to a number of ideas relating to child welfare as well as to corrections, and stimulated thought and action in these fields. In particular, it prompted the members of the Prisoner's Aid Association (of Ontario) to make the advocacy of penal reform a more important part of its propaganda.[29]

A succession of congresses provided similar inspiration to the forestry movement. In 1882 the American Forestry Congress met not once, but twice—in Cincinnati and Montreal—in the first 'parliament of forestry' in North America. The meetings 'served to focus all the hopes and criticisms that had been freely ventilated for so long on both sides of the border' and 'established a platform for leadership by outstanding forestry experts'.[30] They triggered institutional responses on the part of government and business whose effects were still felt decades later.[31]

These were not isolated events. Criss-crossing western Europe and North America, the new middle classes[32] were taking advantage of fast, luxurious railway and ocean travel, not simply to see sights and sounds previously accessible only to the wealthy and intrepid, but to discover a world of ideas and a host of issues that cut across political boundaries. The dehumanizing consequences of urban industrialization, the reckless exploitation of natural resources, the imperfections of democracy, and a multitude of other problems were to be found abroad as well as at home. Furthermore, like-minded people were to be found there. It became common for the leaders of movements in one country to visit and support their colleagues in another. The history of the temperance and women's suffrage movements, for example, is replete with instances in which Canadian, British, and American leaders visited one another, gaining inspiration and support.[33] It was a meeting in 1877 of the American Association for the Advancement of Women that encouraged Dr Emily Stowe to establish the Toronto Women's Literary Society, which in 1883 became Canada's first national suffrage association. The Chicago Women's Club served as a model for the Montreal Women's Club, established in 1891. The British National Union of Women's Suffrage Societies had some influence in Canada, and it was a prominent British woman, Lady Aberdeen, who founded the National Council of Women to promote the interests of Canadian women.[34] Across the spectrum of interest group activity—from reform groups to business groups, to labour organizations—this pattern of interaction and co-operation recurs, inspired by the discovery of common interests and made possible by the revolution in transportation and communication.

Paradoxically, voluntarism and localism continued to be important characteristics of groups during the later 1800s. Visions of reform or of business development may have been international in scope, or even global, but they were still to be attained through local organizations that influenced politicians at both the community and the national level. Most groups continued to be voluntary associations. Those with the resources to employ a permanent staff seem to have been rare. The majority persisted thanks to a dedicated core of volunteers; to the largesse of a patron; or because they formed ties with a larger social institution. The Women's Christian Temperance Union (WCTU) undoubtedly benefited in this way from its ties with the church. In Ontario during the 1890s the work of the Sons of Temperance, the Independent Order of Good Templars and the WCTU—which together claimed more than 40,000 members in the province—was vigorously supported by the Methodist, Presbyterian, Congregationalist, and Baptist churches.[35] Some evidence suggests that where church organizations did not encourage the formation of voluntary groups, reform efforts languished. Judith Fingard attributes the failure of the Quebec public to respond to suggestions for sailors' homes in part to 'the relative weakness of the Protestant middle class. It was the members of this group who were responsible for voluntary associations that promoted amelioration and social control in urban society.'[36]

The fruit growers' associations of Ontario initiated a new trend when they drew on government resources to support their organization. Most of these associations were located in south-western Ontario in fairly close proximity to one another. Their members were chiefly farmers keenly interested in the region's potential for fruit production. As local associations they could accomplish a good deal: they explored new methods of cultivation, developed new varieties, and exchanged information. But they lacked the capacity for concerted action on a wider scale—such as promoting the creation and expansion of the agricultural college at Guelph or disseminating scientific information from and to more distant communities. This was a weakness of another solidary group that had interests in common with the fruit growers and that was simultaneously moving towards interest group status. Its members were drawn from the forest industries, particularly from the lumbering and forest-products industries of the Ottawa valley and southern Ontario, where forest depletion had begun to have adverse economic effects. Led by several farsighted businessmen, these interests had established contact with like-minded Americans. They had participated in and hosted lively, well-attended international and national conferences like the Cincinnati and Montreal congresses of 1882. They had even created a national organization, the Canadian Forestry Association. But they too lacked an organizational infrastructure above the local level.[37]

Both the fruit growers and the forestry interests solved their problem by persuading the Ontario government to establish the Ontario Bureau of Forestry. Because it was small—staffed mainly by only one man, grandly called the Commissioner of Forestry—the Bureau was ill-equipped to play an operational role. Instead the Commissioner devoted his energies to promoting the conservation cause: encouraging local volunteer groups, particularly those interested in farm forestry; helping to organize exhibitions and publishing voluminous annual reports that detailed the activities of local associations and catalogued progress in the field. He thus provided, at public expense, the institutional support needed by local interest groups in the conservation-agriculture field. It was a mutually beneficial relationship; while the Commissioner of Forestry served as a sort of corresponding secretary to a loosely organized provincial association, the local groups who called on his services provided the political support needed to maintain his office. Together they helped to keep alive a number of policy concerns—reforestation, forest fire protection, the maintenance of forest reserves—that became central to twentieth-century forest management policies.

We do not know how many such relationships would have existed before the First World War. Our knowledge of both administrative and pressure group history for that period is pitifully limited. Certainly the kinds of groups served by the Ontario Commissioner of Forestry existed in Nova Scotia and New Brunswick, and offices similar to his could be found in several American states.[38] In Ontario, prison inspectors were ready to support the organization of prisoners' aid societies.[39] But in Quebec a different pattern seems to have developed: a preference for a decentralized state led the provincial government to entrust some aspects of administration to societies organized by the interests most concerned. Instead of creating its own agency the government encouraged Le Conseil de l'agriculture, representing farmers and colonization interests, to organize agricultural circles, or societies, and colonization societies. Similarly the government, instead of creating its own ministry of health called on doctors to organize the Conseil d'hygiène publique. These and similar bodies flourished until the turn of the century; they then gave way to government sponsored independent commissions structured to include representation from concerned interests.[40]

It appears that local voluntary groups represented the height of institutional sophistication for the period. They constituted the core of interest associations. National organizations with permanent headquarters and regular conventions were rare, though local groups seem to have corresponded regularly with one another on a provincial, national, and even international basis. National or provincial co-ordination—when it existed at all—was largely achieved by drawing on the good offices of a stronger social institution, such as religious denominations or, in some cases, the government. A reading of the history of the period suggests that most other interest groups were local in orientation and dependent on volunteer support.

All of this was consistent with, and can be explained by, the political economy Canada had developed during the nineteenth century. A limited degree of sectoral representation, much of it short-lived and issue-oriented, had been encouraged by the structure of colonial government. As Confederation was achieved, however, pressure group politics seems to have developed principally at the local level and seems to have been run almost exclusively on voluntary labour. Sectoral representation progressed only slowly. It represented a minor part of the political life of the late nineteenth century, even though some groups were extremely influential. Far more important was the political party, which was the great engine of political communication. This was the heyday of grass-roots party organization, when, for a few decades, systems of political communication were sufficiently compatible with the structure of the economy for elected representatives to speak equally for the spatial and sectoral interests of their constituencies.[41] Political communication in this period was based on the assumption that the private Member of Parliament, or member of the legislature, was the person best equipped to mediate between the demands of the constituency and the broad requirements of the national or provincial interests. This assumption had taken hold during the late eighteenth and early nineteenth centuries when our present institutions of respresentative government were germinating. They continued to be appropriate in the decades following Confederation because they meshed neatly with the emergent industrial fabric at the time, which was composed of innumerable relatively small enterprises—farms and resource enterprises as well as manufacturing concerns—that, though increasingly interdependent, were owned by local interests and were rooted in communities that in geographic terms corresponded more or less to the new political constituencies.

As party systems developed, the local élites who owned these firms found formal and informal organizations that surrounded the party in each constituency a viable tool for conveying their demands to policy-makers. Local owners might have boundless international visions, but their interests were still solidly parochial and could be safeguarded through particpation in constituency organizations. Because industry, though part of an interdependent world economy, was still locally owned, and because agriculture with its strong spatial orientation still employed a large part of the labour force, the heart of the party system was found in the single-member constituency. Both the local member and the riding association tended to be sympathetic to the needs of the community business leaders and could be counted on to exercise their influence on their behalf in party conclaves. Party leaders had not yet imposed rigid discipline on their parliamentary followers; they therefore had a powerful incentive to accommodate local needs, even as they grappled more and more with regional, provincial, and national issues.[42] In Nova Scotia, for example, the fate of provincial governments hinged for decades on purely local matters, such as the maintenance of roads and the introduction of municipal government.[43] The Lieutenant-Governor of British Columbia, Thomas R. McInness, was dismissed because, as Prime Minister Laurier told the President of the Vancouver Board of Trade, 'so long as he was in office, business interests would be jeopardized and . . . the province would make no progress'.[44] Ontario's Sir Oliver Mowat, at the instigation of a supporter, secured the passage of a Rivers and Streams Act four times, only to have each version disallowed by the federal government, responding in its turn to demands of an influential party member.[45] Sir J.D. Hazen, MP for Saint John, claimed that

> . . . he had boldly risked his political career for the city. At that time, Portland, Maine, served, under subsidy, as Canada's winter port for overseas mail shipments. The Beaver Shipping line offered to operate the service from St. John if it could get a federal subsidy of $25,000 annually. When the government procrastinated Hazen and his colleagues wired the government stating that they would resign their seats if the subsidy were not granted in twenty-four hours. It was granted immediately, and within a year it resulted in thirty-six steamers handling three million dollars in goods through the port.[46]

Such were the demands, and the power, of local interests in late nineteenth-century Canada. Thus, though organized and persistent pressure groups were becoming relatively common and a few had national, and even international presence, a decentralized party system made sophisticated pressure-group politics unnecessary.

CENTRALIZING TRENDS

As the structure of the economy changed at the turn of the century, a need for organizational complexity and institutionalization emerged in interest representation. A revolution in transportation was making the world more and more interdependent; less obvious but ultimately even more powerful, were the changes in international finance—particularly the evolution of modern banking systems and the emergence of corporate concentration—that were radically altering patterns of industrial ownership. It was now possible for provincial, national, and international financiers to take the ownership and control of firms out of the hands of local élites.[47]

Political communication was profoundly affected by these changes, which dissolved the symmetrical relationship that had grown up at the local level between the party system and community business élites. The new corporations and their owners had little concern for local matters—unless they impeded efforts to integrate and rationalize production or otherwise affected business operations. Furthermore, because they sought economic integration between geographically distant enterprises, the new owners preferred to negotiate with government officials who had some authority to secure public policies that would encourage integration. Cabinet ministers and senior departmental officials could do this, but not individual constituency representatives. Consequently the new owners preferred to approach government at its centre rather than at the community level. The individual MP or MLA became less influential, and so did the machinery of political communication that had been built around them—the constituency organization and, ultimately, the legislature. This decline forced local interests to appeal to the same key decision-makers who were increasingly being besieged by industrial moguls. Local delegations trekked more frequently, and with less effect, to Ottawa and the provincial capitals.[48]

The experience of a northern Ontario community illustrates this. Nipigon had grown up at the turn of the century around the logging and sawmill industries. These industries were composed of a number of small concerns whose individual demands for timber holdings were relatively small and were generally processed in consultation with local riding officials of the party in power. The advent of the pulp and paper industry changed that procedure. Pulp mills required long-term leases of timberlands that were extensive enough to ensure a perpetual supply of wood on a sustained-yield basis. It became quite common for them to lease concessions of several thousand square miles—often exceeding the boundaries of an entire constituency. Consequently the promoters of pulp and paper companies insisted on dealing with the centres of power, arguing that because their affairs were associated with the province as a whole, and not with any locality, they should bypass the local party machine in their dealings with government . Furthermore the spokesmen for these concerns usually, though not always, represented large corporations or groups of important financiers and were accustomed to dealing with governments rather than with intermediaries. As a result, though local political organizations occasionally played a significant role in the decision-making process, power came to reside almost exclusively in the hands of the leaders of the party in power. A letter of February 1926 to an Ontario MLA from a riding official in Northern Ontario, protesting the apparent allotment of three townships to a pulp and paper company, illustrates the impact of this development:

> When in Nipigon you announced the deal that Hon. G. Howard Ferguson has promised to the people of Nipigon, that the townships of Booth, Purdon and Ledger would be open for settlement in the near future.
>
> Nipigon as you will remember gave the largest proportionate Conservative majority in the last elections in your constituency.
>
> Is that the reason why the interests of the people of Nipigon *are first to be sacrificed* by our Provincial Prime Minister? Do you expect me as President . . . to be forced by unprecedented nasty dealings apparently going on with the knowledge of the Prime Minister favoring the Nipigon Corporation to the exclusion of everyone else—do you expect me to be forced to announce that Hon Howard Ferguson, whom I praised to my friends before the last election, is a man who does not honour his given word? If your Nipigon association can't trust in the word of our Prime Minister, can't have faith in the promise of the first citizen of the province, then who are they ever to trust in the

future? I sincerely hope that such despicable action has not been confirmed, as yet, and that you will find some means to prevent it, so that I will not be made a liar among my political friends, in having advocated the interests of the Conservative party.[49]

The corruption of senior party officials, never entirely absent from Canadian politics, became particularly prevalent in this period as powerful interests (some formally organized, the majority not) discovered and enlarged the authority of the centre. The Taschereau regime in Quebec, the United Farmers of Alberta, and the Ferguson government in Ontario all succumbed to corruption by major financial interests and were replaced, in Quebec and Ontario at least, by regimes that eventually followed the same path. The federal level, too, was touched by scandal, as Mackenzie King's difficulties with the Beauharnois affair demonstrated.[50]

The decline of local influence during the first three decades of this century was not confined to the forest and mining frontier. It also occurred in the larger centres where, for decades, the business community had used social clubs as convenient forums for conveying informally to politicians their concerns as individuals and as members of solidary groups. Two or three such clubs could usually be found in each major centre; they facilitated the informal élite interaction that was the essence of political communication in the late nineteenth and early twentieth centuries. The new political economy, however, reduced their influence. Most effective when they sat at the heart of an economic region dominated by their active members, they lost their usefulness when outsiders took over large portions of the map of their hinterland. The clubs could not help business élites sound out solidary-group feeling when important interests were not in any real sense 'part of the club'.[51] Nor could élite members use traditional informal methods of influence and persuasion when the increasing resort to bureaucracy and bureaucratic methods required that propositions eventually would have to be put on paper and subjected to formal review. The informal and social orientations that had made these institutions such useful vehicles for interaction in an élite-dominated policy-making system became outmoded as the élites themselves moved to a few international centres, and as formalism came to play a larger part in policy formation. Though businessmen's club still survive in regional centres, only the most important—Montreal's St James and Mount Royal Clubs, Toronto's York, Toronto, and National Clubs, and the Rideau Club in Ottawa—perform their original socio-economic function, and even their influence has been circumscribed by the introduction of bureaucratic processes into policy-making and by the shifting of economic power. Lesser clubs faded away, or concentrated on social features. The importance of clubs as political entities declined immensely in the first half of this century.

The diminishing policy influence of local élites and party organizations was scarcely noticed by the general public. The razzmatazz and glitter of the party machine prolonged the illusion of power. Party leaders caught the eye. Strong personalities, they dominated the headlines and appeared to exercise almost despotic control over their cabinets and officials. The arrogance and arbitrary behaviour of men like R.B. Bennett, Howard Ferguson, Jimmy Gardiner, Maurice Duplessis, and Mitchell Hepburn created legends, but also symbolized the changes occuring within the parties.[52] Power was accruing to the leadership. The grass roots—losing policy influence and becoming instead simply 'a fighting machine'[53]—delivered votes and dispensed petty patronage, and the centre of government, where policy was now made, became the focal point of lobbying activity.

Eventually these changes affected the representation of interests across the political spectrum. New institutions emerged, better adapted to aggregating special interests and organizing representations. By the First World War these institutions had established their presence in the policy process; boards of trade and chambers of commerce were becoming prominent at the national and regional levels, and sector groups were making their presence felt.[54] The Canada Grain Act of 1912, for example, was the product of much debate and of representations from various new groups,[55] whose appearance reflected a need for a higher degree of organizational development, of institutionalization. Interests that previously had been able to resolve problems or promote policies satisfactorily through their local member found themselves building more formal organizations in order to express their special concerns. As local influence declined, and as the costs of interest representation increased, community groups merged into provincial and national federations. Not only did amalgamation ease the financial burden of speaking to government, but wider representation enhanced both the legitimacy and demands of groups. Furthermore, they found that by pooling resources groups could hire permanent staff to keep an eye on government policy-makers and to take care of the day-to-day representations that seemed essential as administrative structures developed around the executive.[56]

The first of these more institutionalized pressure groups were making their presence felt by the turn of the century. The best known—one of the few that have been properly studied—is the Canadian Manufacturers' Association (CMA). As early as 1900 it was actively and continuously engaged in lobbying federal and provincial policy-makers; by the end of the First World War it seems to have become an accepted part of the policy process. Although in its early years the CMA found it useful to have legislative spokesmen, the growth of unions and other organizations with a strong popular base soon forced the association to try to exercise influence in other ways:

> The success of the Association, in the end, depended upon its ability to create opinions among the general public favourable to its policies, and to persuade members of Parliament and Cabinet ministers to translate those policies into

governmental action. Thus its really significant influence was exerted through propaganda carried on in the country and lobbying directed by its representatives in the federal and provincial capitals.[57]

The CMA's attitudes and behaviour offer an insight into the emerging pattern of pressure group politics. Even before the First World War the association concluded that its activities should be focused on the Cabinet, thus confirming the decline not only of local party influence, but of the significance of party politics itself. According to S.D. Clark, the CMA early found it desirable to avoid identification with any one party: 'The Association was interested in issues rather than in parties. "My politics today", said one manufacturer, "are my business." By concentrating upon clearly defined objectives, pressure could be exerted upon the Government no matter which party was in power.'[58] As the century progressed and interest groups spread, this non-partisanship became an accepted feature of pressure group politics. Even in Nova Scotia, where party politics has retained a vigour almost unknown outside Atlantic Canada, a tradition of group non-partisanship developed. J.M. Beck, writing in 1972, reflected on a long tradition:

> The province's pressure groups normally do not work through the political parties, or their members as such; they present their requests to the cabinet, in some cases through annual briefs. Sometimes the opposition takes its cue from the government's failure to meet an interest group's demands, but since the membership of these groups usually cuts across party lines, they are often reluctant to have their interests adopted by any one party . . . The exception to the general rule is trade unionism, which has been largely responsible for any success that the Independent Labour Party, the CCF, and the NDP may have had. However, the unionists, too, are pragmatic Nova Scotians, and they support the old parties when their interests seem to warrant it. Thus Nova Scotia pressure groups barely disturb the even tenor of the party system.[59]

Non-partisanship and the decision to focus on the cabinet were the first stages of the access-oriented pressure group politics that came to be considered characteristic of the Canadian system by the late 1960s. In Nova Scotia and some other provinces this style of pressure-group politics was associated with the long tenure in office of particular political parties.[60] It thus continued to reflect the general centralizing forces—economic and political—that were at work in early twentieth-century Canada. At the federal level, however, and eventually in the larger provinces, access-oriented pressure-group politics came to be associated with the growing influence of the bureaucracy.

THE FIRST STAGES OF BUREAUCRATIC INFLUENCE:
HANDMAIDEN TO THE HANDMAIDEN

Accompanying the centralizing trends of the first four decades of this century was the emergence of a new policy actor, the bureaucracy. Called into being by government's growing involvement in the technical aspects of economic development and by public demands for social services, administrative agencies expanded rapidly and were relied on increasingly for policy advice.[61] Their enlarged role introduced a series of new factors into policy proceedings that, by the 1940s, altered the entire process of policy-making. In the early stages of this evolution—the years of the First World War and the 1920s—the policy role of bureaucracy was limited, but gradually a few able senior officials—Adam Shortt, Graham Towers, Clifford Clark—won the confidence of the executive and came to exercise considerable influence.[62] Until the Second World War, however, political leaders seem to have doubted neither their own ability to 'work' the public service nor the soundness of their policy judgement. Bureaucracy was the handmaiden of the political executive. As political leaders absorbed the lessons of the Depression, and as the war forced governments more and more into managerial roles, policy-making became increasingly technical and a second generation of 'mandarins'—W.A. Mackintosh, John Deutsch, Norman Robertson, among others—acquired a prominent part in the policy process. In subsequent decades that role was enlarged still further, to the point where the influence of senior officials came to be feared as a serious challenge to the legitimacy of the elected government.[63]

These developments are mainly responsible for the proliferation of pressure groups since the 1920s and for their expanded role. We attribute both proliferation and policy influence to the fact that the administrative arm of government, in exercising its own enlarged role, has found pressure groups a source of both information and legitimation. We argue that as power has leached through the administrative strata of government the nature of the Canadian state has changed; and that as the state has changed, so has pressure group politics. We contend that these changes have centred, first, on the failure of institutions of representative government to accommodate both spatial, or territorial, and sectoral concerns in the messages they send to government and, second, on the political system's consequent need to discover legitimate means of expressing sectoral needs. Our presentaton here concentrates on the inter-war years and has two concerns: the effects on pressure group politics of the early stages of bureaucratic influence, and the relations between pressure groups and the bureaucracy when the significance of widespread administrative intervention was first coming to be appreciated. In the next chapter we see how these developments contributed to the diffusion of power that bedevils policy-makers today.

The first effect of increased administrative involvement in the policy process was superficially innocuous, but presaged change: the processes of élite interaction simply became more bureaucratic, requiring the standardization of rules; the precise delineation of responsibility between offices; and the recording of official decisions. As bureaucratic methods invaded the corridors of power, politicians, élite members, and leaders of groups became entangled in a procedure that was inimical to their earlier *modus operandi*. A word in the right ear was no longer enough; officials had to be consulted, regulations checked, and the dangers of creating precedents thoroughly canvassed. Whimsey, personal inclination, friendship, chance— all became less regular ingredients in the alchemy of policy-making. The written record, justification on the basis of law and precedent, and formal procedures of review became more significant. The friendly support of a minister or a senior official might be helpful and in borderline cases essential, but it could no longer serve as a means of bypassing paperwork and the need to 'go through channels'.[64]

The centralizing trends that were making their presence felt in the economy and in politics at the turn of the century also injected formalism into interest representation. Local groups petitioning central authorities found that the very logistics of their pilgrimages to power required more advance planning, and more organization, than had ever been needed in the days of local consultation with the local member. As well, the increasingly centralized decision-making process was inherently less sensitive to the realities of local situations and the nuances of local power structures. Ministers and their advisers had difficulty evaluating delegations and the significance of their demands. More had to be explained; more had to be written down. Groups had to establish their credentials to prove that they spoke for responsible opinion in the community. In other words, they had to establish their legitimacy, which had seldom been necessary when their demands had been addressed through politically sensitive local members. All of this encouraged the formation of formal groups. Formal organization made it easier to prepare delegations, to put together briefs, to orchestrate the adoption of weighty and impressive resolutions and, above all, to demonstrate that the group was properly representative of the community; that its demands were legitimate.[65] The formal structure of the interest group was becoming a factor in its negotiations with government. As a result local interests were gradually forced to make the transition from solidary to interest group status.

Bureaucracy begat bureaucracy. To deal with the burgeoning agencies of government, pressure groups found themselves establishing their own offices and filling them with permanent officials. In some cases a spiral of institutionalization developed. As the permanent staff of pressure groups took up their positions, they found that their work exposed new fields for policy development. Thus the administration of collective agreements led unions to monitor not only remuneration, hours of work and conditions surrounding hiring and firing, but also conditions of work, workmen's compensation, the employment of women and juveniles, and so on. Anomalies and abuses were brought to the attention of government, and as government responded it also expanded to take on the new work-loads. As it expanded, so did the union organizations, for there was always more to monitor and always room for improvement in the conditions of work.[66] Similar spirals of institutionalization developed in many fields, though not, in most cases, until after the Second World War. The basic framework for the explosion of the policy-making system that followed 1945 was created in the inter-war years.

This spiral of institutionalization fed on a fundamental characteristic of bureaucracy: its capacity for differentiating function; that is, for dividing up work and assigning responsibility for specific tasks to different groups within the administrative organization. As each unit develops to meet its responsibilities, it also tends to divide up its work and create a more elaborate organizational structure. These tendencies are mirrored in the pressure group world, since each separate government agency strikes up a liaison with the parts of the public it serves, deriving from the relationship information facilities, administrative assistance, and a source of support in its dealings with other parts of the bureaucracy—and ultimately with the political environment. In other words, the handmaiden to government needed a handmaiden of her own and, in the policy system emerging in Canada between the wars, found that pressure groups admirably filled the role. It is from that time that we date an increased tendency for government officials to encourage special publics to develop their own organizational structures in order to facilitate these supportive relationships and to benefit both themselves and their bureaucratic partners. H.H. Hannam, president and managing director of the Canadian Federation of Agriculture, was encouraged in just this fashion by the Deputy Minister of Finance, during a discussion of the need for agricultural representation on the first board of directors of the Bank of Canada:

> In the course of our early remarks, Dr. Clark said to me, 'We want to get one representative of agriculture . . . We want to do that, the government wants to do that, and we are soliciting your help.' He went on to say, 'You have not a national organization representing agriculture, have you, which is a national interest group?' I said, 'No, we have not.' He said, 'It is too bad, isn't it?' That was a remark I will never forget. I used it quite often in the days when we were organizing the Federation. . . . , that was the early part of 1935. We started and organized our Federation in the fall that same year.[67]

Thus was the development of formal interest groups encouraged.

Overtly political activity was not necessarily the first goal of this encouragement. Interest groups can perform, for example, para-administrative functions, which cannot be as effectively achieved through the myriad unorchestrated contacts that take place between agencies and the public at large. The great flow of immigration to Canada in the first half of the twentieth century could not have been handled by government officials working alone. Local and national groups were needed to greet immigrants at the docks, to provide translation services, to help them through the first formalities, and to start them on their way across the country. Other groups were needed at major railway stops to guide the newcomers to their proper destinations, to make medical help available, to explain what was happening. Still more were needed in the settlement areas as the immigrants selected and began to work their new lands.[68]

Some of the information-channelling activities of groups were also non-political and have been used by agencies to facilitate administrative work. Vincent Lemieux points out that the 'relayers' or popularizers of information, whether independent journalists or groups associated with particular agencies, play an important role in transmitting and translating data to the public. In André Holleaux's phrase 'l'association décode les messages administratifs et les recode dans le langage du public.'[69]

Interest groups, however, also perform semi-political functions that make them valuable allies of government agencies. They aggregate demand, they channel information, and they legitimize both the demands they make and the agencies that respond to them. Demand aggregation, for example, has been particularly important in industries where medium-to-small labour-intensive firms predominate—the textile, fishing, and many service industries, to name a few. Such industries could express their needs effectively to government agencies only if they possessed formal organizational structures and procedures for discussing and reconciling their many divergent points of view; without them government received a flood of conflicting advice and was often at the mercy of the few interests who could command attention.[70] During the interwar years, Canadian bureaucrats and politicians discovered that those structures and procedures could be provided through interest associations.

The work of interest associations to canvass demands, and to reconcile conflicting ones, within special publics also served the double purpose of enhancing both the legitimacy of group demands and the policy proposals agencies developed to satisfy them. An administrative proposal reflecting group-agency consultation and clearly having group support was more likely to win ministerial approval than one that could be described as merely a department project. Furthermore, an agency that clearly had the support of the groups most affected by its work would also gain in stature. Finally, such support represented a counterpoise to the legitimacy of elected representatives. It permitted officials to claim that they too had a constituency—a functional one. It is no accident that officials often refer to their client groups as 'constituencies'.

These trends were developing throughout the inter-war years, though they could be perceived only dimly. S.D. Clark in his study of the CMA, gives an illustration:

> The development of lobby organizations by the Manufacturers' Association and other organized groups indicated the growth of a functional representative system outside the formally constituted machinery of government. Cutting across

the boundaries of constituencies and provinces to give representation to groups organized upon the basis of common interests, the lobbyists expressed, more completely perhaps than members of Parliament, the diversified needs of the national community. They found it unnecessary to compromise principles or modify demands to meet the wishes of a great variety of groups.[71]

Not surprisingly, administrative agencies not only encouraged group participation in the policy process, they began actively promoting the creation of special-interest groups. We noted an instance of this in 1873, when the Ontario Inspector of Prisons and Asylums recommended the establishment of prisoners' aid societies, but the practice seems to have become more common during the First World War. The official history of the Department of Trade and Commerce records, for example, that during the war years the department 'adopted a policy of encouraging the organization of industry-wide associations to seek out orders for their member companies. . .'[72] Similarly N.J. Lawrie writes that at the end of the war the federal government, concerned with reconstruction, 'sought the close co-operation of industry. This it believed, could best be fostered by dealing with associations representing industry's various components, and it was consequently desirous of having as many national organizations as possible. . .' He quotes A.K. MacLean, chairman of the Reconstruction Committee of the Privy Council, stating that if the founding meeting of the Canadian Construction Association had not already been planned ' "I had myself intended requesting such a gathering." As it was, various federal officials attended the meeting, urged collaboration and promised government cooperation.'[73]

Thus was entrenched a practice that has continued to the present day. In the 1930s it contributed to the founding of the Canadian Federation of Agriculture and in the Second World War to the development of the Consumers' Association of Canada. Early in the Trudeau administration there was a spate of pressure group formation as new co-ordinative agencies, such as the Ministry of State for Urban Affairs and the Department of Regional Economic Expansion, sought grass-roots reinforcement for policies of social and economic change.[74] Romeo LeBlanc, from the beginning of his period as Minister of Fisheries, devoted a great deal of time, effort, and regulatory encouragement to persuading the independent fishermen of the east coast to organize themselves. 'If I had to write the manual for dealing with government,' he told one group in 1978, 'I would put two main rules of the road: carry a flag—that is, have an organization—and sound your horn. Let people know you are there.'[75]

Though the sponsorship of pressure groups by government agencies was not entirely new, and though the practice was by no means as common in the inter-war years as it has since become,[76] its increased occurrence was symbolic. It indicated that even though the role of pressure groups in policy-making was still modest, and groups were very much under the tutelage of the state, they were acquiring a more significant role in the policy process. Since the beginning of the century many Canadian interest groups had become national and regional institutions. Responding to the centralizing influences of the concentration of economic and political power, they had grown beyond the local organizations that had given them their character during the nineteenth century. They had also acquired full-time professional staff, which equipped them to deal on a continuing basis with the bureaucracies that were becoming increasingly influential in the Canadian state. Local organizations continued to exist and volunteer labour was still the life-blood of most groups, but a growing number of interest associations now possessed the capacity and the stature to participate regularly in national and provincial policy debates and to work on a daily basis with officials as they implemented government programs.

The expansion of pressure group activity in the first third of the twentieth century sprang from two related but somewhat distinct causes. On the one hand it was inspired by public realization that the most efficacious route to influencing public policy lay along the path of interest group organization. On the other, the state itself, finding its own tasks more numerous and complex, concluded that group participation sometimes facilitated policy formation and program implementation. Working generally through its administrative arm, but occasionally through its political arm, the state consequently encouraged group formation. Fundamentally both of these trends originated in the changing structure of the economy and its closer relationship with the state. In the next chapter we will examine these changes and look at how, during and after the Second World War, they precipitated the re-alignments of policy-making institutions that we now associate with the diffusion of power and that have brought pressure groups close to the centre of our policy-making system.

CHAPTER 3

'To Have a Say, You Need a Voice'

Dramatic changes have taken place in Canadian pressure groups since the Second World War. They have become more numerous, more public, and more attentive to Parliament. Above all, they have come to occupy a more influential—and controversial—role in the policy process. This transition is rooted broadly in the changing relationship between government and the economy in the modern state, and more specifically in the expansion of bureaucratic influence and in the declining policy role of political parties. Hence, to understand how and why pressure groups have changed so much in recent decades, we must first review the transformations that have taken place in the role of the state and its policy-making institutions.

This chapter will show how business and political leaders came to depend on their professional advisers during the twenties and thirties and how that dependence precipitated a shift of policy-making capacity from the political executive to the middle ranks of the bureaucracy and its affiliated groups. Since pressure groups are adaptive instruments of political communication, we will not suggest that this change was the consequence of group action, but rather that groups have for the most part responded to the evolution of central institutions in the policy system. Thus we will contend that the growth of government, with its inevitable elaboration of specialized bureaucracies, has precipitated a diffusion of power. That is, that the authority of the political and administrative executive has dissipated, leaching down into the middle ranks of the bureaucracy. The diffusion of power, we suggest, has transformed the methods used by government agencies to compete for resources and has forced them to look beyond the traditional relationships between Cabinet, bureaucracy, and Parliament in order to secure legitimacy for government policy. These two developments have been instrumental in bringing about the most recent changes in pressure group politics, especially a renewal of pressure group interest in Parliament—and possibly a revival of parliamentary influence in policy making.

THE AGE OF THE TECHNOSTRUCTURE

By the late thirties governments had become equal partners with the private sector in the management of the economy. Governments had become involved

46

in management because contemporary economies cannot function effectively without a harmonious intermeshing of the human skills and physical resources needed to produce goods and bring them to market. Though this is achieved largely through the self-adjusting mechanisms of the market itself, the organizing ability of government is necessary to ensure that resources flow to industry as and where they are needed and that the economy can sustain demand for the goods produced. In other words, government plays an essential role in demand and supply management.[1] A second reason for government's management function is that public-sector intervention is required if the world's depleting natural resources are to be prolonged effectively.

The evolution of this new role for government was related to the development of modern business organization which, as we have seen, radically changed the character of public policy-making in the late nineteenth century. As corporations in the twentieth century sought to integrate geographically distant resources, complex technologies, and sophisticated human skills, they became increasingly dependent on government to organize and manage the supply of resources to enterprises, and even to take a hand in the regulation of demand. Again, the forest industries provide a good illustration of these needs.[2] In Ontario, New Brunswick, and Quebec in particular, but to a lesser extent in other provinces, traditional lumbering gave way to pulp-and-paper operations. These enterprises could not be built around the principle of 'cut out and get out', which many lumber barons had been applying. They involved huge expenditures on plant and machinery and, to some extent, on the hiring of a skilled labour force. Capital expenditures had to be amortized over decades, not years. This meant that companies had to be supplied with forest reserves that could be made to last for a very long time indeed—preferably 'in perpetuity'. Even these vast tracts, however, would prove inadequate unless they were managed. Governments, which for the most part owned the forest resource and were in any case anxious to encourage its development, were drawn into co-operation with business to address the problems of forest management.

Each province handled the situation differently. Nova Scotia and to some extent Quebec, gave the companies virtually a free hand to develop and apply their own management plans. Other provinces, like Ontario, tried to monitor the companies' use of the forest. All took a growing part in the management process, first through forest protection work, then through reforestation programs, and ultimately in direct forest management. Nor was supply management confined to the resource itself. The companies needed large amounts of electricity, a need they sometimes met themselves but that was often provided through government-owned corporations such as Ontario Hydro, B.C. Power, and Hydro Quebec. The demand for human resources—for instance, competent people to carry out forest maintenance and protection work—was also met in part through government action. Forest ranger schools were established in several provinces, largely at public expense. At a more senior level, both private and public sectors also required professionals capable of supervising forest management and developing forest policy. By the 1920s Quebec, Ontario, and New Brunswick had each established university-level professional training programs to meet this need. The cycle of business-government interaction did not end there. Government also had to take a hand when transportation infrastructure was needed to get pulp and paper to market; when demand management became significant, and favourable tariffs had to be negotiated. Some provinces forbade the export of pulpwood and wood pulp in an attempt to protect the markets of companies manufacturing paper in Canada. At the height of the Depression the Ontario and Quebec governments became deeply involved in rationing demand among surviving companies—it was the only way to keep most of them in business. Such examples of government intervention can be replicated, in differing forms, in the context of any modern industry. In aviation or fishing; atomic energy or automobile production; brewing, baking and possibly even candle making—government's role in supply or demand management has become essential and pervasive because government is generally the only actor possessing sufficient authority to orchestrate the flow of resources to business or to harmonize demand.

In addition, there are times when government alone can help the community at large cope with many of the consequences—the externalities—of business activity. For example, the exploitation of any new resource or new technology involves social, environmental, and economic costs that can be met only through the careful management of other existing resources. Tapping the oil reserves of the Beaufort Sea involves enormous expenditures of public and private money, serious problems of environmental degradation, and the disruption of regional societies.[3] Likewise technological change alters many aspects of social and economic life. Though some of these changes will occur regardless of government intervention, most will generate some kind of public debate and government intervention. Communities that expand too rapidly will demand infusions of public moneys to maintain equilibrium; other communities, pushed into decline, will demand similar support to prevent, or at least to mitigate, the attendant human misery. In either pattern of development government will be deeply involved in the calculation and use of public resources, and in the channelling of private sector energies.[4]

These examples underline the high level of interdependence that was becoming increasingly central to state-business relations during the interwar years and that has a determining effect today on public policy-making. To cope with interdependence, government and industry needed a much more sophisticated system of policy communication than had been created by business and political leaders in the early part of this century. The need was met through the creation of what J.K. Galbraith has called the 'technostructure'—a sophisticated communications network of technically proficient specialists that cuts across the lines dividing government and business and in which technical knowledge is the currency of power.[5] The technostructure, so far as the development and implementation of public policy is concerned, is the lace that ties the shoe. Through its network of professional relationships it pulls together the complementary capacities of government and business. It is strong because it works at virtually all levels of both systems; all participants speak a common specialized language, and its operations are largely informal. The technostructure enables the two sectors to make both large-scale policy and the day-to-day adjustments necessary to implement it, and in so doing has made possible the evolution of the modern economy.

At the same time the technostructure has exacted a heavy price from democratic institutions, because it fostered the dominance of technical competence in the policy process. It did this in three ways. First, in Gerard Timsit and Céline Wiener's words, it 'short-circuited' traditional institutions of political representation.[6] Second, it changed the language of policy-making in a fashion that excluded lay people, including politicians. Third, in promoting neutral competence it denigrated political participation in both administration and policy-making and substituted for it technical expertise.

Only to a very limited degree did these actions reflect conscious attempts on the part of technical experts to exclude the political element from policy and administration. For the most part these patterns emerged informally and grew out of the situations in which specialists were working. Technical advisers and officials in government came to bypass elected policy-makers and spoke directly with technicians in corporations and social institutions because they shared a common knowledge base, spoke a shared language, and often genuinely believed that the problems they discussed and resolved were 'technical' and not 'political'.[7] Only when they were looked at in their totality would it become clear that these informal, low-level exchanges between technicians created a framework of understandings and petty decisions that allowed the 'policy-maker' no freedom of action.

The effect of changes in the language of policy-making was equally unintentional but just as devastating.[8] The language of public sector-private sector discussion became detailed and technical. In forest administration, for example, lumber barons increasingly found themselves negotiating with professional foresters whose concerns, and language, were entirely different from those of the party bosses. The bosses were concerned with jobs for the faithful and contributions to the party. The new forestry officials were steeped in the science of 'silviculture' and were conversant with the 'growth cycles' and 'succession' of trees. They allocated cutting rights according to 'forest management plans' that were based on 'forest inventories' and they insisted that lumbering 'operations' should be carried out in a fashion that promoted 'regeneration'. They even spoke of 'wood fibre' instead of trees.[9] The traditional party system could not cope with the new language; nor— except on rare occasions—could political leaders master its intricacies. Reviewing a seminar on the subject of government-citizen communications in Quebec, Jacques de Guise commented that the average Member of the National Assembly had been spoken of 'comme d'un fossile'. At the National Assembly, even in legislative committees, the MNA toes the party line, and while he or she is provided with a constituency office, it is not used as a place where local views on policy matters are discussed, but rather as a consulting room where constituents ask their representative to mediate between themselves and government. It is 'une sorte de confessional où chacun va demander à son ''parrain'' une réponse personnelle sinon privilegiée à un problème personnalisé.'[10] Even the MNAs present at the seminar concurred in this assessment, confessing that their offices were not places where citizens could develop and promote policy ideas. Like their counterparts in English Canada they saw themselves as ombudsmen. [11] Politicians are naturally alert to and understand a different language from that spoken in the technostructure. In the course of performing parliamentary and ministerial roles many politicians develop a good grasp of specialized fields, but their political survival depends on their being first and foremost 'community specialists', fluent in expressing the needs and aspirations of their constituents, but not in debating the merits of rival technical processes, the intricacies of corporate finance, or rarefied social and economic theory.

The promotion of neutral competence was more self-consciously directed at reducing the influence of politicians in policy and administration. The policy problem created by the gap between the politician's capacity to speak for the human needs of his constituents and his ability to engage meaningfully in debate with government's expert advisers served as the pretext for advancing the technostructure. Public dissatisfaction with the legislative branch's ineptitude in policy formation or its distaste for the corruption of machine politics—made apparent in the Beauharnois affair at the federal level and in numerous disputes over the distribution of mineral, forest, and other resources at the provincial[12]—grew during the interwar years. The distributive politics of colonial and late nineteenth-century Canada that reached its peak in the 1920s had become less acceptable by the late 1930s. Its cost, particularly the wasteful management of resources and the corruption of the political machine, was too apparent.

By contrast the competence and purity of technical administration appeared to hold great hope for the future. The implantation of neutral, professional competence in the public service was seen as part of a reform movement. In the United States, in fact, the divorce of politics and administration was an article of faith with many reformers. It struck a responsive chord in Canada as well, achieving its clearest manifestation in the federal Civil Service Acts of 1912 and 1918, which established the federal Civil Service Commission and provided that civil servants would be appointed on the basis of merit and not because of their affiliation with the party in power.[13] Provincial governments took longer to reach a similar stage, but there too the need for professional competence brought neutral expertise into the government service and eventually into positions of authority.[14]

Frequently the reformers' allies in their battles with party politicians were the professional associations that stood at the heart of each newly emergent profession. These bodies had many roles. They knit practitioners together as a group; they helped to determine what knowledge was required to practise each profession; they certified the competent; they worked to secure recognition of professional qualifications on the part of employers and they monitored professional performance, particularly professional ethics. In several respects these functions automatically aligned professional bodies with those who were fighting party patronage. The security of the profession depended on a security of tenure in the work-place that was unattainable in the traditional 'spoils system' in which civil service positions were taken away from the appointees of the 'losers' and handed out to a new group of government supporters each time the reins of power changed hands. Patronage politics were not compatible with professional practices. A forester trained in university to strive for good forest management through crop rotation could only feel that his or her efforts had been wasted when local political leaders applied their own principles to the allocation of forest resources. During the 1920s and the 1930s as the professions developed, these objections to party patronage became more widespread and generally known. They contributed to a growing public view that party-dominated policy-making and administration were inappropriate in the modern world, and they sometimes brought the administrative arm of government close to engaging in open warfare with party organizers. In the eyes of some administrators at least, the campaign assumed the proportions of a crusade against corruption and they sought to replace the influence of local party barons with administrative machinery run by technically competent professionals.[15] In so doing they complicated still further the efforts of elected representatives to speak to both the spatial and sectoral concerns of their constituents, and they enhanced the representative functions of sectorally-oriented institutions. That is, they promoted the political growth of the administrative arm of government and of its satellite groups at the expense of the legislative system and party government. In short, the technostructure, necessary though it was, diminished the role of politicians in politics and administration and changed the relations between policy institutions. Just as the development of business concentration in the first part of the twentieth century drained power from the legislature to the executive, from the party organization to the party leaders, so the emergence after the Depression of technologically sophisticated professionals in business and government effected a further transfer of power from the political executive to the administrative branch of government. While the loss of power by the executive was certainly not complete, it was substantial; and it reduced appreciably the scope of the executive and its decision-making capacity.

As the accession of administrative power diminished the role of politicians, it enhanced that of pressure groups. Communication within the technostructure can, and frequently does, occur without the assistance of interest groups; but there are many occasions when that assistance is useful, and often necessary. Because interest groups, like bureaucracies, are usually built around the principle of division of function, they easily link specific sections of administrative agencies and the parts of the public that are affected directly by those agencies' policies and programs. As well, while many aspects of the day-to-day administration of policy can be dealt with through one-to-one discussion between bureaucratic specialists and their opposite numbers in industry, the determination of industry-wide attitudes and needs can best be achieved through interest groups. They can draw together the various participants in each sector and can bring about some agreement over their conflicting demands. If necessary, interest groups can muster support within the specialized public for the policies that emerge from group-agency consultation. In other words, because interest groups can perform communication and legitimation functions they constitute an essential part of the private sector/public sector relationship.

This pattern of interaction and interdependence evolved gradually, beginning in the First World War as governments encouraged some solidary interests to organize themselves for the war effort. After the war, the new Crown corporations, boards, and commissions that were being set up proved as assiduous as traditional departments in fostering interest-group support. A number sought group representation on their directing or advisory bodies, much as Clifford Clark looked to H.H. Hannam to organize the farm community so that it could be represented on the Board of Directors of the Bank of Canada.[16] Interest groups were equally interested. According to S.D. Clark 'the increasing importance of administrative orders of the Government' was one factor leading the Canadian Manufacturers' Association to change its focus. 'Emphasis tended to shift to influencing the policies and activities of government boards, commissioners, and department officials, and to the extent that parliamentary leaders became dependent upon such agencies, these influences were more effective than pressure exerted upon the party organization.'[17] Before the end of the Second World War, which on a country-wide basis accelerated the trend towards government participation in the organization of the economy, a pattern of technically oriented agency-industry-group interactions was in place in many industries.

GROUP POLITICS DURING THE REGIME OF THE MANDARINS

By the end of the Second World War pressure groups had become an essential part of the policy process, but they had not won a corresponding acceptance from the general public, or even from the officials who found them useful. This was because, first, group politics was antithetical to popular perceptions of democratic government, and, second, the mutual dependence of groups and agencies was not yet fully developed.

As recently as the 1960s the general public treated pressure-group participation in policy-making as illicit. Robert Presthus has called this 'a culturally determined orientation, semantical rather than substantive', attributable to the 'deferential style of Canadian politics'.[18] There were, however, more significant causes. There was a general tendency to equate pressure group activity with 'lobbying', which the public tended to associate with the corrupt and venal side of politics. This was probably a reaction to the publicity surrounding the exposure of American lobbying activity by the Muckrakers at the turn of the century and to the various scandals that plagued Canadian politics in the 1920s and 1930s and were often attributed to the demands of 'special interests'.[19]

However, 'guilt by association' only partially explains the animosity that frequently greeted pressure groups in the first two decades after the Second World War. A more important influence may have been the fact that pressure group intervention in policy-making offended public perceptions of democratic government. The institutions of representative government—the single member constituency and the structure of political parties in particular—were sustained by myths that recognized no distinction between the representation of spatial interests and of sectoral concerns. Despite the growing incapacity of parties and legislatures, the belief persisted that they and they alone had the responsibility for articulating the needs of the people; that interventions on the part of other institutions were illegitimate. In Chapter 2 we cited J.M. Beck's observation that groups in Nova Scotia learned to avoid being identified explicitly with either of the main political parties. This approach stemmed partly from a fear of offending the leadership of one party or the other, but also from a public belief that interest groups had no business intervening in partisan politics. Beck quotes a 1911 editorial in the Halifax *Chronicle* reminding the Union of Nova Scotia Municipalities that its status was only that of 'a body of private individuals banded together for the furthering of what they conceived to be social progress. The Independent Order of Good Templars is another such.' Accordingly the Union should 'leave politics severely alone if (it) wish(ed) to accomplish any good'. The demands of pressure groups, though not necessarily inimical to the public interest, were those of *special* interests and were therefore to be treated with great suspicion.[20]

Such attitudes were still prevalent in the years after the Second World War and provoked earnest debates when the public-spirited members of certain groups realized that their efforts to promote change in government policy bore an uncomfortable resemblance to pressure politics. Helen Jones Dawson, describing in 1963 the activities of the Consumers' Association of Canada, noted: 'through the years there has persisted a considerable body of opinion in the CAC that the Ottawa office, by being constantly in contact with the government, is turning the Association into a "pressure group"; there is very strong resistance to such a development.' One group within the organization 'felt quite strongly that CAC should not be submitting briefs to government as this turned it into a pressure group and did not contribute toward the education of the public on consumer matters'. Dawson came to the conclusion that 'there seems to be only one point on which virtually all members of the Executive during the past fifteen years could find agreement and that is that CAC must not become a "pressure group" or indulge in pressure group methods. It might be more difficult to get them to agree on what a pressure group is and does.'[21] Though these views seem naïve today, in the early 1960s the leadership of the CAC was probably reflecting fairly accurately a broad public distaste for pressure group politics.

These attitudes touched on fundamental philosophical issues. Though not always clearly articulated in public discussion, they were, and are, critical to any attempt to incorporate interest-group representation in public policy-making. (They will be discussed later in this study.) Probably their most significant effect on pressure groups in the fifties and sixties was to inhibit the development of pressure groups and thus to retard the resolution of the problems posed by the increasing incapacity of traditional representative institutions to express sectoral as well as spatial concerns. Inevitably too public skepticism affected the impact that pressure groups could have in the policy process. In their dealings with group leaders politicians and officials exploited the fact that pressure group legitimacy was constantly in doubt. It was never tactically sound to admit too enthusiastically that groups might be useful as sources of information, or as legitimizers of government policy.[22] The structure of the Canadian policy process reinforced the utility of this approach as far as government policy-makers were concerned, for the mutual dependence of groups and agencies was not yet well developed.

Unlike the American system—from which many Canadians, including many academics and policy-makers themselves, derived their ideas about pressure group politics—the policy process in the years after the Second World War operated through two relatively closed structures: the party system and the bureaucracy, both of which culminated in the Cabinet. The major political parties had, as we noted in Chapter 2, turned their grass-roots organizations into 'fighting machines' for delivering votes and dispensing petty patronage. With the power to determine the distribution of party resources concentrated at the leadership level, the party hierarchy was able to impose on elected members a degree of discipline previously unknown in Canada. The same control extended, albeit less explicitly, through the party organization. Its framework was not likely to encourage vigorous internal party debate on policy issues. In fact, in the late 1960s, when the Liberal Party attempted to engage its constituency organizations in policy discussions, the grass roots had difficulty coping with its re-discovered role, and at the provincial level most Conservative regimes proved almost as hamstrung by power as the Liberals in Ottawa.[23]

The structure and mores of the civil service contributed to this malaise. As far as the Ottawa civil service was concerned, by the 1960s it was 'generally accepted by students of Canadian Government that the senior public service has had a crucial position in the overall structure of power.'[24] It was the epoch of the mandarins, a period when the advice of some senior officials vastly outweighed that of most ministers; when more than one senior official could, like W.A. MacKintosh, confide to his colleagues that he virtually alone had written a major policy document (the *White Paper on Employment and Incomes* of 1945, which served as the base for Canada's post-war economic policy) and had inspired the original policy idea.[25] MacKintosh, R.B. Bryce, Norman Robertson, and A.D.P. Heeney and a handful of others derived their power from the trust confided in their considerable professional competence by the Prime Minister and his closest colleagues. Their position was strengthened by the factors we have already discussed: the unfavourable public repute of pressure group politics; the not yet fully appreciated decline in the policy capacity of the political parties and the neutral competence of the public service. (The last had not yet been called into question, since it had not been widely recognized that the public service could be neutral in terms of partisan politics, but very much a supporter of specific policies.)[26]

Pressure group politics meant little to the mandarins. Some senior officials seem to have believed that they did not operate in this country. One confessed to a meeting of the Institute of Public Administration of Canada (IPAC), in 1953, that 'before I entered this meeting, I was under the impression that I had had no experience with pressure groups.'[27] At the same meeting Wilfrid Eggleston quoted a remark by George McIlraith, then Parliamentary Assistant to C.D. Howe, to the effect that lobbying 'is most damaging but fortunately it is practically non-existent in Canada today'.[28] Others were not so insensitive. K.W. Taylor, deputy minister of Finance, probably expressed a representative mandarin view when he remarked that

. . . the rapid expansion and growing complexity of modern government greatly increases the importance of administration. This means that policy is not so much a series of conscious decisions, but rather grows out of a stream of administrative decisions. For this reason there has been a growing tendency in recent years for lobbyists, the people who want to bring pressure to bear, to direct their attention as much to administrative officers as to political heads; for if you get a stream of administrative decisions started in a certain direction it tends to grow into established policy.[29]

The proceedings of successive meetings of IPAC indicates that senior officials dealt regularly with interest groups and believed that they served a useful function in communicating with special publics and could sometimes be counted on to help with the delivery of programs.[30] Some departments—Veterans' Affairs, and to some extent Agriculture or Labour—might have very close ties with certain groups and might even be said to depend on them for support;[31] but for the most part senior administrators in the fifties and sixties were not prepared to admit that pressure groups had an essential role to play in policy-making. The idea of being in some way politically dependent on pressure groups would have been considered far-fetched, though instances of agency manipulation of groups were noted and condemned.[32] The consensus was that senior public servants had a special responsibility to guard the public interest and therefore should be concerned to test the legitimacy of the interest groups communicating with them and to maintain a polite but correct distance from them. According to Taylor, 'the public administrator has a very real interest in the techniques, in the tactics and in the varying degrees of subtlety with which administrators are approached. Among the things we have to develop in public administrators is a high order of sales resistance and a considerable skill in assessing the validity of representations that are made to us.'[33]

The mandarins presided over a disciplined bureaucracy. Today in Canada the media and the Opposition look to the public service for a constant flow of information concerning policy discussion within the executive and administrative branches. Competing agencies, interest groups, and even individual public servants committed to specific policy positions have discovered that public debate can be used to influence policy decisions. Consequently in Ottawa, as in Washington, the leak—authorized and unauthorized—has become an everyday occurrence. In the war years and the subsequent two decades such behaviour was considered unthinkable, and the discipline of the bureaucracy was strictly enforced to prevent it. This discipline extended not only to civil servants but to those whose dealings with government touched upon policy formation. Pressure groups in particular were affected by these constraints.

Attitudes and mores were reinforced by the mechanics of the policy process. Helen Jones Dawson pointed out that 'working in a Parliamentary system, it is inevitable that Canadian organizations find it essential to

Table 3-1. The Stages of Legislative Development in Canada during the 1950s and 1960s, with Points of Interest Intervention

1. CONCEPTUALIZATION

Traditionally the most elusive step in the policy process. Who conceives a new policy? It is usually argued that while specific individuals may initiate action leading to new policy positions they themselves have been inspired by a host of cumulative environmental and specific events. Obviously interest groups may have contributed directly or indirectly to these events.

2. DEPARTMENTAL PRELIMINARY EXAMINATION

Once initiated the policy review or policy preparation process would call upon interdepartmental study groups to prepare background studies, policy alternatives, and draft policy documents. At this point groups were generally invited to make their views known and were, in fact, most active in trying to influence the direction of policy, their rationale being that once a departmental position had been taken and advice tendered to cabinet it was extremely difficult to change that advice, unless cabinet itself called for change. Although one observer reports that groups were invited to participate in this process as a matter of course, there is at least one well-documented case in which key—and powerful—groups were not given an opportunity to influence discussion at this stage, and, in fact, remained ignorant of proposed policy until the parliamentary stage was reached.

3. MEMO TO CABINET

This document, the product of the previous stage, was considered the most important document in the entire process. It laid out the general principles of the proposed policy and its financial implications. In its final form it was, and remains, a highly confidential paper and was not shown to group representatives or any others outside the decision circle. Cabinet might accept the proposal in its entirety or order changes. If changes were required, some of the steps already detailed were repeated. If not, the policy proposal would go to the formal drafting stage.

4. LEGISLATIVE DRAFTING

Drafting was carried out by the Department of Justice and seems to have been considered by some a purely technical process in which groups were not consulted. Anyone who has ever had any contact with the strictly legal aspects of policy-making will find this difficult to believe and will be more inclined to accept Dawson's statement that interests were consulted on matters of detail. It may have been true, though, that interests were not shown *final* drafts of legislation before submission to Parliament. Dawson quotes one minister explaining that interest groups were not provided with advance copies of a particular bill, 'because that insults Parliament. Parliament was the first to see the Bill. However, we did show many of these groups very carefully, specifically worded . . . drafting instructions'. It is unclear how widespread such practices were.

5. PARLIAMENTARY STAGE

In the view of some civil servants of the day, the only really appropriate occasion for interest group intervention in the policy process came at the committee stage of the legislative process. This, naturally, was not a view that sat well with the spokesmen for established groups, and even the less experienced leaders of many issue-oriented groups realized that in the cabinet-parliamentary system it is extremely difficult to modify proposed legislation once the government has formally committed itself to putting it before parliament. During the 1970s this practice was modified somewhat and some legislation was considerably changed or even withdrawn at the Committee stage, but in the 1950s and 1960s only highly technical amendments stood any chance of success at the parliamentary stage.

*Sources: Helen Jones Dawson, 'National Pressure Groups and the Federal Government' in A.P. Pross (ed.) *Pressure Group Behaviour in Canadian Politics* (Toronto: McGraw-Hill, 1975), 27-59, and David Kwavnick, *Organized Labour and Pressure Politics* (Montreal: McGill-Queen's, 1972). Accounts of the procedures used to prepare legislation for parliament in this period differ somewhat. We have assumed that these differences reflect inter-departmental variations in procedure, as the fixed points in the process were relatively few and procedure was apt to vary, not only between agencies but from time to time within agencies.

Table 3-2. Interest Group Interaction with Legislators

Conventional wisdom in the 1950s and 1960s asserted that interest groups had little to do with Members of Parliament. Robert Presthus's 1969-70 survey of approximately 1,000 interest-group directors generally confirmed that view. Asked which three elements of the policy system their groups targetted first, in general, Presthus's sample ranked the following first:

Major General Targets of Interest Groups

Proportion ranking each target first

Target	Proportion	
	%	
Bureaucracy	40	(158)
Back-benchers	20	(80)
Cabinet	19	(74)
Legislative committees	7	(27)
Executive assistants	5	(19)
Judiciary	3	(11)
Other	6	(24)

A comparable U.S. sample ranked the same targets as follows:

	%
Bureaucracy	21
Legislators	41
Cabinet	4
Legislative committees	19
Executive assistants	3
Judiciary	3
Other	9

(Source: Robert Presthus: *Elites in the Policy Process*, Toronto, 1974, p. 255)

Presthus also investigated some 400 specific 'cases' in which he sought a similar identification of targets. As might be expected, in the particular circumstances surrounding each case that target of representations tended to shift according to the nature of the case and the needs of the group:

Substantive Issues Presented to Government Elites by Interest Groups, Case Study

	Proportion ranking each target first					
Issue	Back-benchers	Cabinet	Bureaucracy	Ex. Ass'ts	Other	
	%	%	%	%	%	
Laws	11	51	19	4	15	(92)
Bills	30	33	19	4	13	(90)
Intraorganizational policy	15	26	16	4	22	(27)
Licensing	13	54	21	—	13	(26)
Administrative regulations	13	41	21	3	19	(79)
Fund-raising	7	13	60	3	17	(30)
Group jurisdiction	—	23	31	15	31	(16)
Other	6	36	24	1	22	(70)
	(60)	(154)	(107)	(15)	(50)	(406)

Presthus comments: These data provide an overview of both the substance and process of interest group-government interaction, in the case study context. Forty per cent of all groups contact the Cabinet; 26 per cent turn mainly to the bureaucracy; while only 15 per cent focus on the legislature as their primary target. Putatively administrative issues, such as licensing and regulations, exhibit a similar valence. Only regarding pending legislation do groups approach back-benchers with an intensity similar to that accorded the Cabinet. And only in fund-raising and problems of group jurisdiction is the Cabinet's dominance superseded by the bureaucracy. Even the final 'other' category, consisting of a *pot pourri* of issues, neither significant nor structured enough to warrant detailed categorization, remains primarily a Cabinet province. Here, in sum, we have the clearest evidence of Cabinet hegemony in the process of elite accommodation.

Source: Robert Presthus, *Elite Accommodation in Canadian Politics* (Cambridge, 1973), pp. 230-1.

influence policy and legislation before the Parliamentary stage is reached.'[34] One senior civil servant put it more bluntly:

> People who really want to guide and influence government policy are wasting their time dealing with members of Parliament, senators and, usually, even ministers. If you want results—rather than just the satisfaction of talking to the prominent—you deal with us, and at various levels . . . To produce results you need to see the key planners, who may be way down in the system, and you see them early enough to push for changes in policy before it is politically embarrassing to make them.[35]

In effect this meant tackling senior politicians or the bureaucracy, or both. For the reasons we have already described, neither was easily susceptible to influence; this is reflected in the sequence of policy preparation summarized in Table 3-1. None of the stages reported in the table offered interests a very wide opening for exercising influence. In theory, as some members of the public service argued, groups opposed to new policies could make their views known at the legislative stage and, by capturing media attention, whip up public opposition to the proposed legislation. In practice this was seldom a viable strategy. Not only were governments reluctant to back away from legislation that they had formally presented as government policy, but the very attempt to discredit the proposals would incur the displeasure of senior officials who might capitulate on a single issue, but would punish the group on future occasions by withholding information or foreclosing opportunities for representation.[36]

It is therefore hardly surprising that Canadian pressure groups focused their attention on the mandarins and their departments, according the Legislature only perfunctory attention.[37] This does not mean that the groups themselves necessarily favoured such one-sided relationships; but they were adaptive institutions that accepted the exigencies of the policy system.[38] As late as 1969-70, when the effects of a reformed committee system were beginning to be felt, Robert Presthus found, on interviewing 139 MPs concerning their relations with group representatives, that 58.2 per cent of them saw group representatives occasionally, seldom or rarely. Admittedly, the largest proportion of them saw group representatives occasionally, rather than less frequently.[39] (See Table 3-2.) However, contact about twice a month (Presthus' definition of 'occasional') hardly constitutes a significant degree of interaction and contrasts sharply with Jean Piggot's comment, a little more than a decade later, that as an Opposition MP she was 'overwhelmed' by pressure group representations.[40] Presthus's data, however, is consistent with Dawson's impression that while groups in the late 1960s were paying more attention to Parliament, particularly to its committees, their contacts were not extensive and their tactics were by no means as sophisticated as those used at Westminster or Washington.[41] Even in dealing with Committees, groups tended to confine their interaction to presenting briefs. There seems to have been little attempt to cultivate informal ties with committee members, to persuade them to pursue issues of concern to the groups, or to brief them in advance on technical aspects of their presentations. Contacts with private Members were even more limited, seldom rising to such heights of sophistication as lobbying them through constituency members of the organization; asking them to sponsor legislation; feeding them questions for Question Period; or even visiting them in their offices more than once or twice in the life of a Parliament. According to Dawson, some groups did not lobby private Members 'as a matter of policy'. The Canadian Federation of Agriculture was cited in this category. These and similar findings led Dawson to conclude that 'traditionally Canadian pressure groups have not paid much attention to Parliament, its institutions, or its private Members.'[42]

Thus in the two decades following the Second World War pressure groups developed in a contradictory climate. On the one hand the Depression, the war years, and the growth of the technostructure had all contributed to the extension of group participation in policy-making and the elaboration of pressure group organizations; on the other hand, negative public attitudes, the residue of power concentrated in the hands of the political executive, the disciplined structure of the policy process, and the dismissive attitude of the most senior public service advisers all militated against that expansion.

The groups that survived in this era did so because they came to terms with a central fact: the key to exercising influence in the relatively closed policy-making system that prevailed from the war years to the beginning of the Trudeau era was access. Oriented towards obtaining access to the policy-makers whose decisions had a vital impact on the concerns of their members, pressure group leaders concentrated on developing their capacity to communicate specialized, often highly technical information, and on their ability to engage officials at various levels of policy development and implementation. In order to maintain such an intimate association with the bureaucracy they also developed a high regard for discretion and a readiness to accept agency domination of the relationship.[43] This usually meant that the group would try to avoid public criticism of existing or proposed policy and would never indulge in media-attracting publicity that would arouse public opinion. Consultation, and the search for consensus, became the outstanding characteristics of government/pressure group relations.

These methods affected both group structure and organization. The need for expert knowledge dictated the hiring of specialists, or dependence on elaborate committee structures capable of tapping the expertise of group members. Equally important was the need to employ group representatives who had both intimate knowledge of the bureaucracies they had to deal with and an ability to work at the various levels at which policy was made. Publicists and animateurs, on the other hand, were not needed; nor, in general, was a large staff. As long as the information resources of the membership could be tapped fairly efficiently, and as long as group representatives knew their way around Ottawa, or the provincial capital, groups could function effectively from a modest base. More important than the scale of resources was the extent of their institutionalization. An effective collective memory, a relationship of trust with officials, and an intimate acquaintance with process and issues were vital, and these could only be acquired with time. Hence, few groups could be effective unless they established an institutional presence.

POWER DIFFUSED, POWER CONFUSED

In 1946 the *Canadian Almanac and Directory* listed some 1,700 societies and associations. Nine years later there were approximately 100 more. By 1970, however, about 2,300 were listed. In 1978 4,500 were listed and in 1983, 5,500. A similar progression is recorded in Land's *Directory of Associations in Canada*; and the Institute of Association Executives (an association of professional association leaders founded in 1951) grew in numbers from 1,200 in 1977 to 1,900 in 1982.[44] Even more striking is the extent to which pressure groups, including institutionalized groups that formerly avoided publicity, now attract public attention. In the media they are ubiquitous; many advertise through newspapers, magazines, television, and radio to put their views before the public. They are assiduous in appearing before comittees of enquiry, regulatory bodies, and reviews.[45] Nowhere is their presence more noticeable than in the parliamentary arena. In 1960, according to H.G. Thorburn, a particularly contentious public-policy issue— the regulation of resale price maintenance—saw twenty-nine groups attempting to influence government policy; of these only twelve appeared before the relevant parliamentary committee.[46] Twenty years later, by Hugh Faulkner's estimate, seven parliamentary task forces looking at issues ranging from federal-provincial fiscal relations to regulatory reform in general heard some 2,500 witnesses, many of whom represented 796 interest groups.[47] The activity of parliamentary committees shows the increased dynamism of public debate, of which pressure-group activity is only a part. Committees working in the first session of the 32nd Parliament (1980-1) heard 3,326 witnesses. By contrast, during the record-breaking length of the first session of the 27th Parliament (1966-7), 1,115 witnesses appeared before comittees.[48] If the growth of pressure-group activity in other parts of the policy system is any indication, a significant number of these witnesses probably represented organized groups. These signs of change reflect deep-seated alterations in the way policy is made and in the role of the institutions that make it. They are part of a long process of evolution that affects the legitimacy of our most important democratic institutions. Though much of this evolution is beyond the scope of this book, we must take account of its influence on pressure group developement, and we must consider how it was itself affected by the proliferation and changing behaviour of groups. Broadly speaking we can divide our discussion into three parts:

 (i) The Growth of Government
 (ii) The Diffusion of Power
 (iii) The Search for Legitimating Institutions

(i) *The Growth of Government*

The 1960s was a decade of frenetic activity in public-policy formation.[49] Vast new programs were undertaken in medical care and education. Major reforms were initiated in income-maintenance programs and regional economic policy. Other programs were proposed in the core policy field of taxation. Anachronistic policies relating to Canada's native peoples began a long, and still incomplete, process of review and reform. Three major movements—the women's movement, the environmental movement, and the consumer movement—began to demand government attention. Shifting demographic patterns precipitated debate over appropriate urban development policies. At the same time, government confronted sweeping technological changes and major new demands in traditional fields of activity, such as resource development and communications, where capital-intensive methods of production rendered obsolete long-standing approaches to industry, labour, and trade. Above all, the country faced cultural and regional tensions of an order that it had not previously experienced.

All these factors precipitated growth in government activity. They also affected policy processes and the role of pressure groups. No longer could policy-making authority be contained in the hands of a small and intimate community of leading politicians and high officials. Policy-making had become so extensive and complex that it had to be divided up and parcelled out to the agencies and interests most concerned with what was happening in each particular field of government activity.

There followed an explosion of pressure group formation and participation, much of it stemming from the expansion of government.[50] That is, as government grew, interaction with its many agencies became increasingly difficult, both for smaller pressure groups and for individuals. Group formation, the elaboration of established groups, and the formation of 'peak' associations became a necessity. (Peak associations are organizations that aggregate the demands of other organizations in order to express their collective demands to the state.) Similarly, group activity encouraged more group activity. Here a teaching role was played by television, which exposed the publicity-seeking activities of groups in one part of the country to appreciative eyes elsewhere. Because so many groups were now participating publicly in the policy process a more receptive climate for interest-group activity existed. 'Pressure-group tactics' were no longer considered politically unacceptable. Above all, the mounting clamour around the policy process made organization essential. 'To have a say, you need a voice,' advised a headline in the *Financial Post*.[51] 'Shout when not listened to,' admonished the *Bulletin* of the Canadian Association of University Teachers.[52]

Much of this increased activity was spontaneous. As David Truman, and other pluralist writers, have argued, when governments take steps to change policy or to create new programs, many affected interests coalesce to protect themselves or to take advantage of new opportunities.[53] Similarly, interests that have benefited from earlier policy become defensive and take a more active, often more public, part in policy debate. Many of the reports on pressure groups that appeared in the press in the late 1960s and early 1970s can be seen in this light. A.E. Diamond, president of the Canadian Institute of Real Estate Companies, told his group in 1974 that they must 'make the public more aware of the difficulties faced by developers' in order to counteract 'the power that various interest groups have captured over the development process'.[54] Interest groups, according to the *Montreal Star*, were 'a new political force', and business reaction to much new legislation and regulation—such as the federal consumer-protection proposals of the late 1960s—suggests that the business community was taken by surprise by the influence of environmental, consumer, and women's groups.[55] By 1976, according to the chairman of the Canadian Association of Equipment Distributors, businessmen were 'no longer suprised, though still dismayed, that government listens more to the consumer and environmentalist than the investor'.[56] His group was urged to learn the political process, and the role of its full-time president was redefined, making his chief concern that of achieving 'a closer liaison between the association and the federal government'. Other groups were taking similar steps. Small businessmen, led by John Bulloch and his Canadian Federation of Independent Business, were reported in 1972 to be 'building up their political muscle', and subsequent achievements—such as the appointment of a Minister of State for Small Business—were an object lesson to other interests.[57] Across the board businessmen sought 'more input in government decisions' and to that end were told by experienced lobbyists that they 'should do a better job of participation'.[58] Nor were businessmen and citizens' groups the only ones engaged, like the Canadian Importers' Association, in 'widening the channel of communication' with government.[59] Long-established groups and newcomers alike found themselves building more and more elaborate organizations in order to keep up with policy discussions and to promote their own interests. The 1974 reports of the president and the executive secretary of the Canadian Association of University Teachers echoed many others when they dwelt on the growing lobbying role of the organization.[60] Not long after, CAUT appointed a full-time government liaison officer and—in an effort to halt the decline of research and university funding—was deeply involved, with other university-based groups, in organizing one of the most elaborate lobbying blitzes that Ottawa has ever seen.

Not all of this activity occurred spontaneously, however. As the critics of the pluralists have pointed out, many interests do not have a sufficient sense of solidarity or the necessary resources to participate fully in the policy process.[61] Governments, therefore, have considered it in the public interest to take a hand in group formation, identifying latent and solidary interests and encouraging them to organize themselves. Hugh Faulkner describes one of the several methods used to achieve this:

> One of the greatest innovations initiated by government in this field was the decision to permit public funding of interest groups. A variety of interest groups have been receiving money from the federal government since the 1960s. Consumers and native people have been the principal beneficiaries. The capacity of the people to intervene before the National Energy Board on the Norman Wells pipeline, for example, was a result of federal funding over the years. Government core funding has allowed groups to participate in the political process who up to that time had been unable to be effective for lack of money. That public funding achieved that end is evident in the results of the Berger inquiry, where $1.2 million was granted to Indian organizations to make representations. Another $540,000 assisted a coalition of interests, including the Canadian Arctic Resources Committee, the regional associations of municipalities and the Métis Federation. Funding is particularly important for regulatory agencies. Without funding, the full range of interests will not be heard. Regulatory agencies have their own proceedings, schedules, requirements and bureaucracy—and are every bit as complex as a line department of government. To effectively penetrate these agencies, an interest group needs expensive legal and expert help. A good illustration of the levels of funding needed for this sort of participation is found in the decision of the Beaufort Environmental Assessment Panel to provide $250,000 in 1981-82 for public intervenors wishing to make representations on the commercial exploitation of the Beaufort Sea. A further $150,000 was set aside for the 1982-83 fiscal year. Among the groups seeking support for this work were the Canadian Arctic Resources Committee, the Nature Federation, Energy Probe, the Yukon Conservation Authority and the Arctic International Wildlife Range. The money was to be allocated by a committee chaired by the senior scientific advisor to the Department of the Environment and composed of distinguished individuals from both within government and from outside.[62]

Other methods of encouraging group formation and participation include the development of consultative bodies that solicit representation from weakly organized groups; the creation of regulatory regimes that force solidary groups into forming associations; and straightforward rhetorical encouragement. We have noted that group promotion of this sort is not entirely disinterested—a point we will return to shortly. Nevertheless it reflects in part the code of neutrality of the professional public servant: the public interest can be served best if all special interests are properly heard.

(ii) *The Diffusion of Power*

Interests and interest groups were not the only elements in the political and economic environment that had to adapt to the expansion of government activity in the 1960s. Government policy-making systems were themselves overwhelmed by the profusion and complexity of new undertakings. One response to the problems of overload thus created was to parcel out policy-making responsibility to those most competent and most interested in each field, preserving for the Cabinet and its immediate advisers the authority to create global policy and to monitor the work of individual agencies. By the mid-1960s the flaws in this approach were becoming evident. Ministers, preoccupied with their own departmental affairs, were less and less capable of developing in Cabinet the broad conception of the public interest expected of them. The Prime Minister and his closest colleagues—usually the Ministers of Finance and Justice and the Secretary of State for External Affairs—because their responsibilities gave them a perspective on the work of all departments and often forced them to co-ordinate the work of agencies, were better able to develop a view of the national interest than the majority of Cabinet members. However, the prime ministerial careers of both John Diefenbaker and Lester Pearson often revealed that their ability to achieve an informed view of the sweep of public needs and government policy was hampered by their preoccupation with the major national and international issues facing the country.[63]

In their fields of jurisdiction individual agencies had considerable freedom, which was often reinforced by the competence and stature of senior administrators who exercised great, though scrupulously non-partisan, authority over their departments. Unfortunately it was not sufficient for the departments to be well administered and to propose and implement intelligent and competent policies. Those policies had to avoid encroaching on the work of other governments and other departments and to respect the overall goals of the government in power. As the work of the Government of Canada expanded, the attainment of these objectives became more and more difficult—just as it did a few years later in the majority of the provincial governments. The response was to strive for centralization of policy-making by reorganizing the work of Cabinet and by creating for the Prime Minister and for Cabinet a series of central policy institutions that could co-ordinate the policy process and help the political executive develop global policies within which individual departments were expected to find their own mandates.[64] To reinforce the co-ordinative effects of these changes in structure and process, successive governments introduced a series of reforms in budgetary procedures and financial management that affected the distribution of power and, consequently, pressure group politics.[65]

Reform foundered on three obstacles that frequently impede efforts to bring about better co-ordination through centralization. First, a power struggle developed among the co-ordinating agencies over their respective duties, and over the planning philosophy that was to guide policy-making. Thus, instead of achieving the structured development of policy envisaged by the reforms, the Privy Council Office, the Treasury Board, and the Department of Finance fostered confusion within and beyond government about which agency was actually co-ordinating policy-making and advising Cabinet.[66] Unsure of where sub-Cabinet decision-making was actually taking place, interests had to redouble their efforts to gain access to the process, expanding their physical presence and their lobbying activities.[67] Often finding their way to the centre barred—by the limited resources of the co-ordinating agencies, by the crush of rival groups, or by the policy-making procedures themselves—they changed their lobbying strategies, engaging more frequently in public discussion of issues in hopes of influencing the policy makers through public opinion. Complaining that line agencies, such as Industry, Trade and Commerce; Transport; Agriculture; the Fisheries and Marine Service; and the Canadian Forestry Service, with which they had traditionally worked, had been stripped of their former substantive role in the policy process, they sought to restore to them some of their former power. In doing so they added their weight to two other forces that were resisting the reforms: line agencies' unwillingness to give up power to the centre and concern that co-ordinating officials would pay too little respect to the more technical aspects of department advice.[68]

Thus motivated to resist the new co-ordinative regime, the line agencies employed various devices for avoiding, short-circuiting, or limiting central control—strategies that nearly always exacerbated the centre's penchant for extending its supervision. A vicious circle developed that gradually diffused power throughout the institutions of government, so that though to some extent power still resided at the centre—particularly where the need to take critical decisions galvanized the executive—for the most part it simply trickled down through the bureaucracy, creating pockets of authority even at fairly junior levels. The phenomenon led Andrew Roman to remark that '. . . the Government of Canada is secretly being run by persons earning no more than $20,000 a year,'[69] but in general the influence of each policy actor was so restricted that power came to be expressed most frequently and most effectively in checking the activities of other actors. 'If power in our political system is diffused,' two students of British politics have observed, 'the power that is most widely diffused is the power of the veto.'[70] Canada's situation has been similar. 'Ottawa is full of "no" bodies,' one official commented after some months in the capital, 'all they do is press "no" buttons.'[71]

We can attribute much of the increased influence and growing public presence of pressure groups to this tug-of-war. Initially valued for their capacity to communicate with special publics, interest groups gradually came to be seen as allies of line agencies in their struggles with the centre. Within agencies themselves specific services would cultivate the support of groups particularly affected by their programs and policies. A 1968 report to the Canadian Citizenship Council complained that the Citizenship Branch had

> . . . no non-governmental institution which is in a position of supporting or criticizing the overall organization, budget, policies or methods of the Branch . . . [This] means that the Branch competes in the jungle warfare in this government for scarce resources all by itself. It gets no help from the public it serves. In fact, those publics who may depend on the Branch for support of critical experimental and innovative programs, may not even know that an internal struggle is taking place which will hamper their efforts.[72]

Other agencies drew the same conclusion and set about creating supportive institutions, or strengthening their connections to existing ones. The close affiliation between the federal Forestry Branch and its associates in the forestry profession, for example, succeeded in 1969 in securing the elevation of the Branch to departmental status. The March 1969 edition of *The Forestry Chronicle* applauded the success of a major campaign, and made it clear that professional foresters expected to be rewarded with 'adequate representation on the Forestry Development Board, and a substantial program of continuing research by graduate students and forest school staff members supported by the new Department'.[73] A few years later the fledgeling Department of the Environment considered a recommendation that it develop

> . . . a coherent Departmental policy, including structures and procedures, which would encourage and regularize participation by public interest groups, private interest groups, professional associations and the public at large within a general framework that would allow for flexibility in its application by the various parts of the Department and would permit the continuance of on-going program-specific activities. By providing a consistent framework and ground rules, such a policy would contribute to the development of sustained relationships between interest groups and decision-makers which are an essential part of the mutual learning process required for effective public participation.[74]

In effect agencies were building policy communities.[75] This was the self-serving aspect of the campaign described earlier by Hugh Faulkner to ensure that the weak and under-represented could participate in policy-making. A great many latent and solidary groups—like the independent fishermen of Canada's east coast—found themselves exhorted to organize themselves into interest associations.[76] For those who could not afford to organize themselves in this way, agencies provided financial incentives.

Core funding was an important factor in developing the modern Canadian Indian movement.[77] It has been made available to other minority groups and to organizations representing the economically disadvantaged.[78] Special grants have been made to groups preparing submissions to regulatory bodies and to established groups with limited means, such as learned societies, while contract research has been purchased from others.[79] Separately, or in conjunction with funding assistance, positional policies have been used to enhance the mandates of favoured groups or to co-opt unruly but influential ones.[80] Hence the proliferation of advisory boards remarked by some observers. Where moral support, funding, and positional inducements have failed, regulatory coercion has been applied. Thus fish quotas in the east-coast fishery are divided up in consultation with sector committees representing the various elements in each fishery, an arrangement that may at last quell the individualism of the region's independent fishermen.[81] In these various ways federal agencies have sought to develop interest communities capable not only of creating a link with a specific clientele or sector constituency, but also of supporting each agency and its policies in the turbulent policy process that currently prevails.[82]

These relationships have not developed solely at the departmental level. Within agencies themselves specific services have cultivated the support of groups particularly affected by their programs and policies. In fact, it is probable that the natural grouping for most policy communities occurs at the administrative level, where the functional responsibilities of agencies closely parallel the organizational structure created by interests. Thus a small department with very clear, relatively narrowly defined responsibilities, such as the Department of Labour, would relate as a department to its policy community.[83] The Department of the Environment on the other hand, with responsibilities ranging from weather forecasting to parks management, to environmental impact assessment, to name but a few, relates only with difficulty to its global constituency and so allows its individual branches, and often sub-branches, to discover and cultivate their own policy communities.[84]

During the 1970s policy communities became prominent as line and central agencies struggled for influence in the policy process. At the centre the weight of the collective authority of Cabinet, and the capacity to influence budget allocations, weighed heavily on the side of the Privy Council Office, the Treasury Board, and the Department of Finance. On the departmental side the ability to generate public support through affiliated pressure groups transformed the latter from useful adjuncts into vitally important allies whose support enhanced the legitimacy of the departmental mission. However, in order to exploit the new group-agency relationship several changes had to be wrought in previous practice. It became less and less true to argue (as this writer argued in the mid-1970s)[85] that agency-group relations tended to be dominated by the government side. A dependency relationship became an exchange relationship. The agencies today need their pressure group allies to a much greater extent than they did in the heyday of the mandarins. For example, as financial constraint bit deeply into agency budgets, officials turned to their policy communities for help, asking them to approach senior officials, members of the relevant Cabinet committees, and parliamentarians with a view to representing the urgent needs of each agency and service. Sometimes these efforts have been successful, as one official demonstrated in a 'thank you' letter he wrote to individuals and groups that had lobbied ministers and MPs on behalf of his agency:

> The numerous examples and suggestions were extremely useful. [The deputy minister] did obtain the strong support of the [other] departments and agencies belonging to the [budgetary] sector, and the two press releases indicate that his efforts were successful. I would also like to extend our thanks to those who have themselves approached politicians and high ranking officials to make them aware of the [agency's] difficult budgetary situation. It is obvious that taken as a whole, the actions undertaken have had a considerable impact on the decision ultimately made.[86]

Agencies pay a price for this sort of public support. They have had to accept greater public involvement in policy and budgetary discussions in order to generate public support. Similarly, as the policy process becomes more dynamic, and as more interests are stimulated to participate, agencies and their traditional policy communities lose their capacity to direct the course of policy debate.[87] Operating in a more uncertain environment, they must expect the policy process to take much longer than it did in the war years, and in the two decades following.

Obviously there are many ways in which the political system benefits from these changes in the policy process. The public agenda has been broadened and the policy-making system is more dynamic. Groups have been recognized as a viable part of the policy process and group intervention today is more generally accepted than it was in the 1960s. The new dynamism is extremely important because—as we shall argue shortly—it has strengthened the role of Parliament in the policy process. And yet, despite the enhanced role of Parliament and increased public participation, this dynamism is flawed by its *raison d'être*. It grows out of a power struggle within the executive-administrative branch of government, rather than out of improved democratic institutions of government. Although those institutions have benefited from recent changes in the policy system, the principal effect of the changes has been to diffuse power and to elongate the policy process. In fact, it can be argued that these changes have introduced a new kind of pluralism into Canadian politics: bureaucreatic pluralism. Agencies fight agencies intragovernmentally, thereby exciting the participation of pressure groups, which support their own respective positions. While this engenders more open discussion of policy issues from which the general public can benefit, experienced observers do not consider that democratic government has improved as a result; they see instead an excessive diffusion of power that emphasizes the political executive's lack of real control over the administrative branch. Even J. Hugh Faulkner—who argues from his own experience as a member of Cabinet, that the system's legitimacy has not been compromised so far by these developments—expresses concern:

> Short of an ideal definition of what is in the public interest, it becomes necessary to find a legitimate process for defining it in an on-going manner. That is clearly the role of Parliament and the executive. For them to fill this role effectively, they in turn have to enjoy widespread legitimacy as the final arbiters of the public interest. The process of accommodation and adjustment requires that the political act of initiation, leadership and arbitration must proceed from sources that command political legitimacy. The present Canadian context demonstrates the risks and dangers to the system when that is not present. The system of decision-making that I have referred to here is excessively dispersed. It leaves many Canadians confused and uncertain about how public policy is made; it increasingly puts a premium on group interaction—generally well-organized interaction—with the political and bureaucratic executive, and it leads many to conclude that the heart of the system, Parliament, has become weak and futile. All of these undermine the legitimacy of the policy-making process and they should command our concern.[88]

In the next section of this chapter we address the concerns raised by Faulkner.

(iii) *The Search for Legitimating Institutions*

'It makes me very, very nervous', an interest group leader commented in 1981, 'that people out there look at our organization as being more legitimate at representing them than the government.'[89] The diffusion of power we have discussed above considerably strained the legitimacy of Canadian governments.[90] Expansion of government tends to erode public respect under the best of circumstances. A remote authority concerned with external relations, defence, and a few great national enterprises can, with a modicum of forethought and care, retain public confidence over a long period. An obtrusive, questing government, perpetually encroaching upon the private sector and diminishing the freedom of the individual, is bound to generate resentment, however necessary its expansion may be. When, as in Canada, the growth of government is particularly rapid and engenders intergovernmental conflict, mistakes are easily made, public respect is undermined and, over time, the community's willingness to accept the authority of public officials diminishes. This is what we mean by a decline in the legitimacy of government.

Declining legitimacy has materially affected the roles and interrelationships of our three most important political institutions. Cabinets and bureaucracies at both levels of government, after a long accession of authority, have experienced a diminution of public regard. Parliament, and to a lesser extent the provincial legislatures, though often said to be institutions declining in influence, have in fact been more active in the policy process in recent years. We will argue that this may be partly attributed to reforms in parliamentary procedure, and to a decline in executive legitimacy. Finally, the changing status of these institutions has been reflected in new forms of pressure group politics, including an enhancement of the role of pressure groups in the policy process. Before looking at these developments, however, we must explore what it means to say that the legitimacy of Cabinet and bureaucracy have declined.

Ultimately, the authority—the legitimacy—of the political executive depends on two intimately related factors: its capacity to control the legislature and its ability to direct the government. The need to select from the legislature a group of men and women able to oversee the public service in the execution of policy and to derive from civil servants advice necessary in policy formation has been largely responsible for the development of modern Cabinet government. Thus on the one hand, Cabinet, as the executive committee of Parliament, must secure its confidence. Equally, however, it must be able to show that it is in command of the public service. Inability to do so reduces the Cabinet's claim to public support, exposing it to a loss of legitimacy. It also casts doubt on the legitimacy of the service itself, for if the Cabinet is not seen to be in command of the public service, we cannot be sure that policy is being implemented in a fashion sanctioned by duly elected public authorities.

The conviction that the federal Cabinet has lost control of the machinery of government has gradually been taking hold of public consciousness since the late 1960s.[91] The need to reassert political control of the administrative arm was one theme of Pierre Elliott Trudeau's leadership campaign.[92] Yet, despite the vigorous pursuit and elaboration of central-agency reorganization, many observers soon came to feel that the bureaucracy was even less amenable to control and direction than it had been a decade earlier. As an assistant deputy-minister put it to a journalist in 1975, 'I always knew the politicians could never control the bureaucracy. But when you reach the point where the bureaucracy can't control the bureaucracy, you know its time to look for another job.'[93] In other words, the alliance between the political leadership and the mandarins, which had ensured ultimate Cabinet control in the forties and fifties, was effectively dead. Such cocktail-circuit views were reinforced by a succession of reports issued by the Auditor-General that drew attention to weaknesses in financial control and problems in policy implementation, going so far in 1976 as to argue that the government had 'lost control of the public purse'.[94] The stature of the Auditor-General is such that his concerns ultimately led to the appointment of the Lambert Royal Commission on Financial Management and Accountability. The Commission *Report*, though more soothing in tone than the Auditor General's reports, nevertheless confirmed the existence of a serious problem. Released a few months before the 1979 election, the *Report* prompted major innovations in the budgetary process, financial management, and the institutions of accountability. Although the preliminary results of these improvements have drawn optimistic reviews, it will take a decade to discover whether they have achieved the desired effect.[95] In the meantime many politicians remain convinced that the problems of control go far deeper than the present program of reform admits. Flora MacDonald, for example, after her stint in 1979 as Secretary of State for External Affairs, concluded that personal attitudes and long-established patterns of behaviour in the public service were as much at fault, and inherently much less susceptible to remedy, as weaknesses in financial and personnel management systems.[96] Understandably members of the Mulroney Cabinet have been less outspoken since their election in September, 1984. Again, it will be some years before we can evaluate the effects of the measures they took—including the Nielsen Task Force review of government programs—to reassert Cabinet control of the bureaucracy.

Perhaps more important than the decline of Cabinet have been repercussions from the declining legitimacy of the public service.[97] The general public as well as informed observers perceived that diffusion of power had weakened the authority of the political executive. Traditionally Canadian government bureaucracies have acquired legitimacy first because they serve the political executive, which derives its own legitimacy from the support it receives in the legislature; and second because agencies apply neutral professional expertise to the development of policy and the delivery of programs.[98] Since the 1950s there has been a steady deterioration in the potency of these sources of legitimacy and thus in the status of the bureaucracy, particularly that of the federal public service. Flaws in the merit system were the first to cause concern. It was accepted that the public service was scrupulously non-partisan and highly competent, but in the eyes of many these advantages were offset by a system of management that undermined efficiency and effectiveness.[99] Later it was realized that the merit system also tended to exclude certain parts of the population from the public service. French Canadians were poorly represented, as were native peoples and, in the senior ranks, women.[100] Efforts to create a more representative and responsive service, particularly the attempt to build a bilingual public service, outraged many who had benefited from the system, but did not necessarily appease those who had not. These difficulties were lumped in the public mind with other problems of public administration: the seemingly endless growth of government; the extensions and sometimes arbitrary use of power;

strikes in important services; the inflationary effect of some wage settle-
ments and, above all, the growth of public-sector spending. The public has
grown increasingly skeptical of the authority of professional expertise and
of the disinterestedness of bureaucratic advice. It became aware that political non-partisanship should not be confused with policy non-partisanship
and that officials can be tempted into supporting policies because they
enhance their own organizations or are administratively convenient. The
public, therefore, began to question the legitimacy of the policies and
programs developed by government departments. Respect for a neutral,
highly professional service gave way to outspoken dissatisfaction. Public-
service management became a political issue; critical journalism abounded,
and the decline of public confidence was registered not only in the polls and
the election of governments pledged to austerity, but in the publication of
books like *Cover Your Ass*, a derisive vignette of civil-service life, which
sold vigorously across the country.[101]

Bureaucracies sought to meet the decline of traditional sources of legitimacy
in two ways: they surrounded themselves with their own form of representative institutions and cultivated the legitimating authority of Parliament.
The first of these strategies is evident in the trend towards representative
bureaucracy, observable particularly in agencies dealing with social policy
or minority groups.[102] The most widely used strategy, however, has been
the expansion and institutionalization of the policy communities operating
in each field of government concerned. This approach seeks to enhance the
legitimacy of agency proposals—and of the agencies themselves—by trying
to give all who are most affected by specific policies an opportunity to
influence them; agencies can then argue that such policies are a product of
consensus within the affected sectoral constituency. The advantage of this
strategy over others is that as long as agencies do not artificially limit
participation, they can convincingly repudiate charges that they have manipulated consensus formation among their 'clients'. Thus we can see in the
development of policy communities not only a response to the changing
power relationship of central agencies and line departments but a groping
towards more comprehensive representation of interests, which would
enhance the legitimacy of agencies themselves.

Among the most important consequences of the search for legitimating
institutions have been its effects on the role of Parliament. We have shown
that in recent years pressure groups have paid increasing attention to
Parliament. This does not mean that interest-group leaders have revised
their assessment of Parliament's capacity to effect immediate changes in the
policies proposed by the Government. While it is true that the number of
witnesses appearing before House Committees increased significantly after
1968, and that a number of bills have been withdrawn, revised, or amended
as a result of public intervention at the Committee stage, experienced

lobbyists seem to expect very little from their encounters with Parliament and parliamentarians.[103] John F. Bulloch, founder of the Canadian Federation of Independent Business, sees his early attempts to influence MPs and Parliamentary Committees as the misguided exertions of a 'very naive' apprentice lobbyist. With more than ten years' experience behind him, he approaches parliamentarians only when 'it makes sense . . . We do not have time to talk to people who have no influence.'[104] Other lobbyists agree and wonder why 'groups and companies persevere, given [the] limited pay-off'. They still believe that 'the important time to be having discussions with the government is before they actually draft legislation, or during the course of the drafting'.[105] The apparent futility of a time-consuming and expensive process is underlined by the fact that MPs themselves frequently bemoan their inability to effect real changes in legislation. One MP estimates that 'maybe' in 20 per cent of cases 'committees are useful in terms of decision-making, policy-making, or involvement of Parliament'.[106] A sense of inefficacy, not to mention the time constraints imposed on MPs by their other duties, often leads them to prepare inadequately for committee sessions, so that group representatives and other witnesses are often discouraged by Members' apparent ignorance of the issues under review.[107] Yet groups seem to appear more frequently and acknowledge that the days are gone when a major pressure group can conduct a national policy campaign with virtually no direct communication with Parliament, as the Canadian Medical Association did during the medicare debate.[108] It is considered essential to invest time and effort in cultivating Parliament. As one labour representative has put it, 'we wouldn't lose any opportunity [to influence Parliament]. We'd always go and hope that somewhere, sometime, someone will take up some of the things we are saying. We would never back off from doing that.'[109] In the words of Ernest Steele, President of the Canadian Association of Broadcasters, it is 'a very necessary part of what we program for our association.'[110] Even John Bulloch maintains that 'if . . . you want . . . to put pressure on the system, there is nothing more effective than going to your Member of Parliament' and focusing public attention through caucus and question period.[111]

Two factors account for this anomalous behaviour. Simply by giving a hearing to challenging interests, Parliament first confers legitimacy on them and, second, publicizes their demands. Furthermore their participation galvanizes opposing and competitive groups who also want to mould public attitudes and promote new policies. In the increasingly competitive environment of pressure group politics, the leaders of established groups have to anticipate these interventions, or at least respond to them. In other words, the search for legitimating institutions resulting from the diffusion of power has alerted policy actors in the private and public sectors to the legitimating capacity of Parliament. As agencies sought to create in policy communities a source of external legitimation, they found in Parliament a vehicle through which those communities could publicize issues and secure their ultimate legitimation. Ironically, then, the diffusion of power has contributed to the stature of Parliament.

Many would disagree. A 1982 report of the Canadian Bar Association, for example, stated that 'Parliament is not only inefficient and ineffective, but . . . its reputation within the country is at an all-time low.'[112] Perhaps, but so is the reputation of the Cabinet and bureaucracy. Comparatively speaking, the status of Parliament has improved. Kornberg, Clarke, and Goddard, for example, have analysed Canadian Institute of Public Opinion data to show that 'the *position* of members of Parliament is held in great esteem by the public . . . The mean score for parliamentary office (82.3) was exceeded only by those for the Prime Minister (86.3) and the police (83.3)'. Civil servants, the Governor-General, and the Queen scored much lower (68.4; 61.3 and 57.8 respectively).[113]

A diffused power system enhances the status of Parliament because it places a premium on what had previously been undervalued: the legitimating capacity of Parliament. Of all the political institutions in Canada, Parliament— the House of Commons in particular—is the pre-eminent legitimating institution. In this Canada differs notably from the other political systems that have influenced the country's development. No single institution in Britain, the United States, or France stands for the political community and acts to legitimate its activities to the extent that the House of Commons does in Canada.[114] The system in Britain comes close, but there—for historic reasons—the Crown has more status than it does in Canada. In the United States and France the capacity to legitimate is shared to a much greater extent. Legitimating capacity is shared in Canada as well—Cabinet confers legitimacy on public policy by presenting it to Parliament; and the Crown, represented by the Governor-General, confers legitimacy on legislation by proclaiming it—but neither possesses legitimacy of the same order as the duly constituted, properly representative Parliament, particularly the House of Commons. And of course the legitimating capacity of the Cabinet is derived from its ability to command a majority in the House.

The centrality of Parliament as a legitimating institution ensured that the collective groping for public support on the part of agencies and interests would in the long run bring public servants, pressure groups, and even the political executive to petition for the two benefits within its gift: publicity and legitimation. The government used Parliament to these ends during three important public debates in the early eighties: constitutional reform, the National Energy Program, and the negotiation of federal-provincial fiscal agreements.[115] In each case the federal government, after long and unproductive discussions with the provincial governments, took its own case to the public, via Parliament. Similarly, public servants—in the past reluctant suitors for parliamentary attention—have recently espoused reforms that would give them greater access on matters not involving the House's confidence.[116] Officials sometimes see in greater access a means of using parliamentarians and parliamentary committees to 'sell' favoured policy proposals to the public, even though, as Nord reports in a study of the Green Paper on Immigration Policy, such attempts sometimes fail in the face of determination on the part of committees to play a more independent, mediating role.[117] The Levesque government was more successful in its use of a committee of the national assembly to publicize the case for its language legislation—selecting for public presentation and discussion 62 briefs of the 270 submitted—on the grounds that they were most representative of the various viewpoints held within the Quebec comunity concerning the legislation.[118]

In their relations with Parliament, public servants are constrained by the constitutional provisions of Cabinet-parliamentary government. In effect they may speak only when spoken to, and in all exchanges must be careful to respect the ultimate responsibility of the minister. For officials ambitious to foster policy development, or to secure the well-being of their institutions, this is a major impediment. The cultivation of policy communities offers an effective way around it. Interest group representatives are not bound by governmental agenda-setting. Intimately aware of the needs and objectives of agencies, they can express those needs when necessary in a manner that can be readily disowned by the sponsoring agency. Furthermore, in the sometimes competitive atmosphere of committee hearings friendly interest groups, rather than agencies themselves, are at times the most appropriate defenders of agency positions and proposals. Thus in cultivating policy communities, agencies simultaneously achieve two types of legitimation. On the one hand they reinforce the support of their own functional constituencies, and on the other they use them to tap Parliament's capacity to publicize and legitimate agency goals and programs. In so doing they contribute to a revival of Parliament's role in the policy process.

This revival has not depended solely on a renewed interest in Parliament's capacity as legitimator and publicist. Parliamentary reform has facilitated, and perhaps encouraged, this trend. In particular the expanded use of committees to review legislation, scrutinize public expenditure, and investigate policy issues has made possible a greater interaction between Parliament, public servants, individuals, and interest groups. According to Rush, between 1945 and 1965 only 10 per cent to 15 per cent of public bills passed in each Parliament were referred to committee. After 1963, however, a growing number found their way there. In 1966-7, 23 per cent of bills were sent to standing committees. The number dropped drastically to 3 per cent in 1967-8, a period dominated by the Liberal leadership contest, but with the introduction of new procedures in the 1968-9 session, the proportion expanded to 75 per cent and in 1969-70 dropped only slightly to 70 per cent.[119] Impressionistic evidence suggests that, with the further integration of committee review in the legislative work of Parliament, this proportion has been maintained. The figures cited earlier leave little doubt that the public, including interest groups, has found committee hearings a useful forum for comment on proposed legislation. Case studies reinforce the point. Nord, in his study of the parliamentary review of the Green Paper on Immigration (referred to above), reports that the Joint Committee conducted well-publicized cross-country hearings that netted 1,400 letters and briefs and heard 400 individuals and groups.[120] The Commons Committee on Justice and Legal Affairs, which is credited with having pushed the 1968 reforms 'as far as possible',[121] has conducted several important inquiries into proposed legislation and into the penitentiary system, at times having to limit the number of briefs it would formally hear and on other occasions specifically inviting pressure groups—clearly members of the Justice policy community—to comment on legislative proposals. Some of these hearings clearly influenced public opinion. The hearings on the 1976 Omnibus Bill to amend the Criminal Code generated so much public opposition to certain aspects of gun control that the bill was withdrawn and a revised version was eventually passed.[122] These committees are but two of the many standing and special committees that have conducted similar reviews of legislation and investigations since 1968 and have attracted considerable public attention. The recent use of parliamentary task forces to investigate developing policy issues can only reinforce this pattern of behaviour.[123]

Although the search for legitimation, together with the effects of parliamentary reform, largely explain recent interest group attentiveness to Parliament, several other factors associated with the public aspects of policy formation also contribute to the changes we have observed. First, developments outside the governmental arena have placed a premium on publicity. Television in particular encourages demonstrative public participation. It also tends to encourage groups lacking established access to agencies to imitate the attention-catching behaviour of groups in other countries. Parliament, because it is able to focus attention to an extraordinary degree, becomes a target for Canadian groups. Challenged publicly by newcomers or the less privileged, established groups find they must respond publicly in order to safeguard their position and the policies they espouse. For them too Parliament is an important vehicle for gaining publicity and generating support.

Second, while it may appear to many MPs, and to those working to influence them, that the power of Parliament is extremely limited, so too, increasingly, is the power of other institutions, as our discussion of the diffusion of power has demonstrated. Relatively speaking, Parliament's authority in the policy process has expanded simply because that of other institutions has declined. While this does not mean that Parliament can actually formulate or determine policy, it does mean that interests must take into account Parliament's capacity to influence both policy and public opinion. Finally, the evidence suggests that Parliament today can effect changes in legislation that would have been unheard of twenty years ago. Several major pieces of legislation have been withdrawn and/or revised, apparently as a consequence of committee review: the Competition Bill of 1977; gun control legislation, and proposals to revise the Crow's Nest Pass freight rates are examples of occasions in the last fifteen years when interest groups have been able to take advantage of parliamentary hearings to generate public debate on specific issues and thereby change government proposals.[124] On a less dramatic scale, a good deal of legislation seems to undergo revision at the committee stage. Not all such revision is technical in nature. Rush quotes Hockin to the effect that the Ministers of Agriculture and Justice 'spent many hours in the summer of 1969 consulting with committee members on proposed legislation, thus recognizing the political reality that both the Agriculture and Justice Committees were developing atittudes of their own—attitudes sometimes at variance with Government policy.'[125] More recently Jim Hawkes, PC member for Calgary West, has argued that the diversity of witnesses before the Special Joint Committee on the Constitution 'changed public opinion and ultimately changed the government's mind'.[126]

Parliament, then, has become an important target for interests wishing to publicize their demands and/or receive the cachet of the legislature's support. This attentiveness to Parliament denotes a significant change in the behaviour pattern of groups. It enlarges the opportunity for issue-oriented groups to enter policy discussions, and draws the more traditional institutionalized organizations into the public debate they once eschewed. It weakens the hold of government agencies on affiliated interest groups, diminishing their capacity to dominate the relationship and creating something closer to partnership in group-agency relations. It contributes, in short, to more dynamic public debate.

THE EVOLUTION OF A POLICY ACTOR

In these two chapters we have seen how pressure groups, never entirely absent from the policy process, have come to prominence in Canadian politics. Today national organizations lead public debate on many issues and are involved on a daily basis with the refinement and implementation of public policy.

Group politics, which played a limited role a century ago, has become an integral part of policy-making. Pressure groups now perform a vital communications function, linking special publics to government and often supplanting the élite interaction and party intervention that was the norm in 1900. They are often used to secure the legitimacy of government actions, something that would have been considered most unusual in the early part of the period we have studied.

Their form and behaviour has changed too. In the nineteenth century group activity occurred largely at the local level and depended on volunteer support. As the century reached its close national associations were becoming prominent. Some of them employed a small professional staff, but they still owed their vigour and influence to the enthusiasm and dedication of volunteer supporters working in local chapters scattered across the country. We have seen how this decentralized group politics was superseded by the institutionalization of groups clustering around governments at the federal and provincial capitals. Local organizations did not disappear but their influence—and their spontaneity—declined as national associations developed, co-ordinating the views of individual branches, passing those views through the mill of committee review and convention ratification and, in general, 'aggregating' demand. Institutionalization turned pressure groups into complex organizations with elaborate federal, provincial, and local structures employing professional staff. Pressure groups also became more numerous.

Their behaviour became more complex. Early groups used petitions and personal lobbying with government leaders to obtain their ends. By the late nineteenth century the equivalent of today's mass media campaigns were not unknown—witness the public meetings organized by temperance groups and the extravagant parades of fraternal associations like the Orange Lodge— but Canadians seem to have exercised restraint in lobbying from the outset. As government expanded and the role of the bureaucracy in policy formation became more pronounced, restrained behind-the-scenes lobbying became the norm. Mass meetings, marches on Ottawa, demonstrations and appeals to the media occurred but they came to be seen as the last resort of groups that had exhausted every other avenue of persuasion, or did not understand the policy process. The most influential groups eschewed publicity, accepting instead the norms of acceptable behaviour laid down by government. Ultimately, however, the scale and extent of government activity expanded beyond the control of senior administrators and leading politicians, fragmenting the policy process and unleashing an unprecedented level of group intervention—both public and behind-the-scenes—in policy-making. As a result, Canadians today possess a diffused policy-making system in which group politics is at the heart of policy communication and legitimation.

We have linked the transformation in the role of pressure groups to the evolution of Canada's economic and political life. The shift from a decentralized economy to one in which corporate concentration affects every aspect of life could not have been achieved without major changes in the role of the state and in the relations among political institutions. Governments became managers as corporations realized the need to plan. Supply and demand management became the common object of both the private and public sectors. Technostructures, often operating through the medium of interest groups, spun pervasive, binding threads of communication between the two. The role of specific political institutions varied as the modern political economy evolved. Representative legislatures brought responsible government and paved the way for the political party and the Cabinet-parliamentary system of government. A decentralized, developing economy fostered confederation and the emergence of the party system, giving only a minor role to interest groups. The latter, active at the local level, mitigated the harsher effects of industrialization and development and laid the basis for our modern system of social welfare. The party system and the provincial and federal governments were the preserve of business interests who saw the state as the guardian of law and order, the defender of the country and, above all, as the mechanism through which economic development would be achieved. Thus, at the local level benevolent societies established hospitals and shelters; fraternal organizations provided their members with insurance against the vicissitudes of life, and boards of trade brought pressure to bear on MPs and MLAs and party leaders to secure through the national and provincial governments the building of railroads, the settlement of new territory, the distribution of natural resources, and the erection of tariff barriers behind which an industrialized economy could emerge.

Industrialization, however, precipitated further changes in the relations among political and economic institutions. Initially corporate concentration fostered the dominance of the political executive and started the decline of party and legislature. Subsequently, as the complexity of economic management became apparent, the bureaucracy grew in influence, the technostructure emerged, the political executive became less competent at directing the public service, and Parliament reached such a low ebb of influence that many despaired of its revival. A revival of sorts has been achieved, however, growing out of the diffusion of power that complexity has spawned and based on Parliament's capacity to bestow legitimacy and publicity on those interests it chooses to hear. In this most recent evolution of our state and economic institutions, pressure groups have flourished, becoming more numerous and pervasive as they carry messages between interests and agencies; agencies and Parliament; Parliament and the media; and as they work to secure the legitimation of their demands. Their adaptability; their skills in communication; their capacity to represent interests; and, above all, their understanding of the policy process—all these give them an importance today that they never had before.

Part II

The Analysis of
Pressure Groups:
What They Do
and
How They Work

CHAPTER 4

Function:
The Context of
Pressure Group Life

Pressure groups perform the same functions wherever they are found. They promote the interests of their members. They communicate between members and the state. They legitimate the demands their members make on the state and the public policies they support. They regulate their members and they assist the state to administer policies and programs. However, they carry out these functions to different degrees from political system to political system and they behave differently in each. In this chapter and the next we will use our knowledge of the universal functions of pressure groups and our appreciation of the idiosyncratic behaviour that develops in each political system to build a typology of groups that will help us organize and interpret our knowledge of how pressure groups have adapted to Canadian political life.

Most pressure group studies have focused on individual countries. Few scholars have made comparisons across countries, though many use American findings as a benchmark, and frequently warn that pressure-group behaviour in the country under study is not quite like that in the United States. S.E. Finer, for example, found that interest groups in Britain work 'more cordially' with government departments than they do in the United States, where they are 'still regarded as piratical' and are obliged to resort to public campaigning.[1] Robert Presthus, in comparing élite accommodation in Canada and the United States, found many instances of differing behavioural and organizational patterns. Some of these differences—such as public attitudes towards groups—he attributed to fundamental differences between the two political systems.[2] Henry W. Ehrmann, summarizing a series of papers examining group behaviour in several countries, also argues that differences in political systems affect the development and behaviour of pressure groups: 'the political system, as well as the social structure, will often decide whether claims raised in the name of special interests will be successful or not; it may determine the "style" used by pressure groups when raising their demands.'[3] The constitutional arrangements found in each country will also be important, conditioning in part the 'methods by which pressure groups penetrate parliament . . . [A] parliamentary system, a system in which the separation of power prevails, a federal system, and a unitarian system will of necessity place the organized interests in a different position.'[4] Another scholar, Harry Eckstein, argues that pressure-group politics are a function of the variable attitudes of individual members and of the society at large, the structure of governmental decision-making, and the patterns of policy-making in the political system.[5]

These findings are not conclusive, but they suggest that there are important variations in pressure group politics from country to country and that they are probably rooted in the different political systems of the countries involved. Each system obliges the pressure groups working within it to adapt to its particular characteristics, since pressure groups survive only if they are willing to adapt. The cumulative effects of individual group adaptations is the creation in each country of distinctive patterns of behaviour. We see this illustrated in the patterns of voluntarism in different countries. The Americans tend to be a nation of joiners. Their groups are characterized by a high degree of voluntarism. Broad-based 'grass roots' support for groups and their demands is often a prerequisite to being recognized and heard by government. This is contrasted by some scholars, like S.E. Finer, with the situation in Britain, where close working relationships between groups and government departments appear to be a more noticeable characteristic than massive public involvement in group activity.[6] The French, on the other hand, seem to engage in very limited group activity at the popular level, though there is usually a good deal of discussion between ministries and their specific 'partners'—heads of corporations, businessmen's groups, unions, associations of professionals—when changes in policy are being considered.[7]

Canadians seem as ready to 'join' as Americans, and are more attuned to a voluntaristic approach to political life than Europeans.[8] Canadians expect and demand a role in policy-making that is certainly not expected in France, nor for the most part in Britain. In each setting a long history of political development—the centralism of France, for example, or the openness of the American system, or Canada's adaptation of parliamentary-Cabinet government to federalism—has created idiosyncratic attitudes and relationships.

The movement to win the vote for women offers an illustration. The campaign for women's suffrage in Canada that began in the late nineteen-hundreds was part of an international movement. Its leaders were well aware of the strategies used by their counterparts in other countries. Often they participated in the demonstrations and conferences held elsewhere, and they in turn were aided, in this country, by visits of the movement's foreign leaders. Yet they did not imitate foreign pressure tactics. Laura Bacchi, one of the historians of the movement, reports that their approach was 'cautious and undemonstrative, in keeping with the country's reputed character'.[9] For them, the petition was the principal weapon of policy communication, though they also used mock parliaments, plays, exhibits, postcards, and other similar vehicles to demonstrate to politicians that they wanted the vote. J.P. Whitney, premier of Ontario, was presented in 1909 with a petition supported by over one hundred thousand signatures. In Manitoba 39,584 people signed the petition that preceded the extension of votes to women in 1915. In Bacchi's opinion caution was induced by an appreciation of the political culture of the day and of the capacity of the movement itself. In many respects these were unique to the Canadian environment:

> The movement was still young and had not faced the long years of rebuke and ridicule which enraged British women. Moreover, Canadians had a reputation to uphold as non-violent, law-abiding citizens. More significantly, the movement lacked the cohesiveness and strength necessary for a concerted drive. The associations were widely dispersed and poorly organized, fragmented both by geography and ideology. Sectionalism, a problem for most Canadian social movements, troubled the suffragists as well. Although the (Canadian Suffrage Association) claimed national status, in fact, it had few affiliates and even less control outside of Toronto. Suffragists in British Columbia considered themselves autonomous. Suffragists in Saskatchewan, Manitoba, and Alberta co-operated with one another but wanted nothing to do with a national association directed by Eastern women. The Montreal Suffrage Association became a CSA affiliate but it too conducted its own campaign with little guidance from Toronto. With the exception of occasional encouragement to New Brunswick, the CSA also had little to do with the Maritime provinces where the [Women's Christian Temperance Union] led the campaigning.[10]

Few groups have escaped these peculiarities of our political and social system.

Having demonstrated that pressure group politics varies a good deal from one country to another, we must return to the other side of the view we presented at the beginning of the chapter: that there are many important similarities. The French, for example, may not be great joiners, but they wave placards, sign petitions, and in other ways use groups to influence government. Journalists covering the 1983 student riots in Paris noted that demonstrations developed with an almost ritualistic rhythm into violent confrontations between students and police, suggesting that even at this extreme, interaction between government and organized interests is a recognized part of the French policy process. Though American group politics places unusual emphasis on grass roots involvement, this has not inhibited the development of the world's most sophisticated machinery for interacting with government agencies; an activity Finer, for example, associates more clearly with British groups. So faithfully have environmental groups around the world copied the mass demonstration techniques of American environmentalists that a casual observer of the television news must often listen and watch carefully to determine where the latest demonstration is taking place.

The key to this apparent contradiction is suggested by Robert Presthus when he refers to pressure group politics as 'a process that seems functionally essential in any political system'.[11] If pressure groups perform one or more essential functions in each system, the functions are probably similar whenever they occur, and in carrying them out the groups are likely to develop comparable techniques and structures. Examination of group activity on a comparative basis suggests pressure groups perform one function—the promotion of members' interests—that serves the needs of members and four others that meet the needs of the community in which they work. The most important of these are communication and legitimation functions. Less significant are the steps they take to regulate their members on behalf of the state and the assistance they give governments in administering programs. In the following paragraphs we examine each of these functions and identify their appearance in Canadian pressure group politics.

INTEREST PROMOTION

In chapter 1 we said that pressure groups seek 'to influence public policy in order to promote their common interest'. They draw together people who see themselves as having common interests; they bring about agreement on which interests are indeed common and on how they can be best served, and enable these people to express their interests to government in a way they hope will influence public policy in their favour. In the jargon of political science the first part of this activity is known as *interest aggregation*, the second as *interest articulation*. Taken together they constitute the function of promoting member interests. As we shall see, not all members join groups out of a desire to promote their own narrowly defined interests. Furthermore, few pressure groups exist *solely* as pressure groups; many also act in the political realm as an inevitable extension of their other concerns. But whenever they engage in the policy process, such groups do so to promote what the members conceive as their common interest, whether it be a broadly stated public interest—such as will excite the Canadian Civil Liberties Association, for instance—or a narrowly conceived one like the majority of issues pursued by trade associations. From the point of view of the members at large, the interest promotion function is the chief reason why the groups they belong to should interact with government; should, in effect, act as pressure groups. Interest promotion, then, is a fundamental function of pressure groups.

THE SYSTEMIC FUNCTIONS

The desire to get some personal advantage from government policy is a common characteristic of interest group members. But can the self-interest of group supporters explain the fact that pressure groups are not only formed around the world, they are often welcomed and fostered and are tolerated even in many states that on ideological grounds should be hostile? The promotion of self-interest is a subsystemic function: it helps those who are in the subsystem—that is, the group members—but at first glance it does not do very much for the rest of us who are in the larger system, the broader political community. Surely to justify their prominence pressure groups must perform some functions that render them useful in the system at large. There must be what some scholars call a benefit-exchange relationship. To survive as effective political institutions they must offer services needed by their host political systems, receiving in return specific benefits for themselves and their members. The functions of communication, legitimation, regulation, and administration do this. They not only meet the needs of members, they facilitate the workings of the political system. We can therefore call them 'systemic functions'.

(i) *Communications*

When groups engage in the communications process they act as relay points, sending messages in four different directions. Best known is their role in transmitting demands from special publics *to* governments. When the federal government suspended commercial salmon fishing in New Brunswick and parts of Newfoundland, Denis Monroe, president of the Fisheries Council of Canada, complained that 'we simply weren't consulted. We learned about it third hand.' He urged the fishery interests to build up the resources of the Fisheries Council to enable it to make the fishermen's views heard when similar decisions had to be considered in future. 'You need a rifle, not a popgun to get through to the government,' he concluded. [12]

Besides transmitting messages to government, groups often convey the views, demands, and decisions of public officials *from* government to special publics. For example, the Union of Nova Scotia Municipalities began life as a ' "common" pressure group, trying to influence the government to follow the wishes of its members', but soon became a 'quasi-administrative' arm of the province, passing on to local governments the views and policy decisions of the government in Halifax. [13] Public officials encourage groups to act as the main conduit between themselves and group members, partly because this promotes dialogue, but also because they have found that interest organizations frequently offer the most effective means of reaching special publics. One government agency working in the Lac St-Jean region of Québec had a typical experience. Letters, use of the media, audio-visual displays, demonstrations, flyers, and press releases brought the agency's message to less than 18 per cent of its target audience. The officials concluded that members of the public create a wall of indifference to protect themselves from the barrage of information they receive daily from and about government. They might attend to those messages that seem to affect them personally—'Ils ne sont touchés que par ce qui les pogne aux tripes. On les attrape avec leur bol de café, avec leurs oeufs, leur pain'[14]—but even these will not register unless they appear in a context and form that the individual is attuned to. Interest associations understand how to catch the attention of their members; to show them how their vital interests may be affected by government messages, and perhaps even to translate the officialese of press releases, forms, and regulations into everyday language. On occasion, where the special public is numerous or has a recurrent contact with government, it is possible to convey information through officials. 'Ag reps' have often served as links between farmers and departments of agriculture; the unemployed can be reached through Employment and Immigration Canada offices. In many ridings MPs and MLAs see communication with distinct parts of the public as one of their prime responsibilities. For the most part, however, members of interest communities are too dispersed to be contacted in this way, and the vital link between citizen and government has to be provided by interest group organizations.

The two-way flow of messages between groups and governments is the most important communications process groups engage in, but not the only one. To a limited extent groups can facilitate communication *within* government, carrying messages between agencies, cutting across the barriers that separate levels in the administrative hierarchy or divide the political and administrative worlds. They may simply be needed to interpret one part of government to another. They can at times render even more valuable service in intergovernmental communication. In 1876, after repeated protests from the provincial government had failed to persuade Ottawa to begin work on the British Columbia end of the transcontinental railway, a group of Vancouver Island businessmen organized themselves into a club to lobby in support of the British Columbia government's demands. Ultimately the combined lobbying of government and business convinced the federal government that work should be started and that Vancouver—not New Westminster, whose own lobbying was in part responsible for the delay—should be the western terminus of the railway.[15] On the east coast the Atlantic Provinces Economic Council took a leading role in promoting communication between governments, advocating intergovernmental meetings, supporting the work of the Deutsch inquiry into Maritime Union and later championing establishment of the Council of Maritime Premiers. In itself APEC serves as a mechanism through which governments can talk to one another on economic matters. Governments commission research that cuts across provincial jurisdictions; their representatives sit on APEC committees and study groups, and they participate in the Council's many conferences and seminars. Daily these interactions provide the means through which governments can send messages to one another.[16]

Finally, groups spend a great deal of time communicating *among* themselves; more so as issues appear to be increasingly interrelated and as budgeting systems, such as the federal 'envelope' system, are developed to encourage co-ordination between policy sectors.[17] The extent to which groups communicate and co-operate with one another can be observed readily enough during any public debate. The discussion of 'freedom of information' legislation offers an illustration. To promote more open access to government information, the Canadian Bar Association, the Social Sciences Federation, the Canadian Association of University Teachers, and the Canadian Library Association, to name but a few organizations, co-operated extensively in presenting their views to government and bringing public pressure to bear. As the campaign developed an umbrella group, ACCESS ('A Citizens Committee for the Right to Public Information') emerged and assumed most of the burden of co-ordinating the campaign.[18] Intergroup co-operation and communication has a long tradition in Canada; nearly a century earlier the temperance movement promoted not only temperance but votes for women, the elimination of sweat-shops, the extension of educational opportunities for women, and so on.[19]

The direction of communications received and emitted by groups is important, but equally so is their content, which ranges from the routine to the urgent; from the banal to the extraordinary. Trade associations advise governments on appropriate standards for new products; fishermen's associations complain about inadequate weather forecasting and rescue services on the Pacific and Atlantic coasts; monarchists keep a watchful eye on governmental attitudes towards the Royal Family; and so on. Even the more unusual interest group communications are part of the flow of information government needs to exercise its vital functions. Consider, for example, a series of messages delivered to the federal and Ontario governments by the Ontario Federation of Hunters and Anglers and the Ontario Trappers' Association, among others, concerning the introduction into Canada of an Asian dog, known as the coon dog. The dogs had been imported in 1980 by a Madoc, Ontario, fur rancher who proposed to use their fur as a substitute for raccoon fur. The scheme had received the approval of the Ontario Department of Agriculture and it was only after the animals had arrived that wildlife groups learned that the importation 'had the potential for being the biggest environmental disaster since the introduction of the starling and the carp in the last century'. The coon dog, it appeared, is a voracious hunter of small game and a prolific breeder. Any dogs that escaped from the fur farm could, in a short time, extend their range throughout the eastern provinces and the northeastern United States. Urged on by the wildlife groups, federal authorities acted on two fronts. First, the Export and Import Act was amended to prohibit further importation. Second, after their owners were compensated, the dogs themselves were put down and a potential threat to Ontario wildlife was eliminated.[20]

Despite their variety and the diverse ways in which they are transmitted, interest group communications have two common features. First, they concern the vital interests of the groups engaged in transmitting and receiving them. Second, they are seen by public officials as essential to the business of government. The first makes them valuable to the groups originating them, and renders functional the formation of organizations capable of articulating them to government. The second renders those same groups valuable to government. Without that multi-directional flow of messages modern government could not respond effectively to its environment, influence that environment, or attempt to create within it an element of order and stability.

Nowhere is this more clearly evident than in the recent experience of the east-coast fishing industry. Here the role of government has steadily expanded, particularly in the period after January 1977 when Canada established the 200-mile limit and in effect undertook to manage the supply of fish to Canadian and foreign concerns. Not only is this resource highly unpredictable, the product of a complex environment we understand only inadequately, and prone to sudden and inexplicable fluctuations, but the industry itself is excessively fragmented, technologically diverse, and rent by deep ideological differences. For years federal officials have sought to achieve order within it, to attain a degree of predictability sufficient for even minimal planning of stock management. This has been easy enough where the major fish companies have been concerned; capital-intensive firms, they have experts who relate easily to the bureaucratic world of regulation and negotiation and who serve as the technostructure for the industry and government. The companies' trade association, the Fisheries Council of Canada, was for many years the main interest-group contact between the federal Department of Fisheries and the industry; federal officials assumed that independent fishermen and small fish processors would communicate adequately with government through political parties and provincial governments. As the resource has been depleted, however, and market access has become more problematic this assumption has had to be abandoned, and federal officials have sought ways of persuading the 'unorganized' fishermen to build organizations through which they could hear and speak to government. Romeo LeBlanc, Minister of Fisheries and Oceans in the Trudeau Government, has pointed out that 'most groups and professions have some means to influence events. But in my first speech as Minister I had to urge fishermen to organize, not just to deal with processors but so we in government could begin to hear their views.'[21] Time and again since the early 1970s incentives have been offered to independent fishermen to organize themselves. When incentives have failed, regulatory regimes have been established to coerce them into collective decision-making and communication. These efforts have had only limited success, and the measure of their failure is the slowness with which regimes of stock management have been accepted across the industry; the lack of appropriate and coherent federal policies; and the difficulty Ottawa has had in explaining the needs of the industry to the voters of central Canada whose tax dollars support the expensive—and too often unsuccessful—programs that sustain the industry. The east-coast fishery needs a stable environment—consistent regulation, sufficient and predictable catches, orderly exploitation, and secure markets—but without effective communication within the industry, neither industry members nor governments can determine what policies will best secure these objectives, nor can they ensure that members of the industry will respect fisheries policy and make them work. Organization of the diverse interests within the fishery would go far to securing stability; it would facilitate the flow of communication government needs to fully play its role in demand and supply management.[22]

(ii) *Legitimation:*

Interest groups confer legitimacy when they acknowledge and support the work of a particular individual, institution, or policy and use their influence with the community at large to extend that support throughout the political community. The legitimating functions of pressure groups are by-products of their comunications activities and supportive of them. As well as expanding the range of information available to government, group involvement in policy discussions can be used both to neutralize group objections to proposed legislation and to engage support for it. Government thus finds in the pressure group system a device for testing policy proposals and a means of securing support for them. A typical instance occurred in 1983 when the Minister of Consumer and Corporate Affairs attempted to end nearly fifteen years of debate over reform of competition policy by drawing leading business groups into a privileged advisory position. Officials and some two dozen representatives of the Chamber of Commerce, the Business Council on National Issues, and the Canadian Manufacturers' Association met behind closed doors to work out the latest proposals. Consumer groups were pointedly ignored. Their support was not essential to passage of the bill; that of the business groups was. As one newspaper report put it, 'Ottawa has tried six times in the past dozen years to update its competition laws but has failed each time after colliding head-on with business.'[23] This process ultimately gave birth to a policy that appeared to have business endorsement.

The doubly supportive function of legitimation has encouraged some government agencies to stimulate pressure group activity within the community and has also been rewarding to compliant pressure groups, since government recognition enhances their own stature and guarantees a measure of influence over policy decisions that are of concern to them. Above all, the relationship can serve the function of keeping the political system abreast of changes within the social system as a whole, thereby promoting general political stability. The successful performance of this last function, however, will depend on the sensitivity of governmental and pressure group sub-systems to changes in their own and immediate environments. Through a failure to absorb external demands, closed and captive agencies and groups may compound rigidities existing elsewhere in the system. Quasi-judicial tribunals, such as motor carrier boards or natural product marketing boards, are prone to do this. Because they deal with complex, highly technical matters they often depend on the information resources of the groups they are meant to control and even—by defining very narrowly the public's right to intervene in regulatory hearings—lose the capacity to assess the broader public interest.[24] Eventually such atrophication can lead to policies that are so clearly self-serving that an offended public repudiates their legitimacy and imposes new rules, new terms of reference, and new decision-making processes on the policy community. In the field of tax policy, for example, Kenneth Woodside suggests that the 'closed and secretive' character of federal tax policy-making undermines the legitimacy of many tax measures. He finds in the politics surrounding recent budgets a struggle between those who have traditionally influenced tax policy and reformers who want measures that would meet the needs of 'the full range of interests within Canada'.[25] To achieve reform, he argues, the federal government must either brave the attacks of those whose influence has created policies that suit their needs and/or 'it must mobilize new support to offset the opposition of aggrieved interests'. Both groups, and government itself, would treat their ability to proclaim or undermine the legitimacy of the government's measures as important weapons in the policy battle.

(iii) *Regulation and administration:*

Finally, pressure groups frequently act as the agents of government to regulate their members and to administer programs. Their role in the regulation of professional activity is perhaps the best-known example of this function. The governing bodies of the professions decide what lawyers, doctors, chartered accountants, engineers and other professionals need to know before they can be allowed to practise.[26] In many cases they test recruits to the profession and establish periods of probation. They determine some of the conditions that govern the conduct of professionals—lawyers must not solicit business, for example; accountants must observe strict rules when they report the financial affairs of clients—and they discipline those who break the rules, sometimes by dismissing them from the profession. The state permits the profession to exercise this legislative, executive, and judicial authority over their members partly because neither politicians nor administrators feel competent to regulate matters that are often highly technical and complex and partly because our political culture tries to limit the intervention of government in the conduct of economic activity. For these reasons the community is prepared to entrust a great deal of power to the self-regulating professions, hoping that a sense of public trust will encourage their governing bodies not to abuse their authority.

There are many other occasions when the work of interest groups supplements that of government agencies. Our earlier survey of the evolution of Canadian pressure groups discussed the role charitable associations played in establishing and supporting hospitals and shelters for the poor. As the state assumed the burden of responsibility for these institutions the role of voluntary organizations declined, but did not disappear. Increased state responsibility brought some groups new duties, and even occasioned the creation of others, as officials suggested that volunteers might assist them in carrying out their duties. Thus we saw Ontario prison officials foster the development of prisoners' aid societies. Freda Hawkins, in a study of Canadian immigration policy, found that 'over the whole post-war period . . . voluntary agencies have given considerable (and largely unpaid) service to the government in the reception, welfare, settlement, and adjustment of immigrants'.[27] Many social-welfare agencies such as Children's Aid Societies provide similar administrative assistance to government.[28] An indication of how extensive this form of 'privatization' of government activities has become appeared in 1982 when the Ontario government, in imposing spending cuts on the public service, insisted that the restraint measures extend to salaries of individuals working for charitable institutions under contract to the government.[29]

Research and data collection are frequently assigned to interest groups by governments and the interests themselves. The Alberta government's Environmental Trust enables non-government bodies to carry out environmental research. In Ontario the Canadian Environmental Law Association has been assisted to carry out research into environmental impact assessment; toxic waste disposal; sand and gravel extraction; and other procedures and practices that are in dispute. Such research assists regulatory tribunals and informs legislation.[30] Throughout Canadian industry associations carry on research activities that aid the public, governments, and industry. The Canadian Home Builders' Association conducts research into energy efficiency; the Canadian Masonry Contractors Association and the Machinery and Equipment Manufacturers' Association of Canada fund research on behalf of government and industry.[31] In the health field the National Cancer Institute is known to all Canadians for its work in channelling government and private funding to medical research. Less public is the work of the Institute of Public Administration of Canada in supporting research and publication concerned with the management, operations, and conduct of government. Our list could go on and on.

On occasion government and industry attempt 'co-management' and even co-regulation through interest associations. The Department of Fisheries and Oceans, arguing that it spends 'too much of its efforts and resources doing the jobs that fishermen should be doing themselves', has looked to newly formed fishermen's organizations to assume regulatory and administrative responsibilities.[32] To this end, in 1976 the Department modified its regulation of the Bay of Fundy herring stock in such a way that various industry groups could form a herring fishermen's co-operative. The co-operative not only negotiated fish prices on behalf of fishermen, it also policed vessel quotas, distributed surplus quotas across the fleet, supervised certain sales procedures and collected statistics, all functions frequently performed by government officials.[33] For a variety of reasons the Bay of Fundy scheme failed, but the idea of interest group participation in co-management of the fishery has continued to tantalize policy makers. The Task Force on the Atlantic Fishery, in 1982, called co-management an intriguing idea 'if it means that fishermen's organizations might take more responsibility for the development of and follow-through on policy in the harvesting sector.'[34] More recently, officials have pointed out that the highly regulated in-shore ground-fishery could be made less cumbersome if monitoring of the catch could be carried out through fishermen's organizations.[35]

We treat the administrative and regulatory functions of pressure groups as less significant than their legitimating and communication functions because they have less impact on the operation of the political system. They are, nevertheless, important in the delivery of government programs—many government functions could not be performed without them—and in the maintenance of economic relations, particularly the relations between professional groups and the community at large. In the climate of government restraint that currently prevails it is quite possible that these functions will become more important as governments attempt to turn over to the private sector responsibilities and activities that they can no longer afford. If this should prove to be the case, it is also probable that increased responsibilities will bring to interest groups increased influence in policy-making.

CONCLUSION: THE FUNCTIONS OF PRESSURE GROUPS

In order to understand the role and behaviour of pressure groups in our political system we have assumed that pressure groups behave differently from one political system to another even while they perform functions that are similar. This strategy is useful because it helps us avoid the risks of adopting too freely the conclusions about group behaviour reached by students of other systems, while at the same time it helps us order what we know about groups in general and Canadian groups in particular. It suggests that we look for two types of characteristics in pressure group systems; those that are universal, and those that seem to vary from country to country and can be called system-specific. We applied the strategy by identifying the critical functions groups perform for their members and for the system at large: (i) interest promotion; (ii) communication; (iii) legitimation; (iv) regulation; (v) administration.

The first of these is subsystemic in orientation. It is far more immediately important to group members themselves than to the political community as a whole. Nonetheless, interest promotion is the *sine qua non* of pressure group politics, since very few pressure groups would exist at all if group members did not feel a need to combine in order to forward their own interests. While the remaining four functions are of varying significance to group members, they play a vital part in the life of most modern political communities. To the extent that each of these functions is indispensable to a given polity, pressure groups will develop and take the shape peculiar to that specific system.

PRESSURE GROUPS IN THE POLICY PROCESS:
THE ROLE OF POLICY COMMUNITIES

Our perceptions of pressure groups have been permeated by the pluralist philosophy espoused by American scholars. The pluralists saw the political system as a dynamic mass of activity in which new groups constantly evolve and old ones are killed off as society adjusts to change; any change will advance some interests, but will have an adverse effect on others, which will come together to solve their common problem. Quite likely the new group will seek a political solution. In the process of maintaining equilibrium, the pluralists argued, society will naturally produce groups to champion an interest disadvantaged by a recent change in social and economic conditions. The same dynamic forces will ensure that there will always be challengers to groups that seek to dominate policy-making. An atomistic, bustling, vibrant, self-organizing interest-group politics is, they believed, healthy, natural, and optimal.[36]

Pluralism has been under attack for several decades largely because of its implications for democratic theory. Here we are more interested in criticisms of its tendency to think of group politics as highly atomistic, with each group preserving a one-on-one relationship with government. Years of conducting case studies of single groups reinforced this bias, and the slow development of concepts of the general policy process did little to offset it. Scholars in Europe were among the first to challenge it, pointing out first, that interest groups do not interact with the state individualistically, but combine with one another to persuade state agencies to pursue preferred policies. Second, European scholars noted that interest groups often work in concert with state agencies as well as other groups in order to exert influence on the government and the public at large. In 'corporatist' Germany and Scandinavia, according to these scholars, relations between groups are highly structured and to some extent orchestrated by the state.[37] American critics also attacked the pluralist view that groups act individually in the market-place of policy demands, but they found that policy tends to be made by 'sub-governments' composed of the executive agencies, congressional committees, and interest groups chiefly interested in specific policy fields. These sub-governments—or 'iron triangles' as they have been called—dominated the policy process in the sectors that concerned them.[38]

These conclusions drew attention to an aspect of the policy process that is integral to our understanding of the policy role of groups: the entire political community is almost never involved in a specific policy discussion; specialization occurs throughout the policy system. The existence of pressure groups offers the most obvious evidence of this, but specialization occurs elsewhere as well. Government departments, however large and multi-faceted they may appear, are confined to precisely defined territories. Even the political executive finds that only major issues are discussed by the entire Cabinet. The rest are handled by individual Cabinet ministers or by specialized Cabinet committees. Richard Crossman, a former member of the British Cabinet, remarked in his diary that 'we come briefed by our Departments to fight for our departmental budgets, not as Cabinet ministers with a Cabinet view.'[39] Only prime ministers and presidents play roles that encourage them to consider policy comprehensively, but their schedules are so tight that only the most urgent and significant issues come to their attention. In short, political society permits special publics to dominate decision-making in fields of policy where they have competence, interfering only when larger concerns must take precedence, when systemic or techno-logical change necessitates intervention, or when conflict within the special public spills over into the larger political arena. In a sense any special public can be seen as the narrow end of a funnel, bringing issues from the general public to the decision-making apparatus of the state. In another sense, though, such special publics supplant the general public and the greater number of issues are never debated beyond its purview.

Various terms have been coined to describe these specialized publics: iron triangles, networks, and policy communities are the most prominent.[40] We will call them 'policy communities'. The triangular concept developed in the United States seems inappropriate in Canada, where there is no real counterpart to the Congressional committee, and where the relationships in sub-governments are more permeable than the term 'iron triangle' suggests. Networks, on the other hand, tend to be highly open-ended, stretching infinitely into the general public. To describe the Canadian context we need a term that will suggest communication that is both continuous and contained, and that will evoke the notion of a social pattern encompassing not only gradations between its members but shared, or at least commonly understood, belief systems, codes of conduct, and established patterns of behaviour.[41] The term 'policy community' seems best suited to these needs.

A policy community is that part of a political system that—by virtue of its functional responsibilities, its vested interests, and its specialized knowledge—acquires a dominant voice in determining government decisions in a specific field of public activity, and is generally permitted by society at large and the public authorities in particular to determine public policy in that field. It is populated by government agencies, pressure groups, media people, and individuals, including academics, who have an interest in a particular policy field and attempt to influence it. Most policy communities consist of two segments: the sub-government and the attentive public. In effect, the sub-governnment is the policy-making body in the field. It processes most routine policy issues and is seldom successfully challenged by dissident members of the policy community.

As the core—the policy-making centre—of each policy community, sub-governments consist primarily of government agencies and institutionalized interest groups. Only institutionalized groups and agencies with substantial resources and the incentive to dedicate them to sub-government work can manage day-to-day communication between agency officials and representatives of companies or groups; automatic group inclusion on advisory committees and panels of experts; invitations to comment on draft policy; participation on committees or commissions charged with long-range policy review; and continual formal and informal access to agency officials. Because they do not have unlimited resources, and because the policy process seldom allows time for full, meaningful consultation, sub-governments consist of very small groups of people: the minister in charge of the agency that is primarily responsible for formulating policy and carrying out programs in a field; the senior officials responsible for that field of policy, and perhaps their most important federal or provincial counterparts; and representatives of the few interest groups whose opinions are vital and whose support is essential. Representatives of other agencies may also be included, if those agencies are deeply involved in the policy field. For example, the federal Department of Health and Welfare is often a sub-government actor in the formulation of policy affecting native peoples; the Departments of Energy, Mines and Resources and of Indian and Northern Affairs are usually involved jointly in decisions concerning the exploitation of northern resources. Other actors who may appear in the sub-government from time to time are parliamentarians whose constituency interests or committee responsibilities give them a special, if intermittent, authority in a specific field, and officers of the Privy Council Office who are responsible for maintaining liaison between Cabinet and agencies.[42]

The attentive public, by contrast, is neither tightly knit nor clearly defined. It includes any government agencies, private institutions, pressure groups, specific interests, and individuals—including academics, consultants and journalists—who are affected by, or interested in, the policies of specific agencies and who follow, and attempt to influence, those policies, but do not participate in policy-making on a regular basis. Their interest may be keen but not compelling enough to warrant breaking into the inner circle. Often they may be excluded from it—particularly if they are opposed to prevailing policy trends.

The attentive public lacks the power of the sub-government but still plays a vital role in policy development. Conferences and study sessions organized by professional and interest associations offer opportunities for officials at various levels to converse with the grass roots of their constituency, and with journalists and academics who have been studying public policy. They usually have views on government performance and are quick to put them forward. Though most are heard skeptically, sometimes patronizingly, they contribute to the gradual process through which policies and programs are amended, extended, and generally adapted to the changing needs of the community. Similarly, the newsletters, professional journals, and trade magazines that circulate through the policy community give both the sub-government and the attentive public plenty of opportunity to shore up, demolish, or transmogrify the existing policy edifice. In this turmoil of theories and interests, officialdom—which is almost never monolithic, nearly always pluralistic, and seldom at peace with itself—discerns the policy changes government must make if it is to keep nearly abreast of circumstance. The main function of the attentive public, then, is to maintain a perpetual policy-review process. It introduces into the policy community an element of diversity inhibited at the sub-government level by the need to maintain consensus.

Figure 4-1 represents the kind of policy community that might be active in a field in which the federal government is prominent. At the heart of the community are the key federal bodies involved: the agency primarily responsible for formulating policy and carrying out programs in the field; Cabinet, with its co-ordinating committees and their support structures; the Privy Council Office, Treasury Board, the Ministries of State, and so on. None of these are located at the very centre of the figure because no single agency is ever consistently dominant in the field. But because so much policy-making is routine, the lead agency tends to be most influential over time. Clustered around, keeping a sharp eye on 'the feds' and taking part in the sub-government, are the key pressure groups and provincial government agencies.

Figure 4-1. The Policy Community

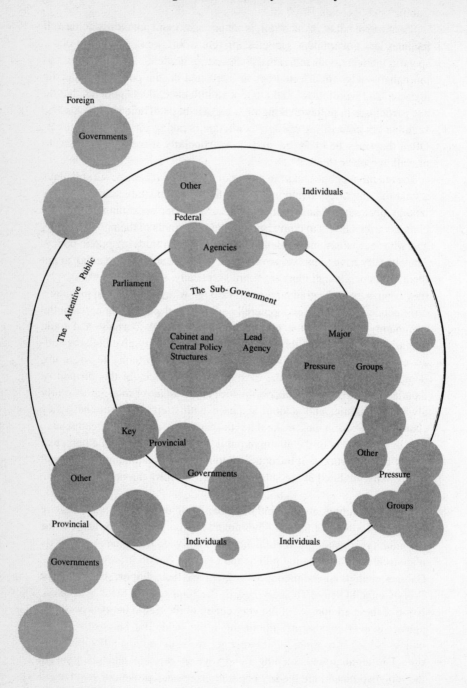

Foreign

Governments

The Attentive Public

Other

Federal

Agencies

Individuals

Parliament

The Sub-Government

Cabinet and Central Policy Structures

Lead Agency

Major

Pressure Groups

Key

Provincial

Governments

Other

Pressure

Groups

Other

Provincial

Governments

Individuals

Individuals

Source: G. Williams and M.S. Whittington *Canada in the 1980s* (Methuen Publications, Toronto, 1985).

Figure 4-2. The Canadian Farm and Food Policy Community

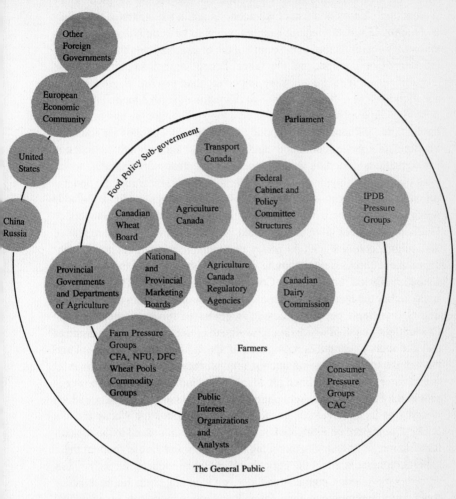

Legend: CFA = Canadian Federation of Agriculture. NFU = National Farmers Union.
DFC = Dairy Farmers of Canada. CAC = Consumers' Association of Canada

Source: J.D. Forbes, *Institutions and Influence Groups in the Canadian Food Policy Process* (Toronto, IPAC, 1985).

In Figure 4-2 a modified version of the policy community model, developed by J.D. Forbes, illustrates this structure. In the setting of food policy Agriculture Canada and its related agencies are at the centre of the policy community. Even the federal Cabinet seems to be a little distant from its customary position close to the centre of the community. Marketing boards, the Dairy Commission, and the Wheat Board, next in importance to the Department itself, are even more important than provincial governments and their agencies, despite the fact that the British North America Act gives the provinces concurrent jurisdiction over agriculture. Consumers seem to have limited influence on food policy. Their pressure groups are found on the edge of the policy community and government agencies created to speak for consumers' interests do not appear at all. Transport Canada—which must oversee the shipping of food products—plays a larger role. So do farm pressure groups. Forbes concludes that farmers' groups dominate the food policy process 'almost to the point of excluding other food system members'.[43] Coleman and Jacek give us a detailed picture of how the Department of Agriculture consults with its policy community and particularly its sub-government through an elaborate committee system that focuses on the Canadian Agricultural Services Co-ordinating Committee. This committee is chaired by the Deputy Minister of Agriculture and includes the provincial deputy ministers; but policy advice is generated through seven 'Canada Committees', each of which is empowered to create specialized committees called Expert Committees; composed of specialists from government and the private sector, including interest groups, they are extremely powerful within their narrowly defined jurisdiction. An indication of their power is provided by the Canadian Agricultural Chemicals Association (CACA), which claims that its involvement in the Expert Committee on Weeds and the Expert Committee on Pesticide Use in Agriculture is 'critical to the agricultural chemicals industry'. According to Coleman and Jacek, 'both of these expert committees affect the agricultural chemical industry directly. CACA describes the Weeds Committee as the only means in Canada for establishing weed control recommendations for new and in use chemicals on a regional basis. The pesticide committee is described as the "single most important Committee of its kind in Canada". The policy on the use of pesticides in terms of which pesticides may be used, used where, how frequently, and in what amounts apparently is formulated in part, here.'[44] At first glance these arrangements may seem banal, routine, and not worth the effort the CACA and other groups make to have a voice on such committees. But their value lies in the fact that it is extremely unlikely that any review body, either in the Department of Agriculture, the government, or Parliament, will have the technical competence to challenge the decisions of these committees, and in the fact that Canadian farmers spend a great deal of money each year on agricultural chemicals. The amount of energy expended by consumer and environmental groups to challenge and curtail the use of certain agricultural chemicals indicates the extent to which this use of expertise in the making of policy hinders those who oppose prevailing policy trends.

Despite the prominence of the lead agency, its activities are closely monitored by other federal agencies whose overlapping mandates bring them within the sub-government. Working through interdepartmental committees, they usually review and often greatly alter agency policy. For example, Canadian fisheries policy has often been influenced by External Affairs, which worries about Canada's relations with trading partners who fish off our coasts. Hovering on the edge of the sub-government is Parliament—perennially interested, intermittently involved, sometimes influential. Provincial governments are variously involved: some might wish to be part of the sub-government but lack the resources to maintain a presence; others are simply not interested and are content to observe the activities of the sub-government, interfering when necessary. In the final analysis provincial governments may be no more influential than the major pressure groups active in the community, some of which overlap one another, having common memberships, sitting together on advisory boards, and frequently combining their efforts to present a joint position to government and the public.

Finally we should note that Canadian policy communities are not composed exclusively of Canadians, nor do they function only within our borders. Foreign governments follow closely our policies in fields of concern to them, as the American government demonstrated when Ottawa implemented the National Energy Policy. As Canadian nationalists frequently claim, foreign governments sometimes come close to participating in our sub-governments. So do multinational corporations. In the chemical industry, for example, as Coleman and Jacek demonstrate, the boards of directors of the peak industry associations are usually composed of the senior executives of multinational chemical firms who strongly influence the views presented by those associations when they participate in sub-governmental deliberations.[45] Other external participants in Canadian policy communities include international organizations—such as the Organization for Economic Co-operation and Development, which regularly reviews Canadian economic policy, or the International Labour Organization, whose views on labour matters are often influential—and international pressure groups, like Greenpeace and other groups that have used international public opinion to oppose the sealing industry. Conversely, Canadian policy communities try to influence the actions of foreign governments, through, for example, international trade discussions or international aid activities.

Although figure 4-1 suggests orbital movement around the lead agency and the federal executive, the other members of the policy community are actually in constant motion. As governments and key personnel change, provincial government participation varies, or changing economic factors compel provincial agencies to retreat or advance into the sub-government. In the energy field, for example, Alberta became prominent after the Leduc discovery, and Newfoundland after Hibernia. Similarly, pressure groups move back and forth from the centre.

Mobility is particularly evident in the attentive public, whose pressure groups and individual members are the most mobile participants in the policy community. They are in constant motion, coalescing around or breaking away from more powerful actors, advancing towards and withdrawing from the core as their resources, their interests, and the public agenda change. In the early 1960s, for example, Douglas H. Pimlott, a University of Toronto biologist, was a prominent critic of Ontario forest policy. A decade later, even though his views on that field were probably unchanged, he had shifted his energies to national environmental policy and become a leading academic figure on matters touching northern development.[46] While individuals are more likely than organizations to shift focus in this way, groups do so as well. In the early 1970s the Social Sciences Federation of Canada became involved in the environmental movement, establishing an interdisciplinary committee on the human environment that attempted, for approximately a decade, to monitor social science activity in environmental studies and to represent the social sciences in some of the policy communities concerned with environmental issues. Among its varied interests were codes of ethics applied by the federal government to social scientists working with native communities; the development of environmental and social-impact assessment; national parks policies. Eventually, however, other more appropriate institutions developed for representing the social sciences in these matters and the SSFC disbanded the committee and ceased being a part of the attentive public in the environmental field.[47] Such behaviour regularly occurs in any policy community. Organizations and individuals are constantly changing their interests, responding to new situations, developing new capacities, and shedding old ones.

The composition of the attentive public ranges from institutionalized group members and government agencies to issue-oriented groups and individuals. The degree to which a group is institutionalized need not dictate its status in the community, or its level of participation, which may be determined by the strength of the interest of group members in the policy field and by their power in the economy and society. Prior to the 1970s the chemical industries evinced very little interest in what we now call environmental policy, and their participation in the formation of policies relating to water quality, for example, was minimal. With the growth of environmentalism the industry mobilized itself to contribute to environmental policy. The Petroleum Association for the Conservation of the Environment, in particular, became a prominent actor—or member of the sub-government—in certain closely defined policy fields, such as that of oil pollution control. PACE has become an institutionalized actor, but not all members of the attentive public need be as well organized.[48] The academic groups taking part in the foreign policy review of the early Trudeau years were linked to the Canadian Institute of International Affairs but could not otherwise be described as a highly institutionalized group.[49] To a considerable extent their meetings had to be arranged by the Department of External Affairs, whose readiness to do this indicated the value it attached to academic 'legitimation' of the policy review, even though the department seems to have paid very little attention to the advice it received. Even less organized, and generally less welcome, are the issue-oriented groups whose spontaneous eruption into a policy field shatters the carefully contrived appearance of consensus, and challenges both the routinization of policy and the conventional wisdom prevalent in the sub-government, and to a large extent in the attentive public. These interventions, though usually detested by long-time members of the policy community, draw attention to inadequacies in policy; force the pace of change; and, to some extent, introduce new blood and new ideas. They may at times precipitate a total restructuring of the policy community—as in the early 1970s when several older communities were reorganized and combined to serve the newly defined field of environmental policy—but more limited interventions also create shock waves.

The attentive public tends to exercise its greatest influence on long-range policy. Its lack of ready access to the key agency and the sub-government precludes its influencing day-to-day policy to an appreciable degree, though some groups or corporations may periodically have a stake in intervening on specific issues. Occasionally members of the attentive public may be called in to defend existing policies from some outside threat, as in 1968, when Prime Minister Trudeau directed a new set of perspectives at Canadian foreign policy and the Department of External Affairs looked to the academic community for assistance. But the attentive public is more likely to be engaged in discussions of medium-term and long-term goals, chiefly because it cannot maintain the regular communication—virtually daily contact—with decision-makers that is necessary in order to be involved in day-to-day policy. The average member of the attentive public, who is seldom physically close to the decision centre, and whose work does not make regular contact necessary, turns to more readily available links with the policy community. These may be local chapters of national organizations; national conferences; study seminars; or various types of print media, ranging from trade journals to academic periodicals. Such links keep members of the attentive public adequately informed, though not on short-term issues, many of which are resolved before information has filtered through these channels. Consequently the organizers of conferences and the publishers of journals concentrate on general trends and the larger picture.

The fundamental hypothesis that policy communities participate significantly in the policy process leads to a subsidiary hypothesis that the structures and functions of policy communities will vary from policy field to policy field.[50] Though most policy communities will contain common elements, the functions performed by specific components will vary significantly. In some fields, for example, citizens' groups, the media, and the academic community may play a larger role than they would in others. The structural relations between community members will differ accordingly. The determinants of variation will be extremely diverse and include such factors as the nature of the field, the longevity of government involvement in it, the extent of agency power and responsibility, the agency's significance in the power structure of its own government, and the resources and characteristics of the non-governmental members of the policy community.

While the policy field is an important variable in determining the nature of the policy community, so is the jurisdictional framework surrounding it. The structures and functions of policy communities will also vary according to the policy field's jurisdictional location. This is particularly important in the Canadian federal system, especially where vast differences exist between policy communities operating exclusively within provincial jurisdictions and those operating on the national level. For example, in some of the Atlantic provinces government bureaucracies are much less aggressive and powerful than they appear to be at the federal level. The structure and organization of the policy communities are likely to vary accordingly. Similarly, a policy field restricted to the federal domain would be expected to possess a policy community significantly different from one that is continually engaged in the niceties of federal-provincial diplomacy. Contrast, for instance, the policy community that seems to surround the Department of National Defence with the one formerly associated with the Ministry of State for Urban Affairs. The intense pressure brought to bear by provincial and local governments whenever the Department of National Defence talks of closing a military base, or when the acquisition of new equipment involves the purchase of components from Canadian suppliers indicates that while these governments and interests are not part of the defence sub-government—which appears to be a small, tightly knit group very much dominated by the military and including members of the international military organizations to which Canada belongs—they are very much a part of the attentive public. The short-lived Ministry of State for Urban Affairs, by contrast, had a very loosely structured sub-government that contained one extremely cohesive element, the sub-government surrounding the Central Mortgage and Housing Corporation, and a coterie of groups concerned about the co-ordinative and long-range policy roles of the Ministry. Several of these, like the Canadian Confederation of Mayors and Municipalities, had considerable influence inside and outside the Ministry's policy community, but the majority—issue-oriented and institutionalized citizens groups, research organizations, professional planners' associations, and so on—were unable to form an effective sub-government. They constituted a policy community so deeply divided that the Ministry and its supporters were ultimately unable to resist the attacks of those who wanted the federal government to abandon its venture into urban policy.[51]

Before concluding our comments on the policy community we should note that the most prominent of its members are not primarily interested in making or reformulating policy. For them the policy community is a protective device, limiting rather than expanding the opportunities for the public at large to achieve major policy changes. The goal of the sub-government is to keep policy-making at the routine or technical level, thereby minimizing interference. Often, however, circumstances outside its control—economic changes, the development of new technologies, changing public concerns— overwhelm the sub-government's system of formal communications and informal networks. Controversy develops, new issues emerge, and more and more interests want to take part in policy-making. Policy debate broadens as levels of conflict rise, so that eventually central issues are taken out of the hands of the sub-government and the policy community and resolved at the highest political levels—by Cabinet and by the First Ministers' Conference.[52] When this occurs, both the policy community and policy are often vastly altered.

Without the policy community's special capabilities for studying alternative courses of action, for debating their rival merits, and for securing administrative arrangements for implementation, governments would have great difficulty discerning and choosing between policy options. Within policy communities pressure groups are equally important. It is in the policy community that they most frequently perform the functions we have attributed to them. They draw together the interests associated with the community and articulate their concerns. Their ability to secure the support of special publics for policies is often indispensable. They at times hold the collective memory for policy issues. With their annual meetings, newsletters, regional organizations, and above all, informal networks, they have an ability to cross organizational lines denied to other more formal actors, such as government departments. They can therefore act as go-betweens, provide opportunities for quiet meetings between warring agencies, and keep the policy process in motion. They may also act as emissaries to other policy communities. These services, together with their ability to evaluate policy and develop opinion, make pressure groups integral members of the policy community. Pressure groups are vital to the life of policy communities and policy communities are essential to the development and implementation of public policy.

CHAPTER 5

Types of Groups

In this chapter we will construct a typology of groups out of the following assumptions:

1. As political analysts we want to categorize groups in a manner that helps us explain their power relationship to the political system.
2. Pressure groups are adaptive instruments of political communication; they tend to work within the framework established by government, rather than impose their own structures and procedures on the power centres they deal with.
3. The complex bureaucratic structure of the modern Canadian state has a decisive moulding influence on the form and behaviour of this country's pressure groups.

The typology we will build from these assumptions uses organizational characteristics to arrange groups along an institutional continuum. The continuum, we will argue, is particularly helpful in identifying the capacity of groups to relate to the structure of policy-making in the modern state.

POWER, ADAPTATION AND BUREAUCRATIC ORGANIZATION

Political analysts view pressure groups as actors competing with others in the political system for a say in how the power of the state is articulated in public policy and exercised through programs. We are concerned, in other words, with a power relationship. Hence we must analyse pressure groups from the perspective of their relationship with the state. (We do not deny the possibility of analysing interest groups from other vantage points—for example, from the perspective of the psychological benefits members derive from participating in them—but such analysis would take us out of political science and into the domain of other disciplines.) We want to be able to explain the success or failure of specific groups in political terms and to understand their methods of organization and patterns of behaviour as part of the process through which a community establishes public policy. Similarly we want to be able to trace the connections between the evolution of pressure groups in a political system and the development of the system itself. This would not only help us understand the development of both state and groups but would enhance our ability to predict the behaviour of policy actors.

Pressure groups, according to our definition, act to influence public policy in order to promote the common interests of their members. Furthermore, they are motivated by the limited resources available to groups and by the limited tolerance of members—particularly those whose interests are vitally affected—to search out the most efficient means possible of identifying key decision centres. Successful group leaders husband their resources and learn to understand the policy systems they have to deal with. They generally act to influence the decision centres that can best effect the changes they desire: they do not waste time persuading the uninfluential. For example, because they appreciate the fact that public discussion invites public discussion, they avoid open debate and try to deal directly with key decision makers, hoping through behind-the-scenes discussions to effect desired policy changes before other interests can marshall opposition. Fortunately, from the point of view of democracy, few groups are single-minded or knowledgeable enough to be quite as efficient as this suggests. Nevertheless our survey of the evolution of Canadian pressure groups, and the evidence of attempted efficiency presented throughout our study, leads us to suggest that, other things being equal, pressure groups act to influence the decision centres that can best effect the changes they wish to bring about. This in turn leads us to agree with Presthus, who maintains that 'interest group behaviour provides us with a nice index of power in the sense that groups mainly seek access at that place in the Canadian legislative apparatus where the authority and power to make decisions reside.'[1]

In this particular power relationship it is clear that the state is the dominant party. If governments possess the capacity to exercise the coercive authority of the community, and if pressure groups strive for efficiency in bending that capacity to their own ends, then they will adapt themselves to the opportunities for exercising influence that each individual system presents. Hence the character of pressure groups in any particular system will be the product of interaction between the internal resources of the groups themselves and the political system in which they are found. Because the points of access to policy-makers differ in each political system, and because groups must avail themselves of the access points peculiar to the system in which they operate, pressure groups perform comparable functions differently in different systems. Collectively their patterns of adaptation will, as Presthus says, indicate the location of power in the system. Individually their attempts to take advantage of appropriate access points or targets cause groups to adapt their behaviour and structure to the conditions imposed by the sector of the political system in which they operate, so that particular groups stress some structural and behavioural patterns rather than others. Different targets call for different structures and different strategies. The character of a specific group is determined in part by its internal resources, but also by the policy environment it attempts to influence, for its effectiveness as a pressure group will be governed by its ability to adapt to that environment. Thus a policy-making system that stresses decision-making at the centre, rather than in the field, will tend to foster pressure groups that are highly centralized.[2] Engelmann and Schwartz speak of groups attempting to maximize access to the Canadian political system's federal structure and therefore adapting themselves to it: 'The result is that most of Canada's major interest groups have a federated organization'.[3] In France and Britain centralization goes further: groups tend to be unitarian rather than federated.

Changes in the distribution of power will also lead to pressure group adaptation. At the turn of the century Canada was experiencing a shift of political power from the legislatures to the political executives at both the federal and provincial levels. As a result groups learned to focus their attention on the executive and to pay correspondingly less attention to the legislative branch. Their behaviour suggests that groups working in an environment dominated by the executive are inclined to organize themselves to develop reasonably well-informed arguments on the broad features of policy and to study the political needs of ministers. They do not need complex organizational structures since they depend on personal contacts with a few key actors and on a sophisticated understanding of the inner workings of élite politics. During the heyday of the mandarins established groups elaborated their ability to communicate with the bureaucracy and government leaders, becoming in the process more complex organizations with an orientation towards technical expertise. In contemporary Canada, the diffusion of power that has spread through our governmental system compels effective pressure groups to add to these political and administrative capacities an ability to present themselves to the public. Only if they do so can they generate public support for the policies they favour. As well, at the federal level in particular, the tendency to delegate a great deal of responsibility to the administrative branch affects the structure and behaviour of groups. Organizational complexity is forced on each pressure group as it tries to cope not only with the political environment of senior policy makers but with the voracious appetite of the administrative apparatus for technical adjustment of policies. The group becomes adept at research in order to master the required technical detail; it acquires legal and public relations skills to ensure the effective presentation of its position; and it builds a capacity to monitor the implementation and further development of policy.[4] The environment is bureaucratic; to work effectively in it, the pressure group must become bureaucratic.

To appreciate why the bureaucratic character of modern policy-making should so profoundly affect interest group character and behaviour, we must briefly consider what bureaucracy is and why today's governments cannot live without it.[5] Bureaucracy divides complex undertakings into comprehensible and manageable units of work, and then, through hierarchy, provides a means for co-ordinating the separate activities that specialization has created. Specialization reduces all-encompassing projects to a scale that individuals can understand and, by working together, accomplish. Hierarchy makes the common endeavour possible because it provides for the direction and control of everyone engaged in it. Through specialization, tasks—and the skills needed to perform them—are identified and arranged in a sequence that will allow their successful performance to create a flow of work that ultimately produces a product, be it an automobile, a memo to cabinet, a social assistance payment, or a transportation system. The responsibilities and attributes assigned to each position in the sequence of work are made explicit in job descriptions and regulations, then recorded, and finally enforced by those who hold authority in the hierarchy.

Bureaucracy is the most highly developed of social organizations. Max Weber, the nineteenth-century social scientist who first formally identified and described bureaucratic organization, maintained that 'the future belongs to bureaucracy' because it is impersonal, relentless, methodical, and capable of both great and small undertakings. Our survey of the evolution of Canadian pressure groups corroborates Weber's prediction. In particular, we saw how the party politics of the late nineteenth century—with its random, personal style of policy-making—ceded ground to the bureaucratic methods introduced with the development of a technostructure. Patronage was gradually eliminated from the civil service because individuals working for government had to possess the skills needed to perform the job described for each position. We noted that professional associations became prominent as a result, while the significance of local party organizations declined. The influence of experts on policy-makers grew apace in both business and government, and as it did so specialized organizations developed to facilitate communication between the pockets of expertise in the public and private sectors and to persuade lay policy-makers of the wisdom of expert advice. We ascribed the centralization of government administration to a need to keep pace with centralization in the economy. Bureaucratic organization made centralization feasible; in turn, centralization made necessary the emergence of sectoral organizations concerned with the affairs of relatively narrow segments of the economy. The Canadian Construction Association was founded to assist communication between road builders and governments; the Canadian Pharmaceutical Manufacturers' Association was established in 1914 to deal with government on production, manufacturing, and importation problems; the Canadian Life Insurance Officers' Association lobbied federal and provincial governments for supportive regulations.[6]

Today the bureaucratic structure of the modern state imposes its form of organization on all those who must work with and through governments. To interact effectively with its complex machinery over a period, any interest must develop an organizational capacity compatible with the policy system. This applies to élite groups as much as to those with small resources. Even the banks have an association. George McCullagh, the influential publisher of the *Globe and Mail*, once said of Ontario Premier Mitchell Hepburn's actions during a major strike: 'Whatever Mr. Hepburn did as a government leader was only as a result of information I placed before him in regard to government and trade unionism, a subject on which I have some knowledge.'[7] Today it would be extremely hard for McCullagh to make the same boast. Political leaders, even those in the smaller provinces, are expected to engage in such a wide variety of activities and to monitor so broad an area of public policy that they can take a directing hand in very few policy initiatives. Their participation is intermittent and generally confined to sketching the broad outlines of policy or to the more difficult aspects of conflict resolution. Most other aspects of policy development and implementation must be left to officials. As a former member of the federal cabinet put it, 'ministers are far too busy to adjudicate disputes between an interest group and officials, so you have to start with officials'.[8] Working with officials means working in an environment of organizational complexity. The only way a group can do that is to develop its own organizational capability. A group that fails to do this may win a single policy battle, but it cannot win a major campaign. Many protest groups have had to learn that lesson.

The significance of organization was implicit in our discussion of the policy community. Policy communities symbolize the application of specialization of function to the determination of public policy. As we pointed out when we introduced the concept, modern cabinets are unable to address in detail the innumerable policy issues that come before them. Equally, individual members of the public at large resist devoting their energies to all the many causes they are asked to support; they frequently refuse even to interest themselves in matters they know to be worthy and important. The behaviour of both cabinet and public is a rational, though not necessarily desirable, way of coping with overwhelming demands. By assigning responsibility for all but the most significant of these matters to policy communities, the political executive and the general public conserve their energies for dealing with the issues they believe are paramount.

But specialization does not end at the delineation of a policy field. In fact, it only begins there. Within each major policy field are many subfields; agriculture, for example, contains dairy farming, grain production, egg and poultry production, and frequently specializations within each subfield, such as butter production, cheese manufacturing, the production of fresh dairy goods, and so on. Bureaucratic organization ensures that each field, subfield, and sub-subfield is attended by its own group of specialists who deliver programs and contribute to policy development. Specialists in government and interests in the private sector find that they work most effectively together if they organize at the level of their specialization. The resulting structure of organized representation in agriculture is a common one: nationally two organizations, the Canadian Federation of Agriculture and the National Farmers' Union represent agricultural interests on a variety of issues, but the detailed work of administering agricultural policy is carried out by subordinate, semi-autonomous or independent government agencies, each of which has close ties to groups representing the interests of producers of the commodity it regulates. The Canadian Egg Marketing Agency, for example, may have dealings with the Canadian Federation of Agriculture and the National Farmers' Union, but its day-to-day relations with the industry would be conducted through such organizations as the Canadian Egg Producers' Council; the Canadian Hatchery Association; the Canadian Egg and Poultry Council; and the Canadian Poultry and Egg Producers' Council.[9] In another policy field, librarians interested in securing, at minimum cost, government documents for their collections do not usually address their concerns to the Deputy Minister of Supply and Service, whose department is responsible for federal government publications. Instead they organize themselves into a committee of government documents' librarians, a group within the Canadian Library Association, and they attempt to work directly with those officials in the Department directly responsible for publishing and distributing federal documents.[10]

Our description of the policy community emphasized the extent of organizational commitment interests must make if they wish to play a prominent role in it, particularly if they wish to be become members of the sub-government. We noted, for example, that sub-government members must be ready to contribute advice frequently on a number of issues; to serve on advisory boards; to represent their interests to the public; to co-ordinate their own activities with those of others; and to engage constantly in a host of undertakings that demand organization. We suggested that only those with a vital interest in the policy field and the resources to sustain full membership in the sub-government attempt to become full members. Others must be content with membership in the attentive public or they must neglect the field entirely.

Interest organizations are more likely to perform the functions of communication, legitimation, regulation, and administration within the policy community than elsewhere in the policy system. To perform them interests must possess the attributes of organization: formal structure, clear definition of roles, a system for generating and allocating resources, a collective memory, rules governing behaviour, and, most important, procedures for reaching and implementing decisions. In an earlier chapter we called interests that lacked these attributes latent and solidary interests and we noted that their political influence is often limited. Members of solidary and latent groups lack the means to share information, to reach agreement on positions they should take, and to act in common. Organized interests, on the other hand, are able to communicate among themselves and to take concerted action. Modern policy systems are so constructed that some degree of organization is a prerequisite to participation. Without organization a strong strategic position is of limited value to an interest, but strong organization considerably enhances a weak strategic position. Organization is the key to the exploitation of power in the modern community.

AN INSTITUTIONAL TYPOLOGY

If organization is the key to the exploitation of power, a concept of organizational capacity may serve as the foundation for a typology of pressure groups designed to relate varieties of such groups to one another and to the policy system at large. Such an approach is suggested by Philip Selznick's concept of the institutionalization of organizations, a process through which an organization—a 'technical instrument designed as a means to definite goals'[11]—becomes an institution—'a responsive, adaptive organism'.[12]

> Beginning as a tool, the organization derives added meaning from the psychological and social functions it performs. In doing so it becomes valued for itself. To be sure, the personal and group bonds that make for institutionalization are not wholly separable. As the individual works out his special problems . . . he helps to tie the organization into the community's institutional network. Personal incentives may spark this absorption, and provide the needed energy; but its character and direction will be shaped by values already existent in the community at large. Similarly . . . the internal struggle for power becomes a channel through which external environmental forces make themselves felt. This is, indeed, a classic function of the American political party system; but less formal and recognized groupings . . . follow the same pattern. Organizations do not so much create values as embody them. As this occurs, the organization becomes increasingly institutionalized.[13]

According to Selznick, 'as institutionalization progresses, the enterprise . . . becomes peculiarly competent to do a particular kind of work.'[14] This suggests the applicability of a sequence, or continuum, to the classification of pressure groups, positing at the one extreme 'issue-oriented' groups (a designation we will elaborate below), and at the other, 'institutionalized' or 'institutional' groups, which will be described first.

Institutional Groups

(i) **They possess organizational continuity and cohesion.** There will be fairly clear delineation of responsibility and well-defined channels of communication to permit the orderly flow of information within the organization and to ensure that individuals perform the tasks assigned to them. Usually this will require an elaborate organizational structure—to carry out the many specialized functions involved in preparing briefs, organizing representations to officials, sitting on advisory boards, rallying membership support, and creating a positive public image, to say nothing of the many non-political activities engaged in by most large interest groups. Continuity is essential to ensure the long-term implementation of favourable policies and to maintain a watchful eye on the evolution of new policies.

(ii) **They have extensive knowledge of those sectors of government that affect their clients, and enjoy easy communications with those sectors.** The organization's officials have ready access to appropriate government officials and are aware of the procedures necessary to bring the group's views to their attention.

(iii) **There is a stable membership.** For many members affiliation with the group has benefits quite separate from, and in many cases more important than, its work in the policy sphere. In some groups these rewards are of a solidary nature. Like-minded people with similar backgrounds provide mutual support for one another in a sometimes hostile world. Many Canadian ethnic groups fall into this category. In professional associations the ties that bind are powerful indeed: it is illegal to practise one's profession without the certification of, and affiliation with, the formal professional association. Other groups, lacking such powerful inducements, have found that many people will join the organization, or remain in it, because membership brings special benefits—the rewards of collective bargaining, or even 'fringe benefits', like group life insurance, group travel rates, and so on. Such inducements, which we call selective benefits, play an important part in ensuring that the group's membership remains relatively stable.[15] Attracted largely by these secondary inducements, the membership generally acquiesces in the policy directions taken by career and elected leaders and is willing—within limits—to assign them the resources needed to carry out the group's political objectives.

(iv) **They have concrete and immediate operational objectives.** General philosophies are usually broad enough to permit each group to bargain with government over the application of specific legislation or the achievement of particular concessions. In consequence the tactics of negotiation are devised pragmatically.

(v) **Organizational imperatives are generally more important than any particular objective.** Because leaders of groups generally work to make their environment safe for themselves and their groups, they adhere to informal rules: 'The rules enable political leaders, government officials and group leaders to achieve their organizational goals more readily and more assuredly than would be possible in the absence of rules.'[16] But such rules also prohibit certain kinds of action—for example, public condemnation of civil servants—which could incur sanctions against the group. Most leaders of institutional groups seem to feel that it is better to return to bargain another day than to damage the organization's 'credibility' in the eyes of those whose decisions may in future make or break the group and its clients. Hence the reluctance of most institutional groups to avail themselves of the wide range of pressure techniques—particularly the manipulation of public opinion—that exist in most western systems. The degree of manoeuverability open to groups varies, of course, between political systems and is one of the determinants of the characteristics of pressure group behaviour within specific systems.

The vision of a highly complex, multi-faceted organization that this description conjures up is somewhat misleading. Though a number of Canadian groups—major unions and leading business-interest associations, for example—possess considerable resources, most are chronically unable to meet all the demands made of them by members and governments. A fully institutionalized group is an ideal type, a model rather than a working reality. J.D. Forbes, in his study of the powerful food-producer groups, was able to identify only a few groups—including the Canadian Federation of Agriculture, the Dairy Farmers of Canada, the Saskatchewan Wheat Pool, and the United Grain Growers—that closely resembled our model institutionalized group. He found that

> . . . élite members of this group and their government counterparts to whom I spoke sound remarkably similar. They were constantly aware of the legislative process, dates and deadlines for policy development, and of all the other things which constitute policy-making. And although staffs of some of these organizations are not large by any measure, they manage to have broad, selective objectives, use their resources effectively, are skilled in public and press relations and, above all, maintain extensive, regular contact with government élites and with their own members, and have been able to put themselves or their members on appropriate administrative and regulatory bodies.[17]

Since relatively few groups display the traits of full institutionalization we use two other categories to describe and analyse the majority of working groups. We speak of 'mature' and 'fledgeling' groups. Mature groups possess many of the attributes of the fully institutionalized group, but are less developed. Their organizational base is narrower. Their behaviour may not reflect a complete grasp of the relations that prevail between institutionalized groups and governments. Forbes' characterization of the Canadian Cattlemen's Association and various poultry-marketing groups, suggests that they fall into this category since they 'appear to be less broadly based, have fewer resources devoted to food policy, and have less depth and regularity of contact with government élites'.[18] Fledgeling groups on the other hand are only just emerging from the issue-oriented stage that we will now describe.

Issue-oriented Groups

Issue-oriented groups have the reverse characteristics of institutional groups:
(i) **They have limited organizational continuity and cohesion; most are very badly organized.**
(ii) **Their knowledge of government is minimal and often naïve.**
(iii) **Their membership is extremely fluid.**
(iv) **They encounter considerable difficulty in formulating and adhering to short-range objectives.**
(v) **They usually have a low regard for the organizational mechanisms they have developed for carrying out their goals.**

Issue-oriented groups possess a limited organizational base because they allow their concern with the resolution of one or two issues or problems to dominate both their internal affairs and their relations with government, with the public, and with other groups. They spring up where there is strong feeling about particular issues and tend to be led by people who have little previous experience of the policy process. The magnitude of the issue is of little consequence for the long-term evolution of the group. Nor does it matter whether the group's concern is with material benefits or is ideologically or attitudinally based. As long as the group is concerned with one issue to the exclusion of all others, that concern will dominate the group's organizational arrangements, producing the characteristics we have just described. This is because the group's preoccupation with one or two issues prohibits it from developing selective inducements, apart from the largely psychological rewards it can offer the leadership and a small group of supporters for whom the organization is a centre of social life.[19]

Their weak base does not in itself render issue-oriented groups ineffective. Many groups concerned with preventing action of a particular kind can achieve their objectives through techniques that institutional groups consider crude and self-defeating. In 1968, when Canadians debated this country's attitude towards civil war in Nigeria, issue-oriented groups did not hesitate to challenge the federal government's reluctance to recognize the secessionist state of Biafra. Although these groups were not able to win Canadian recognition of Biafra, their demonstrations, media events, and inflammatory rhetoric caught public attention and greatly embarrassed the newly elected Trudeau government, persuading it to take the unusual step of assigning Canadian Forces planes to fly food and medical supplies into Biafra.[20] Issue-oriented groups can do this because they have no commitment to their own long-term survival; they are not bound by the considerations that often render institutional groups powerless. The pro-Biafra groups, for example, were not as dependent on the goodwill and services of the Department of External Affairs as were church groups and humanitarian organizations.

A weak organizational base does not guarantee an early death. Issue-oriented groups built around strong ideologies often exist for years on minuscule resources, attempting to contribute to the development of public opinion. Nevertheless many more issue-oriented groups die in infancy than survive. Many succumb to discouragement, others cannot muster sufficient resources to hold together even a small group of dedicated supporters, and a few disappear after they achieve their goal. Of the survivors many remain substantially unchanged. But some, like the Canadian Federation of Independent Business, broaden their base, form coalitions with like-minded groups, create selective inducements, and become institutionalized. The CFIB 'began in anger', but rapidly mobilized into a highly organized nationally federated association offering its members valued services, such as tax counselling, and representing them individually, as well as collectively, before government.[21]

Even though issue-oriented groups are usually small, they frequently serve important functions in the political system. Their chief advantage lies in their flexibility. Because they can develop extremely quickly and are unencumbered by institutionalized structures, they are excellent vehicles for generating immediate public reaction to specific issues. Because their stake in the future is usually limited, they can indulge in forms of political communication that institutional groups are reluctant to use. This was particularly true in Canada during the regime of the mandarins, when established groups tended not to resort to publicity for fear of disturbing relations with administrative agencies. Even in today's more open policy system issue-oriented groups are less constrained than institutionalized groups. They and other less influential members of policy communities have good reason to excite public discussion of the issues that concern them: generally they have little standing in the policy community, and quite apart from lacking access to it, they may have only limited knowledge of its methods, its language, and its philosophy—the essentials for participating in its discussions. Consequently an appeal to public opinion is the best way, sometimes the only way, to challenge a specific decision or to object to an undesirable policy and to embarrass governments into taking action. Campaigns of this sort command daily media attention, whether they be challenges to urban redevelopment schemes; efforts to promote—or eliminate—bilingual government services; petitions to restore, or rescue, rail passenger services; or any one of the countless other causes espoused by an active citizenry. On occasion institutional groups avail themselves of the services of issue-oriented organizations, allowing members to work with their more radical counterparts in hopes of winning through publicity what conventional methods have failed to achieve. Again the debate over recognition of Biafra offers an illustration. Leading church groups, concerned about the Nigerian civil war but anxious not to damage their ties with the

Department of External Affairs, gave considerable quiet support to the militant issue-oriented groups attacking federal policy towards Nigeria and Biafra.[22] In general systemic terms, issue-oriented groups enhance the adaptive capacity of the overall system, permitting a responsiveness to emergent issues that is not easily achieved by more cumbersome mechanisms of political communication. The early environmental groups, for example, were loosely structured organizations that emerged to protest particular abuses, and though most of them were short-lived they succeeded in drawing public attention to the need for more effective methods of environmental protection.

Institutionalization of Issue-oriented Groups

The conditions under which institutionalization occurs will vary a great deal but will usually depend on members' capacity to accept the extension of the organization's concerns and activities in order to attract new membership; and on the acquisition of permanent staff and the assignment to it of an increasingly influential role in group management and leadership. Accompanying these developments will be a heightened understanding of public policy processes; governmental recognition of the group's claim to speak on issues of interest to it; and a growing sophistication and specialization in techniques of communication with official bodies—though contacts with the general public will probably atrophy as staff members exert a preference for the more easily managed communication links between group leaders and government officials.

Sometimes government recognition is the major incentive for groups to institutionalize. In the early 1970s particularly, Canadian governments, especially the federal government, anxious to enhance communication links with specialized constituencies, encouraged many issue-oriented groups to become institutionalized. Community development projects were sponsored by government—on condition that local groups, often volunteer groups, contribute some manpower and administrative capacity. Government support enabled such groups to obtain the professional and secretarial assistance needed to give them organizational cohesion, but also at times forced some groups to adopt a particular role, often a co-ordinative or facilitative role that permitted other similar groups to avail themselves of the services developed within the central group while, in theory at least, retaining the autonomy to make their own representations to government. As a result of this sort of assistance, endowed groups experienced more rapid institutionalization than they might otherwise have achieved. However, they still faced considerable difficulties, the most significant being: (i) the problems inherent in organizing any issue-oriented group; (ii) difficulties in identifying, embracing, and adhering to the facilitative role; and (iii) difficulties arising out of confrontations with other branches of government. The last was often

Table 5-1. The Continuum Framework

CATEGORIES	GROUP CHARACTERISTICS							
	Objectives				Organizational Features			
	single, narrowly defined	multiple but closely related	multiple, broadly defined & collective	multiple, broadly defined, collective & selective	small membership/ no paid staff	membership can support small staff	alliances with other groups/staff includes professionals	extensive human and financial resources
Institutionalized				■				■
Mature			■				■	
Fledgeling		■				■		
Issue-oriented	■				■			

| CATEGORIES | LEVELS OF COMMUNICATION WITH GOVERNMENT | | | | | |
| | Media-Oriented: | | | Access-Oriented: | | |
	publicity-focused protests	presentation of briefs to public bodies	public relations; image-building ads, press releases	confrontation with politicians, officials	regular contact with officials	regular contact, representation on advisory boards, staff exchanges
Institutionalized						▓
Mature		▓	▓		▓	
Fledgeling		▓		▓	▓	
Issue-oriented	▓			▓		

the most serious problem of all. B. and K. Devaux attribute the early demise of community-development work within the Indian and Métis communities in Manitoba to the spread of community development concepts to the Métis population, which brought the program into conflict with provincial agencies that then moved to curtail its activities.[23] Similar difficulties were encountered by the Company of Young Canadians when their community development activities led to the establishment of local groups prepared to challenge established traditional interests.[24]

Not every issue-oriented group that broadens its base develops into an institutional group of the conventional type. An extremely small number are able to retain the public interest and achieve sufficient cohesion to develop into political parties. In Germany environmental groups have combined to play a role in national party politics by forming the Green Party.[25] Its electoral successes have been minimal, but by threatening the electoral base of traditional parties the Greens have drawn attention to environmental issues and may have forced European governments to consider revisions to their policies concerning the use of nuclear power for generating electricity. In the 1950s the Poujadists—a movement of small business interests—achieved a similar feat, thereby encouraging the French government to be solicitous of small business interests.[26]

A graphic representation of the continuum framework appears in Table 5-1. To reduce complexity only four points on the continuum have been identified—groups are treated as issue-oriented, fledgeling, mature, or institutionalized—and three chief descriptive categories are selected: organizational objectives, organizational features, and levels of communication with government. Within each of the latter, however, a further categorization is attempted so that the objectives of groups are classifiable as single and narrowly defined ('Stop Spadina'); multiple but closely related (those of the Indian-Eskimo Association); multiple, broadly defined, and collective (those of the Canadian Civil Liberties Association); or multiple, broadly defined, and both collective and selective (those of the Canadian Automobile Association). Organizational features have been confined to four: (i) the small group that relies on its own membership to do the office work, meet with officials and the media, and to prepare briefs and press releases and perform leadership and aggregation functions. This is the least sophisticated level of formal organization. (ii) The association that possesses resources sufficient to maintain a small support staff; perhaps one or two individuals working part-time. These individuals may have professional training, but they probably are not being paid at the rates professionals would normally receive. (iii) A much more advanced level of organization is achieved when professionals are brought on staff at appropriate salaries and with secretarial and clerical support. At this point the organization is likely to expand its physical resources and invest systematically in a library and in equipment such as word-processors and photocopying machines. The organization's staff will work regularly with the staff of similar associations. (iv) At the furthest extreme is the large multi-faceted organization that at times appears to be run by its professional staff rather than by the membership. Its employees staff offices in major centres and provide services—such as the travel assistance given members by automobile associations—that are often unrelated to the group's political activities. Labour unions and large religious denominations possess organizational structures of this sort.

Levels of communication are divided into two broad categories—media oriented and access oriented—that are intended to cover the activities groups undertake in order to win government concessions as well as their orientation towards non-public communication with officials. Media-oriented categories include, predictably, publicity stunts and protests designed to draw public attention to an issue; public presentations of prepared briefs to officials, commissions of inquiry, regulatory boards and so on; and finally the discreet attempts of well-established organizations to cultivate a favourable climate of public opinion, through, for example, public-service advertising and a range of public relations gimmicks. Media-oriented communication attempts not only to influence public opinion, but to win specific decisions from government officials. Access-oriented communications, on the other hand, focus on generating a receptive attitude at the political and administrative levels, as well as on achieving more narrowly defined goals, such as the sympathetic interpretation of the regulations group members must comply with. Confrontation is at one extreme of this continuum, but a more frequently used technique is the cultivation of regular and private meetings with officials and politicians. Helen Jones Dawson, describing in 1960 the development of Canadian farm organizations, reported that the Canadian Federation of Agriculture had worked closely with civil servants to establish a relationship of respect and trust that would facilitate a two-way flow of information and ideas:

> The Federation has had and used many opportunities to strengthen its personal relationship with senior administrators in the federal service and particularly in the Department of Agriculture and the various boards and agencies associated with it. The necessities of wartime resulted in a rapid development of close consultation and co-operation: The Federation has continued this policy to the discontent of more militant members of the farm community . . . [I]n its public statements [it] is careful not to criticize civil servants; in fact it is more common to find praise of departmental co-operation.[27]

The more militant National Farmers' Union, on the other hand, was inclined to use confrontation tactics and did not enjoy such intimate relations with the federal government. 'It is possible', Dawson reported, 'to detect hostility toward the Union among some officials.'[28] Today's civil servants are more used to public criticism, but pressure groups are still warned against attacking officials too vigorously. Native groups, for example, have found it difficult to reconcile the aggressive rhetoric demanded by their members with the niceties of bureaucratic negotiation.[29] Even the patrons of *Canadian Business* have been advised that they should 'show respect. Be patient. Take him seriously', if they wish to get their way with a bureaucrat.[30]

At the other extreme of group-agency relations, close ties between group leaders and officials can lead to the movement of group members into the public service, and vice versa. Beryl Plumptre, for example, was a leading figure in consumers' associations prior to her appointment to several senior positions in Ottawa's anti-inflation bureaucracy. W.A. Neilson, after spending several years promoting the reform of federal and provincial consumer-protection legislation, became British Columbia's first deputy minister of consumer affairs. Donald Chant, one of the founders of Pollution Probe, became chairman of the Ontario Waste Management Corporation. At lower levels there is a continuous flow of personnel between the public bureaucracy and interest groups. A former official of a governmental research council may take a position in a private foundation promoting public-policy research. Organizations active in the field of international aid, such as Canadian University Services Overseas or the World University Service, often lose their career staff to government agencies like the Canadian International Development Agency. In this way group interests and public policies are integrated and become mutually supportive.

Sally M. Weaver's studies of aboriginal groups in Australia and Canada illustrate some of the processes of institutionalization our diagram describes. She finds, for example, that as national aboriginal organizations became politically active their leaders came to appreciate the value of policy support staff. The National Aboriginal Conference in Australia has worked towards building policy secretariats at both the national and state levels in order to monitor government activity and to research and formulate policy positions. Similar steps were taken by the National Indian Brotherhood.[31] Experience with group-government relations also led national leaders of aboriginal associations to recommend major organizational reforms to their followers, so that the associations could become more effective in exercising influence and communicating politically.[32]

If we consider the evolution of specific groups in the terms suggested by Table 5-1, we will find that a left-to-right upward movement occurs as the characteristics of each type of group are identified and located within the table. Generally this movement will occur whether the characteristics identified are group objectives, organizational features, or levels of communication with government. The blocked sections of the table illustrate this tendency.

The tendency is not, however, universal and the predictive capacities of the continuum are not infallible. We should expect institutionalized groups to behave in the way we have described, but we must not be surprised if they sometimes act like issue-oriented groups. Given different resources, different concerns, and the variation in the levels of political communication that occur within any complex political system, it is inevitable that few groups will conform exactly to the pattern described here. The pattern is a mean, a central tendency. An incident involving the Canadian phamaceutical industry illustrates the point. In the late 1960s the industry was surprised by public concern over the price of prescription drugs. For the first time in its experience it faced a parliamentary inquiry and responded by lobbying the relevant parliamentary committee. If the industry had possessed a deeper under-standing of how policy was made in Ottawa during the period, it would have looked behind the scenes to a group of senior officials who were conducting their own inquiry into the problem. The Parliamentary enquiry aroused public demands for new policies to regulate prescription drugs, but it was the report of the civil-service group that formed the basis of the legislation that was introduced following the Parliamentary enquiry. Perhaps because it was dominated by US-based companies, the industry failed to appreciate the influence civil-service advice would have on the formation of public policy. In consequence, pharmaceutical manufacturers found themselves working under new and unwelcome legislation.[33]

Business interests found themselves in similar disarray when the first Trudeau government, following up an election promise, moved the Combines Investigation Branch from the pro-business department of Trade and Commerce to a new Department of Consumer and Corporate Affairs, and began revising anti-combines legislation. The business community's attempts to influence the proposed legislation made little impact on a department dominated by consumer activists. Business interest groups—the Canadian Manufacturers' Association, the Institute of Canadian Advertising, the Canadian Real Estate Association, to name a few—engaged in much public outcry. Eventually, by dint of persuading the Prime Minister to undertake some important personnel changes in the new department, the business community re-established its traditional influence over business regulation policies.[34]

In these two instances groups normally expected to have mastered the techniques of influencing public policy faced radical change in policy and policy-making, which left them, temporarily at least, ineffective in the policy process. The pharmaceutical industry was unable to adapt to the changed procedures in time to prevent passage of legislation that it opposed. The business community, on the other hand, was able to reassert its influence over competition policy and secure the demise of the offending legislation. In each case, the affected industry groups reacted to a sudden shift in the environment of policy-making in much the same way as less experienced, issue-oriented groups: they engage in public debate.

Animal-rights groups present us with a different analytical conundrum. It is not clear why such groups continue to use the publicity technique of issue-oriented groups after they have attained a high degree of organizational sophistication. We would expect them to develop close working relationships with officials responsible for securing the survival and expansion of wildlife species. We would not expect the frenetic, publicity-seeking behaviour that is the hallmark of Greenpeace, the International Fund for Animal Welfare, and similar groups. The adaptive capacity of groups does, however, suggest an explanation. The discrete, diplomatic behaviour we associate with institutionalized organizations can be endorsed by group members only as long as it appears to forward their goals. Institutionalized groups hope to achieve their goals by influencing the responsible agencies in their policy communities. Government agencies, however, are not equally powerful. Their authority reflects the priority the community at large attaches to the objectives for which they are responsible. It also reflects the influence and power of the policy community that surrounds them. The goals of environmental preservation are often at odds with the economic objectives of modern societies. Since for most governments the attainment of economic prosperity is a paramount goal, environmental policies, the agencies responsible for implementing them, and their associated policy communities cannot easily compete with economic policies, agencies, and policy communities. The disputatious, publicity-seeking behaviour of a number of institutionalized environmental groups reflects the status of the policy community. Their high level of organization and their capacity to develop sophisticated approaches to promoting environmentalism—which is itself broadly defined—marks them as institutionalized groups; their behaviour stems from the fact that they cannot yet achieve their goals through the policy communities of which they are a part. Where goverments have adpoted policies favoured by environmental groups—as, for example, by implementing parks policies and creating reserves—such groups behave like any other institutionalized interest.[35]

We may also attribute the publicity-seeking behaviour of established groups to the demands of members. Weaver suggests that though Indian organizations tend to rely less and less on protest and confrontation as they become institutionalized, such tactics cannot be abandoned entirely lest Indians in general conclude that they are no longer fighting vigorously on their behalf.[36] She cites the examples of the 1974 Native Caravan that prompted the Trudeau government to establish a joint Cabinet-National Indian Brotherhood policy committee, and the constitutional protests carried out at Westminster in the late 1970s and early 1980s. In Australia, by contrast, the more moderate approach of the national Aboriginal Conference has weakened its credibility in the eyes of its supporters.[37]

In general, Diagram 5-1 illustrates a tendency of pressure group development, not an unalterable pattern. Many variations in behaviour occur because groups differ in their human, financial, and organizational resources. Many issue-oriented groups boast competent staff and access to influential politicians and bureaucrats simply because they are supported by people of influence.[38] For this reason small groups concerned with preserving important landmarks have been remarkably successful in some communities. Again, not all institutional groups have mass memberships, though they pursue broad objectives and enjoy ready access to government. Some academic associations fall into this category. The Business Council on National Issues, with 150 corporate members, is small in comparison to business-interest associations like the Canadian Chamber of Commerce, the Canadian Manufacturers' Association, and the Canadian Federation of Independent Business, but because its members include the country's leading firms many journalists and policy-makers consider it equally influential.[39] We contend, however, that the majority of pressure groups display the characteristics we have attributed them.

CATEGORIZING PRESSURE GROUPS

The categorization of pressure groups, and the definition of their ultimate relationship with the political system, has created difficulties for analysts. Perhaps one factor inhibiting the development of a strong analytical framework has been the tendency of scholars to focus on the objectives or interests of groups rather than on their behaviour and on the nature of their relationship with the state. Eckstein and Potter, for example, divide pressure groups into two broad categories: interest and attitude groups.[40] Those in the first category are concerned with promoting the common interests of their members; those in the second with expressing attitudes about public policy. Most scholars follow a similar approach. Salisbury talks of material benefit groups and expressive groups.[41] Finer, in his study of British groups, goes further and subdivides each category according to the kinds of specialized interests pursued by each group.[42] In the last few years American scholars in particular have used the term 'public interest group' to describe the sort of group that used to be referred to as 'expressive' or 'attitude' groups.[43] The term 'special interest group' has come to be applied almost exclusively to material benefit groups.

These typologies have sometimes proved helpful. The use of the term 'public interest group' in the United States has drawn attention to the fact that expressive groups frequently work for the general interest, and that they often do so with very slender resources.[44] As a result steps have been taken, by regulatory bodies in particular, to facilitate their involvement in the policy process and, through financial assistance, to support their vitally important research work. Some of these measures have been imitated in Canada—as in the early 1970s when the Berger inquiry into the proposed Mackenzie Valley Pipeline provided that assistance be given to native and environmental groups wanting to intervene in the inquiry. Nevertheless the issues surrounding the participation of public interest groups have not been addressed as broadly or as systematically in this country as they have in the United States.

On the whole, however, these typologies have created analytical blind alleys. There are two main reasons for this. First, they do not create clear-cut analytically useful categories. The Canadian Medical Association and the Canadian Manufacturers' Association, for example, would generally be classified as material-benefit groups, yet each has expressive goals. The Canadian Medical Association urges Canadians to stop smoking even though attainment of this goal would probably reduce the work available for doctors. Similarly, the efforts of the Canadian Manufacturers' Association to promote healthy labour-management relations in Canada cannot be considered entirely selfish. On the other hand, as antagonistic politicians like to point out, dedicated supporters of environmental groups are not always entirely totally disinterested.[45] For them personal and public interests are often inextricably intertwined. In short, an approach that divides interest groups into material-benefit versus public-interest or expressive categories forces the data, creating an analytical framework that does not properly reflect reality. It confuses more than it helps.

Another influential approach has been developed by Mancur Olson.[46] Concentrating on material-benefit groups, Olson has proposed a theory of collective action that is essentially a calculus of participation. Group members, he argues, are attracted to groups by the benefits they offer. Some of these are selective, benefiting only members, and others are collective; they benefit the community at large, not simply group members. Group strength, and therefore its influence in the policy process, depends on the extent to which it can provide its members with materialistic reasons for joining and adhering to the group. Olson's work helps us understand the internal life of material-benefit groups and to appreciate the strength they derive from self-interested support. But it does not really help us understand how and why expressive groups come to play a part, often significant, in the policy process. Even more important, it is an analysis oriented to understanding group life without reference to the larger environment in which groups must operate. It considers only one variable—internal capacity—of the two (internal capacity and environmental context), which we have argued interact to create the collective and individual characteristics of interest group politics. Another way to put this is to suggest that Olson's approach, and that of others who have adopted it, considers the role of pressure groups almost exclusively from the perspective of interest promotion, which, as we have noted, is only one of five functions we associate with pressure group activity in the political system. The organizational approach we put forward here takes account of the other four functions served by interest groups. The need for this is underlined by the fact that those four functions are the ones that sanction group participation in the political life of the community because they are useful to the political system itself, rather than to the members alone.

Categorizing groups in terms of their benefit-seeking or expressive orientation leads to an ideological exercise rather than to an analysis of power relationships. Its focus on the object of group activity can be helpful in the normative discussion of group demands, but it does not give much guidance in analysing how groups relate to the political system. Equally, it does little to explain behaviour. Yet political science seeks this guidance and such explanations. They are inherent in generalizations like Macridis' comment that 'wherever the governmental organization is cohesive and power is concentrated in certain well-established centers, the pressure groups become well-organized with a similar concentration of power . . . [T]his parallelism between the political system and the interest configuration is true everywhere.'[47] An institutional approach leads to such generalizations because it classifies groups in terms of their capacity to adapt to the communications devices offered by the state; or, to use Coleman's phrase, in terms of their 'policy capacity'.[48] Even our habit of referring to 'issue-oriented' groups does this, because it draws attention to the fact that their concentration on single issues makes it difficult for such groups to relate effectively to the state; it denies them the organizational capacity to take advantage of the access points made available by the state.

The institutional continuum model presented here attempts to meet some of the difficulties we have discussed. Unlike the ordering of groups according to their attitudinal or materialistic bent, the model with an organizational base provides a means of considering all pressure groups within a single framework. This enhances the possibilities of comparative analysis of groups over space and over time. From comparative analysis we can achieve general statements about the characteristics of pressure groups operating in different environments. The last point underlines the most important feature of the continuum model: it can be used to relate pressure group behaviour to the structures and processes of the policy system—to the structure of decision-making power in the state. When we consider that the major points of contact between groups and governments are organizational, it seems logical to use organizational characteristics as a base for categorization and eventual analysis. The essence of modern government is organizational complexity. The key to understanding governmental policy processes, including the participation of pressure groups, should take account of that underlying fact. That is what the organizational continuum model tries to do.

CHAPTER 6

Groups in Action: Influencing the Policy Community

Discourse, coercion, and corruption are the means groups use to obtain their goals. How they use these methods depends on their concerns, the resources they have at hand, and the environment surrounding the policy process.

Most pressure group persuasion is carried out through political debate. Briefs are presented to royal commissions, hearings of tribunals, and individual officials. Legal argument is used to weigh the validity of government policy. Placards shout distress, anger, hope, despair. Theatre, film, pantomime, music, and every conceivable kind of tactile art express opinions about government and are aimed, however indirectly, at government.[1] Books are written; advertisements concocted; speeches rouse multitudes—or leave them indifferent—all in the name of rational discourse.

Threats and promises are implicit in much political debate. Few demonstrators thrusting placards at politicians or shouting into microphones are simply expressing their right to petition. They are also threatening to use the political process to work—and vote—against the party in power unless it accommodates their demands. Even more ominous are the messages contained in the murmur of voices around a boardroom table, the unemotional recitation of a brief or press statement, as the holders of economic power indicate whether or not they will challenge public policy by withholding investment, cutting back production, or eliminating services. The fury that leads protesting fishermen to burn government patrol boats may be less devastating. More commonly a hint of publicity acts as a powerful solvent for reducing the intransigence of groups and officials who prefer the status quo.

When driven, every interest will use whatever tools it can muster to protect its own. Even illegal means may not be excluded. It is increasingly common in Canada for extremists to explode their frustration at public policy. On another level, it is hard to say whether bribery and other forms of corruption are common. A British student of pressure groups once wrote that his was 'a study of proper, official and recognized activities. There is nothing written here of the underhand. It may be, though I doubt it, that groups resort to such activities.'[2] Canada's record of public morality is not noticeably worse than that of most countries and a great deal better than that of many. Even so, there are enough cases on record of the bribery and corruption of public officials for us to assume that on occasion lobbyists do buy policy decisions.[3] This suggests not that everyone who represents interest associations in our capitals is venal or that corruption is a common tool for pressure groups, but that venality and corruption do exist and can be used to influence public policy.

These are the tools group representatives use to sway the policy decisions of politicians and civil servants. How they go about using them depends, as we have said, on the objectives of each group, and the political messages they give rise to; on the resources the group has to influence policy, and on the conditions that prevail at each gateway to the process. For some groups with extensive resources, sure that their views carry weight in policy circles, the polished tactics of traditional lobbying are ideal. They can afford to give 'the best power parties in Ottawa' where 'Cabinet ministers and deputy ministers mingle with captains of industry'. They can afford professional preparation of briefs and other documentation demanded by our increasingly bureaucratized policy process, as well as the costs of litigation or appearances before regulatory bodies. If necessary they can pay for campaigns of mass persuasion. For other groups access to the policy process, even at the local level, is hard to obtain because they do not understand the bureaucratic ways of policy-makers, because the trappings of democracy are beyond their means, or because their plight is too banal to stir a flicker of interest among crusading journalists.

Within the range of these extremes groups seize on the policy system where and how they can, struggling to insert their claims in hopes of satisfying their demands and interests. We will look at this struggle from the vantage point of the policy community concept. We have seen that from the point of view of a specific interest group, 'the public' can be divided into two parts: the general public and the special public, or policy community, which is concerned with the group's own 'policy field'. Because political society permits policy communities to dominate decision-making in fields where they have competence—interfering only when larger concerns must take precedence, when systemic or technological change necessitates intervention, or when the level of conflict within the community spills over into the larger political arena—for most of the time the policy community, though less significant in global terms than the public at large, is much more prominent in the group's eyes. In keeping with this conceptual framework we will turn first to the policy community, exploring the relationship most significant to the group—that between it and the lead agency. We will then consider how the amorphous and elusive ties that hold together the sub-government influence the way groups in the sub-government behave towards one another. Next we will look at the lively, though not powerful, part of the policy community, the attentive public, and try to assess how it relates to the core members; how it is used by them; and how members of the attentive public try to influence core members of the policy community. In the next chapter we will begin by asking how, when, and why groups bring their messages to the general public. We will also look briefly at the role of other governments in pressure group politics and will glance at the increasing use groups are making of the judicial system.

INFLUENCING THE POLICY COMMUNITY

Policy is seldom the product of general public discussion. There are too many policy issues available for the public to deal with them all. In addition, few of the interests materially affected by particular policies encourage their general discussion. General discussion entails conflict, which reverberates through the foundations of established policy, making them unstable and unpredictable. Those with a vested interest in established policy prefer to maintain its stability by 'organizing issues out of politics', by delegating conflict resolution to administrative tribunals, and by restricting discussion to a narrowly defined special public.[4] For most groups, most of the time, 'the public' means the special public we call the policy community.

The ascendancy of the policy community is a relatively new phenomenon, growing out of the decline of bureaucratic influence and the subsequent search for legitimation. To achieve their goals contemporary public officials must generate support in the policy community, winning the approval of the other government agencies, the pressure groups, corporations, institutions, and individuals with a vested interest or an explicit concern in the policy field. Departments foster constant contact with their 'clientele'— sounding public opinion and obtaining new ideas. Usually this is done by identifying and building on relations with organized groups or specific interests concerned with the work of the agency. If interest groups do not exist, departments encourage their formation.

With this reciprocal relationship comes a growth in the complexity and number of ties that bind the various players in the community. Thirty years ago lobbying and government were much less complicated. David Kirk, an official of the Canadian Federation of Agriculture recalls that it was possible 'to work with just one minister and department. Policy recommendations would come up through the department; the minister would decide what he wanted to do; then he would take his proposals to Cabinet.'[5] Action would be authorized with a minimum of fuss. Interdepartmental committees would not haver forever over the pros and cons of alternative options. If the minister were obstructive there would be little mystery about the reasons why, and it would be fairly clear whether ministerial lobbying would overcome the problem. Today lobbyists know that persuading key officials, or even ministers, will not suffice, since these apparently powerful personages will seldom act without receiving clear signals from other interested parties that they too support the proposed changes in policy. This does not mean that politicians avoid involvement in the selection of policy options; but it does reflect the fact that 'Cabinet ministers are in general enormously overextended and do not have adequate time to devote to any single special interest, unless it happens to be central to the management of the portfolio'.[6] They are forced to rely on their officials. In most cases, the only alternative opinions available to the minister come from affected interest groups:

> These are primary constituencies. Their backing is often essential to maintaining ministerial clout within Cabinet, even of surviving on the job. Their support in the implementation of programs and policies is usually important. A minister who loses the confidence of his primary constituency is in trouble. You can quickly read in the political columns the impending political mortality of a minister who has lost that support. The primary constituency is also a minister's principal alternative source of information for his department. Any minister who decides he can run a department on the basis of the advice he gets from his bureaucrats is bound to be in trouble. Not because the advice from bureaucrats is mischievous or malevolent or badly thought out, but because it represents a particular point of view; and in a world where the public agenda is increasingly broad, a single source of information, a single point of view, can no longer be relied upon . . . The primary constituency . . . provides a minister with grass-roots feed-back on issues and the concerns of its membership. So political heads of agencies need very good communications with that primary constituency to provide intelligence on what programs are working and on how they are working. They need their views on what policies should be changed. In short, they depend on the primary constituency as a source of policy countervail to departmental advice.[7]

Officials, aware that the ministers see key interest groups as a countervailing force, also consult them and attempt to win their support in campaigns for the policies and programs favoured by departments and agencies.

The competition for support on policy issues exacerbates tendencies towards bureaucratic forms of communication. Senior agency officials, however well informed, will want supporting documents from the subordinates who will be responsible for implementing decisions. They know that decisions taken without that support will be carried out half-heartedly at best. Junior officials who are deeply opposed may sabotage the policy or initiate a bitter public debate led by their affiliates in the policy community. Subordinates, consequently, have to be brought 'on side' by being given a lead role in developing an appropriate policy analysis and in generating support within the policy community. To generate that support other units, other agencies, individuals, and groups must be consulted, committees established, and both the unit and the group advocating the change of policy must spend a great deal of time and effort explaining their proposal and then reshaping it into a form that is acceptable to the key actors in the community. What was once a straightforward process involving only a handful of individuals has become a highly bureaucratic one, demanding the time and talents of many.

Because the policy community works in this bureaucratic fashion, a group wishing to be influential in it (i.e. to be part of the sub-government) must possess some of the attributes of bureaucracy. A group may be able to control the flow of human, material, or financial resources to the sector, but power alone is not enough. It may enable the group to have a say in policy development, but the impact of that contribution will depend on how well the group understands and exploits its strategic position in the policy community. Access to decision centres, a strategic place in the information flow, and the possession of technical expertise are also essential. Expert knowledge of the substantive policy field is a valuable commodity, particularly if the group holds a monopoly or near monopoly of vital information. Such information can be exchanged for access to decision-makers and for a continuing place in the information flow, such as group representation on advisory committees or automatic inclusion in technical conferences and consultative exercises. Access to key decision-makers denotes more than recognition—it is an acknowledgement of power in the community, of the possession of vital information and/or the ability to persuade others to support or abandon a cause. Above all, however, it is an acknowledgement of the group's familiarity with the policy process; of its ability to deal with a bureaucratic structure and to share bureaucratic values, such as a high regard for factual information and rational decision-making.

To influence its policy community a group must be prepared to deploy its lobbying activities in four different directions. The most important target will be the sub-government comprising, for the group's purposes, three targets that function separately and must be approached differently: the political executive and its supporting agencies; the lead agency itself, and the other groups and agencies that are regularly consulted in the formation of government policy. Finally, from time to time the group will have to address the entire policy community, including the attentive public.

(i) *The executive*

Most established groups prefer not to take action-oriented messages to the Cabinet and the central agencies. To do so would be to admit that they failed to reach agreement within the policy community and, in effect, are breaking ranks with the other members of the community. Invoking the superior authority of the political executive disturbs the balance of power within the policy community; and even if it achieves its purpose, it does so at the cost of goodwill and smooth working relations with their immediate associates. There are two even more important reasons why many groups do not appeal to the centre. First, they want to avoid Cabinet interference. Cabinet—particularly the inner Cabinet—occupies the overview position in the government: it is responsible for overriding the self-regarding tendencies of departments and their allies; for finding ways of co-ordinating the policies and programs of individual agencies, and ensuring that issues that have been organized out of politics are pushed back in. These responsibilities are often pushed aside by cabinet workloads and the natural tendency of ministers to defend their own departments by not encroaching on others', but since major reforms were made to the central policy structures during the Trudeau years, officials in the Privy Council Office, the Treasury Board, the Prime Minister's Office, and Finance have frequently assumed the task of representing Cabinet's co-ordinative and monitoring roles.[8] Their many interventions during the 1970s, earned them the dislike and bitter opposition of line agencies and their allies, who became determined to contain issues within the policy community and to reduce the central agencies' influence.[9] This determination is given a further edge by the second reason for avoiding the involvement of the political executive: groups have discovered the fact that an appeal to the centre may force them to engage in public debate. The agenda of Cabinet and its committees is so constrained that only a few issues inherently and obviously of national importance find their way automatically to Cabinet consideration. The majority have to fight for a place on the agenda, usually by attracting the kind of media attention that persuades cabinet ministers that the public is concerned and wants policy decisions. This kind of publicity attracts the interest of opponents as well as the support of friends.

Nevertheless circumstances often force issues into Cabinet's purview—as in 1985 when the failure of two regional banks precipitated a major review of bank regulation and inspection. On such occasions groups must contend with the mysteries of central decision-making. It is then that the maintenance of offices in the federal and provincial capitals pays off. Since access to Cabinet is virtually impossible to obtain, groups must focus their attention on the officials of the central policy structures and aides of influential ministers. Groups whose staff are familiar with the workings of the central agencies and who know their officials have a considerable advantage. Familiarity with the policy review process gives them a sense of when to inject supporting information and whether, when, and where to apply pressure, as well as the ability to monitor discussions at the centre and to use personal connections to communicate group concerns to officials. Some may be able to brief key ministers. Groups without staff members able to achieve this level of access—and they are probably the great majority, even among members of the various sub-governments—must secure the services of the many legal and consulting firms who specialize in this type of lobbying. Described as 'door openers for the lobbying trade', firms like Executive

Consultants Limited will, for a sizeable monthly retainer, advise clients on whom to see and what to say.[10] Groups that are not affluent enough to pay for professional lobbying must depend on the pressure tactics we described earlier: communicating with MPs; asking friends and members with influence to intercede on their behalf with cabinet members and party officials; writing to cabinet members, and generally trying to create the impression that the public at large supports their cause.

Influential members of policy communities are chary of taking action-oriented messages to the centre, but they treat the delivery of legitimating messages as a mark of recognition—a telling point in the game of positional politics. Groups with particular influence—either because they represent a broad cross-section of the community or because they can command extensive economic resources—frequently have access to cabinets and from time to time make formal presentations to them. Thus for many years it was a tradition that the Canadian Federation of Agriculture, the Canadian Labour Congress, and business groups such as the Canadian Manufacturers' Association annually presented to the federal Cabinet briefs on the current state of government policy in fields concerning them and urged the executive to further measures that each group favoured. Some of the positions put forward in these briefs were 'ritual demands'—demands that the leadership and the politicians knew could not be met and followed up—that were presented as tokens of the group's long-term commitment to certain goals. Others, however, signalled to the executive the group's current policy agenda. These 'serious demands' were related to the group's mandate, its privileges and prerogatives, and other matters affecting the organizational integrity of the group, as well as to major current issues.[11] Over the last decade, as the proliferation of pressure groups has made it more and more difficult for the federal government to appear to favour even very broadly based specific groups, the tradition of the cabinet briefing has been discouraged and major groups have had to be content with influencing those they hope will influence the Cabinet, namely the members of caucus.[12] Thus in 1980 a representative of the Canadian Federation of Agriculture reported that 'in recent years' his organization had made presentations to the several federal caucuses, rather than to Cabinet.[13] In the provinces, where such meetings still continue and may be more numerous, group briefs may be concerned with immediate issues and problems. In December 1974, for example, when the East Coast fishing industry was experiencing one of its recurrent crises, the Atlantic Chambers of Commerce highlighted the fishery's problems in their brief to the Nova Scotia Cabinet.[14]

Groups reluctant to take specific concerns to cabinet level make an exception in the case of 'their' minister. The minister responsible for the community's lead agency is generally expected to be sympathetic to the community's concerns and to speak for them in Cabinet. Self-interest accounts for this.

The community's successes tend to cast the minister in a favourable light; its failures nearly always find political expression, and unless handled adroitly, can undermine a promising ministerial career.

The policy process itself also enables interests to develop friendly relations with their minister. He or she is in constant contact with the lead agency and its clients and depends on it for an introduction into the details of the community's concerns. Inevitably an element of indoctrination creeps into what is already a mutually dependent relationship, but the process has the advantage of making the minister a member of the community—a person with whom it is possible to discuss issues that many members would not discuss with anyone outside the community. This relationship should, therefore, enhance the minister's understanding and capacity to lead and to represent. Finally, the policy process also puts the minister in a position to arbitrate between officials and private sector members of the community.[15]

The working relationship that makes possible the arbitrator's role, and gives the community the link it needs with the political executive, is developed and maintained in a variety of ways. Community members generally have freer access to the minister than do non-members. Consultations may take place fairly frequently. Some ministers like to meet regularly with a small group of trusted advisers, some of whom will be members of the community. Symbolic appearances—official openings, presentations, keynote and after-dinner speeches—are important and numerous, not because of what is said in public, but because they sustain acquaintanceships, permit brief confabulations and remind the minister of the group's work, influence, and interests. They also have positional importance. The Canadian Club of Toronto takes pride in the fact that, since Donald Fleming addressed its members in 1958, it has played host to every Minister of Finance. The event reinforces the group's image as a gathering of the business élite and, not incidentally, permits a few of those who attend to exchange some words with the minister. In a succession of days crowded with events of this sort ministers establish their affinity with the community, take its pulse, and connect it to the Cabinet and the larger political scene.

(ii) *The lead agency*

The bureaucratic nature of the policy communities is reinforced by the fact that government agencies sit at their centre. Even though agencies may not dominate their relations with groups as easily as they once did, they are still very powerful. Their capacity to dictate terms has diminished, but not evaporated. To work with agencies, interest groups must organize themselves in similar fashion and, to some extent, must abide by the norms of consultation preferred by them. This is particularly true of the relations with the lead agency and, where their authority is significant, the regulatory boards and commissions in the policy community.

On the organizational level, group adaptation to the structure of the target agency begins as soon as it decides to attempt to influence the bureaucracy. To wield influence the group must become familiar with the agency's institutional framework: it must know who in the organization deals with what issues; how much weight their advice carries; who their rivals are and how likely they are to attack. The group must also have an intimate knowledge of the programs administered by the agency: a thorough understanding of how they work in practice; how they affect the public; what their shortcomings and benefits are; and whether or not they come close to meeting the objectives set out for them. To accomplish this the group must, at a minimum, be able to conceptualize issues in terms of bureaucratic rationality. This means that the group must employ at least one professional who is familiar with both the institutional framework for policy development and delivery and the pattern of thought the agency applies to the policy field. Often groups will organize themselves to mirror the structure of the agency and its chief affiliates. They will hire professionals to maintain a continuing liaison with those parts of the agency whose work is vital to them, and they will organize members' committees to evaluate the information derived from monitoring, and to respond to initiatives from the agency and related groups. A recent program-based budget prepared by the Social Science Federation of Canada gives an idea of what is involved:

> A sizeable portion of the Federation's staff, elected officers' and members' time is devoted to liaising with government departments and agencies. The work accomplished in this area by members and elected officers is considerable, but obviously very difficult to quantify. It is possible, however, to give an indication of the nature and scope of the Federation's staff involvement. During the course of the past year, the Executive Director and/or the professional staff have had ten meetings with M.P.s and ministers, more than twenty with senior civil servants, thirty with SSHRC's Committees or members of staff and a dozen with representatives of other Councils or agencies (Science Council, National Science and Engineering Research Council, Economic Council, etc.). In addition, a substantial amount of correspondence is carried out with various departments on topics which concern the academic community.[16]

In support of this work and as part of it, the Federation was preparing and distributing a number of discussion papers, briefs, and reports; conducting several task forces; reviewing the work of a consultative exercise on the strategic concerns of its member organizations; attempting to monitor and react to the policy initiatives and legislative program of the Mulroney government; and maintaining up-to-date data sets on current and projected legislation and departmental programs of concern to social scientists, and similarly current lists of elected officials, public servants, university officials, and members. It was also developing departmental profiles for the five federal departments with which it was most regularly involved: Secretary of State; Health and Welfare; Solicitor General; Environment; and Communications. Its 'public awareness' program and special programs for members were additions to these activities. It is hardly surprising that even a modest interest group like the SSFC becomes a complex organization.

These developments occur over organizational space. Staff is added and new units are created as the group's work evolves to keep pace with government initiatives. Frequently, however, the elaboration and institutionalization of Canadian interest groups takes place over physical space as well. Groups first established at the provincial level, often in only one or two provinces, have frequently moved their headquarters to Ottawa or set up a major office there, and have had to establish a physical presence in each of the provinces. In part this reflects the tendency for sectoral interests across the country to recognize their common concerns and to merge provincial organizations into federated ones able to speak with a national voice.[17] It also reflects the expanded role of government. Organizations that at the end of the Second World War existed only at the provincial level found that in the next quarter century the expansion and interpenetration of federal and provincial responsibilities necessitated their presence at the federal level as well. Without it they were unable to maintain a continuous liaison with the federal officials whose decisions were crucial to group members. This was the experience of the Canadian Trucking Association, which in the 1950s was a loose confederation of provincial associations. A series of court decisions recognizing Ottawa's constitutional role in interprovincial highway regulation, together with the the federal government's Trans-Canada Highway program—which made a national trucking network feasible—drew the federal government into a more prominent and authoritative position in the policy community concerned with motor vehicle transportation. Ultimately the Canadian Trucking Association stengthened its national organization and built up a major office in Ottawa.[18] At least one Canadian academic society, the Canadian Political Science Association, followed a similar route. Until the late 1960s the CPSA's 'head office' was located primarily at whichever university employed the organization's part-time secretary treasurer. By the mid-1970s the association's involvement with federal programs, particularly the Social Sciences and Humanities Research Council of Canada programs in support of national academic associations and the publication of learned journals, had forced a change in policy: head office had to be located at one of the two Ottawa universities. There the association, which still has a part-time secretary treasurer but employs several administrators, can participate readily in the numerous committees and consultative activities organized by the Social Science Federation of Canada to lobby federal agencies, particularly the SSHRCC and the Secretary of State. The experience of these, among many, national organizations suggests that the growth of government activity has fostered a concurrent physical centralization of interest groups, drawing them into an increasingly bureaucratized policy community. Perhaps physical centralization has also reinforced bureaucratization of the policy community, facilitating as it does committee interaction between groups and agencies and fostering the extensive consultation that is a hallmark of politics in modern policy communities.

But the bureaucratic influence of the key agency does not end there. Most agencies will want affiliate groups to accept their own bureaucratic mores, including a high regard for bureaucratic modes of communication. A good deal of emphasis will be placed on formal research and analysis of policy options, and on written presentation of group positions. Above all they will want to ensure that the groups will have little resort to publicity—unless, of course, it promotes the legitimacy of the community and its dominant policies—and even less resort to confrontation.

In the 1970s Canadians became aware of how influential the bureaucracy had become. The widespread realization that in agency-group relations the agency tends to dominate[19] fostered a small mythology of bureaucratic behaviour. An article in the September 1980 issue of *Canadian Business* describes some of the perceptions many interest group representatives developed of the lead agencies in their policy field, and indicates some of the strategies deployed to deal with them. Entitled 'Getting Your Way With a Bureaucrat', its subtitle suggests a power relationship in which the official calls the shots: 'Show respect. Be patient. Take him seriously. Sounds easy, but a lot of businessmen don't know how to get to first base.'[20] According to author Larry Smith, a consulting economist with experience as a federal civil servant,

> The need for business to be able to defend its interests before the civil service has never been greater. But many business representatives not only fail to advance their causes, but actually antagonize the very persons they wish to influence. The ineptness that many lobbyists bring to their relationships with the civil service arises from a single source—their failure to understand the bureaucracy's aims and the way it works. The bureaucracy is not, as too many business people tend to regard it, some inscrutable mandarinate out to thwart the legitimate ends of the free enterprise system. It is a collection of, for the most part, reasonably principled and reasonably intelligent civil servants who can be swayed by reasonable discourse.[21]

To get their way, lobbyists were urged to adopt a set of procedures that reflected a shrewd understanding of how human foibles and motivations mingle with and leaven the operations of bureaucracy. The bureaucratic machine lives on information. It demands raw data from those it serves and sophisticated analyses from those who want to influence it. It is also complex and slow moving. Decisions are seldom made at a single point; they are generally the product of internal consultation and often reflect the public service's mandate to defend the public interest. These rationalistic aspects of bureaucracy intimidate many, who come to resent and fear the quest for information; they see the need for formal analysis and the complexity and slow pace of decision-making as an encumbrance. For the experienced lobbyist, however, the mingling of these classic attributes of bureaucracy with the normal, everyday need of human beings to advance and take satisfaction in their work offers an opportunity to exercise influence. Smith's message is that civil servants are human, 'reasonably competent and conscientious'. They are even 'susceptible to the most basic bargaining techniques'. The artfully prepared brief has greater impact if it is presented 'by someone the civil servant knows and may already have cooperated with. That circumstance alone guarantees a reading, which is the first, most critical step in advancing your case.'[22] The request for information may be an opportunity to establish a contact and to do a favour. Respect for the civil servant's expertise and concern for the public interest builds trust that may be important in future bargaining sessions. Finally, the very complexity of the public service can be put to good use. Smith argues that 'when you are dealing with a complex organization, it is futile to try to impose simplicity where none exists. But handled knowledgeably, the very complexity of the bureaucracy can work to your advantage.'[23] People who complain that 'I cannot find the right person to talk to; everyone refers me to someone else', are turning an opportunity into a problem:

> . . . it is a mistake to take the absence of a single channel of responsibility as a vice; it is an outright virtue. If you are lobbying for a cause down a single pathway, a turn-down becomes a rejection without recourse or appeal. In the more tightly structured private sector, one imbecile often has the power to bring an entire line of activity to a complete halt. But in the civil service, where responsibility is diffused, any particular refusal need be only a road-block around which it is possible to manoeuvre. The likelihood of ultimate success grows in direct proportion to the number of avenues of pursuit.

Aware that a single, knowledgeable official can guide him or her through 'the dark labyrinths of the mandarinate', the effective lobbyist obtains referrals from one civil servant to another.

> The real challenge is to get each of them involved in your problem. Some civil servants, mistakenly believing that if the lobbyist states his problem precisely enough they can refer him to the right person, actually try to do so. Therefore, never state your area of concern precisely; use the most general, ambiguous terms possible without being incoherent. That forces the civil servant to generate a number of alternative referrals in the hope that one of them meets your needs. You, of course, want all of them.

But the canny lobbyist does not simply generate lists of names:

> . . . in your initial conversations with any civil servant, find out exactly what he does. Then try to find something about your problem that fits his bailiwick. Consider, for example, a company seeking support to make an investment in new plant. Each of the following aspects of the question involves *different* civil servants: job creation in general; job creation for a specific region; job

creation for a minority; export stimulation; import substitution; improvement in the competitiveness of the market; enhancement of research and development; environmental improvement; and national unity. And that is a short list, any aspect of which may make the critical difference for obtaining a favorable hearing. Broader lobbying causes, of course, involve an even wider range of possibilities.

Like much sophisticated advice, these suggestions over-simplify the world of policy formation and present too optimistic an account of the benefits to be derived from Machiavellian manipulation.[24] Nevertheless they give us a glimpse of how lobbyists work with the public service and a sense of the rules they often apply. We can condense those rules into several basic strategies.

First, even though the lobbyist may want to exploit the complexity of the bureaucracy, it is essential to have a very clear idea of what the organization wants. Bureaucracy has its own rationality. It divides the world into innumerable activities, which it approaches separately. The group that does not know its own mind may find itself queuing at the wrong wicket, wasting resources in attempts to influence officials who themselves are unable to affect the policies that are of greatest concern to the group. The group that does know its own mind is able to exploit the complexity of the bureaucracy and to apply the second rule in the lobbyist's operational guidebook, which is to know and understand its target. This enables it to look ahead, identify the agencies it is most likely to deal with, and to become familiar with their policies, their programs, and, above all, their problems. This is necessary because working with government is a process of collective bargaining. A group may be able to negotiate modifications in the policy it is concerned about in exchange for support—in the policy community, with other agencies, or with the public—for the agency's pet policy. Alternatively it may be able to barter information or administrative facilities for policy concessions, financial assistance, or position in the sub-government.

Professional lobbyists also get to know the agency's organizational structure and the people who work in it, for civil servants can help or hinder group efforts to influence policy. Knowing who makes which decision can be crucial. With a knowledge of structure and of the people who work in each agency, lobbyists can identify the locus of decisions, and by working on the assumption that the best way to stop an adverse decision is never to let it be born, the lobbyist can familiarize officials with the group's point of view and assess their attitudes towards it. If a cordial relationship has been created, the lobbyist may also obtain advance warning of policy reviews and the guarantee of an opportunity for input at the right time. Obviously a sense of timing is important.[25] Lobbyists know that addressing an issue too soon may be as dangerous as reacting to it too late. Being over-eager may waste group resources and irritate policy-makers, and may even precipitate the very discussion that the lobbyist hoped to avoid. In addition lobbyists learn how to use the budget cycle to put forward proposals and develop a sixth sense about the issues they should leave alone, those they should monitor, and those that demand immediate and decisive action.

Such strategies virtually compel the lobbyist to become professional, devoting his or her entire time to understanding the bureaucracy and attempting to influence it. Being professional is, in fact, the third rule of lobbying; one of the mores that the bureaucracy imposes on its relations with groups. Officials and senior politicians deal with groups continuously and are not impressed by tantrums. As one community activist puts it, 'don't wing it—and don't whine. Don't make outrageous demands, or back government people into corners. Do your homework.'[26] Nor do they tolerate poor organization and amateurish presentations. They expect groups to make the best use of their time. They prefer to read briefs that are crisp, well documented, and effectively organized, culminating in recommendations that are not only clearly set out but take account of the ramifications for program implementation of changes in policy. They like group spokesmen to be well organized in their oral presentations with their facts at their fingertips. They do not like the group's supporters to become abusive and 'physical'—to get out of hand.

The sanctions against confrontation present many groups with a fundamental question: should we try to embarrass policy-makers and expand our public support by public criticism in the media, or is it better to work quietly behind the scenes and forsake a public image? To address this question many groups formulate a fourth, and final, guide to action: avoid confrontation, but remember that sometimes it is necessary to embarrass politicians and officials. On those occasions it is important to avoid the strident exposure that alienates them permanently and may antagonize the public as well. In the words of one activist:

> Avoid confrontation, but don't ignore its potential. Better to be seen as a lion than as a pussy cat! Confrontation—like the theatre that it strongly resembles— can generate emotions; rousing passions, touching people at their deepest levels, stimulating a catharsis. If the media are present they magnify and transmit the images to thousands of people. But confrontation is a two-edged sword: it can ruin an organization's credibility as well as enhancing it. Use it at specific times, to achieve specific goals (media coverage, mobilization of interest, to reach politicians who have ceased to listen). Plan confrontation so that it is effective in achieving these goals, and keep it under control.[27]

It is equally important to avoid boxing in policy-makers. They must have an 'out', a compromise that will allow them to save face and permit them to maintain an equable relationship with the group in the future.

Simply cataloguing the rules lobbyists follow informally as they try to influence the lead agency in the policy community underlines the significant role of the bureaucracy in policy formation, and the extent to which its characteristics colour the policy community. It also emphasizes the inequalities groups face in the policy process. In 1985-6 the Social Science Federation of Canada budgeted over $300,000 for representing the concerns of its members and for fostering 'a greater and more positive awareness of the social sciences'.[28] The SSFC is not a wealthy organization. The Consumers' Association of Canada was reported in 1980 to have revenues of $1.7 million, derived from federal grants and from its 145,000 members. It too is considered a 'brown bagger in the lobbying crowd'.[29] In 1984 the Business Council on National Issues was reported to have a budget of $1 million, but unlike the CAC it does not have to devote a great portion of this amount to providing services to members and maintaining a geographically dispersed organization. Most of its resources can be dedicated to lobbying. Furthermore, the BCNI's influence extends 'far beyond' its budget because the corporate leaders who form its membership possess power, influence, and access to policy-makers in their own right.[30] Such comparisons underline the handicaps that encumber groups with small resources—particularly groups attempting to represent the poor and disadvantaged—that cannot work easily in a bureaucratic environment. Their capacity to help make policy is limited.

Some observers argue that these disparities are not as debilitating to citizens' groups as they might seem. According to Julianne La Breche:

It's important to understand that even a temporary, makeshift lobby can be effective. For instance one of the best lobbies, recalls Walter Baker, was carried out (in 1978) by 35 university scientists representing the Canadian Federation of Biological Societies [sic] (CFBS).

Scientists are rarely political beings, but in this instance a 'freeze' on research funds, administered through the Medical Research Council, had suddenly cut short many of their research projects. Because of this scientists quickly learned how to politicize their pitch. They claimed the public would suffer in the end from the 'freeze' because there would be a brain drain across the border to the US. Their efforts were strengthened because, for the first time, different scientific disciplines were suddenly speaking with one voice.

Baker recalls being buttonholed by scientists from his own constituency (as were 50 other MPs) who spent two hours delivering a persuasive carefully prepared brief. 'I remember going home late that night and saying to my wife, "Now there's an issue we can really get involved with." ' (The freeze was later lifted.)[31]

But the science lobby was not a 'scratch-built' affair. Nor was it a 'one-shot' effort that achieved a permanent and satisfactory conclusion. Rather, it was the culmination of months of planning by a number of associations.[32] It involved identifying the attitudes of politicians and the agencies many of them were associated with and then assigning to them carefully selected representatives of the scientific community. Buttressed with carefully researched fact sheets and position papers, group and individual meetings in 1978 achieved some of the success La Breche notes, but by 1981 much of the work had to be done again. A second visitation in December 1980 revealed that . . .

> The average MP is much better informed [on research and development] than in 1978, but the absence of large scale lobbying by us during the two years of musical chairs in Ottawa has taken its toll. Even some of our old allies in the House now need updating and re-educating to a considerable extent. . . .
>
> As of December 11th, the short term picture for research seems bleak...The only factors which might influence [it] are the lobby just held, the next lobby in March, and resistance from presidents . . . of the granting councils.[33]

It was clear that continued effort was necessary to keep the scientific community's needs before decision-makers. The lobbying coalition developed a long-term strategy that involved supplying MPs with questions for Question Period; being prepared to respond immediately to budget decisions; and extending the canvass of MPs and Ministers to senior civil servants and media leaders. All this was in addition to the normal round of lobbying conducted by most of the organizations participating in the coalition. Clearly this was more than a 'makeshift' lobby. If a lobby with that amount of organization and resources could achieve such tenuous results, how much greater are the odds facing groups that really are 'scratch-built'?

(iii) *The sub-government*

Apart from its concern for promoting its influence with the lead agency, two factors are paramount in a group's relations with other members of the sub-government. The first is position. The second is co-operation.

Status, recognition, and position are essential to being consulted. Securing a recognized position in the sub-government is a first priority for any group intending to exert continuing influence on policy.[34] For many this involves continual struggle and competition. The National Farmers' Union, after many years on the policy scene, still does not enjoy a privileged position in the agricultural policy community.[35] Other groups, however, gain recognition from their work, or else their status was earned so long ago that it is no longer questioned. The Canadian Bankers' Association and the Canadian Tax Foundation, for example, are confirmed members of the policy community that regularly discusses fiscal policy with the Department of Finance. The Business Council on National Issues and the Canadian Federation of Independent Business, on the other hand, have only recently been created and have had to earn a consultative position in the community concerned with the economy. The CFIB mounted a flamboyant, belligerent publicity campaign that asserted the right of small business to be heard. The BCNI was equally flamboyant, but deliberately conveyed the impression that an organization speaking for the wealthiest corporations in the country would automatically have a seat in the councils of the mighty.[36]

Once they have survived the first round in the game of positional politics, groups tend to become less vocal, less inclined to invoke public opinion on issues of the day. Problems of legitimacy give way to problems of communication. Instead of clamouring to be consulted, they are hounded for advice. When governments and their agencies decide that specific groups speak for a significant part of the population and that their views are legitimate, they turn to them frequently, inviting them to sit on advisory committees and consulting them on issues far afield from the immediate concerns of the groups themselves. Responding to these overtures takes considerable effort. Membership opinion may have to be elicited, or specialized knowledge tapped. More frequently the organization may have to dedicate the time of its research staff to the question at hand, diverting it from tasks more important to the group and its members. Even participation on advisory boards can siphon off valuable executive time.[37]

Despite these problems groups hesitate to turn down invitations to advise and participate. Participation helps maintain the organization's position as an integral part of the policy community; taps it into the information flow; guarantees consultation on issues of real concern to the group; and provides opportunities for group representatives to form personal links with civil servants, leaders of other groups, and sometimes senior politicians. The cost of participation is, in short, the price the group pays for acceptance as a full-fledged member of the policy community.

Monitoring is an important aspect of any established group's relationship with its policy community, and particularly with the key agencies. Being a part of the information flow and establishing friendly ties with the representatives of other groups help the group keep abreast of opinion in influential circles, enabling it to anticipate proposals for policy change, and thus to react and adapt to them. Informal ties, and even a prominent place in the community, do not in themselves guarantee adequate monitoring of trends in public opinion and government thinking, however. It is often necessary to introduce more systematic monitoring devices, such as clipping and analysing the general and specialized press; scrutinizing government policy, proposed legislation, and policy reviews in related fields; following academic discussions that have a bearing on the policy field; and even commissioning research into emergent issues. Often groups will themselves organize seminars, workshops, and conferences whose major function is to engage in forecasting activities—summing up the results of current monitoring activities and extrapolating from them.

Position confers the privilege of consultation and of access to strategic information, both of which facilitate the process of bringing influence to bear. These privileges reconcile group members of the sub-government to the norms preferred by bureaucratic members. Indeed, these norms are not necessarily distasteful to groups that have worked their way to the sub-government. While competition and conflict are the hallmark of group efforts to secure the support of public opinion and also play a part in campaigns to influence the political and administrative executive, a search for consensus is an even more important part of the life of the sub-governments. Community members use consenus to keep issues from spilling over into the public arena. But consensus, as much as the predilections of officials, imposes norms and sanctions on group behaviour—particularly norms and sanctions of discretion and confidentiality.

The preoccupation with keeping issues out of politics also has much to do with the tendency to co-operate—the second feature of sub-government relations that concerns most of its members. For as long as organized groups have existed to influence government, they have allied themselves with other groups. There are several reasons for this. First, they promote stable relations between groups. As Kwavnick puts it: 'To leave a group outside the circle of accepted groups is to invite its leaders to adopt unorthodox tactics, to make exaggerated demands and, generally, to be a disruptive and uncertain element.'[38] Second, alliances strengthen group credibility. Third, they broaden the base of support and increase the resources available to specific groups. Fourth, they also reflect the communal nature of policy-making. Most members of the sub-government are aware that they will have to live with one another in the future. Tomorrow they may in fact search out as allies the groups they are tempted to revile today. There is therefore an incentive not only for reaching compromises, and for exercising restraint and civility, but for acting in concert.

At the turn of the century, for example, those who supported 'votes for women' often found themselves working with temperance groups. In 1916 the president of the Saskatchewan Grain Grower's Association, which like many western farmers' groups was strongly prohibitionist, wrote to the Acting Premier, J.A. Calder: 'I am instructed by the executive . . . to memorialize you stating that the body sincerely hopes that provision may be made fully enfranchising the women of Saskatchewan so that they may vote in December next on the referendum on the liquor question.' Though the biographer of the Canadian women's suffrage movement wryly comments that 'the evidence reinforces the hypothesis that women received the vote primarily because they represented puritanical, moralistic values and not because of the growth of genuine sentiment in favor of sexual equality', the fact remains that it was through a succession of alliances of this sort that women in all the provinces influenced public opinion—and ultimately governments—to the point where they won the right to vote.[39]

Such alliances are not always entered into without misgivings. In the early years of the suffrage movement many prohibitionists felt that their association with the suffragists offended many who might otherwise have supported the temperance cause. Later, as the narrow focus of the rural-based temperance movement became a liability in an increasingly urban country, the suffragists themselves came to doubt the wisdom of aligning their cause with one that was considered less and less relevant to modern needs.[40] Nevertheless for a crucial period at the turn of the century the alliance was a great help to the suffragists:

> The connection between prohibition and woman suffrage, like the connection with the social gospel, contributed to the esteem of the woman's movement and to the eventual suffrage victory. The temperance reformers remained a powerful group in early-twentieth century Canada and their endorsement undoubtedly aided the women politically. The close alliance between the WCTU and the suffragists and the actual overlap in the two memberships also convinced the men in power that the suffragists were really quite an inoffensive group. Woman suffrage ceased to alarm.[41]

While the struggle for women's suffrage is uncharacteristic of sub-government behaviour, in that the issue was taken to the general public, it nevertheless illustrates the advantages of co-operation. For the suffrage movement the alliance with the temperance movement, at least in the early days, brought access to leaders of religious groups and others who regularly influenced government policy concerned with moral issues. Elite sub-government support of that kind made an impression on politicians. In the more public aspects of the struggle the mass support for the temperance movement was to some extent transferable to the initially less popular suffrage cause. More commonly, co-operation between members of the sub-government will present opportunities for making joint approaches to policy-makers, reinforcing each other's influence, forestalling challenges to the authority of the sub-government, and trading off benefits between groups. Co-operation, in short, is an essential tool in maintaining the hegemony of the sub-government.

A group's relations with other members of the sub-government is seldom defined explicitly. Admission to the circle of sub-government members is a recognition of a group's policy capacity. It can use the same levers to obtain concessions from officials, politicians—and other members—that other key groups and agencies can use. It is in a position to regulate the flow of information to government and the public; to secure the success or failure of government programs, and to confer legitimacy on public policies. Consciously and unconsciously the group exploits these attributes to form alliances, win support, oppose rivals, and crush the pretensions of groups that would like to supplant it. As in most élite groups, however, real influence is maintained in a more subtle manner. The sub-government is a spontaneous social phenomenon formed because its members share a power relationship with a government agency. Over time, recognition of mutual interests, and the habit of working together, lead to the evolution of a more-or-less cohesive social organization that is maintained through a network of mores, norms, and sanctions that, like many of the bonds between agencies and groups, are entirely informal. Admission to the sub-government sets up a reciprocal relationship in which the privileges of membership are conferred and the leaders of the newly accepted group 'become susceptible to socialization into the mores and modes of behaviour appropriate to interest group leaders'.[42] The most important aspect of this socialization has to do with positional politics, with the continuation of stability.

> By recognizing the mandate of a group, the leaders of other groups provide themselves with someone with whom they can bargain. At the same time they reduce the possibility of another group developing to represent the same interest. Such a group might attempt to consolidate its position among the membership by means of a radical or uncompromising stance or by use of rash tactics, either of which could only hurt all interest-group leaders.
>
> The recognition of the mandate of the group and its leaders by those outside the group, by government and by the leaders of other interest groups is advantageous for both sides since they are both interested in assuring that the equilibrium is not unduly disturbed. So great is the desire for stability that although 'an organized alternative leadership is almost always absent, when it appears, the Government usually refuses to deal with it anyway'.[43]

In the processes of intergroup bargaining, however, these norms are a powerful instrument in the hands not only of those within the sub-government anxious to maintain stability, but also of those who are bargaining with them. Because these norms exist, the threat of publicity becomes the ultimate weapon and a powerful incentive for securing accommodation within the sub-government. Like confrontation, with which it is closely associated, it is a bargaining technique that must be used with care. It is also an important element in the uneasy relationship between the sub-government and the policy community's attentive public.

(iv) *The attentive public*

The attentive public is the lively part of the policy community. It does not share the privileges of access and does not necessarily have a vested interest in keeping issues out of politics. In fact, many of its members are excluded from power and influence and see public debate as one way of obtaining them. They are therefore prepared to challenge the status quo and are less inclined to accept the norms with which sub-government members are comfortable. As a result, relations within the attentive public are more volatile than those within the sub-government—though not always devoid of the same influences—with which its relations are frequently uneasy and at times frankly hostile.

Yet this part of the policy community—the attentive public—cannot be ignored. For the majority of issues it is the sub-government's public, and for those few issues that excite general debate it occupies strategic territory between the sub-government and the public at large. Its capacity to generate informed support or opposition to policy makes it an ally worth courting and an opponent to be feared. The attentive public has value as a source of systemic renewal, even though challenges to conventional wisdom, however apt, are seldom welcomed by those who hold power. New ideas and new approaches must be voiced on the fringes of the community, where they can be explored, tested, and put into practice without disrupting the stability that is so important to charter members of the sub-government.

The components of the attentive public are disparate. Allies and affiliates of sub-governments have a significant presence. Groups, agencies, and corporations whose policy capacity and power base are inadequate to sustain membership in the inner circle will nevertheless share many of the values of the more powerful, and in return for access to information and consultation on issues of great concern to them they can be counted upon to give public support. Many groups, agencies, and corporations with only a secondary interest in the policy field maintain membership in the community primarily to monitor events that might affect that interest. They too are likely to share the attitudes and policy goals of the centre, as are the many individuals and consulting firms that depend on the larger players for their livelihood. Divergent ideas are more likely to come from groups, corporations, individuals, and even some agencies that are avowedly challenging the status quo. Their opposition seldom stems from a sense of alienation or a desire to attack society, but from a conviction that the conventional wisdom is in error and that a new policy paradigm must be put in place. They consequently attract both public attention and the interest of the more venturesome participants in the policy establishment, some of whom hope that supporting important new approaches or concerns will put them in the fast lane to success.

Because of its greater extent and more varied composition, the attentive public lacks the communal qualities that facilitate interaction within the sub-government, though face-to-face contacts between members are frequent. Leaders are often known personally to a large number of people and a great many more know a surprising amount about them; but barriers of time, space, and divergence of interest prevent regular discourse. Intimate understanding of conflicting views is rare and stereotyping is common. The interest group living in this policy climate must work hard to secure the support and understanding of other members. It must monitor their activities, attempt to build alliances with affinity groups, and strive constantly to maintain a position in the community that enables it to hear what is being said and to contribute to debate. At times it may feel compelled to 'educate' not only the public at large but the policy community, and government decision-makers in particular, about certain problems and about the value of the alternatives available to policy-makers who are shaping public solutions.

For these reasons the attentive public tends to use for communicating internally some of the techniques that link it to the public at large. The electronic media play an insignificant role, though populous communities have access to specialized programs—for example, CBC Radio's 'Radio Noon', beamed at the farming community, and 'Soundings', a program for fishermen. Teleconferencing, already popular in medical and educational circles, may eventually become a vital part of the communications used in many policy fields; but for the moment the print media dominate. Many groups publish their own journals and newsletters. Varying widely in format, coverage, and quality of presentation, they all convey information to group members and supporters. Some fields are affluent enough to support an independent specialized trade press that provides a forum for debating policy issues. When community issues erupt into public debate such publications become a source of background material for the general media, and their specialized journalists often act as communications intermediaries between the community and the press at large. Other means of communication favoured by the attentive public are books and pamphlets. Anti-establishment groups favour critical reviews of policy, but other groups also support writers and publishers who can produce commemorative volumes that become a valuable instrument in positional politics and are often an effective method of sending legitimating messages. In recent years, as a number of Canadian groups have come of age—a centennial is a coveted event, but many groups fix on a mere twenty-five years as an excuse for publication—a rising tide of such commemorative volumes has appeared, reaffirming the values and extolling the virtues of one organization or another. It is not entirely clear who reads them—reviewers abhor them—but they do have symbolic value, being quoted frequently at testimonial dinners and generally expressing the permanence and importance of the sponsoring group.

Although there are some similarities between communications in the attentive public and communications with the public at large, the business of influencing the policy community calls for different strategies and skills. The communicating group does not have to start by persuading the community that it ought to be interested, but assumes that it has a definite interest in the policy field. The community is also relatively small, making competition for attention less fierce, so that face-to-face communication is often possible, and language barriers are lower. In most policy communities, professions and trades have devised understandings of the terms that are used in the policy field. Even though a variety of professions and trades may be found, long association with one another has created a basic vocabulary that facilitates discussion about matters of common interest. To the outsider the language is obscure, even arcane; but to the community member it is a useful tool that defines differences precisely and smooths negotiations between groups, corporations, individuals, and agencies. Also implicit in a common language are assumptions about the way in which the community works, about its relationship with the broader environment, and the nature of the processes, materials, and relationships it deals with. Though not all of these assumptions are fully shared, they provide a framework for policy discourse within the community, and they underlie the norms and sanctions that guide behaviour within it.

Conferences are vital to developing opinion within the special public. The most frequently used means of bringing sub-government members into contact with the attentive public, they create opportunities for all sides to try to persuade others, to exchange information, and to attempt to assert community solidarity. A typical event of this sort occurred in October 1983, when the Automotive Parts Manufacturers' Association of Canada and the Japan Automobile Manufacturers' Association—with the Institute for Research on Public Policy, the Canadian Institute of International Affairs, and the Canadian Studies Program of Columbia University—held a one-day symposium in Ottawa on 'The North American Automobile Industry and the Canadian Interest'. The conference tackled the question of 'What to do with the automobile industry?' Should the federal government support restructuring of the industry, or resist its decline? The conference organizers, suggesting that decisions taken in 1984 and 1985 would 'have a critical impact on the employment and exports for several decades', built their agenda around discussions of world trends and 'current Canadian concerns' in particular—concerns that must have deeply interested the JAMA who wanted an answer to the question, 'What are the trade-offs of export restraints?' The conference was clearly intended to influence both the policy community in the automobile field and Canadian government officials especially. Doubtless the JAMA hoped that it would buttress its arguments against the imposition of quotas on Japanese car imports.[44] An active participant in any policy community must devote a considerable portion of its resources to such exchanges, both in order to hear contending points of view and in order to put forward analyses and statements that will advance its interests.

Though members of the attentive public do not enjoy the nearly daily contact with the lead agency, or the almost automatic consultation that is the privilege of sub-government members, they are not excluded from consultation. Some, in fact, are represented on advisory committes and are regulars at conferences and closed-door seminars. Individal members—academics in particular—are likely to be chosen to sit on task forces and royal commissions. The assumptions behind these appointments are two-fold: the appointees are expected not only to represent a point of view, but to be fair-minded about the opinions of others, and they are understood to have considerable knowledge of the field. In general these assumptions are probably correct, but such appointments also offer opportunities for promoting preferred positions and interests.

Alliances and co-operation are valued even more by members of the attentive public than they are by the sub-government. Smaller groups co-operate to the point of sharing office space and resources. In every major urban centre there is an office building (a little past its prime but at a respectable address) where a cluster of smaller groups share space at a low rent, office equipment, and sometimes staff. Similar clusters are found on many university campuses. Usually such groups will belong to the same, or to a closely related, policy community, and their interdependence may extend to sponsoring joint activities and sharing mailing lists and information. Even when it is not necessary, co-operation can be a regular part of a group's relations with organizations close to it in orientation and interests. Co-operation enhances each group's abilitiy to project an impression of legitimacy.

Co-operation is also extremely valuable in winning public attention inside and outside the policy community. An alliance had a considerable impact on the decision to revise freedom-of-information legislation. The extent of administrative secrecy (an inheritance from Britain) had long disturbed lawyers, journalists, academics, and many others concerned with the study and discussion of public affairs. For years individuals—Professors T. Murray Rankin and Donald Rowat and Progressive Conservative MP Ged Baldwin, among others—had written and spoken in favour of more open access to government documents. In 1969 Baldwin proposed a motion to the House of Commons to this effect, but it was not until the mid-1970s that the House and Senate agreed to have the issue investigated by the joint Committee on Regulations and other Statutory Instruments. The hearings, at which a large number of groups and individuals testified, resulted in a strong report that urged implementing freedom of information. Although the report was endorsed by the House, the government responded with a green paper whose 'meagreness . . . . provoked many organizations . . . . to protest and to suggest more wide-ranging legislation'.[45] The Clark government did introduce legislation that, while not entirely satisfactory to the interested groups, went a lot further than that projected by the Green Paper. But that legislaton succumbed with the defeat of the government. The Liberals, while re-introducing the legislation, seemed far less anxious to implement it, and 'seemed gradually to retreat, using the opposition of some of the provincial attorney's-general as an excuse'.[46] At this point the interest groups that had been active in the debate—the Canadian Bar Association, the Canadian Library Association, the Canadian Association of University Teachers, among others—extended the informal alliance that had gradually emerged under the umbrella group ACCESS and joined forces to conduct a series of press conferences that precipitated strong public pressure on the government, which reluctantly honoured the promise to implement legislation like that introduced by the Conservatives.

For the majority of groups in the attentive public the game of interest politics is played with the weapons of communication that we have described. Consultation, the giving and receiving of advice, participating through conferences and the printed word in the formation of the ideas that underlie policy are, even for the majority of those who have little standing in the community, the chief instruments for influencing policy-makers. But the attentive public provides the policy community with its more outspoken critics—those who feel that they will not be listened to unless they can excite support from the public at large. For them the business of capturing media attention is a necessary lever for general participation in the policy process. From time to time they use that lever, but more often they only threaten to use it.

How effective is media attention? Few policy actors know for certain, though many hold strong opinions. A bid for publicity is always a gamble. The media, even more than the public, are fickle. The competition to arouse opinion is intense and probably many more attempts to attract attention fail than succeed. Failure may only confirm the policy community's confidence in the conventional wisdom. Nevertheless, in this media-conscious age even a letter to the editor can sometimes attract attention—far beyond its intrinsic merits—among policy-makers. Many officials and corporate leaders see letters to ministers, legislators, and newspapers, demonstrations, and responses to hot-line shows as litmus tests of public opinion. They reason that for every member of the public who is committed enough to write a letter or to demonstrate there will be many more who, though mute, feel the same way and may express their convictions through the ballot: out of caution, and perhaps with a faint hope of co-optation, they may be persuaded to pay some attention to what the disaffected group has to say. In the long process of policy formation this is a small step, but for many groups it justifies taking issues to the general public.

CHAPTER 7

Beyond the Policy Community: Strategies for Working in the Broader Environment

Not all issues are resolved within policy communities. Some are considered too important to the country at large to be left in the hands of a small number of government agencies and their associated interests. They have to be resolved by the political leadership after full-dress debate in the media, Parliament, and often at intergovernmental meetings. Policies that affect relations between the English and French communities often require such debate. At other times issues may be discussed by the Cabinet and the public at large because they have generated conflict between two or more policy communities. Environmental issues often precipitate disputes between the policy communities that surround environmental protection agencies and the communities associated with economic development. Finally, when serious disagreements occur within policy communities it is sometimes necessary to remove issues from the communities and secure their resolution through the larger political system.

Groups concerned with issues that have escaped the policy community have to deal with processes and institutions quite different from those they are accustomed to work with. They may have to engage in debate with members of the general public who know virtually nothing of the circumstances that have led to a particular dispute, but who have strong opinions about it. The debate may force policy community members to meet the intense, hectic agenda of the media and Parliament. Alternatively, dispute may take groups to the courts or to intergovernmental meetings. Often a variety of institutions will participate in policy discussions that are highly contentious.

Wherever the path of conflict resolution leads, the affected interests must be prepared to follow, and they must be ready to adapt themselves to the conditions established by each new policy environment, whether it be the judicial environment, the arena of high policy, the court of public opinion, or any other forum in which major policy debates take place. In this chapter we consider how groups approach several of these: the public at large, the courts, and intergovernmental bodies.

155

INFLUENCING PUBLIC OPINION

Groups have one of two ends in view when they seek to influence mass opinion: they hope to use an aroused public to dictate a specific decision, or to create, through public education, an environment of ideas and attitudes that will encourage policy-makers to take certain kinds of actions rather than others. In general we are more aware of the first kind of action-oriented campaign; but the transmission of legitimating messages is probably more widely practised, and perhaps more effective. Each of these endeavours is precipitated by entirely different circumstances and makes very different demands on both groups and the policy system. Attempts to influence specific decisions are often reactions to a proposed or adopted course of action. They may entail appeals to the general public through the media, the use of demonstrations, perhaps even attempts to force candidates and parties to address certain issues during an election campaign. In contrast, the creation of a broadly supportive environment is a long-term process involving the regular and steady seepage of ideas into the public consciousness.

Groups attempt to influence public opinion in three ways: they try to capture media attention; they advertise; or they take their messages directly to individual citizens. The first is the most significant and most frequently attempted, and we will deal with it last. Advertising is engaged in by groups with sufficient financial resources. Direct lobbying is relatively rare.

Few groups in Canada rely on advertising to influence the public. It is not a standard pressure technique here, as it is in the United States. One commentator, Isaiah Litvak, calls it 'a tactic to be used only when more traditional methods fail'.[1] While it is unlikely that this reflects policy-makers' frequent assertions that they are not influenced by mass mail-ins or pressure tactics clearly related to advertising campaigns, it may reflect the assumption behind such statements: that decision-making power in Canada is focused and is less susceptible to external manipulation than it is elsewhere. In any event, as Litvak has noted, 'of late, it is being used more often.' He points out that in the late 1960s 'the trauma of tax reform made the [mining] industry public-relations conscious.' As part of its battle against changes in mineral industry taxation, the industry launched its first major radio and television campaign.[2] During the 1970s such campaigns became more familiar. Litvak cites the efforts of the Auto Parts Manufacturers' Association, whose advertisements invited readers to cut and send to the Prime Minister a coupon calling for an embargo on Japanese car and truck imports, and the work of the Canadian Petroleum Association to persuade Canadians to abandon their negative perception of the oil companies and to accept the legitimacy of the industry's attack on the National Energy Program.[3] Similar legitimating messages were widely broadcast during the debate over the building of the Mackenzie Valley Pipeline. The oil industry used television extensively to present a series of advertisements intended to persuade the public of its respectability, its regard for the environment, its respect for the culture and way of life of the native peoples, and its concern for energy conservation. Action-oriented messages are common. The campaign against sealing made dramatic use of television and newspaper advertisements urging the man and woman in the street not only to boycott seal products but to express their abhorrence of the hunt to their legislators. At election time the National Citizens' Coalition purchases advertisements in major newspapers exhorting the public to challenge candidates to adopt the conservative posture favoured by the Coalition. During recent elections various groups have used advertising campaigns to inject their concerns into the election debate and, occasionally, to attack specific candidates.[4]

Such campaigns are still uncommon. They are part of a slight shift towards the increased use of advertising as a part of Canadian pressure group politics. This shift probably reflects the adaptation of groups in this country to the diffusion of power we have described as occuring in the last two decades. Since in other respects Canadian groups have begun to adapt to a redefinition of the power system by exploiting a more open policy style, it is quite possible that advertising will become more prominent in the future.

Legitimating and action-oriented messages can also be conveyed directly to members of the public. A traditional direct approach is often used at the local level. Door-to-door canvassing, meetings organized to attract concerned citizens, and campaigns to obtain signatures on petitions are all believed to affect the thinking of municipal politicians and public officials. Provincial, national, and international groups 'go direct' in more sophisticated fashion. Mailing lists obtained from magazine publishers and sympathetic interest groups can be used to identify individuals likely to respond positively to a blitz of flyers, appeals, and 'personal' letters from prominent figures urging 'Mr and Mrs Citizen' to write or phone their MP or MLA to express support for the group's position.[5] Often, too, the literature will solicit funds to support the group's work. In California Cesar Chavez, whose long campaign to win better working conditions for agricultural labour has drawn international attention, has recently used computer technology to bring a new dimension to this approach. In a boycott designed to discourage a supermarket chain from using a particular supplier, Chavez and his United Farm Workers dedicated $1 million to a postal and television campaign that would last two years. The main feature of the boycott was a mail campaign based on computer selection of households within a certain radius of the chain's 600 supermarkets. Using 1980 census data as the base of the selection, the UFW intended the campaign to convey a 'negative image' of the chain among Hispanics, white liberals, Jews, blacks, and trade union families.[6] Similar techniques have been favoured by wildlife preservation groups.

The most widely used technique for influencing public opinion is to capture media attention, largely because it brings a double benefit. It lends legitimacy to a campaign, and it can be used to whip up public support for a cause.[7] These benefits are not easily obtained, however. Competition for attention is fierce and once the novelty of a situation has evaporated a high degree of organizational competence is called for. Furthermore, because of their fundamentally different characteristics, the electronic media and the print media demand different strategies and techniques from those who seek to exploit them. We will look first at the relationships between groups and the electronic media.

The electronic media search out and focus on dramatic action that vividly expresses a group's feelings. Demonstrations, riots, bizarre happenings, and harrowing personal events grip media attention, serving both as a backdrop to a group's message and to drive home its point. Radio and television time is precious. Only events high on the national agenda can be assured exposure. Competition for air time is intense, and is not confined to each group's own backyard. A local group attempting to capture the attention of its immediate community must vie for air time with the latest atrocities in the world's trouble spots. Like its competitors working on the larger stage, the local group must strive to exploit the dramatic, to force complex issues into snappy slogans, to seek the essence of issues and, inevitably, to caricature them.[8]

Groups attempting to attract media attention must become skilled in staging media events. Those with action-oriented messages have the greatest choice, ranging from demonstrations to carefully staged conferences that give leading members of policy communities a podium from which they can expound a group position. At the furthest extreme are the violent techniques used by revolutionary and profoundly disaffected groups. Legitimating messages are less amenable to dramatization, though their proponents can still take advantage of the same techniques. Drama is diminished, but symbolism is more readily available. Conferences can be used to reaffirm a group's support of a widely accepted public position. Historic events can be commemorated, citizens honoured, worthy causes espoused and materially supported. All of these techniques serve to associate the group and its message with sentiments engrained in the public consciousness.

The policy process offers opportunities for legitimating communications that are not as readily seized by proponents of action-oriented messages. Public hearings are important opportunities for doing this. Ironically, though public hearings are often seen as occasions for groups to influence policy recommendations, they are probably more important for providing groups with an opportunity to educate the public to their concerns and points of view. Many groups appear at public hearings principally for this reason. Presenting their views at such hearings generally assures them media coverage, and thus free advertising for their cause. Such considerations may explain the pattern of representation before the Royal Commission on the Economic Union and Canada's Development Prospects that troubled commission chairman Donald Macdonald. Although the business community submitted over 1,000 briefs to the Commission, Macdonald felt that business representation had been uneven. The leading representatives of some important fields did not testify. The *Financial Post*, reviewing representations to the Commission during 1983, noted that the major steel companies had presented no formal briefs to an inquiry whose recommendations, like those of the Rowell-Sirois Commission forty years earlier, might influence economic and political development for several generations.[9] No briefs had been received from the influential financial firms based in Winnipeg, and only a few from the major oil companies. By contrast an unprecedentedly high number of interest groups appeared, an indication that though individual firms saw little advantage in appearing before the commission, they felt that their representative interest groups should treat the occasion as symbolic and as an opportunity for public education.

When they take advantage of public hearings groups are aware that they are stepping from one level of interaction with the media to another. The electronic media may draw attention to public hearings and outline for the public the issues and rival policies under debate, but the format used at hearings does not lend itself to television and radio reporting. The presentation of briefs, the testimony of expert witnesses, interventions from lawyers, and questioning by commissioners make for pallid television, forcing a group anxious for a spot on the evening news to mount a side show—a demonstration, perhaps, or a dramatic, visible example of its concerns—to capture camera attention. For the print media, however, public hearings are a source of good copy. The sequential elucidation of issues and concerns, the analysis of underlying causes, the presentation and explanation of data are the basis of the in-depth background reporting and analysis that newspapers, magazines, and public-affairs books do best. Astute group leaders consequently strive to use the electronic media to draw public attention to an issue and to create a mood of concern, and the print media to convey reasoned proposals that will have some bearing on the formulation of a policy response. They know that policy-makers will be influenced as much by the groups' briefs, the mass of clippings flowing from public hearings, their internal analyses, and by more immediate political concerns as they will be by the frenzied cacaphony of conflict transmitted by radio and television.

Parliament, of course, is a perpetual public hearing—a vehicle not only for transmitting demands and proposals to policy-makers, but for engaging public concern and creating receptive general attitudes. Here too the different media fasten on and exploit separate features of the policy process. Question period is the focal point for all journalists, but it fosters a short, pungent, and pointed style that is more effectively exploited by the electronic media and by groups with an action-oriented message. The routine business of Parliament, particularly the major debates on the budget, the throne speech, and the second reading of the government bills—together with the hearings of Parliamentary committees and task forces—are, like public hearings, more effectively reported by the print media and are likely to attract the attention of groups with long-term policy concerns.

In recent years lobbyists have paid increasing attention to Members of Parliament, and even to provincial legislators. The more open policy process that has evolved has encouraged more groups to channel issues to question period and has swept away the reticence that used to bar institutionalized groups from parliamentary discussion. But while the diffusion of power has freed groups, it has also imposed new burdens on them. It is now necessary for them to cultivate Parliament. MPs report that they receive a constant flow of background material from groups—much of it related to issues being debated, but a good part of it intended to educate the MP to a broader understanding of the group's concerns.[10] Some campaigns are intensive, and though individual MPs are not lobbied as persistently and continuously as are American Congressmen, there may be a growing tendency for groups to seek to speak to caucus. Backbenchers are considered capable of influencing policy while it is still in caucus, particularly where regional issues are concerned.[11] But the independent views of members can be truly influential only during 'free votes', when the member is permitted to vote according to his or her conscience. Consequently, on those occasions the average back-bencher is submitted to a degree of persuasion comparable to that normally endured by Cabinet ministers. Votes on capital punishment produce the most notable examples of such pressure, both in Canada and elsewhere.[12]

In some countries prominent groups secure the election of legislative spokesmen.[13] This ensures not only that the group has a sponsor and speaker in the legislature, but that it is tapped into the flow of policy information as it circulates through the country's busiest talk-shop and rumour mill. The small size and the spatial orientation of the House of Commons inhibit this tactic in Canada, though special interest representation has long been a feature of the Senate, where a number of Senators identified particularly with business interests articulate group concerns on Senate committees.[14] Nevertheless prominent interest communities often believe that a good way to influence public policy is to win the election of individuals who can broadly represent them. This has been true of the women's movement which, despite continued male domination of politics, has had a good deal of success both in persuading women to run for political office and in electing them. Similarly businessmen often urge one another to enter politics in order to secure a more sympathetic hearing for the business point of view in Ottawa and the provincial capitals.

Electing representatives to Parliament, however, will not ensure their constant adherence to a point of view endorsed by the interests that sponsored them. Members of Parliament, as representatives of a geographically located community, must strive to speak for its broad needs rather than for the needs of a sectoral interest.[15] They must also consider the general needs of the country or the province. When elected, business people are not seen as delegates for groups such as the Canadian Manufacturers' Association or the Canadian Federation of Independent Business, even though they may be expected to sympathize with the views of the business community and to have ties to specific organizations. In the words of Robert Stanbury, general counsel and secretary to Firestone Canada Ltd. and a member of the first Trudeau Cabinet, MPs from business must accept that 'in government, whether it is the bureaucrat or politician, there is a different point of view that has to be adopted', and that they do not speak only for business. 'You're forced to think in national terms.'[16]

Some groups have tried to influence public opinion by intervening in the electoral process. Though it is not easy to influence party platforms—and many doubt the utility of engineering inclusion of a favourable plank in the platforms of the major parties—groups often expend great effort trying to win friendly promises from the parties and their leaders. Prior to the 1984 federal election campaign the business community worked to persuade party strategists 'that the best contribution Ottawa could make to future growth and stability would be to regain control over federal finances'. However, by the end of the campaign, when each of the three major parties announced that the cost of their election promises would amount to about $5 billion, the Investment Dealers Association, the Business Council on National Issues, and the Canadian Chambers of Commerce, among others, admitted despairingly that the politicians had been more prone to promise new programs than to pay other than lip service to the need for deficit reduction and financial housecleaning.[17] Nevertheless the groups' efforts forced the public to debate issues that concerned business. And though the election campaign itself generated little of the 'responsible leadership' that business people (perhaps naïvely) hoped for, the Mulroney government, once elected, put at the top of its agenda a number of issues of concern to the business community. In particular, it maintained that it had been elected with a mandate to cut the federal deficit. In other words, by successfully injecting business issues into the electoral debate the business community laid the ground for the government to claim that deficit reduction was part of its electoral mandate.[18]

Several recent elections have witnessed more focused interventions, some of them directed at specific candidates and parties. In 1977 *Maclean's* reported that gun associations had effectively intimidated some MPs by threatening to encourage their members to vote against them if they supported gun control.[19] The NDP's Svend Robinson was vigorously attacked during the 1980 campaign by groups opposed to his and the NDP's position on the abortion issue. Though

Robinson's majority was sustained and the party's position unaffected—in the Canadian party system a campaign against an individual candidate would be unlikely to have a significant effect on policy—the Chief Electoral Officer, Jean-Marc Hamel, was sufficiently disturbed by the attack and by similar recent American experiences to recommend changes in the Elections Act.[20] Parliament took his advice and on October 25, 1983, with remarkable unanimity, the House of Commons adopted Bill C-169, an amendment to section 72 of the Canada Elections Act, which declared that Canadians might not 'incur election expenses' in support of, or in opposition to, a party or candidate during an election campaign, unless the benefiting party or candidate consented. Parties or candidates accepting such support would have to include the cost of the advertising in their allowable election expenses. Anyone convicted of advertising in violation of the act could be liable to a fine of $5,000 or five years in jail.

The amendment opened a new chapter in an important but not widely known debate over the role of parties and pressure groups in election campaigns. The issue is rooted in the 1974 revisions of the Canada Elections Act, which regulates public donations to political parties and limits the extent of election expenses. According to Toronto lawyer Aubrey Golden, 'restricting candidates' spending was a cornerstone of the act', but 'if candidates and their parties were to be restricted, the obvious loophole that others could spend in their support had to be closed.'[21] The 1974 act did this in part by providing that only registered candidates and parties could spend money campaigning to oppose or support some other registered candidate. However, since Parliament at that time was not anxious to restrict the right of individuals and groups to debate issues of public policy, the act also provided that a citizen who was not a candidate could spend money for 'the purpose of gaining support for views held by him on an issue of public policy'.[22] He could even support a non-political organization engaged in the same quest, as long as the debate involved an issue in public policy and was entered into 'in good faith'. This 'good faith' clause, when tested in the courts, acquired an interpretation so liberal that it permitted campaigns like the attack on Robinson. In Parliament's eyes it was clearly too liberal.

The new provisions were soon challenged by the National Citizens' Coalition, a group described as 'right wing' by the press.[23] The Coalition, which claims 30,000 members, was supported in its challenge by a variety of other organizations, including the Canadian Daily Newspaper Publishers' Association and the Canadian, Ontario, and Atlantic Provinces Chambers of Commerce.[24] Maintaining that the amendments represented an undue limitation on freedom of expression, the NCC attacked Hamel's position by arguing that since the revision of Canada's electoral laws in 1974 it had become increasingly difficult for new parties to establish themselves. In effect party activity had become 'a closed shop', a barrier to citizens seeking to put new issues on the public agenda. The Coalition's argument was accepted by Mr Justice Donald Medhurst of the Alberta Court of Queen's Bench, who ruled that because the sections limited freedom of expression they would have to pass the test established in the Charter of Rights, which requires that 'the limitations must be considered for the protection of a real value to society and not simply to reduce or restrain criticism, no matter how unfair such criticism may be.' As far as Justice Medhurst was concerned 'fears or concerns of mischief that may occur are not adequate reasons for imposing a limitation.' He ruled that the amendments violated the freedom of expression guaranteed in the Charter and therefore were unconstitutional.[25]

When the federal government—faced with hostile editorial opinion[26] and on the eve of an election—decided not to appeal the decision, it closed a chapter in the debate over freedom of speech during election campaigns, but it did not close the debate itself. The issue remains: if candidates themselves must observe limits to the amount of money they may spend on election campaigns, how can they be protected from the irresponsible use of advertising by groups and citizens who face no similar constraints? Chief electoral Officer Jean-Marc Hamel stated that he would recommend a complete overhaul of federal election spending laws in his next annual report to Parliament. He called a system that limits election spending by parties and candidates, but not other interested groups, an 'exercise in futility'.[27] He pointed out that in 1980 candidates were allowed to spend only $1 for each of the first 15,000 voters in their ridings; $0.50 for each of the next 10,000 and $0.25 for the remainder; parties could spend $0.30 for each voter in ridings where they fielded candidates. According to Hamel most candidates in 1984 would be allowed to spend $40,000 to $50,000, while the two major parties spent about $4 million each in 1980. Although he drew no comparisons between the spending limits imposed on candidates and the actual expenditures of interest groups, Hamel was clearly anxious to avoid a Canadian version of recent American experience. There 'Political Action Committees' have spent many millions supporting their preferred candidates. In some situations the level of support has been grossly lopsided. The public-interest group Common Cause calculates that in 1980 political action committees pumped $12.2 million into campaigns that paralleled the Reagan presidential bid, but only $46,000 in support of Jimmy Carter; yet both candidates were confined to a total expenditure of $29.4 million each for their official campaigns. This type of expenditure is growing. Overall PAC spending in the elections of 1981-2 amounted to $190 million in contrast to $77.4 million in 1977-8. One Senator, Republican David Durenberger of Minnesota, received more than $1 million from PACs for his 1982 campaign. Such support has led Common Cause president Fred Wertheimer to call the PACs 'a corrupt system. It is a visible national scandal totally undermining the integrity of Congress.'[28]

The question for Canadians is whether or not the problem is likely to reach similar proportions in this country, and, if it is, whether Canadian electoral laws should emulate those in the United States. American politicians, faced with a more serious problem, have not gone so far as to virtually ban interest group participation in elections. Rather they have tended to hope that public indignation at PAC abuse of their freedom to participate will discourage politicians from accepting their support. Those who feel that this may not suffice have promoted measures to encourage individual donations to politicians and to limit the level of PAC contributions. The 1983 Canadian legislation went well beyond this and may be seen as an over-reaction. Furthermore, while the chief electoral officer makes an interesting point, it is worth remembering that candidates and parties receive a great deal of free publicity that other participants in elections to do not receive. As well, while interest groups might from time to time be able to spend enough money to influence the outcome in a few ridings, voters are generally believed to vote for national or provincial parties, either on traditional grounds or because they support the party leadership. To influence the vote significantly on a national or even local basis, interests would have to spend a great deal more than is available to most of them.

* * *

The preferred technique of groups wishing to influence public opinion is that of trying to persuade the media to focus public attention on them. Not only does this give broad, relatively cheap exposure, but it also implies legitimacy and is achieved both through attention-catching activities and through exploitation of the policy process and the political system. In attempting to influence the public at large, groups assume either that strongly expressed public opinion will in turn influence the decisions of key policy-makers, or that they can foster a climate of opinion that encourages some kinds of decisions rather than others. The first assumption applies when groups send action-oriented messages to the public; the second when legitimating messages are sent.

To transmit either type of message to the general public, groups must fight hard for attention. This nearly always means they must catch the eye of the camera and the ears of the microphone, and must be skilled in exploiting the fleeting opportunities presented in the brief exposures the media allows. To do so they must understand the needs of the media as well as the rhythm of the policy process, and must be able to generate resources of imagination, expertise, organization, and manpower. Though many smaller, less-experienced organizations are successful in obtaining public support and sympathy, the long-term demands of influencing public opinion place a premium on knowledge, material resources, and organization. But a group that has won public support cannot assume that its policy preferences will be implemented. To translate public acceptance into policy action, the group must secure the co-operation and support of the policy community, particularly the bureaucracy.

VARIATIONS ON A THEME: ADAPTATIONS IN PRESSURE GROUP TACTICS

As adaptive instruments of political communication pressure groups have been quick to take advantage of changes in the Canadian policy system. We have already seen how, in responding to the diffusion of power, they have expanded their legitimating role and have paid increasing attention to Parliament. Their quest for influence has led them to other points of access. Though sometimes baffled in their attempts to exploit intergovernmental relations in Canada, they have been assiduous in their efforts to influence the first ministers and their colleagues. Some have been quick to seize opportunities to influence international public opinion and, most recently, to take advantage of the growing policy role of the courts.

(i) *Influencing intergovernmental negotiations*

Over the last thirty years many public-policy issues have been debated at the intergovernmental level, either at meetings of the first ministers or at conferences of ministers responsible for particular policy fields. Not surprisingly interest groups try to influence these negotiations. Observers differ over their rate of success. Richard Simeon suggests that while the mechanics of federal-provincial relations appear to offer interest groups a multiplicity of access points to policy debate, in actuality the mechanics of the process constrain interest group participation in the bargaining process.

> Affected groups are not invited to participate or make their views known. The relative secrecy of debate means group leaders may often be unaware of developments in federal-provincial negotiations which might involve them. To the extent that the mechanisms . . . become a central arena for policy formation and form the major preoccupation for both federal and provincial policy-makers, the process thus limits the number and scope of participants in policy-making.[29]

Simeon bases his argument on case studies of the development of hospital insurance and pension schemes, negotiations in which the federal and provincial governments, as well as private interests, had a great deal at stake. However, other case studies offer evidence that interests and the representative groups can influence federal-provincial diplomacy. Bucovetsky shows that by persuading key provinces that their economies would suffer if tax reforms proposed by the Trudeau government were adopted, the mining industry lobby, particularly the oil lobby, brought about major revisions in the proposals.[30] Other examples of the oil lobby's exploitation of differences between Ottawa and the provinces are well documented.[31] Similar cases abound in transportation policy. Many interest groups have exerted influence on the evolution of the Crow Rate, for example.[32] In the Maritimes business interest groups have, since the 1920s, been able to use provincial governments to lobby on their behalf for transportation subsidies. Most recently, in 1982-3, they were highly successful in persuading the provincial governments to attack the federal government when it sponsored an enquiry that appeared to be directed at recommending the removal of the subsidies. The subsidies were retained. In the Maritimes at least, business interest organizations have led government in the articulation of regional needs and the creation of regional institutions, particularly the Council of Maritime Premiers.[33]

It may be that in cases such as those examined by Simeon, in which the federal and provincial states have to defend vital interests of their own, governments do accord a low priority to group demands. Given the extent of government intervention in the economy, there can be very few instances when the state, federal or provincial, has no stake. Every bureaucracy has a vested interest in its programs and jurisdictional territoriality. However, in situations where the state's interest is negotiable or not seriously threatened, there is probably considerable opportunity for groups to exert influence. Furthermore, as Thorburn points out, the fact that groups are not always represented in the final stages of intergovernmental negotiation does not mean that their interests are disregarded. Each government is likely to remain faithful to the interests that it has supported in the past.[34]

Do groups operate any differently at the intergovernmental level than when they exert influence on a single government? To some extent, yes. The most obvious differences are organizational. Groups that interact with more than one level of government tend to be organized 'to facilitate interaction with both levels of government. This has meant, in most cases, either a federal structure or a confederal one in which the major power rests in the provincial or regional offices.'[35] Group behaviour is affected as well, however. In Cairns' view 'each government transmits cues and pressures to the environment, tending to group the interests manipulated by its policies into webs of interdependence springing from the particular version of socioeconomic integration it is pursuing.'[36] Cairns' analysis suggests that interests virtually become hostages of the governments to which they are beholden, but Thorburn argues that even groups whose fortunes depend primarily on one level of government and that consequently are often compelled to support that government, are careful not to be totally committed to it. 'It is in the interest of a group to have friends in all governments and on all sides.'[37] Group behaviour is also profoundly affected by the conditions that prevail in the forum in which intergovernmental debate takes place. Almost by definition an issue important enough to be on the first ministers' agenda is also on the public agenda. That means that groups will not be able to rely almost exclusively on the tactics of consultation that are effective within the sub-government. They will have to publicize their concerns. They will also experience problems of access. Meetings with premiers are not easily obtained and the Prime Minister is nearly inaccessible. Even if access is obtained, meetings have to be so short as to be almost symbolic. This not only reinforces the tendency to resort to publicity; it compels the groups to act through intermediaries, senior politicians, the ministers active in the policy field, caucus, other group leaders, and above all the officials around the leader. Since few of these will be fully aware of the nuances of the group's position, it is quite likely that the group will achieve less than it would like. Probably the most difficult intermediaries will be the officials of the leaders' support staffs. Used to the overview position and sometimes predisposed to suspect the importunings of groups whose normal allies are the line agencies, these officials are often elusive and difficult to persuade.[38]

At the provincial level many of these problems will be less acute, particularly in the smaller provinces. Provincial policy communities are less complex than those at the federal level and access to key decision-makers is easier to arrange. Often if a provincial government is persuaded that an important interest will be damaged by a proposed national policy, it will champion that interest vigorously at the intergovernmental level. In such circumstances the interest's chief concern is the extent of its champion's own influence. The smaller provinces can do very little for local interests if their concerns run counter to those of Ontario and/or Quebec. The problems posed by inter-regional rivalries led Maritime business interests to encourage the formation of the Council of Maritime Premiers, and experience has shown that when the Maritime Premiers can be persuaded to speak collectively they are more likely to obtain the concessions the interests want. To achieve this, however, groups must themselves achieve a high degree of agreement and they must become sophisticated diplomats, juggling the concerns and shibboleths of provincial administrations as they search for the compromises and convincing arguments that will hold the premiers together at the bargaining table.[39]

These efforts also impose strain on national organizations. Intergovernmental tensions generally reflect differences of interest from region to region. What is good for the southern Quebec milk industry is not necessarily good for milk producers in Ontario and the Maritimes.[40] Provincial branches of organizations can have as much difficulty working out differences between one another as the first ministers. That is one reason why some issues escape the policy community. Again, regional and provincial branches of organizations often find that they are at odds with the national office. This was the experience of the Atlantic region branches of the Canadian Manufacturers' Association in the 1983 dispute over freight subsidies. Arguing that transportation subsidies are essential to a healthy regional economy, the regional branches of the CMA vigorously participated in a campaign to maintain them. The national office, committed to a policy of subsidy elimination, refused to support its affiliates, even to the extent of compelling regional representatives to organize their own meetings with Ottawa politicians and officials.[41]

All intergovernmental negotiations are not as tense and conflict-ridden as the televised meetings of the first ministers. Certainly many issues that have to be resolved at the intergovernmental level are the product of significant tensions. Many are not, however. They are the subject of intergovernmental discussion because joint programs are essential to social and economic life in Canada. The plethora of intergovernmental conferences to which Canadian have become accustomed are at least as concerned with maintaining intergovernmental agreement as with coping with disagreement. Outside groups are permitted to attend a number of these meetings and even to participate in forging compromises between jurisdictions and interests. Federal officials and mining representatives attend the annual conference of provincial ministers of mines, for example.[42] In a sense many of these meetings are simply the conclave of the national policy community in their specific fields. They are important opportunities for consultation and joint decision-making, rather than occasions for resolving burning issues, and they offer very little that is of moment to the mass media. They do, however, testify to the fact that interest groups are significant and active participants in intergovernmental affairs.

(ii) Domestic/external influences

Many Canadian groups are involved with intergovernmental relations on quite a different level: that of international relations. Nor is Canadian public policy free of external influence from foreign interest groups. Although we do not have space here to explore the many ways Canadians use groups to influence events outside the country, or are in turn affected by international pressure groups, we should catalogue the several manifestations of international pressure group activities that are significant to Canadians.[43]

The first has to do with economic issues. Given this country's dependence on international trade, we should expect Canadian interest groups to keep a watchful eye on the domestic infuences affecting the policies of our most important trading partners, and to try to counteract unfriendly influences. The latter will involve efforts to persuade the Canadian government to take counter measures, but it may also prompt groups to take their campaign into their rivals' camp.[44] It is not unusual for Canadian industries to lobby extensively in other capitals, particularly Washington, for tariff concessions and purchasing opportunities. Frequently this kind of lobbying is carried on in conjunction with more formal efforts on the part of trade officials. For example, in the summer of 1984 the steel industry mounted an aggressive campaign to persuade the American government to spare Canadian steel producers from protectionist quota restrictions.[45] When trying to influence foreign governments Canadian groups must frequently adapt themselves to very different styles of lobbying. In the United States, for example, Canadians have had to learn how to tackle Congress as well as administration officials and the executive. As a columnist in the Kingston *Whig Standard* put it, on learning that the Canadian embassy would lobby more aggressively in the American capital, 'It's about time that Ottawa's striped pants brigade lost its virginity and acknowledged that the grubby business of lobbying is part of the American form of government.'[46] The comment illustrates one of the paradoxes of lobbying in foreign capitals. Despite the numerous provincial and federal trade missions in major capitals, Canadian industries often complain that our officials are not aggressive enough in promoting their products.[47] Those working in the United States urge the Canadian government to adopt the traditional techniques of the Washington lobbyist. It is a role that does not come easily to Canadian officials, who sometimes are accused of preferring to represent Canada abroad but not Canadian manufacturers. The columnist cited earlier gives an illustration:

> Lee Godawn, Representative Richard Ottinger's legislative assistant who drafted the so-called 'domestic content' bill on the auto industry, had 'not heard from the Canadians at all.'
> That bill was passed in the last Congress by the House of Representatives but has not yet been reintroduced. If anything like the original draft ever becomes law, the Canadian auto industry and the thousands of jobs it provides will be in terminal danger.
> But the key legislator had not been lobbied, not been provided with information by Canadians or their hired help. Instead, 'verbal representations' were made to the Secretary of Commerce.
> Such examples are legion. Ottawa's diplomats have shunned the grubby business of business for decades. They would far rather talk about 'global issues' and to emulate their icon, Lester Pearson and his Nobel Peace Prize.

In 1983, at the urging of Ambassador Allan Gotlieb, the federal government allotted $650,000 to pursuing policy goals in Congress as well as at the governmental level.[48] Ambassador Gotlieb himself has urged Canadian business to adopt better co-ordinated and aggressive lobbying campaigns in the American capital. As a result of his efforts the American government is increasingly aware that Canada is the United States' 'largest trading partner' and that Canadians are particularly concerned about such issues as acid rain.

Interest group involvement in trade issues has long been a fixture of Canadian politics. Earlier, for example, we noted Norman Robertson's unsympathetic comments on the Canadian Manufacturers' Association's efforts to influence R. B. Bennett's trade negotiations in the 1930s. The international activities of humanitarian, environmental, and peace groups are generally a more recent phenomenon. In the past many of these groups and their predecessors had contacts in other countries and were influenced by them. The temperance movement in Canada was influenced by its American counterpart. The women's suffrage movement was encouraged by women in the United States and Britain. The forestry movement in the late nineteenth century was inspired in part by American example. The labour movement had international connections. Today, however, many international groups go beyond sympathizing with and encouraging their colleagues in Canada and elsewhere. They take direct action to influence the Canadian government and they work to bring international pressure to bear on it. The International Fund for Animal Welfare, in its attack on Canada's seal hunt, seems to have had relatively little support in this country and was bitterly opposed in Newfoundland. But by enflaming European opinion and embarrassing the Canadian government, it first secured changes in the regulations governing the hunt and ultimately destroyed the market for pelts.[49]

Canadian groups have not been as aggressive in venturing into the domestic policies of other countries, but some have been ingenious in using international public opinion to exert pressure on their own government. Native peoples in particular have done this effectively. The highly publicized lobbying of the British Parliament by Indian groups secured concessions from the Trudeau government as it negotiated repatriation of the constitution. Similarly Indian Women, angry that the Indian Act discriminates against them by depriving women married to non-Indians of their Indian status, have taken their complaint to the United Nations Human Rights Committee.[50]

In sum, for many groups the international environment is an extension of domestic politics. They use that environment—represented by international public opinion and accessible through international organizations, governmental and non-governmental—to influence policy at home, or to create conditions abroad that further their own interests. For other groups the world is truly a global village. They exist primarily at the international level to influence events in whatever country they choose. Oxfam, the Red Cross, Greenpeace, Amnesty International, and many others, though they work through governmental agencies to achieve their objectives, often find that international public opinion is their most effective weapon. Through spectacular stunts as well as through appeals to the consciences of wealthier citizens of the world, they not only acquire resources to carry out their own programs, but goad governments and international agencies into modifying their policies.

(iii) *Using the courts:*

In 1981 John Swaigen, a lawyer with the Ontario Ministry of the Environment, published a book entitled *How to Fight for What's Right*. Described as 'the citizen's guide to public interest law', the book marked a significant trend in

Canadian pressure group tactics: resorting to legal action. Of course the courts and the law have always been available to both groups and individuals prepared to challenge the actions of others, including the actions of government. Until quite recently, however, not many groups seem to have taken advantage of litigation. Though it is difficult to say how many groups go to law today, in comparison with their predecessors their numbers appear to be on the increase. We have already referred to one such case, the successful challenge launched by the National Citizens' Coalition to the 1983 amendments to the Canada Elections Act. At roughly the same time Sabina Citron, a member of the Canadian Holocaust Remembrance Association, pressed charges against Ernst Zundel under section 177 of the Criminal Code, which prohibits the dissemination of false information. Her action was directed primarily at stopping Zundel from publishing and distributing anti-Jewish literature, but it was also aimed at shaming Canadian governments into strengthening and enforcing prohibitions against hate literature.[51] At the level of local government it is commonplace for citizens' groups to engage in long battles before administrative tribunals and the courts in attempts to preserve or improve civic amenities.[52]

The trend towards litigation flows from disparate sources. On a superficial level it might seem to be another example of Canadian emulation of American strategies. In Canada, as in the United States, environmentalists have been particularly forward in using legal mechanisms for delaying and stopping developments they feel would degrade the environment. (Swaigen's book was sponsored by the Canadian Environmental Law Research Foundation.) But this trend does not derive solely from the Americanization of Canadian pressure groups. Changes in legal procedure and in the diffusion of power we discussed earlier provide stronger influences. A community that finds it difficult to locate responsibility and to fix authority, and whose policy process is highly discursive, is almost forced to turn to law. The constitution, the statutes, the body of legal interpretation are perceived as being among its more stable and reliable institutions.

One of the factors inhibiting a resort to law in the past was the fact that the legal system was not, and in large part still is not, friendly to citizens' groups. Swaigen explains:

> The challenges facing public interest groups and their lawyers are difficult ones. In many instances, the full weight of big business or big government can shatter the financial and organizational capabilities of citizen groups before such groups have had the opportunity to effectively present their cases. . . . Citizens can and do fight back. But getting a case into the courts is only the beginning of what can prove to be a lengthy, frustrating and very expensive lesson in how the law works. The question of costs looms very large for individuals or groups who can overcome the standing barrier. Because of the costs involved if a case is lost, few citizens are willing to use the courts to seek redress. A wealthy corporation that stands to lose millions

of dollars because of a consumer protection policy will challenge the policy in the courts. But thousands of consumers who individually lose a few hundred dollars because they have had to repair a defective product will never sue the manufacturer as long as each of them is liable for what may amount to several thousands of dollars in costs.[53]

Swaigen emphasizes the problems of 'standing' and the problems of costs. The two are interconnected. As he points out, the individual or group initiating a legal action has a great deal to lose and very little to gain. A group of Cape Breton landowners discovered this when they challenged the right of Stora Koppaburg, a forest products firm, to spray herbicides on lands sharing their own watershed. The landowners lost the case, and found themselves responsible for paying court costs that far exceeded their resources. Several faced bankruptcy. Ultimately public opinion, including public opinion in Sweden where its head office is located, persuaded the firm to accept a much smaller sum and a commitment that the group would not appeal the case or pursue the issue further. Quite apart from this commitment, the group's experience was a frightening lesson to other groups of the dangers inherent in resorting to law. It cannot help but intimidate other activists trying to 'fight for what's right'.[54]

The question of standing relates to the court's view as to whether a would-be litigant has 'an interest in the subject matter of the legal proceedings that is greater than and different from that of the general public'.[55] In other words the courts, and many regulatory bodies, insist that before they will listen to requests to interfere with the actions of others, the parties making the requests should prove that they are directly and substantially affected by those actions. In general Canadian courts have defined standing narrowly, and have not been very willing to receive the assistance of *amicae curiae* (friends of the court), individuals and groups concerned to show how the public interest might be affected by the outcome of a case.[56] These narrow definitions have limited pressure group use of the courts: they have made it difficult for public interest groups to intervene, and have discouraged efforts to draw larger issues from the particular differences that concern the original disputants. As a consequence many individuals and small groups have to fight public battles on their own, without the financial support, experience, and expertise of the larger and more established public interest groups.

One of the reasons for the increase in group litigation is that these problems are gradually being recognized by legislators, the legal profession, and the courts. There are signs that the courts are slightly expanding the rules they apply to admit argument before them. The increased significance of the Constitution, particularly the promulgation of the Charter of Rights, is expected to foster this tendency. The 'Charter Cases', as they have been called, are only beginning to reach the courts and it is too early to say what effect they will have on pressure group politics. The indications are that the

National Citizens' Coalition case was but one of the first of a long line of group-initiated actions. Ultimately these will have a profound effect in defining the rights of groups as well as of individuals, and we can expect to find that the judgements stemming from them will strengthen the role groups play in the policy process. The legal profession has also shown interest in developing procedures that would help individual citizens and smaller groups. Finally some legislative reform has been attempted to ensure that public interest issues can be brought to the courts through class actions. These are cases brought by individuals on behalf of others who may not have given their consent to the action. In the United States this practice has been widely used by public interest groups. It is intended to overcome the barriers created by court requirements that cases be brought by aggrieved parties, each of whom must plead individually. To date only Québec has introduced a class action law; but though it provides financial assistance to litigants, it is so encumbered by restrictions that it has had very little effect and has led one legal authority, H. Patrick Glenn, to conclude that class actions have an 'inherently problematic character' that makes them inappropriate for use by interest groups and that undermines legal institutions.

> Class actions procedures, where they exist, now appear to be failing, both as significant measures of social reform and as procedures viable even on a limited scale in the court system. There are profound and systemic reasons for this, which no amount of legislative design or fine-tuning can overcome. Parties and counsel are rejecting class actions because they are too onerous and problematical (aside from questions of costs) in a judicial system which responds to radically different priorities. Judges reject class actions because they see them as incompatible with both their procedural and adjucative functions, and in this they are probably correct. Class action implementation therefore accomplishes little, and anything which is accomplished is at the critical expense of judicial authority and the principles of fundamental justice.[57]

The Quebec experience, however, could be the first step towards more effective class action legislation and provision of financial assistance for appellants—part of a larger effort at law reform that, in Swaigen's words, is 'necesary just to ensure that people have the right to speak out about injustice without fear of harassment and to use the courts without paying crushing costs.'[58]

CONCLUSIONS

The last two chapters have discussed the way groups relate to and attempt to influence their environment. We have treated that environment as consisting of two distinct entities: the policy community and the larger world of institutions and mass publics beyond the policy community. To influence policy, groups must influence the policy community. The general public—which has superordinate authority over the policy community—has its say from time to time. But the policy community, as long as it is not disbanded or reshaped, possesses the collective memory for policy and organizes the application of knowledge to the resolution of policy problems. Over time, therefore, it exercises a continuing sway over the evolution of policy and its implementation.

The strategies that win support in the policy community reflect its bureaucratic orientation. To participate, groups must organize themselves along bureaucratic lines—preferably along lines that parallel the structure of the lead agency itself. They must accept many of the bureaucratic mores of the governmental actors in the community. They come to think in bureaucratic terms, finding that elaborate analyses of groups' positions help them push their ideas through the information machine that we call the policy process. Even when groups appeal to the general public they cannot escape the bureaucratic imperative. The media represent a complex organization. They can only be 'used' over time by groups aware of their strengths, weaknesses, and prejudices and able to maintain contact with their many levels of operation. Even the staging of a 'spontaneous' demonstration involves more preparation than most observers will realize. Legislators are often sympathetic to small groups of constituents, but to influence them to the point of securing policy change citizens must bring continual pressure to bear, which also demands organization. Even groups that have won a victory at the public level cannot be certain of translating their gains into programs, unless they achieve organized participation in the policy community.

Bureaucratic strategies are expensive. They demand elaborate organizations, often located in several centres. They call for expertise in the preparation of analyses and in the conduct of lobbying campaigns. Professional help is seldom cheap. The maintenance of position in the community, even if it does not depend on the operation of well-staffed offices, will generally involve member or representative participation in advisory committees, co-operative actions, and the mounting of conferences. The travel and communication costs incurred by these activities are particularly high in a bilingual, sometimes multilingual, country whose major centres are far apart. The commitments of participation do not always end at the boundaries of the immediate policy community. International connections are frequent and sometimes essential supports for domestic campaigns. They too are expensive to maintain. Finally, the resort to law can be the most expensive of all pressure activities.

The cost and level of organization demanded of group actors in the Canadian policy system places an immense burden on most committed groups, but it places the greatest burden on groups that lack a strong resource base—public-interest groups and what are sometimes called 'citizens' groups'—because they emerge almost spontaneously among the citizenry to articulate concerns that seem to be systematically excluded from the public agenda. Even the diffusion of power, which has been a recurrent theme in our discussion, does not necessarily assist these groups. Today they have a wider choice of avenues to policy discussion than they had two decades ago. It is easier to generate policy discussion. But it is not easier to participate in that discussion over the length of time required to form a policy response. Citizens' groups and public-interest groups can therefore make a contribution to the evolution of policy that is far less significant and insightful than their origins and composition warrant. Their limited role may be a comfort to sub-governments, but restricts the benefits the polity at large can derive from group politics.

CHAPTER 8

The Interior Life of Groups

No group, however powerful or worthy it may seem on paper, will achieve political success unless it can sustain the support of its members, employees, and friends. This reality can never be forgotten by those who organize interest representation in the policy process. It is a condition of survival. For that reason the manner in which group support is created and maintained— the interior life of groups—deserves our careful attention.

We will examine the internal operations of groups from three perspectives. First, we will consider the motivations individuals, corporations, and other groups bring to membership in an interest association, arguing that the aims and concerns of members affect not only the success of the group, but the way it works to achieve its goals. This argument will build on the discussion of group types presented in Chapter 5. Extending that discussion still further in the next section, we will review the types of resources used by pressure groups and explore how their availability differs among various kinds of groups. Finally we will consider the complex problem of group management, a seldom discussed aspect of group life that nevertheless can make an enormous difference not only to the successful pursuit of a group's political goals, but also to its capacity to survive.

THE BASES OF SUPPORT

We have argued that pressure groups have a role in the political system because they perform some or all of the four functions of communication, legitimation, administration, and regulation. To carry out any of these functions a group must attract from its potential clientele—from the latent and solidary interest—enough members to sustain its work and, where legitimation is important, to ensure that it can be considered adequately representative of the interest community. This fundamental requirement raises the extremely important question of member motivation. Why do people join pressure groups?

It is sometimes suggested that awareness of the need to promote a common interest accounts for the decision of individuals to join specific groups. Often quoted, for example, is David Truman's argument that formal interest associations are most likely to take shape when the interest community they represent is in some way threatened:[1] a common peril forces solidary group

176

members to recognize their mutual interest and to band together. It is generally argued that recognition of a shared interest is a necessary condition for joining a formal interest association, but is not in itself a strong enough motivation to lead a person to make this sort of commitment. This view, implicit in many early case studies, was put forward as a generalization in the 1950s by V.O. Key, who pointed out that many people did not join pressure groups *per se*: they joined labour unions, voluntary associations, clubs, and many other organizations for the services, personal opportunities, and social life they offered.[2] Pressure group activity was very frequently an unanticipated, and often unwelcome, aspect of membership. In 1965 Mancur Olson stirred a major, still-flourishing, controversy by making this point the centre of a new theory of pressure group behaviour. In *The Logic of Collective Action* he argues that most individuals are rational beings who calculate, even if imperfectly, the benefits and costs associated with taking part in interest organizations, and will not join them unless membership brings with it some benefit they would not otherwise obtain. In the absence of such inducements the only other motive would be that membership is a condition of employment, of practising a profession, or even of enjoying some benefit provided by government.[3] Olson's theory thus rests on the view that human beings are motivated by fear or greed, or both.

For the moment we will not quarrel with this depressing perspective, but will consider instead Olson's explanation of how this view of human nature affects pressure groups. Basically he argues that in the eyes of members and potential members, interest organizations produce two kinds of benefits: 'collective benefits' and 'selective benefits'. Collective benefits are available to everyone in the community (in the 'collectivity') regardless of how much or how little each has contributed to its creation and upkeep. Many individuals will share a common interest in obtaining a collective benefit, but if it can be obtained without exertion on their part they will prefer enjoying a 'free ride' to joining a group dedicated to providing it or to urging the government to provide it.[4] Evidence for this argument can be obtained on any summer day in any of the hundreds of federal and provincial parks. Millions of people enjoy these facilities every year, but very few support in any way at all the Canadian Wildlife Federation and the other organizations that have lobbied for these parks and for the amenities they provide. While many who enjoy the parks systems may be aware that they share that enjoyment with others and that it provides them with a common interest, that awareness is unlikely to encourage them to join the Wildlife Federation, or any other parks-oriented pressure group.

Faced with the free-rider problem, Olson argues, groups develop 'selective inducements'. These are:

. . . private benefits which, precisely because they are private rather than collective in nature, can operate selectively on the membership as a whole:

they can be conferred upon those who contribute . . . If a person wishes to obtain selective incentives he cannot do so by waiting for others to shoulder the costs. He will have to 'qualify' to receive them, which in practice, ordinarily means paying dues and becoming a formal member.[5]

Members of the Wildlife Federation receive special literature about Canadian wildlife and where it can be seen. With other enthusiasts they take part in conservation projects or are offered excursion rates to travel to conservation areas such a Point Pelee where, in weather daunting to the hardiest Arctic tern, they can be been seen floundering through the marshes to participate in the annual bird count. According to Olson these are selective benefits—material, social, and psychic—that are unavailable to non-members of the Wildlife Federation and are an inducement to join that body. Similarly the majority of Canadians cannot subscribe to the group life-insurance plan available through the Canadian Association of University Teachers. Furthermore, Canadian university teachers who are not members of this association are ineligible to obtain the legal and other advisory services the CAUT makes available to affiliate groups engaged in collective bargaining; nor, if they are driven to strike action, can they draw on the association's strike fund. Even business associations, which are particularly oriented towards political intervention, develop selective inducements. As intermediaries between competing firms and government, they are often privy to information that is otherwise available only to individual firms and government regulators. Without breaking confidences, they are thus frequently in a position to offer mediating services to rivals within their membership.[6]

In Olson's estimation selective inducements are in most cases the *raison d'être* of interest associations. Lobbying is, in effect, a by-product of group life:

> The lobbies of the large economic groups are the by-products of organizations that have the capacity to 'mobilize' a latent group with 'selective incentives'. The only organizations that have 'selective incentives' available are those that (1) have authority and capacity to be coercive, or (2) have a source of positive inducements that they can offer the individuals in a latent group.[7]

Other organizations are formed primarily to participate directly in policy-making, but, in Olson's view, they are groups with limited capacity: small bands of idealists; issue-oriented groups whose members are caught up in a wave of public passion; and small solidary groups content to promote very narrow interests for limited returns. In effect these groups, too, are using selective inducements to attract and sometimes to hold their members, but in their case the inducements are the promise of group social life or the psychological rewards of direct participation. Such inducements cannot easily survive organizational growth and when found in larger organizations are accompanied by other, more tangible incentives.[8]

Table 8-1. Reasons for Joining Interest Associations

Main reasons given for joining associations:

Reason given	Association				
	Printers' Union	Retail Assoc.	Hardware Assoc.	Farm Bureau	Farmers' Union
	%	%	%	%	%
Services Provided Members	86	44	56	54	34
Lobbying Activities	0	27	14	25	37
Social Life	2	1	0	4	5
Sense of Collective Responsibility	9	27	26	12	20
Expected to Join by Others	2	1	3	4	4
Total	99	100	99	99	100
N	64	326	391	571	564
Response Rate on Questionnaire	74%	62%	46%	34%	34%

Source: Terry M. Moe, *The Organization of Interests* (Chicago, The University of Chicago Press, 1980), 208-210

Olson's theory explains a good deal about pressure group politics. It forcibly reminds us that for the majority of members participation in the association is related to the specific benefits the group can provide, rather than to the promotion of the public interest. Terry M. Moe, who has developed an extremely perceptive, though highly theoretical, elaboration of Olson's argument, presents the following data derived from a survey of five Minnesota unions whose members were asked, first, what prompted them to join their association, and second, whether they would maintain their membership if the association were to sacrifice selective inducements in favour of lobbying, or vice versa.

Moe's data, though limited, tends to support the Olson thesis. In only one of the five associations polled would more than half the membership stay in the organization if services were withdrawn in favour of intensifying lobbying activities; for none of them would a decision to drop lobbying induce a similar number to quit. The responses suggest that pressure group activity in itself would attract a much smaller membership. Whether the membership would be too small to sustain competent lobbying would, of course, depend on the circumstances of each group; but we can be sure that the legitimacy of each, insofar as it related to the group's capacity to represent the interest community, would be diminished.

Table 8-2. Maintenance of Membership in Interest Associations

How would you react if the association stopped providing services, but still lobbied?

Response	Association				
	Printers' Union	Retail Assoc.	Hardware Assoc.	Farm Bureau	Farmers' Union
	%	%	%	%	%
Stay in:	20	43	40	44	58
Drop out:	80	57	60	56	42
N	65	354	401	587	577

How would you react if the association stopped lobbying, but still provided services?

Stay in:	94	57	70	77	63
Drop out:	6	43	30	23	37
N	65	352	400	583	580

Source: Terry M. Moe, *The Organization of Interests* (Chicago, The University of Chicago Press, 1980), 208-210

Though we have very little comparable Canadian data, one cannot help wondering whether Olson's thesis explains in part the low level of popular support for the Consumer's Association of Canada reported by Helen Jones Dawson:

> Membership has been a grave disappointment to the CAC since its earliest days when it was assumed that every woman in Canada would be happy to pay a fifty cent fee to belong to an organization which would inform her about consumer goods, represent her before the government, and protect her from unscrupulous manufacturers, producers and advertisers.[9]

Olson would diagnose the free-rider problem. He would note that two of the three benefits listed are collective benefits and would ask how the third—provision of information—had been made available. On learning that the organization's capacity to deal with individual concerns was extremely limited, he would conclude that the CAC really offered virtually no special inducements to encourage Canadian women to become members. Considering these deficiences in combination with the other problems identified by Dawson in her 1963 article—lack of money, poor communications, weak organization, and regional jealousies; executive procrastination and lack of agreement on organizational role, and pursuit of too many objectives—Olson would probably wonder how the CAC managed to survive at all.

The CAC, however, did survive these difficult years and survives today, often appearing prominently in the news.[10] Yet its range of selective inducements is no more extensive than it was twenty years ago. Many other well-known organizations have also done as well or better—without offering selective inducements any more appealing than those offered by the CAC. Transport 2000 is an active lobby for public transportation systems that offers its members little more inducement to join than a mimeographed news-sheet and the exhilaration of picketing, as often as not in rain or snow, some forlorn railway station that is about to be abandoned. Yet Transport 2000 regularly prepares elaborate briefs for the Canadian Transport Commission, for ministers and parliamentary committees, and has become a force to be reckoned with. Though some of Transport 2000's members have been put out of work by rail closures or fear for their jobs, many have joined because they feel government policy is misguided and they want a different kind of public transportation system for Canada.[11] For that collective benefit they are prepared to put far more into Transport 2000 than the organization can ever give them in return.

The experience of such organizations forces us to question the Olsonian calculus of participation. If human beings are self-interested, rational, and calculating, why do so many devote much of their leisure time to the CAC, Transport 2000, Greenpeace, Planned Parenthood, and the thousands of other groups whose chief concern is to work for collective benefits? Olson and his supporters offer two explanations. First, non-material rewards inhere in a personal calculation of marginal utility: social rewards, for example. Lifelong friendships can be made camping around a nuclear power station and sharing a paddy wagon. There can also be psychic rewards. Working for the CAC simply makes some people feel good. They may derive a great deal of moral satisfaction from helping to protect the consumer or from making sure that you can still go from Swastika to Moonbeam by train. The second explanation offered by Olsonian theorists is that while human beings are rational, calculating, and self-interested, they must also work with imperfect information.[12] Thus they may underestimate the extent of the resources they will have to dedicate to a cause; they may overestimate the personal satisfactions they will derive from it; or they may simply not realize that they could derive as much satisfaction from doing something else. Such miscalculations doubtless explain the dedication many men and women bring to the often disheartening work of the John Howard and Elizabeth Fry Societies; and the efforts to breathe life and vigour into many parent-teacher associations, and organizations such as the Canadian Cancer Institute.

A third explanation, recently put forward by Moe; introduces another dimension. Individuals, he argues, make assumptions about marginal increments that are shaped by perceptions: 'behavioral expectations are contingent in specific ways upon perceptions.'[13] Thus a person with a well developed sense of personal efficacy will consider that his or her participation in a cause 'makes a difference' in the struggle to persuade public authorities to pursue a particular, desired policy. In other words, both selective inducements and group goals can attract members.

All of these explanations are more or less plausible, but they push Olsonian theory beyond its limits. It may be true that a volunteer in the Elizabeth Fry

Society derives great personal satisfaction from the exacting tasks the organization undertakes even in its policy-oriented aspects, but that satisfaction cannot be quantified in order to make Olson's concept operational. More important is the question of why members of the public should wish to devote themselves to group life when the rewards it brings seldom seem commensurate with the effort they must put into it. Nevertheless, Moe's observation is helpful because it suggests that the desire to participate may be rooted in the individual's experience of the processes of socialization. This supports the argument put forward by students of comparative politics that variations in political culture have a great deal to do with association-joining and political participation in general. A high degree of political efficacy and cognitive orientation in a community increases its chances of producing a lively group life.

We can accept Olson's notion that some groups find it useful to attract or hold members by offering selective inducements, but we cannot agree that the concept of a calculus of participation explains all association-joining. It is true that virtually any satisfaction obtained from group participation can be labelled a secondary inducement; but since the great majority of these satisfactions cannot be quantified in the manner suggested by Olson, it will be more useful to consider them on their own merits rather than to rely on a spurious calculus.

What are these satisfactions and how do they lead people to join interest associations? Those that are social or psychic have little to do with the political aspects of interest group activity. Others, however, are related to political life. As Moe points out, some people have a sufficiently high sense of personal efficacy to feel that their participation *does* make a difference. For example, perhaps such a feeling was experienced by Beryl Plumptre, who for many years was a leading figure in the consumer movement. But it is also experienced by the provincial or regional leaders of CAC and by many local members, who will point out that politicians believe that for each person participating directly in the CAC, many others in the general community hold similar views on issues. They thus feel they play a representative role. Such people provide the core of group life.

Many of these people also feel that they have a responsibility to participate; that a democratic society remains democratic only so long as the public at large monitors the work of government and lets public officials know when they are performing poorly, or unjustly, or corruptly. Such sentiments explain the speed with which a protest movement can arise, and account for the longevity of organizations concerned with improving public policy, whether it relates to the prison system, public transportation, the state of the environment, or what-have-you. We find quantitative justification of this view in the figures presented in Table 8-I. In three of the five associations surveyed over 50 per cent cited secondary inducements as the reason for joining; in three organizations 20 per cent or more were attracted by the association's work in promoting collective benefits. Obviously the latter organizations would be much smaller if they did not offer secondary inducements, but a core of supporters seems willing to work chiefly for collective benefits. Had Moe surveyed public interest groups, he might have shed light on this willingness to work for collective benefits. As it is, he gives us some reason to believe that civic responsibility does play a part in motivating people to join interest groups.

In our view individuals who engage in group life because they feel their participation makes a difference or because they feel a responsibility to work for collective benefits derive their motivations from cultural factors. From childhood, in the family, in school, and in the organizational life that surrounds school and university, they have absorbed ideas about human relationships, about the role of the individual in the community, and about the government's responsibility to promote the general welfare that foster a tendency to take part in collective action. Since individual socialization experience differs—as does the response to it—some members of a political community will be strongly motivated to participate fully in it, while others will not feel that their involvement makes a difference or that they have a responsibility to take part.

Not every active pressure group member wants to take part in group life, not even in exchange for selective benefits. Though potent social and psychological rewards often accompany membership, for many loyal members of interest associations the social contacts and duties of group life are painful rather than pleasant, tedious rather than gratifying. The parent who caps an exhausting, stressful week at the office with a weekend of living out of a suitcase in order to take part in drafting a policy statement for a regional home-and-school association must—if we exclude sheer masochism—be motivated by a very strong sense of collective responsibility as well as a desire to benefit directly his or her own offspring. He or she would be inclined to agree with J.A. Corry when he declares that, 'not many of us derive our satisfactions out of moulding complex collective decisions and carrying a heavy and ill-defined responsibility. We would much sooner leave the burden to someone else.'[14] Given a choice that parent would likely prefer to communicate directly with educational policy-makers; to sit down with curriculum planners, and argue the pros and cons of certain programs, the value of various teaching methods. He or she knows, however, that such opportunities are rare and that even when they do occur they are unlikely to lead to any direct change in public policy, because so many other opinions must be considered. As Leon Dion observes, 'Canadian institutions have evolved in a shape more or less consciously designed to discourage direct personal involvement in the political process.'[15] This is not solely a Canadian problem. André Holleaux, discussing group politics in France, notes that senior officials now see fewer and fewer individuals in the course of their working day, meeting instead with delegations representing groups.[16] Meynaud argues that this situation is a natural outgrowth of the increasing collectivization of modern life: individuals can interact less and less with the state when so many corporate interests—each representing many interests—are also anxious to speak to various authorities. Such groups take precedence. To gain access the individual must combine with others.[17]

In an earlier period the policy-conscious citizen might have chosen to exert influence on decision-makers through the political party; but that option, for the reasons outlined in earlier chapters, is no longer viable. The development of bureaucratic power, the diffuse nature of party concerns, the increasing recognition given to sectoral groups, all suggest to the questing citizen that the only effective way to participate in the policy process is to work through pressure groups active in the field that concerns him or her. In short, there is a strong institutional incentive to join interest associations. This incentive borders on coercion, since the majority of citizens cannot exercise the rights of citizenship apart from group affiliation. Faced with a choice between remaining mute or engaging in group life, most citizens opt for silence. The minority who elect to join associations provide the semi-captive manpower and womanpower that keeps those organizations going.

We have identified five factors that we believe motivate individuals to become members of interest groups: selective inducements, the promise of collective benefits, socialization to a sense of civic responsibility, a strong sense of political efficacy, and institutional coercion. Before discussing the different ways these factors influence the interior life of groups, we should note that they are not mutually exclusive. That is, a person may be led to join a group for one, several, or all of the reasons embodied in our five factors. For example, a lawyer is coerced into joining the bar association, but may also feel the attraction of deriving both direct and selective benefits from it, while at the same time feeling a civic duty to influence the development of the law in the belief that the bar association is a useful vehicle for attaining that end. Because such motivations very often combine in a given membership, both observers and leaders of groups have difficulty in assessing precisely what group members hope to achieve by joining specific organizations—and how those organizations should be made to serve them. This is a point we will discuss in the next two sections of this chapter.

One other point should be made first. We have tended to speak in terms of, and to cite examples of, the motives that lead to participation in institutionalized, or established groups. How does our argument relate to individuals who join issue-oriented groups? While coercion is unlikely to prompt people to join such groups, we suggest that all the other motivations can come into play, though cultural incentives and the promise of direct benefits are probably the most important. An environmentalist, for example, on first learning about the problems created by acid rain, could—if sufficiently endowed with a sense of efficacy and of social responsibility—decide to join with others in creating an organization to combat the problem. Similarly, individuals made aware of an impending public decision likely to affect them personally might be inclined to join a supportive or protest group. The decision to select group action rather than élite action or individual intercession might well reflect awareness of institutional imperatives, even though that awareness might be accompanied by the knowledge that issue-oriented groups do not easily obtain access to the policy system. Finally, even selective inducements may play their part in the decision to join or create an issue-oriented group: the yearning for a sense of solidarity, the gratifications of participation, the sense of leadership—all these can be significant non-material inducements to take part.

GROUP TYPES AND THE AVAILABILITY OF RESOURCES

Interest group resources fall into three categories: knowledge, mandate, or wealth. The capacity of any given group to muster these resources depends largely, but not entirely, on the capacities and inclinations of the membership. There is consequently a direct relation between the type of group that members are disposed to create and the resources available to it. We will first examine what is meant by resources of knowledge, mandate, and wealth, and then will discuss how various kinds of groups use them differently.

(i) *Knowledge*

Interest group knowledge is of two kinds: knowledge about the substance of policy, and knowledge about the policy process. Extensive acquisition of the one does not necessarily entail a grasp of the other, as both specialists and generalists have sometimes learned to their cost. Substantive knowledge is, generally, expert knowledge,[18] which permits one to say to public decision-makers, 'If you do this, that will happen,' and to know that the statement will be accepted. For many groups this is a most precious resource. It is their key to access and influence, for in many instances government has no expertise of its own and no other source of information. Thus critics of the National Energy Board complain that the Board and the Department of Energy, Mines and Resources is totally dependent on the oil companies and the Oil Producers' Association of Canada for their knowledge of the country's resources of hydrocarbons.[19] Coleman and Jacek note that intra-industry surveys carried out by chemical industry associations sometimes offer the only data available to regulators, either because Statistics Canada has cut back on data collection in recent years or has never generated data of the type required. According to them, 'the Canadian Fertilizer Institute suggests that its Canadian Fertilizer Information System is now the only authoritative source on the production and consumption of fertilizers in Canada.'[20] Information monopolies of this sort are doubly valuable in group relations with government: not only do they assure the group of a place in the policy process, but the discreet manipulation of data can be used to shape the thinking of policy-makers. Critics of energy policy have argued, for example, that Canadian reserves of hydrocarbons have at times been grossly overestimated in order to persuade public authorities to allow producers to export to the United States large quantities of oil and natural gas deemed 'excess' to Canadian needs. Even when it is not of strategic importance, information can be valuable currency in winning the regard of public decision-makers, as the following cautionary tale suggests:

> One civil servant conducting a background study on a certain industry needed information that, although in the public domain, required laborious collection. Realizing that these data would have been collected by the industry's trade association, he called, explained his purpose and requested the information. He was refused, abruptly. And what did this refusal accomplish? Because the information in question was still obtainable for the report, the only result was one very irritated civil servant. And since this civil servant was a specialist in the industry he was studying, the next time the trade association might have occasion to lobby Ottawa, this same civil servant would become involved and he would remember.[21]

John Bulloch, of the Canadian Federation of Independent Business, maintains that '75 percent of our time is spent responding to requests by government institutions for advice and assistance on every facet of public policy—federal as well as provincial.'[22] Even allowing for exaggeration, this suggests that the Federation has at its disposal a resource that can, if adroitly used, win it important concessions from government. While the diversity of the CFIB's interests and the size of its membership probably makes it unusual in the information business, it is conceivable that a significant number of other interest groups occupy strategically useful positions thanks to their command of information resources.

Besides being useful in government-group relations, information is of value in the relations between the interest association and its members. An organization that stands in a relation of trust between its members and government not only obtains a perspective on the membership that is not available to individuals, but acquires an authority over and above the willingness of members to support it. This is one of the factors that makes the organization necessary to its supporters and it contributes to the independence sometimes shown towards members by the organization staff and leadership. The tendency of government agencies to use the interest organization as a vehicle for communicating with its members also enhances the stature and independence of the leadership and staff, and gives them core assets—advance intimations of policy change, for example—that can be used in bargaining with members. And government, simply by using the organization as an information conduit, enhances its status with its supporters.

Policy-process information is not the hard currency that substantive knowledge can often be, but it is nonetheless valuable, as the success in Ottawa of many lobbying firms attests. In fact without a considerable knowledge of how the policy process works, the holder of valuable substantive information can easily dissipate much of its value. According to John Bulloch:

> The crucial thing is to know to whom to talk. It follows that you get better at lobbying over time, because it takes so long to infiltrate the system and find out who really makes the decisions. Organization charts are useless. You have to find out who sits on the interdepartmental committees. Every department has its own power structure, and it takes a lot of digging and a lot of contacts to find who makes the decisions. In some cases the ministers are very powerful, but in others they have very little power and major decisions are made for them by their senior advisors.[23]

Knowing who does what, and where, helps the lobbyist place the information he or she possesses. A minister does not want to see a complex brief on a technical point; a deputy minister objects to being troubled with minor questions; a junior official may give useful advice on a major proposal, but is probably not the appropriate person to receive a formal proposal on the agency's behalf. The lobbyist wise in the ways of the policy process selects each contact with care, attempting to gauge the impact of each nugget of information on different policy actors, and its subsequent effect as it works its way through the policy system. Implicit in each decision on the placement of information is a further decision about the overall objective of the policy exercise. If hoping to achieve only a minor modification of policy—or wishing to present as routine a more significant change—the lobbyist will probably initiate the process at the lowest level in the bureaucracy competent to deal with the matter. First contacts may be made with technical specialists. A more complex proposal might involve multiple contacts; lobbyists handling complex proposals are sometimes advised to engage as many officials as possible in the undertaking since each, if properly approached, will develop an interest in promoting the scheme.[24] Major change may take years and engage an entire policy community (a process we discuss in Chapter 6) or may be approached more vigorously via a frontal lobbying of parliamentary institutions and ministers. To quote John Bulloch again:

> . . . if what you want is to put pressure on the system, there is nothing more effective than going to your Member of Parliament who can be influential in caucus—and in the question period. In earlier days, when we were involved in a less sophisticated form of lobbying, the question period was one of our most powerful instruments because Members can obtain information that the

government would not give us. It became a great game of providing the Opposition with material for the question period. We go about our business differently now because we have access to government. But smaller groups which lack clout and access do find the question period a valuable lobbying tool and an important instrument of influence.[25]

Bulloch suggests that the Parliamentary route is used primarily by new issue-oriented groups that lack a sophisticated knowledge of the policy process. However, as we saw in Chapter 3, institutionalized groups have in recent years tended to approach Parliament partly because the changing nature of the policy process demands it, but also because there is a new leverage to be obtained from contesting departmental decisions before Parliament. Labour groups, for example, because they frequently challenge the prevailing economic structure, are often to be seen demonstrating on Parliament Hill and bringing pressure to bear on the government through Question Period and other Parliamentary devices.

The kind of information available to a group is determined by the nature of the policy field the group chooses to participate in; by the composition of its members; and by its organizational structure and ideological orientation. These factors are, of course, often interrelated, and tend to govern the way information is used.

Group type has a profound influence. A group located at the issue-oriented end of the policy continuum we presented in Chapter 5 is less likely than a highly institutionalized group to have at hand process information or to know how to use it. Donald Chant, in his account of the early days of Pollution Probe, noted the naivety of his younger associates when faced with determined attempts by industry to suppress public dissemination of information about the fluoride pollution emanating from the Electric Reduction Company plant at Port Maitland, Ontario.[26] Though many of them were science students at the University of Toronto and were knowledgeable about chemical processes and pollution, they were baffled by the policy process. As the environmental movement gained ground and their own organization became influential, they acquired even greater respect for sound substantive knowledge—their capacity to prepare a thorough and accurate brief helped win recognition—and they became more sophisticated in the ways of policy-making. And yet they did not abandon a lobbying style that many interest representatives consider dysfunctional. A penchant for publicity and a conviction that 'when seeking decisive action . . . one should approach the real centres of power: Cabinet members . . . and other political leaders,' are not recommended for long-term strategy.[27] Nevertheless this approach was effective for Pollution Probe—for reasons that illustrate our earlier point: the availability and use of information reflects group type, membership, ideology, and the policy field it works in. When Pollution Probe was established no distinct field of environmental policy existed; there was merely a series of discrete policy fields, many of them belonging to quite different sectors. Water-quality issues tended to be associated with the Department of Mines and Technical Surveys, because water was used in the production of energy, or was necessary to the majority of mineral-extraction or manufacturing processes. Water purity was seldom considered, except in regard to its potability for domestic or commercial uses. Further issues raised by the environmental movement were treated by other agencies and from different perspectives. Consequently Pollution Probe and other environmental groups could not affiliate themselves with a ready-made policy community. Instead they had to create one, which entailed shaking up the policy system as a whole. Therefore it made sense to tackle the centres of power, as Chant recommended, since only premiers and cabinet ministers could effect the major structural changes needed to create agencies to which environmental groups could attach themselves. Once those agencies were created, environmental groups changed their communication tactics, becoming much less visible and developing the more traditional charactistics of institutionalized pressure groups.

But it was not the nature of the policy field alone that dictated a particular communications style. As an issue-oriented group, Pollution Probe was initially more knowledgeable about the substantive nature of the policy problem than it was about the processes that would have to be pursued to tackle it. We have already quoted Chant's comments on this point. However, because Pollution Probe was part of a widespread movement it did not experience the set-backs endured by other issue-oriented groups when, like them, it insisted on going to the top as well as appealing to the public at large. Nevertheless its strong issue-orientation became an organizational problem for the group as it developed. David Hoffman, observing it several years after its formation, commented:

> The experience of Pollution Probe illustrates an aspect of the question of the most effective strategy for groups who wish to make major changes in the system. It seems that there has been considerable controversy within the organization about what the strategy should be and the discussion has focussed on whether efforts 'within the system' are worthwhile at all. Some of the Pollution Probe staff feel that attempting to influence environmental policy through accepted channels will only bring about short term benefits, and that longer-term results require 'confrontation' strategies—that is, challenges to the entire system of decision-making. Partly in response to this difference of opinion the staff has now been divided into four distinct 'teams', each of which tends to have its own approach to influencing public policy. The energy team, for example, participates actively on various government boards and hearings, but an educational team that operates in Ward 3 of the City of Toronto, on the other hand, is deeply committed to the promotion of citizen participation.[28]

Here we see the intimate connection between group type, ideology, and membership characteristics. Formed around a specific issue (a particular problem of air pollution) and building on a strategy of starting with limited, 'clearly identified, highly visible local issues with which the public can readily identify before moving on to large issues of more far-reaching importance', Pollution Probe took the first step towards institutionalization: it broadened its mandate. But its membership—mainly young people inclined to take strong ideological positions—were oriented more to issues than to process. As the resolution of specific issues proceeded differently, ideological positions developed differently. In the energy sector, where some goals were achieved, members softened their ideological view of the tactics of change. This made them feel more effective; they understood, or felt they understood, how to make the system work for them. But where more resistance was encountered, their ideological orientation to confrontation became a commitment and they used their information more abrasively. Over time these divergent approaches produced cathartic tensions within the organization. Pollution Probe experienced 'horizontally' an information problem that the majority of groups experience 'vertically': the vertical information problem arises as leaders of issue-oriented groups become knowledgeable about the policy process, come to feel more effective in it, and consequently tend to move away from their followers—who begin to worry about the co-optation of the leadership. As one group leader put it, 'we're dealing with incredible anger . . . you have to play a game of taking swings at people just to keep the troops in line.'[29] It is not enough for leaders of pressure groups to have process knowledge; their followers should have it as well.

Pollution Probe offers an illustration of the interdependence of information and organizational characteristics in an issue-oriented group that is becoming institutionalized. The committee system used in the interest associations representing the chemical industry illustrates the way highly institutionalized groups structure themselves to convey technical information. According to Jacek and Coleman, the twenty-six interest associations active in the field involve representatives of their member firms in over 100 specialized committees dealing with matters that range from product development to the transportation of dangerous goods, consumer relations, taxation, planning, tariff matters, and so on.[30] The industry considers many of these committees crucial to the successful representation of its interests; companies are willing to underwrite the travelling expenses and time of their employees selected to serve on them. In certain cases company delegates come from the executive ranks. The Canadian Pharmaceutical Manufacturer's Association requires constitutionally that senior executives serve on its major committees. Coleman and Jacek found that for two associations 32.6 per cent of committee representatives were company presidents; 27.4 per cent were general managers; 24.2 per cent were vice-presidents; and only 15.8 per cent were divisional managers or held lower positions in the hierarchy. To support their activities twenty of the industry associations employed in 1979 an average of 4.85 permanent staff members, though the ten major associations employed an average of 7.25 permanent staff.[31] On the surface these figures seem modest, compared with the 30 permanent staff employed by the one union in the chemical field, the Energy and Chemical Workers' Union. However, it must be remembered that senior executives serving an industry association in this way can, and do, draw on company expertise to accommodate their committee assignments. Unions do not have these supplementary resources. Business-interest associations are expected to devote a considerable proportion of their energies to conveying information between members and government, as well as between members themselves; the scale and complexity of the effort they devote to information-processing alone is impressive. There can be no surer indication of its importance as an interest-group resource.

(ii) *Mandate*

Mandate is the other face of legitimacy. Legitimacy ensures that a group will be heard in policy conclaves, and mandate is the express assignment of representative capacity to a group's leadership by its membership.[32] As long as group spokesmen retain that mandate, what they say is the legitimate expression of the group will. If that mandate is withdrawn or over-reached their legitimacy is diminished—and to some extent so is that of the organization.

Mandate, however, does not depend entirely on membership support, any more than legitimacy is a function exclusively of that support. The other organizations the group deals with, including governments, can, by conferring recognition (legitimacy), also assign a mandate to the group. According to Kwavnick:

> The demands for organizational recognition made upon government by interest group leaders may overshadow the demands which they make in pursuit of the interests of their group's membership and are among the most important demands that they make.[33]

A labour union that wins the support of a collective-bargaining unit has a mandate from the members of that unit; therefore in the eyes of the unit's members the union has legitimacy. However, in the eyes of the public—and possibly in those of the management of the firm involved—true legitimacy is not achieved until the appropriate labour-relations board certifies the union and recognizes that it, and it alone, has the right to represent the employees in that bargaining unit. So it is with most pressure groups. Any entrepreneur can, by establishing an organization, claim to speak for a particular interest. Before being accepted by government as a bona fide spokesman, however, his or her credentials will have to be proven. It will have to be shown that the interest in question—or at least a recognizable part of it—has mandated the organization to speak for it. In other words, government must be assured that the organization adequately represents the interest it purports to speak for, and that the leadership of the organization is itself duly constituted. Failure to provide these assurances exposes government to the difficulties we enumerated in Chapter 4, where we discussed communication and legitimation as functions of pressure groups. On the other hand, once its mandate is secured and its legitimacy established, an organization can obtain from government supplementary mandates that reinforce its legitimacy with members, with government itself, and with other groups.

The quest for mandate, then, is crucially important to pressure group leaders and may lead them to take decisions that affect the structure and policies of the organization. We noted how Pollution Probe had diversified its organization in order to reduce tensions emanating from the different perceptions of strategy and tactics held by members. In part, diversification was an exercise in reasserting mandate. Elements that had difficulty working together on middle- and short-range goals might continue to adhere to the organization if they could work separately on those goals. Thus the overall mandate of the group would be maintained. There is an organizational parallel here with the Canadian Construction Association, a more complex, highly institutionalized group:

> One might wonder how the CCA came to exist at all, let alone survive for over half a century. If the industry was to be organized one would think that its various sections would have formed separate organizations rather than gathering together in one association. In fact, the CCA is unusual in this respect; it is the most comprehensive construction association in the non-communist world. In those other countries where construction associations exist at all, we normally find separate ones for each branch of the industry, many of which spend a good deal of time fighting one another.[34]

In the CCA such disputes are internalized, but not always successfully. By 1969 'it had become evident that most affiliates were either unable or unwilling to participate adequately in organizational structures which were primarily focused on the national level. The result was a deliberate decentralization of the CCA operations.'[35]

Not all group leaderships find decentralization an entirely satisfactory solution to the mandate problem. For many in the Canadian political system decentralization is essential, but not necessarily conducive to reaching agreement on global objectives. The leadership of the National Indian Brotherhood, for example, in working with a specially established federal Cabinet sub-committee to consider major Indian issues, found that its powerful provincial affiliates frequently challenged the mandate of national spokesmen and thus undermined the legitimacy of the NIB in the eyes of federal politicians and officials.[36] Faced with a similar problem, the Canadian Labour Congress responded by seeking to reinforce and extend the portion of its mandate derived from government:

> The weakness of the central organization, the limited role or *raison d'être* of the Congress and the fact that even this is subject to challenge by the larger affiliates and the AFL-CIO have resulted in an attempt by the Congress leadership to institutionalize the Congress as a recognized component of the Canadian political and social system. The ultimate aim . . . is to create a position for the Congress in the minds of the trade unionists, government and the public at large in addition to the position which the Congress occupies within the trade union movement.[37]

As these illustrations suggest, mandate as a resource is subject to constraints very similar to those that affect information as a resource: constraints that stem from the composition of the membership. Organization type and group ideology will affect positively and negatively the leadership's capacity to secure a firm mandate and thus to win recognition from government. At the same time, though, the leadership can secure, or at least reinforce, membership support if it obtains some token of recognition from government. For example, the Union of Nova Scotia Municipalities was established as a mechanism for transmitting the demands of member municipalities *upward* to the provincial government; but even though it was hampered by the reluctant support of some members, the UNSM found that an equivalent factor in securing legitimacy was the provincial government's decision to use the organization as a mechanism for the *downward* transmittal of government views to members. Government recognition and legitimation consequently encouraged member support.[38]

Our illustrations have also suggested some of the strategies used by groups to secure mandate. Clearly these can be too numerous to outline in detail here, but among the most important are:

1. Pursuing issues that members can identify with and that, while associated with larger goals, are limited enough to be resolvable through group action. This strategy is especially appropriate to new, small issue-oriented groups.

2. Development of selective inducements that may persuade members to remain loyal to the group even if they are not strong supporters of primary group objectives.

3. Diversification of goals in order to tap a larger membership pool.

4. Securing external recognition and material support. The former, whether obtained from government or from other groups, heightens legitimacy in the eyes of members; the latter gives group leadership some independence from the membership.

5. Decentralizing group organization along territorial and/or sectoral lines. As we have seen, this strategy creates difficulties of its own, but it broadens participation and helps to resolve conflicts within specialized committees and branch associations.

This list by no means exhausts the strategies available to groups in their efforts to create and bolster their mandates, but it suggests what can be done. In our discussion of organization and management we will consider how they are implemented.

(iii) *Wealth*

Lobbying is popularly associated with illicit distribution of wealth by 'monied interests' anxious to buy political favours. History has shown that this is often precisely what lobbying is all about, but it has also shown that the reality is more complex and that the monied interests are not the only ones that must be prepared to spend considerable sums to achieve their aims. In fact, the nefarious, cigar-smoking lobbyist who bribes public officials very likely spends far less than does the average public interest group which, with the purest of motives, seeks to persuade the community to follow what it conceives to be the community's own best interest. The lobbyist buys decisions, but the public-interest group buys policies—which are far rarer and far harder to obtain in the political market-place.

The point, of course, is that the object of any lobbying exercise cannot be obtained without the expenditure of money, or a money substitute, which for our purposes is the same thing. The modest issue-oriented group defending trees in an urban neighbourhood finds it needs financial resources, just as does the sophisticated, established, institutionalized group fighting its way with batteries of lawyers and consultants through law courts, regulatory bodies, agencies, and legislatures. The pertinent questions to ask, then, relate not to the expenditure of money—though it is important to know how much money must be spent—but to where it can be obtained. Broadly speaking, there are four principal sources:

1. Members
2. Friends
3. Governments
4. The sale of goods and services

We will look briefly at each of these sources and at what their assistance might mean for different kinds of interest organizations.

First, however, we must ascertain the costs of lobbying. Much depends on the type of lobbying. A high profile publicity campaign—such as that mounted internationally by various wildlife groups against the Canadian sealing industry—easily runs into millions of dollars. Less spectacular ongoing lobbying of one or two agencies is, naturally, much less expensive. Coleman and Jacek report that in 1979 the Canadian Soap and Detergent Association cost its backers only $8,000. Of the 20 business associations surveyed by Jacek and Coleman, the average expenditure in 1979 was $303,740, with the most costly, the Pharmaceutical Manufacturers' Association, spending $900,000. In addition, like most business-interest groups, they received various services free of charge from their members. The Petroleum Association for the Conservation of the Environment (PACE), for example, drew from its members some 216 executive man-days of work for each of its committees. At executive rates of pay such activities represent a substantial supplement to formal membership dues. Labour organizations do not as a rule have available money substitutes of this kind, but because their costs are spread across many thousands of members they can generate financial resources equal to, and often greater than, those of the larger business groups. Thus the poor relations in the interest-group family tend to be the smaller professional groups and many public-interest groups. Even they, however, will often work with budgets of over $100,000 a year.[39] Variable though they are, these figures give us an idea of the sums involved in run-of-the-mill interest representation and we can now turn to the question of where the money comes from.

First and foremost on the list of financial supporters are the group members themselves. This is so for two reasons. First, because membership implies a commitment, however modest, to sustain the group's organization in its endeavours, the organization can reasonably expect each member to contribute something—money, labour, or material—to its work. In addition, membership support is a symbol to the members of their own commitment, while to government and other groups it is one of the few indications of the extent to which the group represents the interest it claims to speak for. That is why politicians and officials often question group representatives closely about the number of dues-paying members and other supporters involved with their organizations.[40] Such inquisitions are intended to establish the organization's credentials.

Actual membership dues are often modest, particularly those of voluntary organizations. Labour and professional organizations that can employ an element of coercion to obtain members are generally more pressing in their demands, as are business-interest associations that provide a vital service to their supporters. Dues, in short, reflect what the market will bear. In the case of many public-interest groups, they also reflect a trade-off between the need for funds and the desire for representativeness: it is better to impress government with 30,000 members, each paying $15, than to fix dues at $50 and attract only 8,000 members. Other financial considerations may also dictate lower fees. Some selective inducements may be more feasible if offered to a larger market: for example, if a group publishes a trade journal a membership and subscription fee of $20 may not cover the costs of running both organization and journal; but securing a wider readership may guarantee that the organization can sell more advertising space—and at a higher price—to firms wanting to reach its membership.

Whatever the reasons for maintaining a low membership fee, the revenue derived from fees will not likely be enough to sustain the organization. Alternative sources of funding—some of which we will consider shortly under other headings—will have to be tapped. But other resources can be obtained from the membership itself. Most organizations include members who are more deeply committed than the majority and are prepared to donate their own time, the resources of their firms, or their own personal resources; some organizations can attract supplementary financial support in the form of donations, 'sustaining members' fees, and so on. Charitable foundations and public-interest groups can sometimes count as well on receiving bequests.

For many groups, friends as well as members are a source of support. This is particularly true of public-interest groups, the more affluent of which solicit through the mail, or through advertising campaigns, donations from individuals anxious to support their cause or from corporations that wish to be seen as 'good corporate citizens'. Sometimes such donations are given for specific projects, sometimes for the work of the organization in general. Friends may also include allied groups that are interested in promoting a particular cause but do not wish to undertake all, or even part, of the campaign themselves. Church organizations, for example, gave support to the issue-oriented groups promoting the Canadian recognition of Biafra during the Nigerian civil war, but they were reluctant to jeopardize their own ties with the Department of External Affairs by vigorously and publicly promoting the same cause.[41]

When the support of friends and members is insufficient to sustain the work of a group, the most likely alternative source of funds is government, particularly the federal government. Though such support is at times very generous, it is a mixed blessing; often it is a curse. In principle and in specific cases it arouses controversy, even when given with the best of intentions. For these reasons we should discuss government support in some detail.

Support from government can come in a variety of forms. Perhaps the most bizarre was the catch of squid used to suport the Eastern Fishermen's Federation (EFF) in its first years of operation. Until the late 1970s squid was not a species strongly exploited by Canadian fishermen. At the end of the decade, however, the Japanese sought permission to take squid off the East Coast. Permission was granted, but rights to the fish were given to the EFF, which then acted as middleman in selling the fish to the Japanese.[42] Less unusual forms of government support include secondment of personnel to specific groups—a practice more common in Europe than in Canada—or payment for specific services (such as research services, commissions on the sale of hunting licences, and so on).[43] In general, however, government assistance to groups comes in cash. Just how much is distributed by government to groups is not known. Marc Lalonde, as Minister of National Health and Welfare, once told a parliamentary questioner: 'each year the government receives (from groups) many applications for subsidies amounting to several hundred million dollars.'[44] Quite apart from direct grants, which are generally clearly identified in the Public Accounts, government funding can take the form of special subsidies for publications, consulting fees, subventions for hospitality at conferences, aid for specific projects, travel grants, and so on—the majority of which cannot easily be traced through the Public Accounts. Finally, government financial support is in many cases obtained indirectly through the tax system: businesses can treat association dues and employee involvement in business-interest groups as a legitimate business expense for tax purposes; individuals can deduct union and professional dues from gross income when calculating their taxable incomes; and contributions to a large number of public-interest groups are also tax deductible. In addition to federal government support, groups also receive similar assistance from provincial governments and, to a much more limited extent, from municipal authorities.

We tend to assume that public-interest groups are the ones most likely to receive government support, but this is not necessarily the case. Certainly there is ample evidence that they receive assistance. In 1979, for example, Monique Bégin, replying to a question in the House, revealed that the National Anti-Poverty Association had received $577,273 in grants and contributions from the federal government during the five preceding fiscal years.[45] A good deal of publicity has been given to the funds allotted to public-interest groups making representations to regulatory boards or to commissions of inquiry such as the Berger Commission.[46] Much has been made, as well, of the core funding provided to disadvantaged sections of the community, notably the various native peoples' associations. A glance through the federal and public accounts, however, very quickly reveals that these groups are by no means alone in receiving substantial governmental support. The vast majority of professional and academic groups, for example, derive a significant part of their revenues from government.[47] In many cases they could not exist otherwise. Even some business-oriented groups receive government assistance. We have already cited the support given to the Eastern Fishermen's Federation. Other groups in the same industry to receive assistance include the Nova Scotia Fishermen's Association—which received $50,000 from the provincial government to help organize independent fishermen—and the Bay of Fundy Herring Co-op.[48] In another field the federal and Alberta governments have provided the Sulphur

Development Institute of Canada with a substantial portion of its income since 1973 when it was first established; in that year 78 per cent of the association's income came from government, and six years later, in 1979, it still amounted to 50 per cent.[49]

Government financial support of interest groups raises two important questions. First, is it good for the groups? Second, is it good for democratic government? Because the two questions are closely intertwined, we will discuss them both here, though the second touches on issues that go far beyond the interior life of groups.

Briefly the answer to both questions is a qualified 'no'. In the long run groups do not benefit from being subsidized by government. Furthermore, government support may not promote dynamic public debate. And yet, if public funding were not available to some portions of the community, they would very likely not be heard from at all, which would weaken those sectors as well as the community at large. Consequently some means must be found whereby disadvantaged elements of the community can be heard—without jeopardizing the freedom of public debate.

Perhaps the best indication that public funding is bad for pressure groups is that experienced lobbyists shy away from it. As Don Gamble, director of policy studies at the Canadian Arctic Resources Committee, puts it: 'Interest groups should probably not rely on government for funding. It is unhealthy. Not only does it leave them vulnerable to a sudden policy change, but they might well find that the more effective they become, the faster their funding dries up.'[50] From the group perspective government funding has three serious disadvantages, all of which can be summed up in the word 'dependence': it makes groups flabby, vulnerable, and manipulable. They become flabby because the infusion of considerable sums of money can lead groups to over-extend themselves. They undertake new projects, hire additional staff, move to new quarters, participate in more advisory boards, and generally come to feel that they can do many things that were impossible in the years when they were almost totally dependent on member support. Having established good working relations with officials in their policy community, group leaders are tempted to believe that support will continue indefinitely; they lose the habit of running a lean operation and they stop looking for alternative means of support. In some cases, flushed with apparent success, they indulge in organizational and personal lifestyles that are beyond their means. Group members, too, contribute to the problem: dues are kept artificially low; expansion is approved without sufficient thought for long-term costs; and criticism of leadership extravagance may be muted by fear of reprisals, by the view that group leaders must not look like poor relations when they negotiate with others, and so on.[51]

A flabby organization is a vulnerable organization. As Gamble points out, policies may change suddenly. A new minister; a change of regime at the deputy and service chief levels; a shift in federal-provincial arrangements; a sudden public outcry affecting the group's policy field—all these and more can spell the imminent withdrawal of public funding. A group that has neglected to build up alternative sources of funding and has become over-extended can find itself looking at total collapse. Members may balk at a sudden drastic hike in fees, even when aware that they have been kept artificially low. Kindred groups, foundations, and other governmental agencies may be sympathetic but unable to rearrange their own priorities in time to bail out the sinking ship. This was the fate of the Canadian Council for Urban and Regional Research, which in the early 1970s built a considerable presence in the related policy fields of urban affairs and regional development. It initiated a number of research projects; published a journal in the field as well as several important research tools; and contributed to the lively public debate concerned with federal urban policy—which was probably its undoing, for by the mid-1970s senior officials of the Ministry of State for Urban Affairs let it be known that they wanted major changes in the structure, work, and orientation of the group. When these changes failed to materialize, MSUA funding was withdrawn, leaving the organization to struggle briefly on its own before succumbing.[52] Not all government-funded groups become this vulnerable, but in the majority of cases withdrawal of support would at the very least incur cutbacks in services, laying-off of employees,and extensive rethinking of goals and operations. In the long run these may be salutary, but at the time they are painful.

Any group leader or member who has lived through such experiences knows how easily a vulnerable group can be manipulated by those it looks to for assistance. At such times organizational survival becomes not the means of achieving group goals, but an end in itself, and group leaders are often tempted to comply with virtually any demand if it will ensure that end. This attitude is an extreme extension of the tendency of institutionalized group leaders to prefer returning to the bargaining table another day, rather than risk the 'credibility' of the organization in the eyes of those whose decision can make or break it. In the long run, however, an organization that buys survival at the price of fundamental independence eventually loses credibility in the eyes of its members at large and in the eyes of others in its policy community. Ultimately, unless it can regain its independence it must succumb, for an organization that is seen to be a creature of a government agency is distrusted for that very reason, and eventually ceases to be of value even to that last supporter.[53]

In short, an independent pressure group system is as important to competent and democratic government as are a dynamic party system and a free press. Every effort should be made to eliminate the agencies' existing opportunities for intimidation and manipulation, rather than add to them by encouraging interest groups to look to government for financial assistance.

Nevertheless there are occasions when the public interest is served by government funding of pressure groups. To insist that governments abstain entirely from assisting groups unable to afford the costs of participation would be to ensure that they could not participate and firmly establish the policy process as the domain of the wealthy and powerful. Clearly some middle ground has to be found between this extreme and the dangers of agency domination.

Several possibilities suggest themselves. One derives from the experience of regulatory tribunals and commissions of inquiry where, under closely defined conditions, groups receive short-term assistance to accomplish specific goals. The requirements of the Berger commission offer a useful model:

1. There should be a clearly ascertainable interest that ought to be represented . . .

2. It should be established that separate and adequate representation of that interest would make a necessary and substantial contribution . . .

3. Those seeking funds should have an established record of concern for, and should have long demonstrated their own commitment to, the interest they (seek) to represent.

4. It should be shown that those seeking funds (do) not have sufficient financial resources to enable them adequately to represent that interest, and that they would require funds to do so.

5. Those seeking funds should have a clearly delineated proposal as to the use they intend to make of the funds, and . . . be sufficiently well organized to account for the funds.[54]

Other possibilities include the application of 'sunset rules' to groups looking for seed money. In other words, a group might be granted sufficient funds to finance its initial operations for several years, but the funds allotted would be distributed on a declining scale, so that as the grant ran out the group's organizers would have to find alternative funding or give up. In situations where alternative funding is completely unavailable, and the public interest clearly dictates that an interest be heard, as in the case of poor people's groups, it might be possible to arrange necessary grants through systems of peer review, or perhaps to abandon a group approach altogether, in favour of an advisory board approach. In any event, whenever such support is necessary it should be made available in a manner that minimizes the group's dependence on the key agency in its policy field.

One final note on government support for interest groups: it is sometimes suggested that donations to interest groups should be more generally accepted as a deductible expense for income tax purposes. Some proponents go further and suggest that donations should be deductible from the tax itself, much as donations to political parties are deductible.[55] In theory at least, these proposals would do much to encourage public support for group participation in the policy process. They would not, however, entirely eliminate the need for government support for certain kinds of groups: the person too poor to buy a membership in an anti-poverty group is unlikely to derive much benefit from a tax deduction. Government assistance would still be necessary for groups representing such people.

The fourth and final means of raising funds essentially turns the group away from its primary thrust of serving its members and its secondary thrust of communicating with government. This is the practice of using the organization's strategic position to develop some sort of saleable commodity. Thus a group with a large membership can at times derive secondary revenue from the sale of selective benefits: life insurance for members, for example, or trade journals. Some groups take advantage of their position in the policy community to act as purveyors of information, either by organizing specialist seminars or by publishing specialized journals.[56] While not abundant, such opportunities present an alternative to the pitfalls of government funding and the risk of leaning too heavily on members and friends, but there is the danger that the group's entrepreneurial activities will supplant its other, more fundamental, functions.

ORGANIZATION AND MANAGEMENT

By outlining some of the factors that make each interest organization a unique part of the political community, we have tried to suggest the complexities surrounding the business of organizing, running, and leading groups. Combined with the variety of situations each group finds in its environment, these complexities make group management a fascinating but formidable task.

It is hard to say which feature of a group's interior life most closely defines the work of its leader, whether a full-time manager or a leader in the conventional sense. Membership characteristics; wealth or (more likely) lack of it; ideology; mandate; the nature of the policy field in which the group is situated—all establish boundaries to action and dictate the conditions under which the leader must work. But none, not even the task of carrying the group's goals into the political arena, will likely influence its leader, first, foremost, and continuously; they will be summed up in a presence that is palpable: the organization of the group itself. For the organization of the group is its membership. The organization expresses the strengths and weaknesses of the membership. It reflects the resources the membership can bring to bear, and its structure is the product both of their goals and of the environment in which those goals must be expressed. Supple or rigid; well-endowed or poor; newly created or well-established; issue-oriented or institutionalized—whatever its characteristics and qualities the organization is the instrument through which the leadership must give expression to the concerns of its supporters and achieve their goals.

Two features in particular of the many aspects of group organization will illustrate the challenges that face any group leader: the question of sectoral and territorial centralization versus decentralization, and the task of reconciling staff needs and goals with those of the members.

The first feature is endemic in Canadian group life. Even organizations that concern themselves only with the work of a single provincial government must contend with the divisive influence of territorial or sectoral particularism. Helen Jones Dawson's early study of the Consumers' Association of Canada demonstrates the extent to which the CAC reflects the problems of working in a political system with a strong central core and weak peripheral hinterlands.[57] She found intense feelings of isolation among eastern and western members of the association, and considerable resentment of the concentration of members from the central provinces on the board of directors. Other groups have similar problems, which are not lost on public officials: they frequently question the extent to which a group's leadership truly represents its national membership. Many, like the Canadian Construction Association, add sectoral differences to territorial cleavages. We have already quoted N.J. Lawrie on the effect of these divisions on the CCA, but it is worthwhile to present his views again:

> [Since World War II] the Canadian Construction Association's organiza-
> tional network [has extended] to encompass an impressive array of industrial
> and regional components. This has not satisfactorily reduced the association's
> remoteness from the industry; instead, it now finds itself in competition with
> a multitude of organizations for the attention and support of contractors. In its
> attempts to rationalize its relations with those competitors, the CCA has threat-
> ened to become a confederation of associations, characterized by a decreasing
> contact with individual firms. This may be a necessary price to pay for having
> a sizeable organization; in an industry so varied as construction and in a coun-
> try so large as Canada, it is difficult to see how any national association could
> remain at once highly centralized and broadly representative.[58]

Such tensions impinge heavily on the work of group leaders, and particu-
larly on key staff members. Not only must they spend a good deal of time visiting branch groups and accommodating their sensitivities; they must accept certain organizational inefficiencies in order to ensure the continued loyalty of important constituencies: for example, functions that could be managed more efficiently in a single place are sometimes dispersed across several provinces.[59] Such inefficiencies are not manifested solely in higher telephone bills and higher transportation costs between headquarters and branch office; unless the travel funds of the branch office match those of the head office, the branch may find itself less in touch with the general membership than the centre. In effect, it will be working only for a small local

part of the organization. And because it symbolizes the importance of the regional, or provincial, group, the branch office may resist direction from the central leadership and become a focal point for regionally based internal opposition to the leadership.

Sectoral cleavages are less likely to create such explosive organizational problems for group leaders, but they do produce tensions, which sometimes can be resolved only by allowing organizations to splinter into independent or loosely affiliated units. Thus the Canadian Library Association has become an organizational maze of regional bodies and large specialized sub-groups, such as those representing school librarians and public librarians, and lesser groups whose presence is intermittent and whose organizational status is vague.[60] Many academic associations, on the other hand, have split into independent groups. For example, the Canadian Political Science Association was once considered capable of representing not only political scientists but economists, sociologists, and anthropologists. Today three organizations represent those disciplines. Such divisions are the natural product of growth, but they inevitably interrupt the work of the group and create severe problems of resource dispersion, which group leaders must manage with minimum fuss.

Management of staff demands talents that are in many ways different from the diplomatic and political skills needed to keep a disparate organization functioning harmoniously. The most striking difference is the fact that the job of managing the staff belongs not to the group leadership as a whole but to the professional and permanent head of the organization. It is an internally oriented activity, and if it is managed successfully it is almost unnoticed by the membership. Nevertheless it is crucially important because for many members the attitude of the staff makes or breaks their affinity with the organization. The group manager who considers the members a necessary but tedious part of the organization will soon transmit that attitude to staff, among whom it may be magnified, prompting lack of courtesy in the treatment of members; disregard for their concerns; delay in handling inquiries; and the subordination of members' goals to those of staff. Also, the manager who exploits staff, or leaves personnel matters to an unsympathetic subordinate, is likely to create tensions in the office that can have very similar effects, leading gradually to a falling-off of membership participation and eventually of membership support.

Relations between staff and the group manager are crucial in many other ways. Few groups, for example, have staff resources commensurate either with their ambitions or with the projects they have in hand at any given moment. Consequently staff are called upon to do far more than would be expected of them in government or in the majority of large businesses. This applies as much to the secretary who must give up a weekend to type an important brief as to the specialist who has spent hours of overtime researching it and melding into it the members' divergent views. The group manager, as the one member of the leadership who is in daily contact with the staff and who is their representative before the board, can, by his or her actions, elicit willing, efficient staff support rather than the grudging and careless work that is often the response to inconsiderate pressure. Effective staff management includes the things one would expect of any competent manager: recognition of merit; constructive and sympathetic criticism of failures; support before the board; a flexible approach to the widely varying circumstances in which a group finds itself, and so on. A good manager has the ability to imprint on staff a loyalty to the organization; a sense of sharing in its identity; and a commitment to its goals—in short, an ability to so motivate staff that the organization makes the difficult metamorphosis from organization to institution that we discussed in Chapter 5. This is particularly important where professional staff is concerned. Since most group organizations cannot afford the high salaries that experienced, top-flight professionals command, they must depend on bright, energetic but inevitably inexperienced younger people. This is not necessarily a bad thing. Such people bring with them a vigour and a fresh outlook that are very important in the dynamic, often changing, world of pressure group politics. However, to produce results that will impress senior officials, politicians, group members, and spokesmen for rival groups, these specialists must stretch their talents to the utmost—often beyond what they themselves thought possible. It is a form of apprenticeship that demands of the 'master-lobbyist' considerable talents of leadership and instruction.[61]

A final aspect of the group's relationship with its staff that must be handled with care by the manager and the leadership as a whole is the natural and understandable tendency of staff to superimpose its own goals on those created by the membership. Staff, after all, are far more involved with the organization than are the majority of members. They work for it daily; they have, as a consequence of their strategic location in the information flow, a perspective far broader than that of most members; many are personally ambitious and tend to tie their own mobility to particular policy initiatives; and they are often influenced far more by the views of colleagues in the public service and other groups, whom they see daily, than by the members, whom they see sporadically at best. Their tendencies may be shared by the group manager, who is subject to many of the same influences. They are frequently the source of considerable tension within institutionalized organizations, capable of setting staff and membership at odds with one another unless handled with restraint by the group manager and the elected leadership.[62]

The complexities of group management indicate that the successful group manager must be a paragon of professional virtue, if such an individual exists. Even so, we have touched on only two aspects of the management task. We have not referred to the talents required to make limited financial resources go far beyond what might be reasonably expected; to superintend the development and provision of selective benefits; to organize the more commercial aspects of group work; or even to juggle personnel and staff resources in order to meet the constantly changing set of issues and problems that the group must deal with. Nor have we mentioned the outstanding diplomatic and political skills required by anyone who must lead the group in the public arena, negotiate with officials, and bargain with friendly and competing groups. Finally we have not mentioned the need for substantial, expert knowledge both of the policy field in which the group is located and of the policy process in which it must work. It is highly unlikely that many group managers possess all these talents Nevertheless the proliferation of pressure groups in the last twenty years shows that enough individuals with some of these talents have been available to build groups, to serve them, and to enhance their role in the policy process. There are even enough professional managers to warrant creation of their own interest organization, the Institute of Association Executives, which publishes a professional journal and concerns itself with professional development, conditions of work, and ethical issues. Between 1977 and 1982 its membership grew from 1,200 to 1,900—surely a sign that the recent expansion of the profession of group manager is likely to continue.[63]

Part III

Group Politics
and
Democratic Government

CHAPTER 9

Models of
Interest Representation:
Corporatism

Our experience with pressure groups demonstrates that in many ways they are indispensable to Canadian political life. It is hard to imagine how we could organize policy debate if pressure groups, with their specialized knowledge, did not focus discussion in policy communities. Even our political parties—always suspicious of pressure group influence—are indebted to them. Broad-based middle-of-the-road parties such as Canada's cannot easily reconcile the conflicting demands of their members, particularly when sectoral aspirations in one region clash with those of another. The existence of pressure groups enables party leaders to relegate potentially divisive issues to 'technical levels' where they can be defused piecemeal by officials and interest group representatives.[1] As well, pressure groups are far more sensitive than either political parties or government bureaucracies to subtle shifts in public opinion. For individual citizens they are a more flexible vehicle for articulating policy demands. From the authorities' perspective they offer quick access to public opinion. That same flexibility and sensitivity allow them to render service to the political system generally, helping it recognize and adjust to the changing needs of the community.

Inevitably there are drawbacks. There are great disparities in pressure group influence. Some pressure groups represent individuals and organizations that already possess immense economic power, which gives them a status in the polity beyond that of other groups. Such powerful groups assume that their access to senior policy-makers is a right, not a privilege, and their participation in key decisions becomes a matter of course. To the problem of inequality between groups we must add the problem of group legitimacy and mandate. Is a particular group genuinely supported by the people it says it represents? Have they given it the mandate it claims? Public officials are often at a loss to evaluate these crucial aspects of group intervention in policy-making. Meanwhile the public at large must be concerned about the affinity between groups and the bureaucracies they work with. Does working together lead to scheming together? Do group leaders and bureaucrats manage the public and its elected representatives?

The dynamic of the sub-government makes this a possibility. How can the public monitor the relationship? Finally, there is the difficulty of assigning roles to pressure groups and political parties. The vitality of the party system has caused concern for years.[2] The hoopla of party politics cannot conceal the fact that the party rank and file long ago ceased to play an effective role in policy formation and that the vacuum has been filled by pressure groups and the bureaucracy. Party leaders see that constituency organizations lose touch with the policy concerns of individual voters, and that the party thereby loses sensitivity to public opinion, loses status and support, and appears not to be interested in ordinary Canadians. Resources disappear. Civic-minded individuals devote their time, money, and energy to organizations that seem to care more about their public-policy goals and are better prepared to achieve them. The net effect is to make pressure groups competitors of political parties and to lead thoughtful Canadians to worry about the danger of Canada's becoming a special interest state.

Their concerns can be expressed in many ways, but fundamentally they revolve around a single question: What form of representation is to be paramount in the Canadian state, representation by sector or representation based on place? On the face of it there can be only one answer: the constitution provides for a system of representation based on the election of legislators from geographically defined constituencies. No other system of representation has legitimacy. Sectoral representation, however, has become a potent force. We have seen that bureaucratic influence in the Canadian policy process is extensive, as it is in most industrialized countries. We have also seen that the natural constituency for bureaucracy is the sectorally oriented policy community. Together specialized bureaucracies and their surrounding policy communities are powerful—conceivably powerful enough to be, *de facto*, the paramount system of representation—which makes the problem of representation a crucial one for the Canadian state.

Does this justify putting the problem of representation at the centre of a discussion of the role of pressure groups in the Canadian political system? It does, because in democracies the legitimacy of the state rests on public understanding that the government of the day serves with the formal consent of the governed and is chosen through a process of election in which all citizens have an equal opportunity to select members of a house of representatives, which is responsible for determining fundamental policy and for monitoring the government as it carries them out. Even though we recognize that the complexity of modern public policy prohibits the legislature from actually formulating policy, or supervising its implementation on a daily basis, the legislature is, in the final analysis, able to hold the government accountable for its actions. As long as the general public believes that these conditions prevail, it will consider that the government of the day is legitimate and will accept and abide by its decisions.

Interest group politics threatens the legitimacy of the state when it undermines these broad understandings. Bureaucratic expertise coupled with that of private interests makes the policy community a significant counterweight to the authority of the legislature, even though the legislature derives its legitimacy from the constitution and from its quality as an elected representative body. When the representativeness of its interest group members is added, the policy community acquires an authority that may challenge that of the elected legislature. Ministers and officials often characterize the policy community as 'the functional constituency',[3] a term that implies not only comparability with the constituencies of legislators but a similar legitimacy. Even though the policy community is not truly representative of the sector for which it speaks, its ability to be seen as the 'functional constituency' diminishes the legitimacy of the legislature.

Policy communities do not usually challenge directly the authority of elected legislatures. Frontal attacks would fail in the face of constitutional rights and the legitimacy of election. Nevertheless policy communities do steadily undermine the legislature's authority. By seeking to obtain delegated authority to implement the details of broadly expressed legislation, the policy community acquires an extensive, virtually unsupervised territory for policy-making. This practice has troubled thoughtful democrats for decades.[4] There has been a tendency for ministers and senior officials—who today seek the support of Parliament to a degree that they never did in the past—to come to legislatures armed with the support of the functional constituency. Their claims that 'the affected interests' have been consulted and have agreed to the policies proposed are difficult to refute—especially for legislative committees, whose members have little knowledge of a field. Legislative committees thus have little opportunity to escape the confines of specialization and to consider proposals from the perspective of the broad public interest, while policy communities, through their specialization and the claims they can make because of consultation, effect a steady attrition of real legislative authority. As the public learns the extent of the attrition, it loses confidence in the legislature's ability to monitor government and to review policy. The public also realizes that the policy community by no means fairly represents all the interests its decisions affect—and that the people are being governed through an unequal distribution of power. As a consequence the public's confidence in the legitimacy of the system as a whole dwindles.

Our investigation of pressure group politics began with expressions of the fears aroused by these developments. We then traced the developments themselves and looked at some of their root causes. Now we will examine how practitioners and theorists have tackled these issues and will work out some remedies of our own.

All theorists and practitioners do not, of course, diagnose the problem in exactly the way that has been done here. For several, whom we quoted at the beginning of the book, the issue is one of the rivalry between parties and pressure groups. Others are concerned about illicit influence. Many theorists, focusing on the state's desire to organize functional constituencies and to look for corporatist structures that are truly representative of the sectors for which they speak, pay little attention to traditional representative institutions. Others, writing out of the pluralist tradition, conceive of a less structured, more dynamic group politics than do the corporatists. They share with the corporatists an underlying concern with representation, but recently have shown greater interest in the effects of inequality between groups. Not all of them worry about the decline of legislative authority. American scholars, for example, can still maintain that in the iron triangles that constitute the sub-government, legislative committees are at least as influential as pressure groups and executive agencies. Two British scholars, on the other hand, have gone so far as to suggest that their political system is a 'post-Parliamentary democracy'.[5]

We will look first at the corporatist discussion. Here we see a highly structured system of sectoral representation that makes some attempt to achieve equity beween participants. We conclude that Canada is not, cannot—and should not—be corporatist. We next examine the traditional pluralist position, which we find equally unappetizing. It does not overcome the deficiencies of representation and inequality that we found in our system. Models of the policy process developed by critics of pluralism, like the model of policy communities elaborated here, clearly indicate that the deficiencies originally noted in pluralism have been exacerbated in the evolution of sectoral representation. Nevertheless we must admit that some features of pluralism serve a necessary purpose and that we have to live with them despite their deficiencies. Our task then becomes one of trying to build equality into the system; of creating safeguards against the usurpation of legislative power by policy communities; of strengthening the capacity of weaker groups to exert influence on policy communities; and, above all, of enhancing the role of the legislature. To address that task we must return to the problem of representation, depicting it in terms of two contending systems: the representation of space and the representation of sector. We will argue that in our political system spatial representation must be paramount, but that sectoral representation cannot be discarded. Therefore remedies for the inequities of sectoral representation must be developed and the diffusion of power must be used to provide an opportunity for legislatures to reassert their influence.

WHAT IS CORPORATISM?

A striking feature of modern politics is the extent to which government institutions seek to organize the political world. In democracies as well as in totalitarian states, in countries espousing 'free enterprise' as well as in socialist systems, governments arrange the way in which various interest communities communicate with public authorities. Elaborate formal structures—often called corporatist structures—have at times been created to regulate communication and economic decision-making, as is the case in Austria, Germany, and the Scandinavian countries. In other countries the structure of *concertation*, as the French call it, is not as rigidly defined, but there is nevertheless an intimate and continuous liaison, much of it initiated and regulated by the state, between government agencies and the groups they consider to have an interest in the development of specific aspects of policy. In Britain, Canada, and the United States pluralist approaches are still prominent. That is, governments expect interests to organize themselves as the need arises and to compete with one another for government attention and for influence. Even so, many government agencies in these countries have encouraged some groups to organize themselves and others to expand, and there has been talk of creating more structured relationships similar to those found in northern Europe. More of such talk has been heard in Britain and Canada than in the United States. But even there not only have steps been taken to ensure that certain kinds of groups, such as those promoting the public interest, receive special support, but elaborate, though informal, systems of consultation exist in every field of policy.[6]

The development of highly structured relationships—even the more modest instances of government encouragement of groups that we see in Canada—has set off several important debates. Many observers ask whether these changes are symptomatic of fundamental changes in the nature of the state. Some ask whether the state is being forced to share power more as the activities of government increase and the state becomes more obtrusive; is the state itself less authoritative?[7] Others, particularly in countries like Canada, where the state has never been very obtrusive, ask whether the state is becoming *dirigiste*, as it is in Europe.[8] That is, are government bodies, working through planning exercises and with interest groups, gradually becoming more and more capable of directing every aspect of our daily lives? Still others look at more immediate and less fundamental aspects of these developments, asking the kind of questions we raised in the first chapter: are we witnessing the development of new systems of representation—systems for more effectively bringing sectoral concerns to public attention? If we are, what are the implications for party politics and, above all, for Parliament?

There are many different interpretations of the origins and implications of these developments. It has become customary, however, to divide the proponents of specific interpretations into two classes: the corporatists and the pluralists. Corporatists emphasize the state's role in determining group participation in policy formation and execution, while pluralists focus on the voluntary, competitive, and unorchestrated quality of group involvement in the policy process. However, dichotomizing the various approaches in this way—largely the work of corporatist scholars—oversimplifies both schools of thought, particularly the views of the pluralists, and ignores subtle but important aspects of policy-making:[9] the corporatists tend to ignore the dynamism of the policy system, which is a favourite theme of the pluralists; but the pluralists have no effective explanation of the role of government in promoting and orchestrating group involvement in policy-making. Neither side has properly considered the influence of the bureaucracy in promoting the changes that spark so much heated debate. Despite these problems we shall tolerate the conventional terminology, considering the corporatist argument first.

The first and most difficult problem for anyone investigating the applicability of corporatist ideas to Canada is that of definition. What is corporatism? A great deal of time is spent on this question, which suggests that the concept is less generally applicable than was at first supposed. Furthermore, scholars in various parts of the world have concluded that though the concept says something about their own political systems, it does not say as much as they had hoped.[10] Although we agree essentially with that conclusion, we intend to explore the concept briefly because, despite its deficiencies, it contributes to our understanding of government's growing tendency to orchestrate the relations between groups and the state. Hence we too must dwell a little on the problem of definition.

The most widely accepted definition has been developed by Philippe Schmitter, who sees corporatism as

> . . . a system of interest representation in which the constituent units are organized into a limited number of single, compulsory, non-competitive, hierarchically ordered and functionally differentiated categories, recognized or licensed (if not created) by the state and granted a deliberate representational monopoly within their respective categories in exchange for observing certain controls on their selection of leaders and articulation of demands and support.[11]

This complex definition consists of the following elements:

1. The relationships between the state and the many interests in the community are organized into a system of representation. A structure is consciously imposed on them, which allows some groups to have a recognized role in policy communication and to count on being heard, while other groups are not recognized in the same way and cannot count on being heard. In terms of the continuum framework we developed in Chapter 5, institutionalized groups would probably fit into the first category, but issue-oriented groups generally would not.

2. In this system each group is recognized as having certain kinds of expertise and acquires a role consistent with that expertise. Most, for example, represent quite specialized interests—the United Auto Workers of Canada

might be deemed to represent auto workers, the Canadian Brotherhood of Railway Transport and General Workers some railway workers, and so on—and are expected to speak for those interests. Each of these functionally differentiated groups monopolizes its field, but is expected to co-operate with other groups in such a way that agreement can be reached on their collective views and demands and can be represented to government and to other peak associations by a few superordinate associations, such as the Canadian Labour Congress. This hierarchical system filters policy ideas and proposals in order to reduce them to manageable proportions at the bargaining table. In the process many groups find that demands important to them have been ignored or grossly altered. They generally tolerate such abuses, partly because this is a bargaining process, which—like any other—involves compromises and even the loss of valued position, but also because the system accords each group a definite status and a monopoly position as spokesman for a particular interest community. To object too frequently and too strenuously about the way the system works not only antagonizes other actors, but may lead them to redefine the status of the group and even to reduce its monopoly.

3. This complex of rewards and punishments holds the system together. The state recognizes the monopoly of functional groups but assumes in return that they will respect the hierarchical authority of peak associations. For the latter, participation in the policy process entails not only the advantages of being recognized as the sole peak association in its field, but the responsibility of ensuring that its membership accepts the decisions reached by the state and the peak associations. Participation also involves maintaining a degree of representativeness consistent with popular ideas of legitimacy, which is extremely important because in the long run the acceptability of the policies devised through corporatist processes depends on the extent to which the public at large feels these policies have been properly arrived at. If the general public believes that the developers of public policy are not properly representative of those they speak for, the policies will be considered illegitimate. For this reason the state insists that groups participating in corporatist exercises accept externally devised standards of representativeness and due process.

Schmitter identifies two kinds of corporatism: state corporatism and societal corporatism. State corporatism comes from 'above', from authorities at the centre of power who consciously try to create a system of group-state relations through which they can control and dominate the various interests in the community.[12] At its most extreme, state corporatism resembles the highly structured relationships created by the Fascist regimes in Italy and, to a lesser extent, in Germany. In Italy Mussolini subdued a strong labour movement by transforming various unions and professional groups into corporations that, along with similar groupings of business interests, were substituted for traditional political parties, becoming in effect instruments of the state. They did not survive the restoration of parliamentary government after the Second World War.[13] Schmitter points out that since state corporatism entails almost complete loss of autonomy for hitherto independent associations and may, as in the Fascist states, involve their suppression, it is usually resisted and is unlikely to be effective in the long run. In his view societal corporatism is a more feasible system for harmonizing relations between the state and interest communities. This type of corporatism develops from 'below': from the gradual evolution of 'interassociational demands and intraorganizational processes'.[14] It is the product of the will of associations to achieve consensus among themselves and, in conjunction with government authorities, to agree on public policy and on their own interrelations. This view of corporatism is the one most commonly adopted by present-day scholars. It has the advantage of presenting the development of structures for state-group relations as an interactive process—the product not simply of the state's desire to create order in its communications with its many publics, but of an equally vigorous desire by the business and labour communities in particular to build institutions of communication that not only strengthen their hand in their relations with the state, but help to protect them from its full coercive authority.[15]

For some Marxist students of corporatism the practice of corporatism occurs only in relation to the class struggle, so that it 'mainly pertains to economic policy-making and it is those associations which are based directly on the social division of labour that are drawn into such structures'.[16] Corporatism is, in short, a device through which capital, acting in concert with the state, co-opts working-class organizations and contrives to contain the power of the working class.[17] From our point of view this restriction of the term reduces its utility.[18] We can agree that modern industrial democracies concentrate on economic policy, and that in developing it many states have refined their systems of interaction with key actors in business and labour to a point that is far more institutionalized and representative than that achieved in any other field of public policy.[19] The development of such tripartite structures facilitates the legitimation of economic policy. But corporatism, as defined by Schmitter, captures aspects of state-group relations that are reflected in no other term currently used to describe the totality of relations between the state and interest communities. In particular, the term expresses the will of both government officials and interest representatives in all fields to avoid conflict in the development and implementation of policy, and to do so by creating monopolistic representative groups working through formal structures for collaboration.[20] Because of this we will use Schmitter's term to refer to all forms of corporatism, regardless of where they occur; however, we will use the term 'tripartism' to designate those forms of corporatism concerned exclusively with the development of economic policy.

CORPORATIST TRENDS IN CANADA

At first glance corporatism seems to have very little to say about Canadian politics. We tend to think of ourselves as adhering generally—though a little less tenaciously than our neighbours—to the liberal, pluralist ideology that dominates the United States. We recognize that our governments play a larger part in the economy than does American government, but we tend to agree with Whitaker when he describes this form of intervention as little more than 'private ownership at public expense'.[21] The idea that public policy should be concocted through a system of interest representation such as that defined by Schmitter offends our notions of legitimacy, which hold that public policy should be developed by Cabinet and approved by Parliament. Our reactions when confronted with corporatist, particularly tripartite, proposals have been distinctly negative.

Nevertheless there is a strain of corporatism in Canada, both at the level of ideas and in actual practice. Furthermore, given the fact that corporatism seems to be associated with advanced industrial economies, such as Canada's, it is possible that corporatist trends will strengthen in the years ahead. Consequently we must look closely at what corporatism means in and for Canada.

There are two schools of thought about whether Canada has experienced the historical process to sustain corporatism today. Panitch argues that this country's ideological orientation has always been antagonistic to corporatism and that recent attempts to institute corporatist practices have been the product of new economic forces and have fallen on stoney ground. Robert Presthus and Jack McLeod, however, believe that while it may be an exaggeration to claim for Canada 'a complex and lengthy historical process' leading towards corporatism, the soil is more fertile than Panitch would have us believe. For Presthus corporatism

> . . . is essentially a conception of society in which government delegates much of its functions to private groups, which in turn provide guidance regarding the social and economic legislation required by the modern national state . . . Its essential ingredient is an underlying pluralism which gives groups both normative and functional legitimacy in the political system.[22]

Panitch convincingly argues that this definition is too broad, and that the evidence Presthus musters is inconclusive or even contradictory. However, Presthus's observations deserve to be taken a little more seriously than this, because he is comparing Canada with the United States, and finds a stronger orientation towards corporatism in this country than south of the border. This impression is worth noting. It partially accounts for the greater willingness of Canadians to permit the state to structure its relations with groups, and even to take a hand in creating them.

McLeod's argument is also basically impressionistic:

The essence of corporatism is private or capitalist ownership coupled with state control. Various functional groups are brought into harmony and into more or less direct collaboration with the state, with the will of the state (as the supreme agent of the community) being ultimately decisive. With private property left undisturbed, the objective is to obviate strife or schism between business, labour and the state. Instead of competition between classes or aggressive competition between individuals and groups, corporatism seeks to substitute principles of social harmony and unity through negotiation between capital, labour and the state, usually within tripartite structures. Emphatically the free play of the market is reduced and the state becomes dominant. Cooperation must replace competition; if not, cooperation will be imposed and commanded by the state.[23]

Panitch also finds this definition too broad because, while Canada has indeed experienced a great deal of 'private ownership coupled with state control', its form in this country has been generally pluralist. He warns that the 'normal interest-group and regulatory-agency characteristics of any advanced capitalist polity' should not be mistaken for tri-partism,[24] and points out that McLeod has to conclude that instead of corporatism in Canada 'there seems to exist a strong recurrent desire to create tripartite institutions of a symbolic (if often toothless) kind at the centre of our political economy.'[25]

Panitch is not persuaded by either Presthus or McLeod that Canada has experienced the historical development that leads to corporatism. He is willing to acknowledge some ideological background for corporatism, but finds it in Québec Catholicism, agrarian populism, and Mackenzie King's Liberalism, rather than in the shades of Loyalist 'Toryism' where Presthus and McLeod find it. Panitch identifies two periods when corporatist ideas have reached the public agenda: in the ten years between the First World War and the Depression, and in the 1970s.[26]

During the first period corporatist ideas were espoused by the Catholic Church, which in Québec, as in several European countries, applied them to trade-union organization.[27] Later these ideas were taken up by Duplessis, who spoke in terms of abolishing Québec's upper House and replacing it with 'an advisory economic council in which all "corporations" would be grouped to formulate policy for the economy as a whole'. These corporations would be associations of employers and employees in each industry, and would have 'considerable authority to make decisions regarding prices, wages, and general policy for the industry'.[28] On the Prairies corporatism appealed to the farm community, which saw in it a means to eliminate the corruption of traditional parties and the influence of the eastern interests. The United Farmers of Alberta, like Duplessis some years later, advocated government through groups. In Ottawa no less a figure than Mackenzie King came to the leadership of the Liberal Party with corporatist ideas in mind. Industry, he argued in *Industry and Humanity* (1918), should be controlled by a 'partnership' of labour, capital, management, and the community. As Panitch has demonstrated, none of these proposals were ever put into effect or even seriously discussed, despite their having been suggested by leaders who could have taken steps to implement them.[29]

In the 1970s Canadian interest in corporatism was rekindled—partly as a result of concern over the direction of economic development, and partly as a reflection of institutional imperatives. For Panitch the revival was rooted in the class struggle, notably capital's growing need to channel and contain the demands of workers. The years following the Second World War had created conditions—'a stronger organized working class, conditions that the government considered to be full employment, inflationary pressures, a squeeze on private capital accumulation, the failure of "stop-go" '—similar to those that had fostered corporatist developments in Western Europe.[30] Nevertheless corporatism, in Panitch's view, did not develop. Beginning in 1968 Prime Minister Trudeau initiated discussions with business and labour leaders that eventually led to the creation of the Prices and Incomes Commission; this body, though not tripartite, 'set about a series of meetings with the organizations of business and labour to secure agreement and co-operation in a price and wage restraint program'.[31] Despite some minor successes, the project was constrained by labour's refusal to support it and was abandoned at the end of 1970.

As inflationary difficulties increased during the early 1970s the government again sought tripartite arrangements, but despite generous participatory inducements labour again resisted, 'finding little substantive response to their demands for cheaper housing, higher pensions, full-employment policies . . . and close controls over corporate investment to create jobs.'[32] The Anti-Inflation Program that followed not only earned bitter criticism from labour, and a total denial of support, but led labour to withdraw from the few tripartite bodies that had been established, notably the Economic Council of Canada. Even so, the dispute served to familiarize Canadians with corporatist, and particularly tripartite, concepts. Both labour and government sought a mechanism for achieving tripartite consultation, though neither side was willing to go as far as the other wanted. The Canadian Labour Congress edged towards large-scale social and economic planning under tripartite auspices, while the government, protesting that constitutionally it could not share power and that the CLC proposals would undermine Parliament's role in policy-making, sought safety in numbers and proposed a multi-partite 'consultative forum'. Based on a combination of regional and sectoral representation, the forum would consist of 30 to 50 members and would discuss economic policy. In 1977 the Department of Industry, Trade and Commerce followed up the consultative forum proposal by initiating 'Enterprise 77', a series of interviews with leading businessmen. In response to the very critical view of government that emerged from this exercise, Ottawa embarked on a more elaborate consultative process—known as the Tier I and Tier II discussions—built around the work of 23 task forces, each of which examined the government/business partnership in a particular sector of the economy. According to Coleman and Jacek, business at least was impressed with the 'seriousness with which the government took this exercise'. They concluded that some federal officials had been encouraged to consider creating 'a permanent structure for consultation that can only be described as "corporatist" '.[33] At the very least these initiatives are, in Panitch's words, 'indicative of the tendencies toward corporatism in Canada'.[34]

Brown, Eastman, and Robinson are more cautious. The exercises provided governments with a 'wealth of information' about the private sector's view of the problems and challenges facing Canadian industry, but the sector reports did not 'present government with a basis for making decisions about which sectors should be encouraged to lead economic recovery'.[35] Furthermore, the consultative process used in Tier I 'encouraged each sector task force to make a special case for itself, and worked against the formulation of recommendations which would permit government to choose between sectors and between firms'.[36] The second round of consultations (Tier II) led to 'uneasy compromises' that testified to 'the difficulties involved in formulating proposals for manufacturing industry as a whole'.[37] Brown, Eastman, and Robinson conclude that the 1978 exercise barely went beyond elementary consultation. Certainly 'a broad joint consensus on objectives for industrial policy' was not achieved.[38] The Tier II consultations were, however, 'a step toward more effective collaboration on economic and industrial issues'.[39] They did involve much closer collaboration than had occurred previously—at least within a framework of discussion cutting across sector policy fields—but they were a long way from corporatism itself.

Even less can be said of the 1985 economic summit organized by the Mulroney government. First suggested in 1979 by Robert de Cotret, then Minister of State for Economic Development in the Clark government,[40] the National Economic Conference brought to Ottawa representatives of most sectors of Canadian society. Primed with a series of background papers prepared by government and many of the participating groups, the delegates were expected to address, on national television and radio, an agenda that extended across the economic spectrum. This they did, but with disappointing results. The media and many delegates themselves concluded that most speakers had time only to present established group positions. Dialogue did not take place, much less a movement towards consensus. From a corporatist perspective, however, the exercise did demonstrate an interesting feature: because the number of places at the conference were limited, emphasis had to be placed on major national associations and collectivities of associations. In other words, the conference may have contributed to the development and recognition of peak associations.[41]

Panitch considers fundamental economic forces to be responsible for the limited drift to corporatism observable in Canada today. These may be the underlying forces propelling Canadian governments to undertake tripartite discussions. However, it is important not to 'underestimate the extent to which the impact of new policies depends on the institutional framework within which they are to be used'.[42] Fundamental economic forces may push public policies remorselessly in a particular direction; but the speed with which new approaches are adopted and the extent of their impact at any one time will be affected by the institutional environment in which they are applied. Hence, it is significant that the corporatist solutions proposed in the 1970s came from a new source: the central policy structures. They should therefore be taken more seriously than earlier proposals, for they reflect the views of people and organizations actually engaged in the manipulation of power, rather than those of individuals seeking power and likely to revise their opinions once they have come to grips with the realities, and the pleasures, of office. When the Privy Council Office, for example, issues a document such as *The Way Ahead*, which advocates tripartism, and when the central authorities in the Government of Québec manage to stage a series of high-level meetings organized along tripartite lines, it is clear that corporatist concepts have wafted into the corridors of power and have inspired some of the strategic thinking that goes on there.[43]

Undoubtedly corporatist approaches appeal to 'superbureaucrats'. There is some evidence that 'in advanced capitalist, highly industrialized societies, there is a strong positive relationship between a societal corporatist mode of interest intermediation and relative governability'.[44] That is, where interests can be organized into a hierarchical, monopolistic system for determining and reconciling demands, there is less evidence of popular unrest and some indication that public policies can be effectively implemented.

> Rather than proliferating the 'number of citizens' and the 'sphere of interests', the modern conservative ruler concerned with governability would diminish their number, encourage their centralization and concentration of authority, grant them privileged monopolistic access, and, above all, extend the sphere of governance by licensing or devolving upon them powers to take decisions binding on their members and even on non-members. In this way 'responsible' private governments can collaborate in controlling citizen-initiated protest and in ensuring proper fiscal discipline and management.[45]

Regime governability is not the sole factor that makes corporatism appealing to central policy actors. It also enhances their control of bureaucratic processes. As the term 'superbureaucrats' implies, the men and women working at the centre of the policy process have taken on far more than they can possibly handle.[46] The tasks of serving the political executive and of co-ordinating the processes of policy formation are in themselves monumental. When one adds the tasks of monitoring the implementation of policy and of participating in the inevitable refinement of policy that accompanies implementation, the pressures of the job become overwhelming. And they cannot be relieved simply by adding staff. 'Policy shops' have to be small, talented, and flexible, otherwise they lose the capacity to cope with the rapidly changing pace of the public agenda. Officials of line departments watch with satisfaction as 'the best and the brightest' struggle with their burden. They know that each time a central agency decides to review, or intervene in, the policies administered by line departments, the experience is traumatic but brief.[47] The attention span of central agencies is mercifully short and before too long line officials are back in the driver's seat of a vehicle that may be a little battered—or perhaps even improved— but is once again 'theirs'. Together with their closest interest groups they take charge of the policy field again and do what they can to discourage further depredations by 'whizz kids'.

At the centre this state of affairs is known and distrusted. It is a constant challenge to the capacity of the executive to develop public policy and to be confident that it is being properly implemented. Yet for the reasons we have outlined central officials can do very little about the tendency for power to revert to line agencies. Corporatism offers a solution. By creating a hierarchy within the pluralistic world of interest representation, senior officials can reduce the number of contacts they must have with the interest community to a level compatible with their own resources. At the same time a hierarchical ordering of interests can be used to reduce the number of policy options to be presented to key decision-makers. Thus the efficiency of the policy process can be maintained and even heightened. More important, however, is the possibility that a properly functioning corporatist system will shift bureaucratic power back from the line agencies to the centre. This is because the central policy structures have much more to offer peak associations in the way of recognition, material assistance, and positional rewards than do the line departments. As long as the peak associations can control the centripetal tendencies of their junior affiliates, and as long as the central policy structures can absorb the flood of information that must be mastered if a particular policy field is to be properly served, then it is likely that the centre and the peak associations can maintain a mutually supportive corporatist system.

One final factor makes the corporatist strategy attractive to those who run the central policy structures. It enhances their legitimacy. As we noted in Chapter 3, the diffusion of power that has come to characterize Canadian government brings with it a diminution of the legitimacy of the Cabinet and the public service. In the search for legitimating institutions that ensues, bureaucratic agencies not only look to Parliament for support, but they seek to reinforce the representative capacity of their own associates. For the line departments this is quite easily done. Because they have many contacts with their 'constituency' they need merely to formalize these relationships and to ensure that they encompass everyone who might claim to have a direct interest in the policies administered by each agency (a process we will shortly discuss in detail). This option is not open to the central policy agencies. Lacking the capacity to maintain communications with entire policy communities, and having no direct authority to minister to their day-to-day needs, the central agencies cannot maintain policy communities across the spectrum of government activity. Their only alternative is to build hierarchical structures along corporatist lines, which encompass a good deal of interaction between line agencies and sector organizations in matters of policy detail and program administration, but which are unequivocally associated with the centre on matters of major policy. The centre thus gains a constituency but avoids the burden of administrative detail that comes with running a policy community.

There are three strong reasons why central policy structures should favour corporatist approaches to policy formation: first, they enhance governability; second, they facilitate central control of line agencies; and third, they enhance the legitimacy of the centre. The trend towards corporatism was not solely the ineluctable result of economic movements; it also reflected the contest for power—both in Ottawa and in several provincial capitals—between central policy structures and line departments.[48] In Ottawa the Privy Council Office, Treasury Board, and the Department of Finance had sought for twenty years to co-ordinate and control the activities of line departments, with only limited success. They had also battled among themselves for primacy at the centre. In these struggles corporatist approaches appeared to offer powerful tools for central domination. It is hardly surprising that they should have been promoted by the centre. Institutional factors, as well as the more fundamental economic ones, explain Ottawa's recent interest in tripartism.

Canadian discussions of corporatism use the narrow definition of the term, embracing exclusively economic policy and the tripartite form of interest intermediation. If we allow ourselves a little more latitude we can, while staying within the confines of Schmitter's definition, observe other tendencies towards corporatism. For example, we can see in the field of research and education a number of movements towards close co-operation among interest organizations and some effort to create peak associations. SCITEC, an organization dedicated to promoting the expansion of Canada's efforts in research and development, was established in the early 1970s by the leaders of several interest groups and with the support of the Science Council of Canada, a government-sponsored advisory board comparable to the Economic Council of Canada, and the Ministry of State for Science and Technology. Initially SCITEC sought to act as a peak association for the social sciences as well as the natural and applied sciences, but it was eventually content to co-operate with social-science bodies in promoting policies designed to encourage research and development.[49] The social sciences, while resisting the blandishments of SCITEC, have nevertheless found it convenient to engage in a multitude of co-operative endeavours and to create the Social Science Federation of Canada, which might be loosely termed a peak association. The Federation, governed by representatives of the constituent associations, provides them with certain services, such as organizing annual meetings of all the 'learned societies' at which academics present research papers to one another, hold earnest meetings on the 'state of the discipline', organize themselves professionally, and so forth.

In recent years the SSFC, at the urging of the Social Sciences and Humanities Research Council of Canada, which supervises government funding of social-science and humanities research, has sought to become a peak association in the full sense of the word—that is, to become the sole interlocutor between these academic communities and the SSHRCC. The constituent associations have strenuously resisted, particularly the Canadian Political Science Association, whose members, in Schmitter's phrase, 'prize their organizational autonomy and defend their traditionally pluralistic ways of operating'.[50] Nevertheless the SSHRCC does tend to look first to the SSFC for an expression of social-science opinion on policy issues; it also assigns to the SSFC certain functions—such as the awarding of grants for the support of academic books—that are judged too delicate to be undertaken directly by a government agency. These are clearly corporatist tendencies. It would be going too far to suggest that a 'system of interest representation' has been created, and certainly there is no organization of a limited number of 'single, compulsory, non-competitive, hierarchically ordered and functionally differentiated categories, recognized or licensed . . . by the state'. Even so, a drift in that direction is clearly observable.[51]

These trends are not peculiar to academic and scientific bodies. The Canadian Federation of Agriculture has long been treated as a peak association by the federal Department of Agriculture and many provincial agencies, despite the challenge to the Federation represented by the National Farmers' Union.[52] In the fisheries field, as we noted before, the federal government has encouraged fishermen's groups to organize themselves. A part of this campaign has involved the creation of a peak association, the Eastern Fishermen's Federation, which—subsidized from resource revenues—has worked to create and consolidate local fishermen's groups.[53] At the provincial level we have already noted Quebec's interest in tripartism. In Léon Dion's view this was seen by the Parti Québécois government not only as a mechanism for developing economic policy, but as a vehicle for building a consensus on Québec's national future.[54] In Nova Scotia, exercises in Voluntary Planning have been conducted continuously since the late 1950s. Multipartite sector committees were initially engaged in developing an economic plan for Nova Scotia; but since the plan's ignominious rejection by the federal government the committees have concentrated on periodic reviews of sector policies and on acting as intermediaries beween government and economic sectors, and between members of the sectors themselves.[55]

Finally, we should note the evidence presented by Coleman and Jacek of extensive corporatist development in the chemical industry, where business-interest associations representing discrete elements of the industry have engaged in mutual co-operation for several decades and, as government intervention in the industry has grown, have participated in short-term and long-term policy development through joint government-industry committees.[56] They have also been involved in the direct administration of some policies and, in the definition of product standards, 'have been delegated certain responsibilities for allocating values for the whole society'. Since these relationships are not pursued through a strictly hierarchical system of interest intermediation and are seldom tripartite in form, they conform to neither the Schmitter nor the Panitch definitions of corporatism.

Full-fledged corporatism entails far more extensive rationalization of interest intermediation than that described above. And, despite periodic calls for a march towards corporatism, it is unlikely that we could easily or quickly overcome the barriers standing in the way, even if we wished to. In 1982, when Prime Minister Trudeau urged Canadians to apply the corporatist models of Japan and Germany in order to pull out of the recession, Montreal's *Le Devoir* replied:

> Au sujet de l'Allemagne et du Japon le chef du gouvernement avait raison d'invoquer l'habitude de la discipline et de la concertation. Cette habitude est ancienne dans les deux cas, et de plus en plus fragile dans la République fédérale. Des générations de leaders patroneaux, sindicaux et politiques l'ont patiemment construite et mise à jour. L'expérience canadienne, les attitudes des partenaires économiques et celles des politiciens ont plutôt maintenu le cap vers une autre direction. Nous en payons le prix aujourd'hui. Nos improvisations restent hésitantes. Peut-il en être autrement?[57]

Brown, Eastman, and Robinson, in their assessment of the Tier I/Tier II experience, reach similar conclusions. Attitudinal and ideological barriers inhibit the translation of the consultative exercise into a corporative arrangement. As well, the representative capacity of most groups is limited:

> [N]o single business organization exists to legitimately represent the private sector. The Canadian Manufacturers' Association, the Business Council on National Issues and the Canadian Federation of Independent Business each represents a significant proportion of business, but none are as all-encompassing as, for example, the BC Employers' Council or the conseil du Patronat in

Quebec are for their regions. Nor do they speak with the authority that business, labour and agricultural groups in many European countries do. Foreign ownership is one significant obstacle to this; the cleavage between large and small business and the regional dispersion of business are others. The . . . exercise did bring together firms in the manufacturing sectors (many for the first time) but, as a whole, small business was neglected. . . . The Canadian Labour Congress does not have the same degree of structural weakness for consultation, but it, too, has limitations. Only a minority of the Canadian work force is organized, and a significant minority of unions are not affiliated with the CLC.[58]

We conclude that there is a tendency in Canada towards state structuring of relations with interest groups, and that some elements of the bureaucracy would prefer that structuring to take the hierarchical and representative form embodied in corporatism. We also conclude that groups themselves are inclined towards closer co-operation with one another. These tendencies are fostered by institutional self-interest, and more importantly by economic forces that have encouraged some people to argue that national and provincial economic development has to be achieved within the framework of industrial strategies.

A tendency is not a trend. Both in terms of practice and of ideology Canada has followed a path that is far removed from corporatism. The present hesitant movement towards a more integrated system will not easily displace two centuries of individualism. Powerful ideological convictions militate against corporatist discipline, and these convictions are reinforced by the institutionalized tendencies towards decentralization found in groups and government. Our political structures are in many ways incompatible with corporatism. Divided jurisdiction means that key elements of the economy must be managed by different sets of institutions owing no obedience to one another. It may be possible for the federal government to arrange corporatist structures to deal with matters within its competence, but there are few such matters today that can be handled without in some way affecting, or being affected by, provincial policies. As long as that is the case the integrated hierarchical system of policy development and implementation, which is the essence of corporatism, will not take hold in Canada. Canadian interest representation, as Dawson and Kwavnick have shown, reflects this reality. The voice of local interests, even in organizations that have centralized structures, is powerful and often divisive. Many interest organizations are structured as decentralized federations; a number are organized only at the provincial level; very few accord significant authority to a powerful head office.[49] The recently accelerated institutionalization of interest groups encourages participation in corporatist forums, but as long as power in groups remains decentralized these forums will lack authority. The exercises in consultation that have taken place do not go beyond consultation. Views are exchanged, understanding is extended, and co-operation is achieved, but authoritative agreements are not reached. Even when we move from the level of national consultations grappling with issues that cut across sectors to the level of the policy community, we find that though individual groups are willing to collaborate more closely and to join consortiums, they jealously guard their independence and their right to treat separately with governments. Consultation and collaboration are as close as Canadian groups have come to corporatism.

CHAPTER 10

Models of Representation: Pluralism and Post-pluralism

Pluralism is generally treated as the antithesis of corporatism. Where corporatism is considered to be structured, representative, and monopolistic, the essence of pluralism is the unorchestrated interaction of individual citizens, each striving through political action to improve or defend his or her position and lot in life. Schmitter defines interest group pluralism as

> . . . a system of interest representation in which the constituent units are organized into an unspecified number of multiple, voluntary, competitive, non-hierarchically ordered and self-determined (as to type or scope or interest) categories which are not specially licensed, recognized, subsidized, created or otherwise controlled in leadership selection or interest articulation by the state, and which do not exercise a monopoly of representational activity within their respective categories.[1]

It might be possible to treat pluralism and corporatism as the two poles of a continuum, the one describing a form of state-group interaction in which groups are virtually joined to the state apparatus and exercise an essential representational role in determining and implementing policy, while at the other end of the continuum pluralism could be seen as describing a dynamic, self-regulating political system. Such a conceptualization might aid our understanding of the evolution of group politics in relation to the development of the state. At the least it would help us appreciate more profoundly the subtle distinctions to be found between the state-group relations in one country and those in another.

But such an approach has not achieved critical acceptance. Instead, the more fervent corporatists and pluralists have dichotomized their views of the political world. Having established their camps on separate theoretical peaks, they have spent more time lobbing academic squibs at one another than in explaining the political realities that lend a measure of plausibility to each theory.[2] This is because both pluralism and corporatism are more than simply explanations. Each has profound ideological implications: pluralism is closely associated with liberal individualism, while corporatism embraces a collectivist view of the role of the state. In addition, there is an undercurrent of cultural chauvinism in the attacks each side has launched against the other. Pluralism was the theoretical contribution of American scholars who were the first in the interest group field. The diffused power structure of the American system not only encouraged pressure group activity, but made it more apparent than did the bureaucratically structured and controlled systems that predominate in Europe. It also suggested a particular interpretation of group involvement in political life. Having discovered pressure groups, American scholarship exported the discovery to Britain and Europe, where at first it was accepted somewhat uncritically.[3] In time, attempts to apply pluralist theory led to skepticism and ultimately to the development of corporatism as an alternative theory. Unfortunately academic theories are never completely distanced from the pressures of national emotions. The revision and replacement of pluralist theory in Europe coincided with changes in the European view of America, so that instead of treating pluralism as merely an inadequate explanation of European group politics, corporatist theorists have often treated it as a piece of cultural imperialism, similar to the planting of hamburger palaces on the grand boulevards of Europe's greatest cities.[4]

In the resulting intense debates, theories that seek the middle ground are ignored or disparaged.[5] Corporatist scholars tend to equate non-corporatist interest-group theory with the 'group theory of politics' espoused by the early pluralists. Because of this association, any theory that is not corporatist is often assumed to make the same free-market assumptions that Bentley, Truman, and the more extreme pluralists adopted. However, it is quite possible to conceive of a dynamic and competitive interest group environment without believing that it will naturally facilitate the articulation of latent interests or produce equitable representation in the policy process. Such an approach has been adopted by a number of theorists who have pointed to the weaknesses in pluralist theory but adopt neither a corporatist orientation nor a Marxist one. In the following discussion we will contend that this approach—which we call post-pluralist—is a significant research perspective.

PLURALISTS AND ANTI-PLURALISTS

The bench-mark for post-pluralism is pluralism itself. Arthur Bentley was the earliest and most controversial of the pluralists. He argued that group pressures are the basic force in society. 'The society itself is nothing other than the complex of the groups that compose it.' 'When the groups are adequately stated,' he maintained, 'everything is stated.'[6] If groups are basic, so are their interests. In fact, according to Bentley, the state does not take cognizance of interests in the community unless they are made manifest through some sort of group demand.

> All phenomena of government are phenomena of groups pressing one another, forming one another, and pushing out new groups and group representatives

(the organs or agencies of government) to mediate the adjustments. It is only as we isolate these group activities, determine their representative values, and get the whole process stated in terms of them, that we approach to a satisfactory knowledge of government.[7]

The state, according to Bentley, does not articulate a national, or general, interest except as the consequence of group activity. If the state is nothing more than an umpire in the contest between group demands, it follows that the state cannot formulate a national interest except as a result of group competition. Hence, as Mancur Olson has put Bentley's argument, 'group pressures are the one and only determinant of the course of government policy. All things are determined by conflicting group pressures.'[8]

To Bentley groups were defined far more broadly than we define them here. When he speaks of 'groups that operate in the whole social life' or of the 'underlying' groups in society, he is not talking primarily about organized interest groups but about what we have called latent and solidary interests. Any one person in society belongs to a number of groups whose interests and activities can be separately analysed. Because each of us belongs to several different groups, according to our various interests, Bentley conceives of society as being 'criss-crossed' by groups. Some of them, like our latent interests, are 'underlying': though they are not self-consciously organized, they are capable of being influential simply because they comprise a large portion of the electorate. Others are more clearly defined, or 'differentiated': among these Bentley locates 'semi-political' groups, which closely resemble pressure groups as we have defined them, though he does not insist, as we do, that they be formally organized. They range from 'vague groupings of the population . . . [to] sharply outlined and well-organized interests.'[9] Whatever their state of institutionalization, 'there is no essential difference between them.'

> 'Vague' or 'well-organized' semi-political groups act as intermediaries between the inchoate underlying groups of the polity and the institutionalized structures (themselves definable in group terms) of the state—political parties, the executive, the legislature, the judiciary—which formulate and interpret the law.[10]

Each aspect of Bentley's thought draws a critical reaction from modern audiences. On analytical grounds they ask whether he is right to argue that the state recognizes interests only as the result of group action. Even in today's organizational society it seems rash to ignore entirely the idiosyncratic actions of individuals, particularly party leaders or the extremely wealthy who hold positions of power. Again, critics ask whether it is really helpful from an analytical perspective to view the world as a huge conglomeration of criss-crossing, more-or-less distinguishable groups. As long as the groups in question can be clearly defined and studied as independent entities, much can be learned. But 'underlying groups' or vaguely defined 'discussion groups' lead us into a morass of conjecture. As Bentley himself argues, analysis depends on precision. If we cannot determine who belongs to a group or what exactly the group has done, we cannot really say very much about that group's role in the process of government.[11]

It is the normative implications of Bentley's work that have been most attacked, however. When he wrote that 'we shall never find a group interest of the society as a whole... the society itself is nothing other than the complex of the groups that compose it,' Bentley 'set the stage for a redefinition of democracy.'[12] If the general will—the definition of the public interest—is seen as the product of the clash between competing group claims, very little room is left for intervention by individuals acting through traditional methods of democratic election. In J.A. Corry's words, 'democracy which promised a way for people to control their own destiny has encouraged the structures of government, public and private, which everywhere tax or exceed human control and normal understanding.'[13] Critics, like Theodore Lowi, ask whether it is morally right for the public interest to be simply the residual of group demands.[14]

Bentley's intellectual successor, David Truman, was aware of the growing disquiet over the capacity of democratic institutions to cope with special-interest demands. He too assumed that group conflict is the essence of political life, but he amplifies Bentley's theory by developing an explanation for the origin of groups that seeks to sustain the argument that the group process is consistent with democratic government.

For Truman, groups begin to take part in political life in response to changes in their immediate environment. Latent interests, confronted with threatening activity on the part of the state or other groups—or perhaps awakened to some new opportunity—will recognize their mutual interest and coalesce. Quite likely their new group will seek state support to promote its objectives. This activity, and its consequences, are all part of the process through which society maintains its own equilibrium. Truman saw the political system as a dynamic mass of activity constantly engaged in change, group formation, and development, which enabled him to argue that pressure group politics were entirely consistent with democracy. Society's constant search for equilibrium would impel it to produce groups to champion disadvantaged interests. A natural dynamism would create a diversity of groups whose ability to appeal to the many concerns of each individual would further guarantee that no one interest could monopolize power. Individuals would distribute their support over several groups and would thus be aware of any one group's tendencies towards monopoly and would be prepared to limit or withdraw support. In other words, the dynamism of a pluralist society would safeguard it against the abuse of power that might otherwise flow from the uncontrolled development of pressure groups. Truman's position resembled that of the classical economists who argued that in a properly competitive economy an unseen hand would regulate markets and guard against monopoly. Truman's competitive group activity would similarly safeguard the polity.[15]

Critics tend to describe Truman's position as 'naïve pluralism' and in the context of today's debates it *is* naïve.[16] In their day, however, these writers could make an assumption that has not been possible in either the United States or Canada since the early 1960s: they could assume a consensus in national political thought. The United States held strongly to a liberal ideology. It had a sense of direction and national purpose. It was not deeply divided internally. In this context early students of pressure groups could, and did, assume that pressure groups would express demands that were consistent with a deeply rooted and generally understood consensus. E.E. Schattschneider has pointed out that the pluralists believed that group competition was contained by both the ability of parties to reconcile spatial (or geographic) and sectoral (or functional) interests, and by the impact of an extremely powerful consensus, and would therefore not advocate a political system dominated by unrestrained group competition. After all, as Schattscheider wrote in 1960, about a decade after Truman had published his major work, *The Governmental Process*, 'The diet on which the American leviathan feeds is something more than a jungle of special interests.' Consensus existed and could be taken for granted. '[T]he regime as a whole seemed to be so stable that questions about the survival of the American community did not arise. The general interests of the community are easily overlooked under these circumstances.'[17]

Expressing this consensus was the party system, which in Bentley's time was a lively and extremely powerful force in American society. True, it was often corrupt—corrupted frequently by special interests, such as the railway interests, the anti-labour groups, and the many others exposed at the end of the nineteenth century by the muckrakers and other reformers—but even so, the system had shown itself to be resilient. As Bentley, V.O. Key, Pendleton Herring, and many other prominent students of American politics pointed out, it was also capable of aggregating—one might almost say, superintending—this vast, noisy kaleidoscope of political activity.[18]

The earliest criticism of the pluralist approach came from Marxism in response to Bentley's contention that his group theory was meant to disprove the theory of the class struggle. He and his colleagues believed that individuals are influenced by numerous loyalties and perceptions of self-interest. In their approach to politics individuals reflect these influences by identifying themselves with, and acting through, groups. For Bentley, class could not exist. Economic groups could, but they were subject to so many important cleavages—such as race and culture—that they could not attain the homogeneity and singleness of purpose needed for the class struggle. Indeed, groups may bring members of different classes together. Thus, as a recent commentator has observed, 'if classes in capitalist society are so fragmented that the concept of class is of doubtful analytical utility, then the Marxian analysis and critique of capitalism are seriously undermined.'[19] Marxists, however, do not deny the presence of groups in political life, but suggest that groups tend to reflect class composition—they are subsets within the larger framework of class. This argument is plausible: interest-group involvement often appears to be a prerogative of the middle class and of the most influential élites. The poor seldom have the time and money to affiliate with the interest groups that might appeal to them. When they do join, their associations have quite different structures, customs, and methods from those of similar groups boasting a predominantly middle-class membership; they do not work easily with middle-class groups and may often be opposed to them.[20]

Though the pluralists and Marxists have disputed their rival approaches for many decades, the most important attacks on Bentley's focused on his understanding of the role of pressure groups in democratic society. R.M. MacIver, in 1947, took exception to Bentley's assumption that 'a legislative act is always the calculable resultant of a struggle between pressure groups, never a decision between opposing conceptions of the national welfare.'

> . . . . the whole logic of democracy is based on the conception that there is still a national unity and a common welfare. The fact that the interest in the common welfare cannot be organized after the fashion of specific interests should not conceal from us either its existence or the need to sustain it. Democracy itself is the final organization of the common interest . . . . Democracy affirms the community.
> This affirmation is constantly being threatened by the imperialism of powerful groups. It is the eternal problem of democracy to keep them in their place, subject to the democratic code.[21]

A sustained attack began in the 1960s when American political science came to be riven by an intense argument over the validity of the pluralist understanding of politics. This critique argued persuasively that the natural dynamism of the American system could not ensure the equal representation of all interests or even their partial representation . As Mancur Olson pointed out, Truman's argument 'that "suffering", "dislocation" and "disturbance" will almost inevitably result in organized political pressure' is not sustained by the facts.[22] The evidence brought to light by the civil-rights movement and the ghetto uprisings indicated that the distribution of power, and consequently of the benefits of American civilization, was very unequal indeed. Robert Dahl's pluralist argument that the 'independence, penetrability, and heterogeneity of the political stratum' virtually guarantee that the concerns of disaffected groups would be expressed in political debate was considered to misrepresent the distribution of political power because it ignored the fact that 'political penetrability' is compromised by the capacity of non-decision-making—the determination not to consider policy options known to be disliked by the political and economic élite—to prevent some political issues from reaching the public agenda.[23] Non-decision-making was a potent force because powerful special interests had a fierce grip on the levers of power. They had put the resources of the American state to their own use, creating, as Theodore Lowi put it, 'Socialism for the organized; capitalism for the unorganized.'[24]

Lowi has been one of the most strident critics of the pluralists. His book *The End of Liberalism* proclaims the fall of the system of democratic government upon which the United States grew to greatness, and its replacement by a 'second republic'—the tool of powerful interests who manipulate the system. For Lowi the crux of the problem, the cause of the shift, has been a growing incapacity on the part of American representative institutions to reconcile spatially oriented and functionally oriented demands. The American party system has gradually been overtaken by specialized institutions. He traces this shift to a functional orientation in American government when he discusses the emergent pre-eminence of the national government from the 1930s to the 1960s:

> . . . if the 1930s had established a strong national state as politically feasible and constitutionally acceptable, the 1960s made the strong national state a positive virtue, desirable for its own sake.

In addition,

> The new public philosophy went so far as to redefine majority rule, making the President, not Congress, its true manifestation. Congress was redefined as a useful collection of minorities and was belittled still further by the idea that Congress was only one part of a long policy-making process within which organized minorities had rightful access for purposes of informal and formal participation. And once the presidency was redefined as the true representative of the real majority, the overwhelming inclination was to embrace the principle of embodying maximum legislative powers in the presidency. That ties the package together; new functions, new institutional relationships and a public philosophy which not only justified those developments but identified a presidency and professional bureaucracy uniquely capable of leadership as well as implementation.[25]

The growth of the special-interest state in the United States, then, is associated with the rise of specialization and thus with the increasing power of the bureaucracy in American government. The American party system, with its strong bias towards geographically defined community interests, has been no match for the combined power of the functionally oriented administrative units and their affiliates, the interest groups. It has been reduced, on the one hand, to packaging and selling presidential candidates, and on the other to providing a nominal affiliation for the sectoral chieftains who dispense congressional patronage.

Not all American theorists follow Lowi to this point. One of the foremost American students of pressure groups, Robert H. Salisbury, while critical of the pluralist approach, takes a more clinical, less despondent view of pressure group influence.[26] Similarly Mancur Olson, who is himself critical of Truman and Bentley for their failure to consider properly the impact of individual and national interest on group politics, espouses a rational-choice interpretation of group life and behaviour that is not inconsistent with the pluralist approach.[27]

Nevertheless, even these scholars present data that sustain Lowi's interpretations. Salisbury's view of the origin of groups offers a case in point:

> As a consequence of various processes of social differentiation . . . there is within a given population more and more specialization of function . . . and from this comes greater and greater diversity of interests or values as each newly differentiated set of people desires a somewhat different set of social goals.[28]

Lowi would argue that it is this very process that precipitates the special interest state.

THE POST-PLURALISTS

Emerging from the criticisms of the anti-pluralists was a new perception of the structure of relations between the American state and interest groups. The scholars who built on the critique of pluralism—we will call them the post-pluralists—were not convinced that the political system is self-regulating and capable of maintaining an equilibrium in which all members of society have confidence because they share a common right to participate. On the contrary, though there may be a common right to participate there is no common opportunity to participate. There are, in fact, very great inequalities in political life that reflect enormous social and economic disparities between individuals and that in time will provoke disequilibrium in the system. Where the pluralists had envisaged a dynamic, atomistic environment in which individual groups engaged in one-on-one relations with the offices and legislators whose decisions affected their interests, the post-pluralists described tight-knit alliances between key legislators, influential groups, and the leaders of agencies. Some post-pluralists envisaged group politics as a monstrous engine of inequity capable ultimately of destroying the society that created it.

At the heart of this revised view is the argument that 'some issues are organized into politics while others are organized out of it'.[29] Contrary to pluralist theory, politics is not a competitive market-place for policy options. Instead, the majority of participants consider politics a vehicle for limiting competition and for securing a tranquil environment for themselves and their enterprises. Just as in business many entrepreneurs attempt to control their environment by forming cartels or in other ways limiting competition, so in politics various actors try to achieve consensus and to avoid conflict. The most effective way to do this is to control the instruments that define which issues will appear on the public agenda, and—just as important— which alternatives will be chosen to resolve them. For E.E. Schattschneider:

> [T]he definition of alternatives is the supreme instrument of power, the antagonists can rarely agree on what the issues are because power is involved in the definition. He who determines what politics is about runs the country, because the definition of the alternatives is the choice of conflicts, and the choice of conflicts allocates power.[30]

Of the various institutions engaged in defining issues and alternatives, organized interests are among the most important because they have specialized knowledge—unlike political parties and most of the media—and because they derive a degree of legitimacy from their claim to represent an interest community.

Four factors contribute to organized interests' bias towards articulating some issues rather than others. First, not all interests are represented; in particular, the poor or disadvantaged have no voice. Second, not all elements of specific interest communities are represented by the groups who speak for them. Third, Schattschneider finds that people involved in interest organizations, particularly those who take leadership positions, tend to belong to the more affluent classes of society; thus by dominating both the organizations at large and their executive positions, the upper classes steer interest group concerns towards issues that affect themselves and towards alternatives that favour them. Finally, in this system of unequal representation Schattschneider finds that certain kinds of associations have a great deal more influence than others.[31] Business associations in particular tend to be more effective than most unions or professional groups in attaining their ends and infinitely more successful than voluntary groups. They have resources and commitments that normally far outweigh those of voluntary groups and the majority of unions.

Schattschneider, like other post-pluralist theorists, emphasizes the use of consensus in politics.[32] The majority of political theorists emphasize conflict. Because party competition, international tensions, and class war capture the attention of most observers of political life, the student can be forgiven for concluding that politics is the management of conflict. The post-pluralists remind us that the management of conflict is only a small part of what politics is about.[33] When Schattschneider maintains that some issues are organized into politics while others are organized out, he is suggesting that conflict can be contained through the management of consensus. When Bachrach, Baratz, and Crenson argue that non-decisionmaking is the other face of pluralist democracy, they are also suggesting that consensus is being managed—to prevent issues from being articulated.[34]

The vehicle for achieving consensus management is the sub-government. Because complex societies depend on specialization of function to accomplish the majority of economic, social, and political goals, a tendency towards sub-government is endemic in all modern political systems, but particularly in the United States. There sub-governments are built around three mutually dependent elements: administrative units, congressional committees, and pressure groups. The diffusion of power within the American system of government spawned a triangular symbiosis between these three political elements. Congressional committees, and particularly their chairpersons, with their power to create, halt, or mutilate legislation, and their control over appropriations, are courted not only by officials of the administrative units whose budgets and legislation they influence, but by the interest groups most closely associated with the same sphere of activity. Congressmen also have needs, however. Pet pieces of legislation or budget allocations designed to benefit their constituencies often need the kind of public support that can be generated by interest groups. Groups, too, can often dispense patronage. The decisions of members of business asssociations, for example, can be vitally important for Congressmen worried about unemployment back home or anxious to build on their constituency's economic base. Again, the associations can be important intermediaries between public decision-makers and specific interests, and between agencies and the public at large. For all this, the organized interests expect benefits in return: recognition of their own status; policy benefits for their interest at large and, where appropriate, patronage for individual members. Finally, the implementation of policies desired by legislators and groups depends to a considerable extent on the goodwill of the administrative agency.[35]

According to Ripley and Franklin:

> Most of the policy-making in which sub-governments engage consists of routine matters. By 'routine' we simply mean policy that is not currently involved in a high degree of controversy, policy that is not likely to change very much and policy with which the participants in it are thoroughly familiar and quietly efficient in its implementation and minor alteration.[36]

For Schattschneider this routineness is the nub of consensus management; it enables particular groups and particular classes to define the issues and alternatives put before the public. By not drawing attention to what is being decided, sub-governments can arrange public policy to their own satisfaction. 'Since most policy-making is routine most of the time, sub-governments can often function for long periods of time without much interference.' The key to being left alone is to maintain the fiction that what is done is 'routine'; which involves maintaining agreement within the sub-government and ensuring that potential rival interests, in both the public and private sectors, can be co-opted, suppressed, or safely ignored. 'If the members of a sub-government can reach compromises among themselves on any disagreements about a policy, they can reduce the chance of calling a broader audience together that might become involved in their activities and their output.'[37] Consensus management, then, becomes the main task of those employed at the heart of the sub-government: the key political decision-makers, interest representatives, and agency leaders. By striving to maintain an alliance among themselves, members of the sub-government ensure that as far as the public is concerned new policies are 'routine' and 'incremental', even though they may have engaged in heated debate. Sub-governments have thus been successful in keeping out of politics many issues that, according to the pluralists, should naturally find their way into public debate. The process of mutual accommodation creates an extremely powerful relationship that, as Schattschneider pointed out, for the unorganized, the under-represented, the poverty stricken—the weaker elements of American society—is very difficult to challenge, much less break down.

Post-pluralist theory does not exclude the role of conflict in policy-making. There will always be times when it becomes impossible to contain debate within the sub-government. The issues involved may be so important that leading members will be driven to public disagreement. Proposed policy may trench too aggressively on the domain of another sub-government. The leaders of the sub-government, complacent in their long exercise of power, may have failed to recognize the importance of challenging groups, or of fundamental shifts in public opinion. A probing journalist may have exposed a major scandal in the policy field. Such factors can turn a quiet policy backwater into a maelstrom of public debate. Raising the 'level of conflict', to use Schattschneider's phrase,[38] will nearly always lead to revision of policy and disruption of the sub-government itself, ultimately changing to some degree the conditions operating in the particular policy field. In most cases the traditional dominance of the sub-government in that field, its capacity to dispense patronage and co-opt critics, and the sheer weight of the expertise it can muster ensure that controversy will eventually subside, whereupon the sub-government, somewhat mauled and slightly changed, will be able to retire again to a comfortable obscurity. Nevertheless the penalties for failing to maintain consensus or for incompetently adapting to the changing environment will cause the leaders of the sub-government to redouble their efforts to 'routinize' public policy and to organize out of politics discussion of the issues that most concern them. The elemental force of conflict, always present in sub-government relations, is kept at bay through the mangement of consensus.

APPLYING POST-PLURALISM TO CANADA

Post-pluralism occupies the middle ground between pluralism and corporatism. It takes account of the dynamism of traditional American interest group politics, on which the pluralists focused, but it does not ignore the growing influence of the state, a concern of the corporatists. Unlike the pluralists, the newer generation of American interest group scholars are very much aware of the state's role.[39] One of the key actors in the sub-government, the state is represented in part by members of the Congress, but more significantly by executive agencies. In the traditional pluralist formulation the state plays basically a passive role, responding to the demands of diverse interests. The post-pluralists, by identifying a more active role for agencies of the state, pinpoint an important shift in the structure of American politics—a shift that creates a similarity between the American system and the corporatist regimes of Europe. This is not only intrinsically interesting, but it confirms the arguments of economists, such as Galbraith and Heilbroner, that the American political economy, despite its liberal ideology and pluralistic bias, is adapting to the evolution of a complex economic structure by developing the role of state agencies.[40]

But how applicable are post-pluralist concepts outside the United States? How useful are they to an understanding of Canadian pressure group politics in particular? Are issues organized in and out of Canadian politics? Is consensus management a key goal of state-group decision-makers? Is policy specialization within sub-governments the mechanism through which consensus is managed? If post-pluralist analysis is an aid to understanding Canadian pressure group politics, are the normative concerns of the post-pluralists also relevant in this country?

We can find ample evidence of consensus management outside the United States. It is, as we have seen, an integral part of corporatism and thus common throughout Europe. In Britain—which, like Canada and the United States, tends to elude classification as a corporatist state—a tendency towards consensus-seeking politics has nevertheless been noted. For Richardson and Jordan the essence of modern British political behaviour is conflict avoidance. A political system whose primary object is the minimizing of conflict and disagreement assumes that 'the incrementalist/hum-drum style of policy-making is appropriate and the process of accommodation, etc., is of paramount importance.'[41] The recent evolution of the British economy has made such accommodative approaches, often in a tripartite framework, an essential part of exposing 'the nature of the problem for all participants to see' and persuading them, as they look over the edge of the cliff, to 'accept a solution designed to avoid falling over it'.[42]

Another British observer attributes consensus-seeking to more mundane motives. 'Just as the behavioral theory of the firm tells us that managers in private corporations prefer the easy life,' Robert E. Goodin argues, 'so too must we presume that administrators in the public sector opt unnecessarily for the quiet life.'[43] They seek out the key actors in policy communities and consult them frequently in an attempt to ensure that before major changes are undertaken 'some minimal level of agreement' has been reached among those best placed to disrupt the proposed policy. For Goodin this process involves too much hard bargaining to be called consensus-building. Nevertheless, it is important that the outside observer should believe that a consensus exists:

> That is the whole point of co-option in the first place . . . [I]f all or most of the interested groups' elites can be seen agreeing on an appropriate pace of reform, then their constituents will suppose that that pace reflects some objective facts fixed in the nature of their world and will make no complaints.[44]

Observation of consensus management, in the pluralistic British system as well as in corporatist European regimes, confirms the transferability of post-pluralist concepts. Important differences do exist, however, as is illustrated by the fact that though Goodin adopts the concept of the sub-government, there are significant variations between his allusions to sub-governments and the post-pluralists' conceptualization. Where they speak of a tight-knit group of officials, politicians, and interest group leaders managing the sub-government, Goodin envisages a less cohesive, more divided core that includes the most important interests but ignores some who 'cannot cause enough trouble for insiders to bother co-opting them', and is unsuccessful in drawing in others who are 'proud to stand defiantly outside'.[45] In the same context Jordan and Richardson, who describe rather similar consensus-maintaining processes, avoid using the term 'sub-governments' and imply that the mechanisms they have described are more loosely structured, more divided, and less authoritative than those the post-pluralists found in the United States. In part these variations in conceptualization reflect different understandings of American phenomena. This is brought out in Jordan's analysis of the imagery used in American discussions to describe the relations between sub-government actors.[46] At one point 'iron triangles' were said to dominate decision-making; but recently the imagery of 'networks' has been favoured because it reflects the diffuse communication systems used to discuss policy, and because it suggests that the grip on the policy process of core members of the sub-government is less firm than it once was.

These variations in the application of American concepts suggest that observers of non-American systems apply post-pluralist concepts with the same reservations shown by their predecessors in using the orginal pluralist notions. The analytical concepts of one culture and one system cannot be transplanted without modification to others. In the case of the post-pluralists it is clear that, though many vital elements of the concept—the tendency towards policy specialization and the management of consensus for example—can be found in most modern systems, institutional, cultural, and ideological variations modify the way in which groups, agencies, and legislators interact. The most notable distinction between the American and other systems is expressed in the concept of the 'triangle'. Few systems accord individual legislators the power possessed by members of Congress; outside the United States the image of the triangle does not apply, though the concept of the sub-government remains useful. Similarly, ideology and culture decree a different role for the American state than prevails in many other countries.

Such differences force us to use caution in applying post-pluralist concepts to Canada. In some respects these concepts offer a plausible framework for interpreting the Canadian experience of group politics. It is not hard to find consensus-seeking behaviour, despite the tendency towards confrontation in recent Canadian political history. Indeed, institutionalized pressure groups found for many years that they had to conform to a certain kind of consensus-seeking behaviour if they wished to maintain access to, and exert influence on, governmental decision-makers. Recent studies of Canadian business-interest associations have identified many instances of consensus-seeking behaviour. They take a variety of forms. One approach uses joint committees composed of officials and business representatives to formulate policy, 'with senior level committees discussing its general shape and junior committees deliberating over technical details.'[47] Alternatively agency officials will write to interested groups advising them of proposed changes and inviting comment. In other instances—for example, in the case of marketing boards—agencies will delegate responsibility for policy formulation to bodies representing the various business interests.[48] Despite such evidence of consensus-building within specific industries and policy fields, and despite the interest in tripartite consultation that we noted in Chapter 9, scholars have been forced to conclude that regional differences, jurisdictional rivalries, and the fragmentation of interest associations inhibit the building and maintenance of consensus on the broader policy level.[49] In short, the post-pluralist concept of consensus-building identifies a characteristic of interest group involvement in the Canadian policy process, but we must be careful not to assume that consensus-building occurs in the same way or has the same effect as it does in other countries.

We have also used the post-pluralist concept of the sub-government extensively in interpreting Canadian group politics. However, in applying the concept we have modified it considerably, abandoning the image of the triangle and treating the sub-government as the central core of a greater policy community, which organizes the special public concerned with a particular policy field, providing mechanisms for policy communication, legitimation, and, to an extent, renewal.[50] We have introduced these modifications because, as our earlier discussions have suggested, sub-governments in Canada, like those in Britain, lack the cohesion and authority of the American. We can attribute their lack of authority to the fact that, despite the diffusion of power that has occurred in recent years, the Cabinet-parliamentary system still creates a focal point for power in the Cabinet. Because the Cabinet-parliamentary system still accords an important co-ordinative role to Cabinet, the independence of sub-governments in Canada and Britain is less certain and more variable than it is in the United States. When Cabinet chooses to exert its power, as for example when it chooses to reverse the orders of regulatory boards and commissions, then no sub-government can resist it in the short run, however successful it may be in routinizing policy-making over the long term. Thus, ultimately, the administrative structures bargaining with interest representatives do not need to share power with them to the same extent as do their American counterparts. This was very clear in the days of the mandarins, but is less so today.

Again, the Cabinet-parliamentary system imposes an important structural variation on Canadian and British sub-governments. There is no place for the powerful legislative committees that form the third partner in the American triad. In Canada and Britain sub-governments consist of two sets of partners—the lead agency and the major interests—each of which still needs what the other has to offer, but one of which—the agency—is more authoritative, less dependent, than the other. We must not conclude from this, however, that we can substitute the British model of sub-governments for the American one. The extensive diffusion of power found in our federal bureaucracy is reinforced in Canada by the structure of federal-provincial decision-making and the decentralization that comes with federalism. Thus, while Canadian sub-governments are less powerful than those in the United States, they have more authority than their British counterparts, simply because they have more opportunity to manipulate decision centres.

Throughout our discussion we have emphasized the consensus-seeking activities of policy communities because we accept the post-pluralist argument that the majority of participants in sub-governments are anxious to create and maintain a stable environment. Officials seek the 'quiet life'—not simply because general agreement makes life 'easier', but because consensus equates with legitimation. As long as the policy community, even including its less important members, appears to the public at large to agree on policy fundamentals, the general public is likely to feel that the policies being followed are legitimate, and thus acceptable. Such legitimation permits the modification of policy to be treated as routine, or incremental. The co-optation of interests into policy-making allows issues to be organized out of politics. If this fundamental aspect of consensus management is neglected, dissident groups will circumvent the policy community and almost invariably will appeal to the public at large. Their efforts in themselves may be relatively inconsequential, but they can awaken public unease about the conduct of the policy community. If the dissidents include individuals and groups whose views can be respected, the public may challenge the conventional wisdom prevailing in the policy community and raise questions about issues that in the past had been treated as routine and kept out of politics.[51] In short, the level of conflict will rise to a point where issues escape the control of the policy community—and of the sub-government in particular—so that the environment for decision-making becomes extremely unsettled.

To avoid such eventualities the policy community has to engage in a constant process of assimilation. New issues are raised, new individuals brought into the community, changes in the environment accommodated and so on. This may create more turmoil in a policy community than meets the eye of the uninitiated, but it is a necessary part of building and maintaining consensus. Most community members, even the competitively inclined, prefer a stable environment, but to secure stability they must accept a degree of change.

Occasions when issues do escape the policy community occur frequently enough. They reflect either serious internal disagreements within the community, or major changes in the external policy environment. For the leaders of the sub-government, the former are easier to stomach. Internal conflicts, as the preceding comments suggest, may entail unwanted publicity; the assimilation of unwelcome policy ideas (and often their proponents); and momentary destabilization. But normally the community will remain intact. In fact these minor eruptions can be a source of renewal for the community. Not so the major exogenous changes; they can lead to a dismantling of the policy community or, at the very least, to fundamental changes in policy.

The evidence reviewed in earlier chapters suggested that since the mid-1960s Canadian policy communities have experienced the second kind of challenge to an unusual degree. They are being forced to adjust to fundamental changes in the country's social, economic, and political systems: the spread of new technologies; urbanization; the growth of the multinational; the accelerating interdependence of economies; the decline of traditional communities; general changes in life-style; concern for environmental quality, and so on. Individually such changes introduce, often very rapidly, dramatic alterations in the specific environment of policy communities.[52] Collectively the effect of these changes on policy communities is even more profound because it transforms long standing relations between social, economic, and political systems. Governments, as we noted in Chapter 3, have become inextricably involved in demand and supply management, an involvement that has forced a total redefinition of the relations between the public and private sectors in every aspect of public policy. Instead of being the distributor of public wealth, government has become the redistributor. Instead of maintaining an appropriate environment for social and economic life, government has found itself trying to create that environment. Instead of playing a basically passive role in relation to society, government has had to participate very actively indeed. Over the years it has become increasingly obvious that to manage supply and demand, government must manage the economy as a whole, and that in order to manage, government must plan. This is why talk of an industrial strategy for Canada, and the relative success of undertakings such as the Tier II exercise we referred to earlier are extremely significant. They are the first steps towards national economic planning.[53]

The impact of these trends has been registered particularly at two levels of the political system. It has precipitated the diffusion of power on the one hand, and led to confrontation at the intergovernmental level on the other. Both of these effects have made a considerable difference to the way policy communities function. We turn first to the impact of diffusion of power, which we discussed first in Chapter 3.

In essence the diffusion of power represents a loss of control over the machinery of government on the part of the political executive and the senior public service. A consequence of the rapid evolution of new policies and programs, and thus of the even more rapid growth of agencies, diffusion not only precipitates loss of control, but sets in motion the crisis of legitimacy discussed in earlier chapters. Since Canadian bureaucracies have little inherent legitimacy, and derive public acceptance from carrying out policies laid down by Parliament and Cabinet, the deterioration of that acceptance made the crisis of legitimacy particularly acute for most agencies. They consequently sought alternative points of legitimation within the public at large. These efforts included fostering the elaboration of policy communities.

The development of policy communities capable of generating public support for agency policies has transformed participating interest groups from useful adjuncts of agencies into vitally important allies. Not surprisingly this transformation has occurred at the agencies' cost. The tutelary relationship common in earlier stages of the development of the policy process had to give way to one approximating partnership. A dependency relationship has become much more fully an exchange relationship. In effect, the nature of bureaucratic politics has changed in Canada: no longer conducted within the hierarchy and the discreet, tight-knit circle of interest representatives privy to departmental secrets and strategies, it must now from time to time engage public support. The price of public support is a more open, more dynamic policy system. Pressure group involvement in the policy process cannot be encouraged without elevating the status of such groups. And once groups have outgrown agency tutelage, it must be expected that to some extent they will act independently to promote their own immediate interests, as well as those of the agency and the policy community at large. Thus the diffusion of power has accentuated the tendency for policy to be developed by specialized policy communities; it has led to the more precise definition of those communities, and has led them to act more openly and vigorously in the general political system as they strive to maintain the control of their key agencies over the policy field. All this promotes a more open and dynamic policy system.

In fostering the development of policy communities, agencies and their allies have generated mechanisms reminiscent of those remarked by students of corporatism: a concern for representativeness, and, as one sees in the interest associations of the chemical industry, a tendency to avoid overlap between groups.[54] Such arrangements enhance legitimating capacity and interest aggregation. As well there is some attempt to build peak associations. Throughout, a good deal of initiative has been taken by government agencies themselves in the fostering of groups and the definition of their role. Nevertheless, as we said before, this is far from approaching full corporatism. The policy community itself is too open, too free of regulation, and too inclined towards pluralist conceptions of behaviour to be considered corporatist in anything but an embryonic sense. Consequently we have gone no further than to treat these mechanisms as evidence of a growing tendency on the part of governments and interests to orchestrate their relations on a larger scale, and in a more complex manner, than they did in the years before the Second World War and even during the period of mandarin influence.

In the field of federal-provincial relations policy communities can be effective actors. They are weakest when the desires of group members conflict with the fundamental interests of governments themselves. At other times, because they pivot around line agencies, they have been successful in resisting central direction. Policy communities that have succeeded in reaching consensus between interests and government at the agency and ministerial levels can be a formidable barrier to the efforts of Ottawa's central agencies to secure desired changes in policy: the mineral industries demonstrated this when they and their provincial allies opposed the tax-reform proposals of the first Trudeau government. In fact, we might take Schattschneider's level of conflict theory a step further, and argue that in the Canadian situation, the level of conflict that policy communities strive most carefully to avoid is conflict at the intergovernmental level, particularly at the most senior level of all, the first ministers' conference. Policy conflicts attaining that doubtful eminence are not only subject to modification by central agencies and other actors but are quite likely to miss any kind of resolution at all, falling victim to the confrontation politics and its ensuing tendency to result in deadlock, which has often characterized intergovernmental relations.

Using the concept of the policy community, we explored several notions of how the community functions and how it processes policy information. We also looked briefly at its association with the complex tangle of intergovernmental relations, suggesting that in intergovernmental affairs policy communities serve functions of protection and issue-organization similar to those they carry out in single jurisdictions. Finally, we looked at the role policy communities play in the diffuse power situation found today in several governments, particularly at the federal level. We suggested that policy communities have to some extent been the product of, and have contributed to, the growing inability of governmental centres to control the public service. They act as a source of support for the increased autonomy enjoyed by line agencies in recent years.

All in all, it seems that we can apply a good part of the post-pluralist argument to our interpretation of Canadian experience. The post-pluralist models do not fit precisely; we have had to develop a policy community model instead. But their underlying thrust is similar. The policy community, like the American sub-government, exists because of a systemic need for policy specialization. In both, the leading actors strive to maintain stability within the special public and do so through the processes of consensus management.

If these descriptive and analytical aspects of post-pluralism are relevant in Canada, should we not also be concerned about the normative conclusions the approach suggests? Specifically, does our analysis of the role of policy communities indicate that these systems of sectoral representation threaten to supplant the traditional pattern of spatial representation embodied in our legislatures? Secondly, do our policy communities, with their predilection for consensus management, systematically exclude many Canadians from an effective part in the policy process?

By developing the policy-community concept, we have softened the impact of Lowi's charge that policy is made by the organized at the expense of the unorganized. We have done this by recognizing that the policy community consists not only of the cohesive and authoritative sub-government, but also of the polyglot attentive public with its opposition elements, whose views must be taken into account to some extent. We have argued that the instability of the attentive public can change the policy preferences of policy communities and that therefore assimilation and adaptation are an essential part of consensus management. Instability within the attentive public is a vehicle for adaptation. It reminds the sub-government that it cannot run the policy community entirely in its own way and that new actors must be taken into account because they may signal challenges to prevailing policy paradigms. From the general public's point of view this diversity of activity and the instability in policy communities are counterweights to the consensus-seeking behaviour of sub-governments. They introduce new ideas into the policy field, precipitate institutional readjustment, and in the long run promote the adaptation of policy to the changing needs of society. They help maintain a dynamic, responsive policy system. The early pluralists saw a similar dynamism safeguarding American democratic institutions.

As critics of the pluralists have argued, however, we cannot trust entirely to the spontaneous expression of self-interest to ensure that equity and democracy prevail in policy-making. The adaptive capacity of the policy community is a crucially important quality, but it is not enough. Representation within most policy communities is incomplete and unequal. The communities are dominated by institutionalized actors. Generally agencies and institutionalized groups populate sub-governments and comprise a significant part of the attentive public. Though they may not entirely agree with one another, they understand the importance of consensus management and tend to subscribe to established policy paradigms. Issue-oriented and fledgeling groups, whether they oppose the consensus or simply want relatively minor changes in policy, are puny in comparison to institutionalized power. Their resource base, as we have seen, often prohibits continuing, effective participation in the life of the community, even if institutionalized members do not explicitly close ranks against them. If they do incur organized opposition from established members, they confront formidable barriers. Their efforts will be ignored, or given unsympathetic coverage by much of the media. Volunteer help may be unavailable or even discouraged by imputations of radicalism. Public recognition of legitimacy will be denied. Sources of funding will dry up, or the costs of opposition driven to impossible heights by the use of expensive counter-tactics. At worst, the power of the state may be exerted against them, as it was at the time of the 'On-to-Ottawa' trek of the unemployed in the 1930s, and again in the 1970s when Revenue Canada removed charitable-society status from some groups, thereby curtailing the flow of funds from donors who would expect to claim their contributions against income tax.[55] All these impediments, and many more, constrain the majority of groups that consistently challenge the conventional wisdom of the policy community.

In the case of groups attempting to represent the disadvantaged, these problems are compounded. By definition, the weak lack the wherewithal to sustain a presence in policy-making circles. But lack of resources is not their only difficulty. The very act of organizing representation for the weak often results in transforming the messages they wish to send to the government and the public. Church groups, social-service organizations, representatives of the caring professions, and even subsidized groups staffed by the underprivileged are all well-intentioned, but have trouble relating to their constituency and speaking for it. They speak on behalf of their constituents but do not necessarily speak *for* them. Neither their legitimacy nor their mandate comes from those they represent. The quality of their representation is therefore in doubt.[56]

We have to conclude, then, that though Canadian pressure group politics does much to generate open public discussion of policy issues, and provides our political system with a mechanism for adaptation, its capacity for equitable representation of interests is inadequate. In our next, and concluding, chapter we will look at ways of rendering pressure-group politics more effective, and will address the fundamental issue of the tension between our sectoral and spatial systems of representation.

CHAPTER 11

Space, Sector and Legitimacy: Addressing the Dilemmas of Representation

This book began with Robert Stanfield's complaint that pressure groups threaten democratic government—a concern that has crept to the surface again and again as we have examined the many aspects of pressure group politics and their impact on the formation of public policy. When we looked at the historical evolution of groups we saw how closely tied they have been to—and, at times, how strongly influenced by—bureaucracies. We noted how important it is for pressure group representatives to 'get to decision-makers before the parliamentary stage is reached'. In discussing the interior life of groups we found that many receive a large portion of their operating income from governments; that government policies can encourage certain kinds of groups and force others out of politics. In two chapters preceding this we concluded that corporatism, with its tendency to set aside parliamentary discussion, is not a serious possibility in Canada, but also that policy communities, with their tendency to organize issues out of politics, are very much a part of our policy process.

In addressing the normative issues raised by Canadian pressure group politics, we begin with the proposition that the fundamental concerns of modern government have to do with space and sector. The effectiveness of contemporary political systems depends on how well their institutions reconcile the territorial and sectoral needs of their members. We have touched on this problem repeatedly. We have argued that for most of this century it has been difficult for Parliament to address sectoral issues, much less to provide adequate representation of special interests. Until the 1960s the other institutions of policy-making—Cabinet, bureaucracy, federal-provincial conferences, and pressure groups—met these needs virtually without the participation of Parliament. The effect on Canadian democracy was deleterious. Parliament, the country's pre-eminent legitimating institution, proved less and less competent to cope with the questions that a modern economy places on the public agenda, while the institutions that could effectively deal with those questions gradually came to be seen as lacking the legitimacy that would ensure public acceptance of the policies and programs they had devised. We will argue that it is this fundamental tension in Canadian democracy—not the increasing vigour of pressure group politics—that causes the problems raised by Robert Stanfield. Pressure group politics is a symptom, not the cause. In this concluding chapter we suggest that, though the threat of the special-interest state can by no means be ignored in Canada, our highly visible and active pressure group system is not only far from being inherently perverse, it may actually contain the means of overcoming the space-sector tension we described.

THE REPRESENTATION OF SPACE AND SECTOR

Everyone has an attachment to place. In some degree, whether we live in a remote mountain valley or an urban neighbourhood, we are all deeply affected by both the physical and the social context of our surroundings. They are immensely important to us. They are, for us, an integrated, interdependent whole—what we think of when we identify ourselves with a community. Historically this attachment to physical space has been a cornerstone of political organization. Medieval kingdoms were built on the idea that at each level of the social hierarchy men and women were willing to defend specific pieces of territory. Early parliaments were organized around this same attachment. It is not surprising, then, that a concept of representative government built on the principle that each member of the legislature represents the electors living in a spatially defined area was used by western countries to adapt their institutions of government to the exigencies of the industrial revolution. Nor that the single-member constituency, the institutional device embodying that principle, is still with us today.

We take these arrangements for granted—so much so that it comes as a surprise when we are reminded that representative government might have been based on a different principle: the representation of sectors of social and economic activity rather than those of space. Yet many city states were governed in much this way through the guild system. The British have based their parliamentary institutions on the spatial concept, but from an early date they recognized the significance of sectoral concerns. The Woolsack, upon which English chief justices sit (rather uncomfortably) on state occasions, is a tangible relic of one such interest: the wool trade. In the nineteenth century a group of French philosophers, led by Saint-Simon and Auguste Comte, put forward proposals for reforming the system of representation along sectoral lines: proposals that found an echo in the corporatism of Fascist Europe.[1] Though discredited by their association with Fascist dictatorships, these proposals expressed valid doubts that spatially-based representative institutions were not meeting the demands of modern society. They also addressed two aspects of a significant issue: (i) that for most of us a concern for what we do is nearly as compelling as, and often in conflict with, intense attachment to the place we live in; and (ii) that at times we must give political expression to demands that emanate from what we do. How and why have this tension between our identification with both space and sector, and the need to find a legitimate method of representing sectoral concerns become significant issues?

Modern economies depend on the specialization of function. They operate on the assumption that work can be divided and that each element in any series of tasks can and should be performed by those who can do it most cheaply and expeditiously—in other words, most efficiently. The concept of the division of function can be applied not only on the production line, but in large-scale organizations, and even between geographic regions. Hence, in Canada—which tends to be seen in the international market-place as a source of primary products—certain regions are considered to be the best producers of some products, others of others. From a political point of view economic specialization has been a mixed blessing. Certainly it has made possible a vast increase in the quantity of goods available and has brought prosperity to many centres and regions. But it has also greatly reduced the economic self-sufficiency of countries, regions, and particularly of individual communities. It has also gone hand in hand with growing concentration of economic power and with the centralization of business decision-making. Hence not only have whole communities become vulnerable to sudden and unexpected changes in markets and in corporate policy, but they have also experienced a frightening sense of powerlessness.[2] Invariably the dark side of modern economics is reflected in political movements— regional alienation, protest movements, and so on—while even the bright side forces government to take a larger part in general economic management, at the risk of upsetting important economic and political groups whose well-being is adversely affected by government intervention. Thus economic development brings with it a long list of political perils for government. In this list few problems loom as large as the one created by the great pressure the modern economy has placed on the representative institutions of government. It is not an exaggeration to say that in several industrialized democracies, Canada included, this pressure has threatened to undermine the legitimacy of governmental institutions.

The reasons for this are deceptively simple. They relate to the fact that the pre-eminent legitimating institutions in these political systems have been built on the principle of spatial representation and have not successfully adapted to the specialized, or sectoral, demands of the modern economy. This explanation is deceiving in its simplicity because it glosses over the fact that it is not at all easy for governmental institutions to combine representation of both aspects of modern life. In the early years of modern economic development—which were also the first years of our present system of representative government—members of legislatures and the political parties they developed were able to combine both types of representation; but as the economy has grown more specialized and at the same time more interdependent, it has become increasingly difficult for legislators and parties to achieve this combination. The emergence of interest groups provided an outlet for the presentation of sectoral demands, but at the cost of dissociating those demands from the needs of communities. An American commentator, writing in the 1930s, was one of the first to appreciate the significance of this:

> In the thousands of localities which form the constituencies of the country, these different functional and occupational groups meet separately. Such meetings are indispensable, in order that the members of the group may have an informed understanding of their group interest and a policy for its furtherance. But the very success of their separate discussions may endanger the process of general policy-making unless there is local consultation, local cross-fertilization among the groups going on at the same time as their functional activities. The tendency now is toward the formation of pressure groups which move on Washington in blocs demanding that their interests be advanced. Congress and the President thus become practically the sole source of whatever concept of the general welfare receives attention. So far as the constituencies are concerned, the representative system becomes representation of special interests.[3]

The Canadian representative system—unlike the American, and to an extent the British—has not adapted to the representation of special interests. Rather, local and regional identity has always been more than usually prominent in our political institutions.[4] Thus in Parliament members give a very high priority to constituency and regional concerns. When they break party ranks it is more likely to register solidarity with their constituents than to proclaim a difference in principle. Health and Welfare Minister Monique Bégin's decision in 1982 to join with nine other Québec members in publicly criticizing government decisions concerning job-creation schemes was explained in these terms. She and her colleagues, it was pointed out, all represented areas hard hit by the recession; their constituents were complaining bitterly and the 'group of ten' had to demonstrate that, while they could not change government policy, they had tried to do so. It was probably for this reason that the Prime Minister took no serious disciplinary action against Miss Bégin and her fellow rebels.[5] A similar incident occurred in 1983 when members of the Québec caucus announced that they would not support a government bill introducing changes in the Crows' Nest Pass freight rate. The government modified its proposal to meet some of the demands of Québec farmers, even though doing so aroused bitter complaint in the West.[6] But the strength of constituency ties is not solely registered in such extreme gestures. It is seen in the electoral process itself, in the resistance to the system of 'parachuting' widely practised in European politics. In Canada it is highly unusual for a constituency to elect a representative who has no ties at all with the area.[7] At a broader level the strength of regional ties has led to the institutionalization of regional caucuses. The Saskatchewan caucus of the NDP broke ranks with the party over constitutional reform, for example.[8] The Québec Liberal caucus has been the 'single most important influence in maintaining the Québec textile industry [through persuading the government to maintain tariff barriers], despite the government's policy of opening up trade with the Third World.'[9] Among members from the Atlantic provinces regional affinities create an especially strong bond—so much so that the Atlantic Provinces Economic Council has organized from time to time meetings of all members of Parliament from the region, regardless of party label, and claims to have been successful in urging them to forget party differences in promoting policies favourable to the region.[10]

If territorial or spatial concerns are highly institutionalized in Parliament, sectoral concerns are by contrast hardly represented at all. In Europe members of legislatures are often associated more closely in the public mind with specific interests than with the constituencies they happen to represent. They are the acknowledged parliamentary spokesmen for those interests, expected to lead debate on issues that concern them and to lobby for them on committees and behind the scenes. In fact, so pronounced is this type of representation that it is sometimes blamed for the loss of public regard for legislative institutions.[11] Not so in Canada. Here, if a spokesman for a particular interest emerges in the House of Commons, it is more by chance than by design. The reasons for this absence of sectoral representation in our legislatures are numerous and beyond the scope of this discussion, but some at least should be mentioned briefly. We can in part attribute it to the territorialism just referred to. Constituencies that resist parachuting by parties are equally likely to turn a cold shoulder to sectoral interests anxious to place a spokesman in the legislature, unless a single industry dominates the riding in question, as the fishing industry dominates certain constituencies in Atlantic Canada; the textile industry several in Québec; the automobile industry, Oshawa and Windsor; the public service, the Ottawa area; and mining, agriculture, and the forest industries a number of constituencies across the country. In such constituencies members either know a great deal or become knowledgeable about the dominant industry. But in the majority of ridings no one industry is preponderant and the member has neither the time nor the incentive to become expertly informed about the many different types of economic activity—much less non-economic activities—to be found in his or her riding. Thus the electoral system militates against interest representation in the House of Commons. In the Senate, with its different basis of appointment, a greater emphasis on interest representation can be expected, and in fact the Senate has been called 'a lobby from within'.[12]

However, as a lobby it is far more representative of highly institutionalized wealth than of the diversified interests of Canadians. Furthermore, the functions and status of the Senate do not lend themselves to the kind of interest representation that is involved in vigorously and publicly opposing, or promoting, specific kinds of policy, though Senate review of legislation often goes beyond merely correcting technical problems and improving drafting.[13]

Only recently has parliamentary procedure and internal organization encouraged either effective interest representation before the House or the attainment of expertise by members. For example, until the reforms of 1968-9 the Committee system was quite incapable of generating among members a thorough understanding of the fields they were asked to legislate for. It is hardly surprising that very few interest groups or their representatives troubled to appear before them. In the House itself the lack of informed spokesmen made it difficult for House leaders to organize creditable debate. In the era of the mandarins in particular, *Hansard* presented daily testimony to the poverty of Parliament's role in the policy process. Even more important, the timing of Parliament's involvement in the policy process worked against its ability to consider constructively sectoral concerns. For the most part such concerns could be addressed either in question period or through consideration of specific pieces of legislation. The former is a monitoring device or an opportunity to draw attention to urgent problems and contributes little to the development of long-term policy, which is important to most institutionalized interests. In fact, because question period is a time of rapid, short exchanges, which are highly publicized, it could actually distort government and interest group positions or otherwise damage their relationships. Consideration of legislation does allow more scope for discussion of long-term policy, but here parliamentarians and pressure group representatives were for many years deterred by the conventions of the policy system. By the time legislation was presented to the House it had usually been subject to considerable discussion between officials, interest group representatives and finally Cabinet. Even without the government's customary insistence that each piece of legislation be treated as a government bill and have the unwavering support of all its members, most of those involved in drafting and presenting legislation would have been reluctant to reopen clauses that had been the product of much research, consultation and negotiation. In short, Parliament's involvement in the policy process was mistimed and therefore usually ineffectual.[14]

The strength of territorial feeling, the workings of the electoral system, and the inadequacy of the institution of Parliament itself explain in part why sectoral interests have until recently virtually ignored the legislature and have devoted their attention to the political and administrative executive and to the bureaucracy at large. Other factors have had to do with the greater ease with which sectorally oriented interest groups have been able to organize themselves to communicate with administrative agencies—which are themselves structured around a functional division of labour. Together the inadequacies of parliamentary representation and the compatibility of sectorally organized interests and agencies militated against the presentation of special-interest demands through Parliament and encouraged their expression through other channels. Initially special interests cultivated the political executive itself and in so doing imposed the first great check on legislative involvement in policy-making. They also greatly weakened the policy role of party organizations at large. As the tasks of government became more complex, and as the need for communication with government became more pervasive and more technical, interests turned their attention to the administrative branch, reserving contact with the executive to symbolic occasions or to cases where agreement could not be reached at lower levels. In many respects contacts between interests and agencies related to, and were conducted by, individuals; but there were numerous occasions when concerted pressure had to be applied by interests combined, or when government sought the collective views of those affected by policies. On these occasions the benefits of interest group formation were increasingly apparent. Thus pressure groups became the accepted channel for interest representation and the administrative branch became both the object of, and the forum for, communication.

The effect on parliamentary institutions was devastating. Gradually the administrative arm of government assumed powers that earlier had been exercised by the legislature and the political executive. This was part of a world-wide trend that was usually explained in terms of the growing complexity of government activity. Governments, so the argument goes, were so deeply involved in so many highly technical aspects of social and economic life that politicians, overwhelmed by the extent and complexity of these responsibilities, abdicated decision-making to administrators. Even when they insisted on retaining final decision-making authority, more often than not they felt compelled by the complexity of the issues to follow the advice of their experts.

Canada's experience was similar to that of other countries. Federal and provincial statutes increasingly provided that officials would 'work out the details' by preparing regulations, which would be approved by ministers and cabinets and, through the passage of orders-in-council, acquire the force of law. This delegated legislation seldom received close scrutiny from politicians. Its volume was, and is, considerable; it is often technical; it rarely catches the public eye, and in any case it has usually been cleared with the affected parties—that is, with those identified, by themselves and by officials, as being interested in the legislation.[15]

The net result of this long progression—it took three quarters of a century for the effects of delegation to reach these proportions—was to transfer a substantial degree of political power from the political executive to the administrative arm. Just as at the end of the nineteenth century the evolution of the modern economy forced the locus of power from the legislature to the executive, so by the middle of the present century the invocation of administrative competence had effected a further substantial shift of power from the political executive to the bureaucracy. The size and power of the bureaucracy, warned a policy document prepared by the Progressive Conservatives in 1977, 'offer a constant challenge to the moral and actual authority of the House of Commons.'[16] When the Conservatives reached power two years later they found that the challenge at the executive level was equally great. Gillies and Pigott sum up a widely accepted view of the situation:

> It is well known that the process by which organizations put forth their views tends to bypass Parliament. Skilled lobbyists always begin well down in the system so that they will always have a place to which they can appeal if they lose in their first efforts. Thus when legislation is being prepared the first efforts of interest groups are directed at the department involved, their goal being to exclude from the all-important memorandum to Cabinet recommendations which would adversely affect their interests. They generally recognize that once a position has been taken in that document, it can be changed only with difficulty. If, however, a special interest group does fail in its first efforts, it may meet with senior members of the department; perhaps the deputy minister and then even the minister. If these efforts are unsuccessful and legislation is proposed to which it is opposed, the group may then decide to lobby members of Parliament and eventually appear at the hearings on the bill before a committee of the House of Commons. Parliament, in other words, is the last line of defence.[17]

J. Iain Gow makes a similar point when he speaks of policy-making in Québec, arguing that 'les groupes organisés préfèrent exercer leur pressions à Québec, soit auprès des hommes politiques, le Premier ministre et les ministres, soit auprès de la haute fonction publique' rather than through individual members of the National Assembly.[18] The latter, overwhelmed by the complexity of modern administration, find their own resources and those of their parties and the legislature insufficient. In the words of a British commentator, A.H. Hanson, contemplating the decline of parliamentary institutions in that country, 'we are stuck with a form of government in which bureaucrats and pressure groups play leading roles and in which the legislature can hardly expect to be restored to its former glories.'[19]

The same commentator, however, adds an important qualification to his gloomy view. The decline of Parliament, he maintains, does not imply, 'as the extremer critics have suggested, that Parliament is now no more than a dignified or ornamental institution. Even in the absence of further reform it remains the one institution whose demise would involve the virtual disappearance of everything characteristically democratic about our way of life.'[20]

We will argue that Hanson's crucial qualification is at the heart of recent developments in pressure group politics—in Canada at least.

PRESSURE GROUPS AND THE REVIVAL OF PARLIAMENT

In pressure group politics access is the key to influence. The key to access, however, varies from system to system and from time to time within single systems. The latter variation seems to have occurred recently in Canada. A system of pressure group politics in which access sprang from the ability to provide specialized information has been changed into one in which legitimation is equally important in opening the door to the policy process. From the Parliamentary perspective this change is significant: a system of pressure group politics in which specialized communication obtains access tends to shun Parliament, whereas one in which legitimation is the wherewithal for participation cultivates Parliament. The reasons for this spring from the capacities and functions of Parliament itself.

A system of pressure group politics that emphasizes the search for legitimation enhances the role of Parliament, for the simple reason that of all the political institutions in Canada, Parliament—the House of Commons in particular—is, after the constitution itself, the pre-eminent legitimating institution. We have explored this point in Chapter 3, pointing out that Canada gives unusual prominence to Parliament as a legitimating institution.[21] Conversely, an information-oriented system of pressure group politics shuns Parliament because, while Parliament is the nation's forum, it is not a reliable source of information. Parliament deals in large ideas and sweeping visions, dreadful wrongs and great calamities. Exaggeration is its stock in trade; information is simply the raw material used to spin candy floss for journalists. Of course, there are other sides to Parliament's handling of information: committees deal with tedious quantities of technical detail and may substantially affect specific policies. But even in committee, partisanship or constituency concerns are forces to be reckoned with. In short, the language of Parliament—the language of politics—is not the language of policy formulation.[22] It may be used to promote policy, to support policy, or to attack it, but it lacks the precision needed for the analysis of situations, the delineation of alternatives, or the formulation of policy responses.

To say that Parliament is not well adapted to policy formulation is not to say that those who have an interest in specific policies automatically steer clear of it. Quite the contrary, as we will argue shortly. However, in a situation such as we knew in Canada during the mandarin years, where the policy process is both highly bureaucratic and considered to be thoroughly legitimate, interaction with Parliament becomes for most groups dysfunctional. It might raise the level of conflict surrounding specific issues; it might encourage criticism of government actions or intentions; it could lead to the foreclosing of policy options, or put both groups and bureaucrats to a great deal of extra effort to justify, elaborate, and explain policy. For representatives of established, or institutionalized, pressure groups, anxious to maintain good long-term relations with bureaucratic policy-makers, these are situations to be avoided.[23] The simplest way to avoid them is to avoid Parliament.

However, this condition holds only as long as a policy process dominated by the bureacracy is considered legitimate. In a country such as France, where the legitimacy of the public service derives both from the legitimacy of the president, and the executive, and from a deeply rooted public conception of the state, such a condition may last for a very long time indeed. In a country like Canada, where the concept of the state has only limited meaning and where the public service has virtually no independent legitimacy, it is unlikely that such a condition will long outlast the public's realization that the political executive has lost control of the bureaucracy. It is the political executive that has legitimacy and confers that legitimacy on those who serve it. Once it becomes dissociated from the political executive, the bureaucracy forfeits its claim to legitimacy.

The public became convinced during the 1970s that the federal Cabinet had lost control of the machinery of government. This conviction diminished both the political executive and the public service. A Cabinet that cannot work the public service loses public respect and eventually its own aura of legitimacy. A public service that is believed to be 'out of control' comes to be seen as merely self-serving and is treated accordingly. We argued in Chapter 3 that Parliament has, if anything, benefited from the decline of Cabinet and bureaucracy; that the recent evolution of policy processes has placed a premium on Parliament's legitimating capacity and has thus assured it of an enhanced role. The decline of Cabinet enhances the status of Parliament, for the stability of the political system requires the maintenance of legitimating institutions, and when one such institution is in eclipse we can expect others to become more prominent—particularly those that have been endowed traditionally with legitimating status. Parliament's legitimating capacity, in conjunction with its ability to focus public debate, now makes interaction with the legislature highly desirable in the eyes of many groups and a necessity in the eyes of others. Even John Bulloch, who has a low regard for Parliament's policy-making capacity, admits that 'if . . . you want . . . to put pressure on the system, there is nothing more effective than going to your Member of Parliament' and focusing public attention through caucus and question period.[24] Simply by giving them a hearing Parliamentary Committees confer legitimacy on challenging interests and enable them to claim national attention. Furthermore their participation galvanizes other groups interested in moulding public attitudes and promoting new policies. In the increasingly competitive environment of pressure group politics, the leaders of established groups have to anticipate these challenges, or at least respond to them.

A need to defend their interests in public is only one of the factors encouraging established groups to pay more attention to Parliament. Their behaviour also reflects the changed relations between groups and agencies that we have discussed. On the one hand, institutionalized groups clearly act with more freedom than they did in the past. On the other, it is equally clear that their newly kindled interest is encouraged by government agencies, which, faced with the diminished legitimacy we have pointed out, see the cultivation of friends in Parliament as a means of developing alternative bases of support.[25] In part agencies achieve this through direct interaction between parliamentarians and departmental representatives. The more detailed examination of estimates and legislation that is now possible as a result of the reform of the committee system and the tendency for a core at least of MPs to affiliate themselves with specific committees has encouraged the development of a better understanding of agency goals in the House and has increased public service interaction with Parliament. Public servants appear before Parliamentary committees to an unprecedented extent. But public servants are prevented by their constitutional role as subordinate advisers from engaging vigorously and independently in advocating and defending the policies they prefer. In consequence, we argued, they have looked to their closest associates in their policy communities—the institutionalized groups—to act as proxies, explaining policy, defending it, and promoting it. Self-interest has thus encouraged government agencies and established groups to engage in public discussion of policy and to accept an expanded role for Parliament and people in policy formulation.

The significance of the legitimating role obliges us to take issue with those who have argued that the complexity of modern government reduces to the purely symbolic Parliament's role in the policy process. Some twenty years ago A.H. Hanson, in an article that will be treated here as reasonably representative of the literature,[26] contrasted the then widely accepted Schumpeterian view of Parliament's role with that enunciated a century earlier by Bagehot. The former confined Parliament to (1) sanctioning the formation of a type of government that the electorate, through its vote, may be considered to have approved of; (2) subjecting that government to criticism of a general kind, thereby acting as a forum for the 'competitive struggle for the people's vote'; and (3) securing where possible the redress of specific grievances. In other words, Parliament was performing its role adequately as long as it acted as an electoral college, as a critic, and as an ombudsman, but its policy role was decidedly limited. While we would not exclude these functions, we would wish to cite as well the more distinctly policy-oriented functions perceived by Bagehot, and are more inclined to agree with him that the function of Parliament is to 'express the mind of the people'; 'to teach the nation what it does not know'; and to make us 'hear what otherwise we should not'. We have attributed this somewhat restored role to the loosening of the policy system. Because its capacity to legitimate consequently plays a greater part in the competition over policy, and because its talent for focusing public attention is much sought after, Parliament in Canada seems definitely to be playing a more significant role than it did twenty years ago.

The key questions, of course, are how significant is that role and how far can it be extended? How precisely does Parliament express the will of the nation? If very precisely, then Parliament is playing a major role in policy formation. If only very broadly—to the extent, perhaps, of registering the popularity or unpopularity of the government—then Parliament has not progressed beyond the Schumpeterian definition of its functions. The answer seems to lie somewhere between these extremes. The pessimists suggest that the policy role is minimal and is likely to remain so. The optimists claim that caucus has always played a larger part than most critics will admit; that the present more dynamic system has already enhanced Parliament's policy role; and that the recent experiment with Parliamentary task-force enquiries into specific policy issues is a portent for the future.[27] Neither side suggests that Parliament can or should actually initiate or formulate policy. But even if we were to agree that Parliament's role *should* fall short of policy initiation and formulation, we would still be allowing it a potentially large say in policy formation processes and in the overseeing of policy implementation, which is often part of the 'next round' of policy development. Thus Parliament could play a much larger part in the early stages of policy development, carrying out general discussions with the public, hearing expert opinion, providing an initial reading of the public mind on issues, and contributing to the further development of public opinion. The growth of this kind of activity was implicit in some of the steps taken in the field of parliamentary reform by the Trudeau government from the late 1960s on, notably in the creation of Opposition Days, in the experiments with policy papers of various hues, and most recently in the establishment of the parliamentary task forces. In terms of contributing to long-term policy, the task forces seem the most promising because they avoid the temptation to focus on current issues (Question Period and Opposition Days provide adequately for this) and yet they enable parliamentarians to do more than simply react to White Papers and other preliminary documents when they are tabled. Though care must be taken in selecting topics for investigation by parliamentary task forces, experience to date—and indeed experience in the standing committees from time to time—has shown that Parliament can help express the mind of the people and can perform an educational function. A comment made to the Bar Association committee enquiring into legislative reform illustrates the point:

> Most people's general concern is that the place doesn't work and that it is irrelevant to most people on the street and most MPs. If I hadn't got involved in a special committee [task force], the frustrations that other MPs feel would

> have been mine as well. In the committee you could get out there and talk to
> people. You had investigative powers . . . you really got into the subject. The
> proof that you can be effective is that the government has implemented over
> half of our recommendations.[28]

Parliamentary intervention at this middle stage of policy formation opti-
mizes its legitimating capacity while avoiding confrontation with the
government's need to command the confidence of the House. By encouraging
the general public—groups and individuals—to express their views, it
legitimizes those views to a degree, thus pre-empting the tendency of the
public service to set the parameters for discussion early in the policy process.
At the same time, because the exploratory nature of the investigation is
widely understood, this approach neither threatens government's ability to
make the final determination of policy nor excites the more destructive
aspects of partisanship. In short, to make the best use of the ability its
legitimating capacity gives it to contribute to the policy process, Parliament
should follow a long-standing dictum of Canadian pressure group politics:
to influence the shape of legislation, you must present your case before
Cabinet has decided its position.[29] It has been amply demonstrated that
Parliament is not a suitable vehicle for initiating policy or for formulating
policy, but the logic of its position in a diffused power system suggests that
it can make a major contribution to the pre-Cabinet stages of policy
formation.[30]

We assume that party politics will also benefit from Parliament's revival.
If parliamentarians are seen to play a meaningful role in policy formation,
the party should attract strong candidates, and community leaders should
once again wish to be associated with party organizations. To capitalize on
these trends, however, Canada's political parties will have to transform
their grass-roots organizations from electoral machines chugging away on
the fuel of minor patronage into bodies with a genuine capacity to assist in
policy formation. If parties succeed in restoring a policy capability to the
grass roots, there is reason to hope that the competition of parties and pressure groups will turn into something more productive, not only for the
organizations themselves, but for the general public.

Our discussion has linked several phenomena that have been separately
observed in Canada: the diffusion of power within the executive-administrative branch, the proliferation and expanded role of pressure groups, and
the increased attention Parliament has been receiving from interest organizations. Suggesting that this last may reflect fundamental changes in the
policy system as a whole, we argued that the enhanced role of Parliament
and the proliferation of interest groups can be partially attributed to the
diffusion of power within the executive and administrative branches; that a
tendency towards bureaucratic pluralism has led agencies to develop extra-
governmental support at the interest group level; and that both interest

groups and agencies, finding it useful to exploit the legitimating and publicizing capacities of Parliament, have contributed to the enhancement of Parliament's role in the policy process.

Because we see the proliferation and the growing prominence of pressure groups as part and parcel of the movement that led to this improvement of Parliament's policy role, we do not share Robert Stanfield's concern that an abundance of special-interest organizations threatens democratic government in Canada. We contend that because our pressure groups are less willing, or able, to shelter in the half-light of politics, the public is now more aware than it has been for many years of the debates that lie behind public policy decisions, and our Parliaments are much better informed than were their predecessors of twenty years ago. Recent changes in pressure group behaviour are the product of, and have themselves fostered, a more open and dynamic policy process. Parliament may at last be creating an institutional structure that could effectively reconcile the spatial and sectoral needs of Canadians.

TOWARDS EQUALITY IN REPRESENTATION

Enhanced legislative influence in the policy process ameliorates the tension between our spatial and sectoral systems of representation, but it does little to ensure that all interests in Canadian society have an equal opportunity to contribute to public decision-making. To a degree it promotes inequity, because it imposes on all participants an increasingly complex and expensive procedure that only established and relatively affluent groups can afford.

The problem of equality is second only to that created by the rivalry of spatial and sectoral systems of representation. It has two aspects: first, inequity in group representation lessens public regard for the policies that emerge from the process. A sense of inefficacy breeds alienation. An alienated public will, at best, turn a passive face to public authorities, and at worst will come to see the regime as illegitimate and violently oppose it. Apart from the Québec crisis of the 1960s and 1970s, Canada has not been seriously afflicted by the consequences of inefficacy. Nevertheless that crisis, as well as survey reports indicating surprisingly high levels of inefficacy for a country that prides itself on its democratic qualities,[31] suggest a need for efforts to maintain and improve the opportunities for all interests to contribute to the policy process. Complete equality in representation will always be an ideal, but that is no reason to ignore it or to think that efforts to achieve it will not strengthen public regard for policy.

Equality of access also enhances the quality of public policy. On the one hand policy-makers derive breadth of opinion from it. On the other the free flow of information that generally accompanies equal and open participation raises the level of public understanding and promotes consensus. This of course slows down the formation and implementation of public policy;

but as long as due process is not allowed to serve as a vehicle for indecision, the time and effort spent on developing policies and programs are probably compensated for by their general acceptance and ease of implementation.

On grounds, then, of ensuring the legitimacy of the policy process and of enhancing its quality, every encouragement should be given to promoting greater equality between groups. The means of achieving that are numerous, though imperfect and far from reliable. They entail modifications in the regulation of organized lobbying; in the provision of resources for interest groups; and in the processes of public-policy formation.

(i) *Regulation*

One of the first public reactions to the intrusion of pressure groups into the policy process is to call for their regulation. The pleading, often behind the scenes, for special interests arouses the deepest distrust in a democratic society. It is only to be expected that calls for the registration, even for the limitation, of pressure group activity should be heard once their involvement becomes obtrusive, as it has in recent years in this country. As early as 1969 NDP MP Barry Mather presented a private member's bill to Parliament to regulate lobbyists, and a succession of nearly identical proposals have been put forward by Liberal, Conservative, and New Democrat members since then.[32] In September 1985 Prime Minister Mulroney announced that the government would introduce legislation to establish a system of registration for lobbyists.[33]

This proved to be more difficult than expected. After some months of study by the Department of Consumer and Corporate Affairs, the government decided not to introduce a bill but produced instead a discussion paper entitled *Lobbying and the Registration of Paid Lobbyists*. Critics charged that this was the result of pressure from lobbyists, many of whom had campaigned against registration.[34] Perhaps the lobbyists did have some influence, but the decision reflected as well the government's realization that regulation does not necessarily promote the democratization of interest group activity.

Registration—the minimal first step to regulation—typifies the dilemma faced by public authorities when they try to take the measure of lobbying and limit its harmful side-effects. On the surface, registration seems innocuous and uncomplicated. Examination shows it to be neither, though it may still be desirable. This becomes evident as soon as the legislative draftsman attempts to specify who should be required to register. Most frequently lobbyists are defined as individuals who, for a fee, attempt to influence public policy on behalf of a third party.[35] This definition respects the right of individuals to represent their own interests to policy-makers and it excludes those who altruistically lobby on behalf of others. It is the definition suggested by the government's discussion paper, which adds that individuals who lobby on behalf of foreign governments, corporations, and individuals should also be included. The discussion paper proposes several exclusions, as well: officers or employees of trade or professional associations, unions, and 'national interest groups', and business executives responsible for lobbying on behalf of their corporations.[36] The definition would in effect apply only to independent lobbyists and lobbying firms.

By itself such a definition does not meet the needs of legislators. The impetus behind the government's call for registration is the desire of parliamentarians and officials to know the affiliation of the lobbyists who approach them.[37] They believe that this information will help them assess the motivations behind lobbying efforts and the reasons for the positions taken by lobbyists and interest groups, and so aid negotiation. It might even lead to direct negotiation between officials and interests, and so eliminate 'middle men'. Finally, officials want this information because they have a duty to know who is attempting to influence public policy. They do not want to be deceived into putting forward policies that are not genuinely supported by the public at large or by affected special publics. Similarly the public at large expects a registration system to provide it with more information than it now has about the interests competing for concessions from policy-makers.

To meet these needs registration must entail more than simply recording the name of an individual lobbyist in some central registry. It means providing information about those the lobbyist represents. How much information? Should the organization behind the lobbyist be required simply to file a brief prospectus stating its aims, officers, and address? Such a system could be easily abused. Policy-makers would derive some benefit from the information provided about bona fide groups, but groups fronting for interests unwilling to make their activities known would find it easy to contrive innocuous credentials. The registration procedure would consequently create paperwork for legitimate groups but do nothing to illuminate the interests behind less legitimate organizations.

An alternative approach would require the lobbyist to file much more information about those he or she represents, including statements of lobbying expenses, sources of financial support and, in the case of interest groups, copies of their constitutions and membership lists. Provision of such details of interest group aims, structure, and resources would meet many information requirements of policy-makers and of the public at large, but it would entail substantial costs. The least of these would be administrative, although an effective registration service—with the means to exact, verify, or disseminate information—would not be cheap. Administrative charges, though, deserve less attention than the possible costs to free and open public discussion. Superficially an information requirement conforms with the ideal of democratic government; it is certainly important for the public to know who is influencing public policy.

Unfortunately information can lead not only to clarification but to intimidation. Individuals willing to give unobtrusive support to unpopular causes may be loath to do so if their allegiance is to be made public. Just as there are communities where support for the NDP—never mind more radical political parties—is socially unacceptable, so there are communities, including policy communities, that will not tolerate the alternative views expressed by some interest groups. To oppose sealing in St Anthony's, Newfoundland, takes considerable courage. Vancouver-based opponents of wolf-pack culling were physically as well as verbally attacked when they ventured into the trapping and hunting communities of the British Columbia interior.[38] Usually Canadians apply fewer physical sanctions against those who challenge the conventional wisdom, but such sanctions can be compelling. Many are reluctant to join groups whose aims might conflict with those of their employers. Environmental groups, for example, threaten many concerns, large and small. Loss of employment is a real possibility for anyone supporting a group whose activities might lead to higher costs for the company. Similarly corporate support for such groups is hard to come by. Environmentally aware managers and owners of firms are not necessarily free agents—they depend on other companies for supplies and sales. They find it safe to support symphony orchestras, hospitals, and even universities, but often hesitate to support overtly a group that wants clean air, clean water, and an attractive landscape. Non-economic sanctions are readily available. On returning to St John's after being away from Newfoundland for some time, Walter Davis, a former president of the city's Rotary Club, found that his application for membership was deferred. He claimed that his work as a peace activist was the cause.[39]

Social ostracism, discrimination, harrassment—including vandalism and hate mail—can all be used to discipline errant members of the community, and are not easy to prohibit. Nor is the state always an impartial refuge for those who hold unconventional opinions. Many supporters of the peace movement are convinced that their activities are monitored, recorded, and occasionally used as the basis for harrassment. Their fears may be exaggerated, but from time to time actions of security agencies lend them credibility.[40] For these reasons democracy may be imperilled as much as promoted by the full disclosure of interest-group information.

There are other costs to registration. If registration is to be a necessary preliminary to lobbying, how can our political system sustain its spontaneity? The pluralists venerated the dynamism of American pressure group politics for good reason. It encouraged new groups to form as it became clear that the polity had to address new issues. Established groups are often slow to recognize and speak to new issues, and their ties to other members of their policy communities make them reluctant to raise divisive questions; the internal organization may actively resist them, or give them a low priority.

But the sudden emergence of issue-oriented groups jolts them into a new awareness and often forces them to grapple with the ramifications of existing policies. This dynamic occurs in Canada as well as in the United States and should not be doused by a formal system of registration. The impulse to establish a new group can be undermined if a long process of registration prevents its participation in an immediate and pressing debate. A system of registration that prohibits lobbying until groups have filed considerable documentation, or imposes fixed fees to recover the costs of the registration service would impede group formation and participation even further.

Perhaps these problems with registration led the Department of Consumer and Corporate Affairs to propose a system that requires only the registration of the lobbyist—defined, as we have seen, very narrowly—the name of the client, and the subject of lobbying activity. On the grounds that a more detailed review was needed of the confidential relationship between lobbyist and client, the discussion paper left to a House committee the question of determining what financial information should be required. Its prescription for disciplining lobbyists who fail to comply with these requirements—a prohibition from practice—was severe by comparison.[41]

Although the creators of registration procedures must take into account the problems that accompany different systems of registration, such an approach is too cautious. None of the objections to registration that we have discussed refutes the argument that an effective form of registration is desirable. Democratic politics requires interests to be frank about their reasons for supporting or opposing policy options. The public has a right to know who wants what, and why. The policy-maker has a duty to know. Furthermore secrecy can discredit the policy process, rendering its output illegitimate. It is in the interests of all bona fide groups that their efforts to influence public policy not be considered clandestine. Disclosure, then, is a necessity. The problem is, how can we secure disclosure without precipitating intimidation or fostering the fear of intimidation?

A partial solution can be derived from our experience with electoral law, where the debate over secrecy versus openness is also significant. For the individual voter we have guaranteed the secrecy of the ballot. It is up to him or her to tell the world what party he or she favours. Similarly we can respect the privacy of group membership, and we can do so without jeopardizing our efforts to know what interests are actually mounting lobbying campaigns. The mechanism for pursuing this information is also applied in Canadian electoral law, and is found in the requirement that all financial contributions to parties above a certain minimum be recorded and publicly available. Thus individual donations over $500 and corporate donations over $5,000 could be recorded. Under a regime such as that suggested here, all lobbyists—independent professionals, company executives, interest group representatives, and so on—would be required to provide a statement outlining the purposes of the organization represented, naming its officers, and indicating the number of paid-up members. Registration on behalf of organizations would also require a list of the individuals authorized to represent the organization; an audited financial statement of lobbying expenditures and, if the organization were an interest group, a list of all individual members contributing over $500 and all corporate contributions of more than $5,000. Such a procedure, though not foolproof, would go a long way towards ensuring privacy to citizens while identifying major interests.

Flexibility in regulatory arrangements, along with their impartial administration, would also help overcome the dangers of fossilizing the group process through a regulatory system. While it is desirable that a minimum of information be available concerning all lobbyists and all groups, it is not necessary to put emergent issue-oriented groups through the same hoops that must be applied to established organizations. Initial registration for new groups should be simple, routine, and totally cost-free, in terms of fees or professional assistance. As organizations establish themselves, registration requirements should be more probing. Groups with budgets above certain levels and with some experience in the policy process should be expected to disclose their resources and interests.

American experience with lobby regulation demonstrates that these are only the minimal issues that would be raised by a regulatory regime. Even a highly permissive framework such as that in effect in Washington was fiercely contested and precipitated complex evasive activities.[42] Nevertheless the type of measures suggested here would go far towards installing pressure group politics legitimately and usefully in our policy process. The data collected would not only help policy-makers and the public assess rival demands, but might also serve to categorize impartially organizations that lack pocketbooks to match their concern for the public interest, and are in genuine need of public assistance. In short, registration—with the regulation it implies—is a dangerous but necessary instrument. Poorly defined and badly constructed, registration can exacerbate the problems now posed by pressure group politics. Sensitively created and implemented, it can be used to make pressure group politics an effective and useful part of our policy process.

(ii) *Resources*:

Any regulatory regime has to be the product of a broad philosophical framework for incorporating group activities in the policy process. One such as that described above is naturally based on assumptions—we have articulated some of them—about the need for openness in public discussion and the corresponding need to protect the privacy of those whose views render them vulnerable. But such a regulatory regime would not make fully operational the philosophy behind the concerns we have raised throughout this study. It would help identify the participants in public debate and work against illicit lobbying. But it would do nothing to overcome imbalances created by unequal resource bases. A group with the resources to throw impressive 'power parties', to capture media attention, to maintain full-time representatives in the nation's capitals, and to pay for the elaborate briefs that are part of any sustained policy discussion has the staying power, the authority, and the 'policy capacity'[43] to outlast most of its rivals, particularly if they happen to be public-interest groups. Yet the rival policy objectives may be no less valid—they may even be more representative of the public's wishes. Therefore an important underlying assumption of a democratic philosophy of pressure group involvement in public-policy formation is that every effort should be made to compensate for extreme differentials in the resource bases of competing groups.

A policy incorporating this philosophy is not easy to arrive at. State provision of resources, as we argued in Chapter 8, can have a deleterious effect on recipient groups and on the dynamism of the policy process. It can lead group organizations to lose touch with their members; it can encourage undertakings that cannot be sustained by the groups' real resources, rendering them ultimately dependent on government rather than on their own members. Not only does dependency encourage sycophancy and destroy free public debate, but a dependent group may occupy a position in the policy community to the exclusion of alternative organizations, thus fostering inertia in the policy system. Finally the state must avoid creating an environment in which pressure group development becomes a cottage industry. Neither its procedures to ensure a fair hearing for all interests nor its resource assistance should encourage entrepreneurs to build organizations—ostensibly representing a particular interest—that actually exist, through government grants, to support a small staff of professional lobbyists whose chief effects will be to consume public funds and to prolong and complicate the resolution of the public business. In this welter of conflicting goals two imperatives stand out: the need to promote equality and the need to avoid dependence.

Equality can be promoted in a variety of ways, some of which were described in Chapter 8 and others to be mentioned in the discussion of procedure that follows. The resources of groups can be supplemented directly through grants; through the provision of facilities such as space, office equipment, and access to communications tools; and even through the secondment of government personnel to groups. Indirect assistance can be offered through the purchase of group services, such as research or administrative services. Positional policies, such as those that place group representatives on influential advisory boards, also give indirect support because they encourage members to believe that they are tapped into the flow of vital information.

Crucial to equality are not so much the forms assistance takes, but the criteria used to allocate it, and who decides which group should receive what. In 1977 a study commissioned by the Secretary of State reported that though a number of federal agencies supported voluntary groups, each had 'its own unique set of priorities in this area, not to mention its own unique way of reporting on its activities.'[44] The study group was appalled at the lack of consistency it discovered and the unwillingness of agencies to provide information—much less uniform policies—on their support for voluntary groups.[45] Where direct grants and contributions are concerned, impartiality of the allocative process is essential.[46] A case might be made for removing such decisions entirely from the purview of agencies that have a vested interest in recipient groups' policy field, but in practice this would be counter-productive. Agencies in the policy community, particularly the lead agency, will be reluctant to work with groups they consider to be antagonistic, and will exclude them from the flow of information and use positional politics to render them ineffectual. A more practical approach would vest agencies with authority to make grants to groups, as they now do, but insisting that the granting procedure follow government-wide standards and submit to evaluation by an independent body every five years. While this would not entirely eliminate the problems of dependence, it would assure new groups of a more impartial process of grant allocation than currently exists. To discourage groups from becoming dependent on any one agency the granting process might tie assistance to the development of alternative sources of support.

Indirect assistance offers groups the opportunity to broaden their base of financial support. Here too some measure of reform is necessary. Agencies should not be in a position to exploit the groups in their policy community— insisting, for example, on excluding overhead costs from contract calculations. Procedures for awarding contracts to groups should be standardized in a fashion like that used for awarding contracts to private firms, and should be characterized by impartiality. Furthermore, administrative agencies need not be the only beneficiaries of the research capacities of groups: Parliament's revived role in the policy process could be sustained through extended research support, including enlarging the budgets available to parliamentary committees and task forces for commissioning research by groups and consultants.

As we saw in Chapter 8, because the costs of intervening in the regulatory process are often formidable some regulatory agencies and commissions of inquiry have established procedures for granting to less affluent groups the funds they need to hire expert assistance. As a result such groups have been able to present briefs and arguments that are as effective as those prepared by wealthy interests. Similar procedures warrant adoption in all regulatory situations and could be supported in part—as they are in some American jurisdictions[47]—through charges levied on those who would benefit materially from the changes they have requested in regulations or through permission to develop public resources. The principle of 'who benefits, pays' could be extended to other settings. In our cities, for example, neighbourhood groups are often unable to sustain the cost of representing their interests against the proposals of developers who wish to secure major changes in existing plans. Such costs should be recoverable from those who will profit from change.

Similar problems are found in litigation. The experience of the few groups that have attempted to obtain their objectives through court action discourages others, often at the expense of the public interest. Unless the legal system is to be abandoned entirely to the wealthy, some means must be found whereby groups concerned with matters of genuine public interest may pursue their concerns without undue hardship.[48] It should be possible for the state to establish funds to help sustain litigation deemed by the courts to raise issues of genuine public conern. A procedure that would both discourage frivolous litigation and aid the resolution of public-interest questions should be feasible and would secure a measure of equality in a field of public policy formation that is becoming increasingly important.

Thus far we have been unable to escape from the tendency, long evident in Canada, to look to the public purse to support pressure group activity, particularly the activity of public-interest groups. Even though, as we have argued, dependence on government, and particularly on specific agencies, is deleterious, both for the dependent groups and for public debate, the fact is that Canadians—according to a consensus among pressure group activists— are reluctant to give financial support to groups. Though voluntarism is strongly established in this country, private benefaction is not.[49] Pressure groups are forced to rely on direct and indirect government support. The procedures put forward here take this reality into account and attempt to offset the side-effects of dependence by providing for clear criteria to govern both the awarding of support and impartiality in its administration.

It is possible, however, that private benefaction can be encouraged. The Mulroney government's decision to permit registered charities to lobby in a non-partisan fashion removes some of the uncertainty beclouding the application of donated funds to lobbying activities. Similarly the removal of an automatic basic deduction for charitable donations from personal income tax may encourage more people to make genuine donations to groups that are registered as charities. Governments could go further, however. In particular they could permit individuals and corporations to claim tax credits for such donations—similar to the tax credits allowed for donations to political parties. Tax expenditures of this sort have fallen out of favour in Ottawa. But there is merit in a policy that promises over the long haul to wean interest groups from dependence on the munificence of officials and to return to taxpayers in general the responsibility and authority for determining which groups should exist and which should not.

Finances are generally foremost among the issues relating to the resource bases of groups. But other aspects of the resource base could be addressed by a public concerned about equality between public-interest groups and material-benefit groups. On one level, resource issues can be addressed attitudinally. Voluntarism, for example, can be encouraged still further.[50] So can acceptance and encouragement of group activity, even when it runs counter to the conventional perceptions of the public. Governments and corporations can offer groups assistance in kind; for example, in some communities surplus buildings are made available to groups at a minimal rent. Some governments encourage their middle and senior executives to enter executive interchange programs with the private sector; interchanges with some pressure groups might prove equally challenging and rewarding. These and similar strategies to buttress the role of groups in our political system would help them contribute to public debate. Some of these strategies would enhance government understanding not only of the role of groups but of the communications they transmit.

The problems of dependence and inequality would not be eradicated, even if these measures and many others reinforcing them were put in place. The natural advantages many organizations derive from their place in the economy and their value to policy-makers render unlikely their chances of ever being seriously challenged by public-interest groups. Even so, as Canada moves inexorably into an era when, on the one hand, the state is more pervasive and, on the other, diffusion of power makes the policy process more complex, policies that consciously address the issues of dependence and inequality will not only benefit lesser groups and public-interest groups but will ultimately contribute to a higher quality of public debate and more effective public policy.

(iii) *Processes*

Ultimately successful integration of sectoral and spatial systems of representation and amelioration of problems of inequality depend on the maintenance of policy processes that give groups and legislators their due, while reducing the barriers to equal representation of interests. Under cabinet-parliamentary government, legislatures cannot effectively contribute to public-policy formation if they are unable to discuss options before the Cabinet accepts one alternative over others. Even affluent and established groups cannot make an impression on policy if they are denied access to the flow of information and if they are granted no opportunity to present their case. Assistance to the legislature, development of regulations to guide pressure group involvement in the policy process, even development of groups' resource bases can have little effect unless the process itself recognizes their claim to participation and accords them a meaningful role.

Over the last two decades there has been considerable expansion of opportunities for the public to influence policy decisions. The diffusion of power has helped Parliament elicit opinion from various sectors of the community. Agencies, increasingly aware of the legitimating capacity of interest groups, have paid more attention to public hearings and to advance consultation with interests prior to formulating new policies and revising regulations. Some regulatory tribunals have been receptive to the intervention of public-interest groups. In the field of local government citizen participation in the policy process has been significantly encouraged.

All this bring us a little closer to realizing the potential of group representation in the policy process. There are many shortcomings, however, and some progress from earlier years is being eroded by the tide of 1980s conservatism. Consultation too often depends on the goodwill of officials and influential members of policy communities. Regulatory bodies, sometimes assisted by changes in legislation, have shown a tendency to define more narrowly the interests who may make representations to them.[51] A restricted economic climate is frequently used to discourage interventions in developmental investment decisions or to ignore demands for corporations and governments to observe existing social and environmental regulations. It is clear that uncertainty and constraint will increasingly limit the opportunities for group policy participation unless steps are taken to anchor consultation in the processes of policy formation.

The methods of achieving this are numerous. For example, it should be automatic that major revision of regulations be subjected to an open review process and that all delegated legislation be subjected periodically to formal scrutiny both through agency hearings and Parliament. The public consultation that evolved to meet the requirements of environmental impact assessment during the 1970s should not be allowed to wither, but should be extended and translated to other levels of government. It should be a matter of course for a process of public consultation to occur whenever a major change in public policy is contemplated. Such consultation might be conducted variously in the public service, through the legislature, or through the services of *ad hoc* commissions and task forces, as the exigencies of the public agenda and the importance of the issues determine. Their significance would derive from their taking place at a point in policy formation where the views of the public might influence ultimate decisions. Finally procedures for consultation should accommodate the public's need to influence both the implementation of policy and its preparation. Despite the fact that consultation has improved at the early stages of decision-making in recent years, very little has been done to admit the public to the periodic reviews of programs that have been called for by critics of public-sector management and that have to some extent been implemented.[52]

The dangers inherent in institutionalizing consultation with groups are that the process of consultation consumes vast amounts of energy and that it frequently delays the implementation of change until its impetus has dissipated and the resources accumulated to achieve it are dispersed. But these problems can be addressed by encouraging simplicity, flexibility, and openness in the decision process, and by imposing reasonable but fixed terms to it. They cannot be evaded by ignoring the necessity for consultation, which is a consequence of social complexity and has an imperative of its own. Consultation can be ignored for the short-run benefit of specific interests, but in the long run the public interest dictates that the processes of policy-making must formally engage the views of citizens and the groups they have created to represent them.

GROUP POLITICS AND PUBLIC POLICY

Group politics has become a vital force in Canada. In this study we have examined its origins as well as its current place in the policy process. We have applied a number of analytical tools to understand it better, seeking to establish how groups in this country exercise their unique talents for mobilizing opinion and influencing public authorities.

One of the most important of these tools is the concept of the policy community. We have striven to show how policy specialization accords to a relatively small public a dominant say in the creation and implementation of policy. We have analysed the structure of those special publics and suggested the dynamics that govern them. This analysis brought out both the conservative and dynamic tendencies inherent in the relationships generated within the community. We have argued that though the policy community dominates its policy field and is itself dominated by its sub-government, it is by no means impervious to change but experiences constant internal tension as competing groups—particularly those in the attentive public—challenge established policy paradigms. At the same time we have suggested that this dynamism is only partially spontaneous, and that a lively, dynamic, attentive public must be fertilized and encouraged through a supportive regulatory regime combined with adequate consultative processes and sensitive resource support.

Through the window of the policy-community concept we have looked at the normative issues pressing upon Canadian understanding of pressure group politics. We concluded that policy communities have developed in part from the diffusion of power in this country and have contributed to it, and that Parliament has been an important beneficiary of the same process. We can in consequence express some optimism that spatial representation through our legislatures is beginning to recapture an importance that it lost through most of this century. Again, this process is not entirely self-asserting. It is encouraged by the diffusion of power and particularly by the needs of sectoral influences—within and outside the bureaucracy—for legitimation; but it can be assured only if Parliament, and to a lesser extent party processes, are so structured and placed that they have a genuine influence on policy. Gregory Prycz reaches a similar conclusion:

> [R]eform in the Canadian practice of pressure group politics would require . . . a systematic opening of the Canadian legislative system—at the cost of legislative tardiness and perhaps even impotence—and a further development of noninstitutionalized, weaker pressure groups through state-sponsorship—at the cost of decreased autonomy. Neither of these trade-offs would seem warranted if we were certain that some pressure groups in Canada were not now unjustifiably dominating public policy and that the other institutions of Canadian politics and governments, such as political parties, the media, parliaments, federalism, and public opinion were otherwise sufficient to deliver us a liberal democracy. Even if warranted, they seem, on the surface, not quite up to the task.[53]

Viewing interest group politics from the perspective of policy communities draws us to one final question mark in the landscape. That is the question raised so frequently in American discussions of policy formation: Does the assignment of specialized policy responsibility to specific publics preclude the articulation and enforcement of a general will? Is the public interest superseded by special interests? Undeniably there are many aspects of public policy shaped almost exclusively through reference to special interests. Even so, ours is not yet a special-interest state. The means exist to make it so, particularly the devolution of considerable responsibility to expert advisory committees. We have caught glimpses of their authority at several points. The significance of their role is ably expressed by a student of fisheries management, who remarked that though biologists and fishermen 'are directly involved in the policy process and thus are able to lobby the decision-makers', there is

> . . . no similar interest group lobby attending advisory committees, or lobbying politicians on behalf of the general public. Fisheries issues normally do not elicit widespread public concern. Except for the occasional newspaper editorial advocating a modernized and rationalized industry, the policy process lacks inputs which reflect the view that the fisheries wealth should be maximized directly for the benefit of the public rather than for some sector of the public.[54]

There are, however, institutional mechanisms inhibiting the full flowering of a Canadian special-interest state. Among these the collective responsibility of the Cabinet is paramount and the national perspective of parliamentarians is significant. Cabinet responsibility imposes limits on the diffusion of power that do not occur in the congressional-presidential system. The spectre of the special-interest state does not loom as large for Canada, therefore, as it does for the United States. Nevertheless it is a force to be reckoned with. In Cabinet the pressures of sectoralization are intense. Ministers, particularly junior ministers, hesitate to speak beyond their portfolios, and a national vision can easily elude a political executive that is overworked and overscheduled. The fissiparous tendencies of Canadian regionalism expressed in Cabinet, caucus, and intergovernmentally contribute to the fragmented policy perspective induced by ministerial life. Single-party dominance at the federal level and in most of the provinces has not until recently provided government leaders with periods in opposition to rejuvenate their wider vision. Institutional arrangements can partially offset these tendencies. Cabinet committee systems, though they generally foster an unfortunate and unreal dichotomy between social and economic policy, force ministers to address issues outside their immediate portfolios. The federal budget process, with its emphasis on establishing a framework of priorities, can be similarly helpful.

In the final analysis, though, it is the Prime Minister and his closest associates—the ministers of Finance, Justice, and External Affairs—who must establish and maintain a broad perspective and insist that policy address the general interest. This means not only that they must foster a national orientation among their immediate colleagues and advisers, but that they must also perpetually attend to the maintenance of wide-ranging debate across the many special publics. Consultation, minimization of inequality, and encouragement of party and parliamentary contributions to public debates are the means to this end.

Notes

CHAPTER 1. GROUPS AND POLITICS

[1] Robert L. Stanfield, 'The Fifth George C. Nowlan Lecture', Acadia University, 7 Feb. 1977 (mimeo.).

[2] R. McGregor Dawson, *The Government of Canada* (Toronto, 1946).

[3] John Meisel, 'Recent Changes in Canadian Parties' in Hugh G. Thorburn (ed.), *Party Politics in Canada* (Scarborough, 1967), 33-54. See also W.A.W. Neilson and J.C. MacPherson (eds), *The Legislative Process in Canada: The Need for Reform* (Montreal, 1978) and Allan Kornberg, Harold D. Clarke, and Arthur Goddard, *Parliament, Policy and Representation* (Toronto, 1980).

[4] David Kwavnick, *Organized Labour and Pressure Politics: The Canadian Labour Congress, 1956-1968* (Montreal, 1972); Robert Presthus, *Elite Accommodation in Canadian Politics* (Toronto, 1973) and *Elites in the Policy Process* (Toronto, 1974); Ronald W. Lang, *The Politics of Drugs: The British and Canadian pharmaceutical industries and governments* (Lexington, Mass., 1974); W.T. Stanbury, *Business Interests and the Reform of Canadian Competition Policy, 1971-75* (Toronto, 1977); and A. Paul Pross (ed.) *Pressure Group Behaviour in Canadian Politics* (Scarborough, Ont., 1975). Another major work published in this period was Léon Dion's two-volume *Société et Politique: La vie des groupes* (Québec, 1971). It is notable, however, as a monumental statement of pluralist theory, not as a study of Canadian pressure group politics, which are only occasionally mentioned. A bibliography of Canadian pressure group studies to 1974 is included in Pross, *Pressure Group Behaviour in Canadian Politics*.

[5] Though numerous, these bills frequently replicated one another and, like most private members' bills, were intended to goad the government into action rather than to set in place a practical method of regulation. The late Walter Baker's description of his own bill fits most others: 'It defines lobbying . . . as the actions of any person or any group attempting to influence the course of either legislative or executive action. It establishes a register of lobbyists to be administered jointly by the Clerks of the two Chambers. Lobbyists must set down their names, the person or group on whose behalf they are acting, and the duration of any contact. This information must be supplied before any contacts are made, supplemented with any new information applicable and submitted afresh at the beginning of every year. I have included penalties for non-compliance of up to $5,000 per month and prohibition from lobbying for two years, to show that the register which is set forth in the bill is intended to be taken seriously.' House of Commons, *Debates*, 28 January 1977, 2516. Only three of these bills achieved second reading: Bill C-38 (1969) sponsored by Barry Mather (NDP), *Debates*, 5850; Bill C-214 (1976) sponsored by Walter Baker (PC), *Debates*, 2515 and Bill C-495 (1980) sponsored by Ken Robinson (L), *Debates* 22010. The other bills were: C-176/1969 (Mather); C-131/1970 (Mather); C-121/1972 (Mather); C-89/1973 (Mather); C-115/1974 (Mather); C-248/1974 (Robinson); C-254/1974 (John Reynolds, L); C-432/1976 (Baker); C-268/1976 (Robinson); C-316/1976 (Reynolds); C-328/1977 (Robinson); C-330/1977 (Baker); C-255/1978 (Baker); C-355/1979 (Bill Friesen, PC); C-492/1980 (Friesen) and C-248/1985 (James McGrath, PC). I am extremely grateful to David Harvey for reviewing Hansard from 1946 onwards in order to provide this information.

⁶Prime Minister's Office. 'Notes for a statement by Prime Minister Brian Mulroney in the House of Commons, Monday, September 9, 1985.' Reproduced in part in Canada. Consumer and Corporate Affairs. *Lobbying and the Registration of Paid Lobbyists: A discussion paper* (Ottawa, Consumer and Corporate Affairs, 1985), 2-3.

⁷See Kenneth Kernaghan, 'Codes of Ethics and Administrative Responsibility', *Canadian Public Administration* 17 (1974) 4, 527-41. For lively, journalistic accounts of the impact of lobbying on Ottawa see Doris Shackleton, *Power Town: Democracy Discarded* (Toronto, 1977) and Paul Malvern, *Persuaders: Lobbying, Influence Peddling and Political Corruption in Canada* (Toronto, 1985).

⁸J. Alex Corry, 'Sovereign People or Sovereign Governments,' in H.V. Kroeker (ed.), *Sovereign People or Sovereign Governments: Proceedings of a Conference Sponsored by the Institute for Research on Public Policy and the Government Studies Program, Dalhousie University, April 1979* (Montreal, 1981), 3-13, 5.

⁹The *Globe and Mail*, 31 October 1978.

¹⁰Daniel L. Bon (ed.), *Lobbying: A Right? A Necessity? A Danger?* (Ottawa, 1981). Other publications put out by institutes in this period include Mildred A. Schwartz, *The Environment for Policy-Making in Canada and the United States* (Montreal, 1981) and Fred Thompson and W.T. Stanbury, *The Political Economy of Interest Groups in the Legislative Process in Canada* (Montreal, 1979).

¹¹For a particularly useful comment on the definition of a movement see Frances Fox Piven and Richard A. Cloward, *Poor People's Movements* (N.Y., 1979), 4-5. A more general discussion of the life cycle of movements is found in the introduction ('The nature of social movements') to S.D. Clark, J.P. Grayson, and L.M. Grayson, *Prophecy and Protest: Social Movements in Twentieth-Century Canada* (Toronto, 1975), 1-39.

¹²For a stimulating discussion of the relationship between parties and interest groups see Vaughan Lyon, 'The Future of Parties—Inevitable . . . or Obsolete?', *Journal of Canadian Studies* 18 (1983–84) 4, 108-31, particularly 110-12. Lyon argues that though parties seek direct control of state power directly and the interest groups want only to influence it, and though there are significant organizational and tactical differences between the two, we tend to ignore 'the essential fact that both parties and interest groups want to gain preferential treatment from the state for the core interests which are the *raison d'être*' of each (110). A good case study of the tension and dependence between parties and interest groups is found in Raymond Hudon, 'Polarization and Depolarization of Quebec Political Parties' in Alain G. Gagnon, *Quebec: State and Society* (Toronto, 1984), 314-30. E.R. Forbes, *Maritime Rights: The Maritime Rights Movement* (Montreal, 1979) vividly describes the difficulties the Maritimes had in expressing regional concerns through the medium of political parties and the region's consequent resort to sectoral interest groups.

¹³Peter Aucoin, *Public Accountability in the Governing of Professions: A Report on the Self-Governing Professions of Accounting, Architecture, Engineering and Law in Ontario* (The Professional Organizations Committee. Working Paper #4. 1978), 5-6. For an example of the state's ability to alter the terms under which such groups exercise power see D.W. Emerson, 'Legislation for Professionals in Quebec: Government moves for tighter controls', *Chemistry in Canada* December 1972, 28-9.

¹⁴Such objections are nonsensical. Pressure—whether from groups, parties, élites or from government agencies themselves—is essential to political life, which after all, is sometimes referred to as the routinization of conflict. The term 'pressure group' merely recognizes that reality.

S.E. Finer considers the term 'pressure group' too narrow to describe the activities of what he calls 'the lobby'. It is a mistake, he argues, to use a nomenclature that suggests that these organizations constantly apply pressure to government or that they exist solely to influence government. 'Most groups, most of the time, simply make requests or put up a case; they reason and they argue, but they do not threaten.' *Anonymous Empire* (London, 1966), 3. This is true, but it overlooks the possibility that the threat of sanctions, whether explicit or not, is the ultimate weapon of any lobbying group; it suggests that groups are indifferent to the outcome of their interventions, which seems unlikely. It is more realistic to assume that groups do in fact calculate the costs and benefits of applying the sanctions that lie within their power, and in general refrain from exerting the full extent of the leverage available to them. Their restraint is a product of the institutionalization discussed more fully in chapter 5. For political scientists, who are concerned with the study of power, it makes great sense to characterize a political institution by the feature that best exemplifies its relationship to the state. Nor does use of the term suggest that the political scientist is unaware of the non-political qualities of all groups. Though he must take those qualities into account in assessing the political capacities and activities of groups, they are generally outside his domain.

The term lobby has connotations that are equally difficult to deal with. It is often associated with venal aspects of influencing government. The noun 'lobbyist' can refer to an individual who is part of a group, either as a member or as a full-time employee, but it can also refer to someone who, for a fee, temporarily lobbies on behalf of a group. Generally we will try to avoid confusing these two activities—which have very different implications for behaviour—by referring only to temporary, paid spokesmen as lobbyists.

[15] An extensive discussion of these categories is found in Mildred C. Schwartz, *The Environment of Policy-Making in Canada and the United States* (Montreal, 1981), 14.

[16] Ibid.

[17] See J.S. Frideres, *Canada's Indians: Contemporary Conflicts* (Scarborough, Ont., 1974) and Sally M. Weaver, *Making Canadian Indian Policy* (Toronto, 1981) and 'Towards a Comparison of National Political Organizations of Indigenous Peoples: Australia, Canada and Norway' (Lecture Series at the Institute of Social Sciences, University of Tromso, Tromso, Norway, 19-26 October 1983). An interesting case study is found in Tord Larsen, 'Negotiating Identity: the Micmac of Nova Scotia' in Adrian Tanner (ed.) *The Politics of Indianness* (St John's, Newfoundland, 1983), 37-136.

[18] R. Manzer, *Canada: A Socio-Political Report* (Toronto, 1974), quoting the *Report* of the Royal Commission on Bilingualism and Biculturalism, 140.

[19] Philip Lowe and Jane Goyder review this tendency in *Environmental Groups and Politics* (London, 1983), 15-18.

[20] *Maclean's*, 20 Sept. 1976, 8; *Time*, 20 Oct. 1975, 13-15; *The 4th. Estate*, 21 and 28 Jan. 1976; *Globe and Mail*, 25 Sept. 1976, and *Financial Post*, 9 Oct. 1976, 11.

[21] Sheila McLeod Arnopoulos and Dominique Clift, *The English Fact in Quebec* (Montreal, 1984), ch. 13 'Survival Strategy'.

[22] Ann Pappert, 'A New Life on Lease', *Financial Post Magazine*, June 1985, 28-34. Lars Hjörne, 'Aims and Forms of Tenant Influence: Some Preliminary Considerations', *Acta Sociologica* 24 (1981) 4, 251-79; G. Granatstein, *Marlborough Marathon: One Street Against a Developer* (Toronto, 1971).

[23] For an excellent discussion of the role of legitimation and mandate in pressure group politics see David C. Kwavnick, *Organized Labour and Pressure Politics: The Canadian Labour Congress, 1956-1968* (Montreal, 1972).

[24] While the Economic Council of Canada is not a genuine pressure group, it does very often act like a pressure group and is often treated like one. For example, its reports are made to the government *and the public*, not simply to the government, as are those of conventional agencies. They are frequently intended to excite public demands for changes in government policy. The government's regular advisers are formally prohibited from appealing to the public. Again, though the Council is appointed by the government, an attempt is made to ensure that it is genuinely representative of regional and sectoral interests. It can, therefore, make a modest claim to speak for the interest community. For all these reasons we cannot treat the advice it gives as pure 'withinput', like the advice of a regular government department.

[25] I am grateful to William Coleman and Greg Pyrcz for their views on this point.

[26] A.F. Bentley, (ed. P. Odegard) *The Process of Government* (Harvard, 1967) and David B.

Truman, *The Governmental Process: Political Interests and Public Opinion* (N.Y., 1964).
[27] Grant Jordan, 'Group Approaches to the Study of Politics' in D. Engelfield and G. Drewry (eds), *Politics and Political Science: A Survey Worldwide* (London, 1984).

The literature on interest groups is too narrowly focused, examining in great detail the internal characteristics of groups and their activities in the political system, but not going very far to establish precisely what role pressure groups have in the political system nor why they should have that role. Pressure group politics cannot be understood apart from party politics and administrative politics. It is significant, for example, that the few studies that have considered pressure groups from a broader perspective—Bentley's *The Process of Government*, Truman's *The Governmental Process*, E.E. Schattschneider's *The Semi-Sovereign People: A Realist's View of Democracy* (N.Y., 1960) and Theodore Lowi's *The End of Liberalism* (N.Y., 1969)—still dominate what little theoretical discussion does take place, even though their contributions are either incomplete or badly dated. In 1958 Samuel J. Eldersvelt, reviewing the United States literature on interest groups, wrote, 'there is no question but that, if one reads carefully, intermittently one picks up fugitive insights which may have relevance for a theory of interest groups.' ('American Interest Groups: A Survey of Research and Some Implications for Theory and Method' in Henry W. Ehrmann *Interest Groups on Four Continents* (Pittsburgh, 1958) 173-96.) We are only slightly further advanced today.

[28] Frederick C. Engelmann and Mildred C. Schwartz, *Political Parties and the Canadian Social Structure* (Scarborough, Ont., 1967), 96.

[29] Ibid.

[30] Presthus, *Elite Accommodation in Canadian Politics* and *Elites in the Policy Process*.

[31] A. Paul Pross (ed.), *Pressure Group Behaviour in Canadian Politics* (Toronto, 1975).

[32] See William Coleman and Henry J. Jacek, 'The Roles and Activities of Business Interest Associations in Canada', *Canadian Journal of Political Science* XVI (1983) 2, 257-80 and 'The Political Organization of the Chemical Industry in Canada'. Paper. Canadian Political Science Association (Halifax, 1981). The list of other contributions since 1975 is now too extensive to be compressed into a note. In the bibliography the reader is particularly referred to the works by Stanbury, Schwartz, Pyrcz, Paltiel and Thorburn.

[33] Julianne La Breche, 'The Quiet Persuaders of Parliament Hill', *Financial Post Magazine*, 29 November 1980.

[34] See, for example, the criticisms of conventional pressure group studies voiced by Mancur Olson in *The Logic of Collective Action* (Cambridge, Mass., 1971) and Terry M. Moe in *The Organization of Interests* (Chicago, 1980).

[35] The misapplication of others' experience is illustrated by the 1983 amendments to the Canada Elections Act, discussed in chapter 7.

CHAPTER 2. BEGINNINGS: SPACE VERSUS SECTOR

[1] Andre Holleaux, 'Le phénomène associatif', *Revue Française d'administration publique* 8 (1978), 683-727; p. 683 refers to very early groups in France. J. M. Beck, *The Government of Nova Scotia* (Toronto, 1957) and Gerald M. Craig, *Upper Canada: The Formative Years, 1784-1841* (Toronto, 1963), give several examples of colonial groups attempting to influence Westminster.

[2] H.A. Innis, *The Cod Fisheries* (Toronto, 1978), 240, 244-5.

[3] See Douglas Sanders, 'The Indian Lobby' in Keith Banting and Richard Simeon (eds), *And No One Cheered: Federalism, Democracy and the Constitution Act* (Toronto, 1983), 301-32.

[4] S.D. Clark, *The Canadian Manufacturers' Association* (Toronto, 1939) and N.J. Lawrie, *The Canadian Construction Association: An Interest Group and Its Environment* (Unpublished Ph.D. thesis. University of Toronto, 1976).

[5] Norman A. Robertson to L. Robertson. 2 March 1932, quoted in J.L. Granatstein, *A Man of Influence: Norman A. Robertson and Canadian Statecraft, 1929–1968* (Toronto, Deneau Publishers and Company Ltd., 1981). 40-1.

[6] Khayyam Z. Paltiel, 'The Changing Environment and Role of Special Interest Groups', *Canadian Public Administration* 25 (1982), 2, 198-210, at 205.

[7] See chapter 11, below and A. Paul Pross, 'Space, Function and Legitimacy: The Problem of Legitimacy in the Canadian State', in O.P. Dwivedi (ed.) *The Administrative State in Canada* (Toronto, 1982), 107-29.

[8] Robert Presthus, *Elites in the Policy Process* (Toronto, 1974), 8.

[9] Patricia Hollis, 'Pressure from Without: an introduction', in Hollis (ed.), *Pressure From Without in early Victorian England* (London, 1974), 1-26, 6.

[10] J.M.S. Careless describes one instance of this transfer of ideas in 'The Toronto *Globe* and Agrarian Radicalism' *Canadian Historical Review* XXIX (1948) 1, 14-19, 34-9.

[11] Aileen Dunham, *Political Unrest in Upper Canada, 1815–1836* (Toronto, 1963), 51.

[12] Margaret Angus, 'Health, Emigration and Welfare in Kingston, 1820–1840' in Donald Swainson (ed.) *Oliver Mowat's Ontario* (Toronto, 1972), 120-35, 126. A similar development took place in Saint John, New Brunswick, also a major entry point for emigrants. There Moses Perley, the Emigration Agent for the colony, distressed by the conditions faced by immigrants—particularly the unsanitary and inadequate accommodation for those in quarantine on Partridge Island—engaged the help of the local Mechanics' Institute. In 1847, for example, the Institute raised substantial funds to assist immigrants and in 1843 assisted Perley in setting up the Mechanics' Settlement near Saint John. Allison Mitcham, *Three Remarkable Maritimers* (Hantsport, 1985), 43, 44.

[13] Angus, 'Health, Emigration and Welfare in Kingston', 128.

[14] Richard B. Splane, *Social Welfare in Ontario, 1791–1893* (Toronto, 1965), 76, 77.

[15] The following comments are based on two articles appearing in *Recherches sociographiques* XVI (1975) 2: Yves Lamande, 'Le Membership d'une Association du 19ième siècle: Le cas de Longueuil (1857–1860)', 219-41 and Johanne Ménard, 'L'Institut des Artisans du Comté de Drummond, 1856–1890', 207-19.

[16] Ménard, 'L'Institut des Artisans', 210.

[17] Hereward Senior, 'Orangeism in Ontario Politics, 1872–1896' in Swainson, *Oliver Mowat's Ontario*, 136-53, 137.

[18] Ibid., 150-1.

[19] Splane, *Social Welfare in Ontario*, 176-7.

[20] Quoted ibid., 270.

[21] Douglas McCalla, 'The Commercial Policies of the Toronto Board of Trade, 1850–1860', *The Canadian Historical Review*, 50 (1969), 51-67, 55.

[22] Ibid., 54.

[23] Michael Bliss, 'The Protective Impulse: An Approach to the Social History of Oliver Mowat's Ontario' in Donald Swainson (ed.), *Oliver Mowat's Ontario* (Toronto, 1972), 174-88, 174-5.

[24] Ibid., 184.

[25] Quoted in P.B. Waite, *The Life and Times of Confederation* (Toronto, 1962), 16-17.

[26] McCalla, 'The Toronto Board of Trade', 52.

[27] McCalla, Ibid., 55.

[28] For example, New Brunswick legislatures during the 1840s and 1850s lacked disciplined political parties and cabinet authority to initiate spending programs. 'Consequently, the dispersal of the Assembly's new found revenues was left to the local members. Each MLA used "his share" as a tool for patronage in his constituency. . . .' Even after responsible government the support of MLAs was 'unpredictable. Until the twentieth century, it was a common practice for members who had previously supported the Cabinet to vote against a bill introduced by one of its ministers. Politicians solicited electoral support, based on their own positions on various issues. Their personal popularity was more important than their political party affiliations . . .' Arthur T. Doyle, *Front Benches and Back Rooms* (Toronto, 1976), 17.

[29] Splane, *Social Welfare in Ontario*, 187.

[30] R.S. Lambert with A. Paul Pross, *Renewing Nature's Wealth* (Toronto, 1967), 178.

[31] Ibid., 181 ff. These responses included the establishment of conservation organizations, government agencies and educational institutions, both in Canada and the United States.

[32] Although evidence is limited, it seems that in the nineteenth century, pressure groups were the instrument of the middle class, as, in many ways, they still are today. One of the few systematic presentations of data on this point appears in Carol Lee Bacchi's *Liberation Deferred: The Ideas of the English-Canadian Suffragists: 1877–1918*, (Toronto, 1983), 6. In an analysis of suffrage leaders she shows that all but a very few were professionals, business people or independently wealthy. Only one of 37 male leaders with known occupations was a labour representative and only one of 103 female leaders with known occupations was a union organizer, though two were 'agriculturalists'.

[33] Canadian women were less militant than their British and American counterparts, eschewing demonstrations and violent protest. They did, however, give their support to colleagues abroad, occasionally going so far as to join them in demonstrations and parades. Alice Chown led a group, each of whom carried a stem of Canadian wheat, in a London march; others participated in demonstrations prior to Woodrow Wilson's inauguration. (Bacchi, *Liberation Deferred*, 34).

[34] See Bacchi, *Liberation Deferred, passim*. An extensive account of Lady Aberdeen's work is contained in Sandra Gwyn, *The Private Capital: Ambition and Love in the Age of Macdonald and Laurier* (Toronto, 1985), ch. 20, 'The Remarkable Ishbel'.

[35] Graeme Decarie, 'Something Old, Something New . . . Aspects of Prohibitionism in Ontario in the 1890s', in Donald Swainson, ed., *Oliver Mowat's Ontario* (Toronto, 1972), 154-71. The Women's Christian Temperance Union was established in this country in 1873. Bacchi places its membership in 1900 at 6,000 members in Prince Edward Island, Nova Scotia, New Brunswick, Québec, Ontario and the North West Territories. See L.C. Bacchi, *Liberation Deferred: The Ideas of the English Canadian Suffragists: 1877–1918* (Toronto, 1983), 17. Presumably these are dues-paying members and Decarie is referring to supporters. Bacchi's study of the links between the womens' suffrage groups, the temperance movement, and other reform groups is particularly useful, as are her discussions of the ties between these groups and their counterparts in Britain and the United States.

[36] Judith Fingard, *Jack in Port: Sailor Towns of Eastern Canada* (Toronto, 1982), 220.

[37] See Lambert and Pross, *Renewing Nature's Wealth*, chs. 9, 10, and Pross, *The Development of a Forest Policy* (Toronto, University of Toronto. Unpublished Ph.D. thesis, 1967), ch. 2.

[38] See annual *Reports* of the Commissioners of Crown Lands and the Departments of Agriculture for these provinces as well as the *Reports* of the Canadian Commission of Conservation.

[39] *Social Welfare in Ontario*, 176-7.

[40] J.I. Gow, 'L'Histoire de l'administration publique québécoise', *Recherches sociographiques* XVI (1975), 3, 385-412, esp. 389, 392, and 406-7.

[41] The argument in this and the following paragraphs is a shortened version of a thesis presented by the writer in 'Space, Function and Legitimacy'.

[42] This view differs somewhat from that of Norman Ward, who perceives, even in the early years of the House of Commons 'a strong bias in favour of the executive'. However, Ward qualifies his view by stating that the private member was not only 'a loyal party man' but 'one inclined to be on the make for himself and his district as well as his party; his support of the party was always conditioned by his ambitions in other directions. The hope of patronage, both for himself and his supporters, may have made him dependent on his leaders, but the role he played as the real or potential distributor of favours in his district gave him a stature which few of his successors can enjoy today. . . . The member of Parliament was a strategic figure and a man of note. The House of Commons reflected the individuality of the members; yet the domination of the legislature by the executive was almost never threatened.' Norman Ward, 'The Formative Years of the House of Commons, 1867–1891', *Canadian Journal of Economics and Political Science* 18 (1952) 4, 431-51. In other words,

the member had to juggle the pressures emanating from his riding against those initiated by the executive. At the provincial level, member independence appears to have lasted longer. Doyle, in *Front Benches and Back Rooms* (p. 17) records its persistence in New Brunswick until the turn of the century and Martin Robin, *The Rush for Spoils: The Company Province, 1871–1933* (Toronto, 1972) some years later in British Columbia.

43 J.M. Beck, *The Government of Nova Scotia*, (Toronto, 1957), 155-62.

44 Quoted in Robin, *The Company Province*, 74.

45 Christopher Armstrong, 'The Mowat Heritage in Federal-Provincial Relations' in Swainson (ed.), *Oliver Mowat's Ontario*, 93-119 at 97.

46 Doyle, *Front Benches and Back Rooms*, 80.

47 In the Maritimes these influences were felt acutely. Control of financial institutions slipped away first, to be followed by the selling-out of local manufacturing firms and resource enterprises to competitors and speculators in distant centres. In the latters' hands physical plant and equipment deteriorated and concerns were milked of their assets. By the First World War the region was fighting a desperate and losing rearguard action to retain control of the last element of its economic core, the railway system. The journal *Acadiensis* has published a number of articles dealing with the evolution of the regional economy during this period. See particularly, T.W. Acheson, 'The National Policy and the Industrialization of the Maritimes, 1880–1910', *Acadiensis* I (1971) 2, 3-28; L.D. McCann, 'The Mercantile-Industrial Transition in the Metal Towns of Pictou County, 1857–1931', *Acadiensis* X (1981), 2, 29-64, and David Frank, 'The Cape Breton Coal Industry and the Rise and Fall of the British Empire Steel Corporation', *Acadiensis* VII (1977), 3-34. Ernest R. Forbes has documented the transition in *Maritime Rights: The Maritime Rights Movement, 1919–1927* (Montreal, 1979). Tom Naylor's two-volume *The History of Canadian Business, 1867–1914* (Toronto, 1975) is useful as a general discussion of the political economy of the period.

48 Christopher Armstrong and H.V. Nelles offer an illustration of these processes in their study of the campaign of E.A. Roberts and his associates to control Halifax's electrical monopoly ('Getting Your Way in Nova Scotia: Tweaking Halifax, 1909–1917', *Acadiensis* V (1976) 2, 105-131). They conclude:

. . . they were men who knew a great deal about getting their own way....[L]ike promoters in other Canadian cities, [they] were not satisfied simply with operating profits; they wanted the vastly greater speculative returns offered by a merger and a recapitalization. Thus they had first to deal with rival entrepreneurs, then to oust the management from the control of the street railway, while all the time pressing their case with the city and the province. That they attained their objectives was less a measure of their business acumen than of their ability to command political influence. Sir Frederick Borden's presence in the syndicate was symbolic of this: he could be relied upon to deliver the necessary Liberal votes. The 'grab' for Halifax succeeded only through the acquiescence of Premier Murray. While idealists might argue that he acted out of ideological hostility to public ownership in encouraging Robert's schemes, it is difficult to see why he should have alienated his own followers from Halifax as well as local politicians, when he could have thrown his weight behind the plan to have an independent concern, like the Halifax Development Company, generate hydroelectricity and transmit it to the city for sale to the street railway and to other light and power users. Political influence, perhaps cemented by financial generosity, seems the most plausible explanation for his behaviour, and it was this that enabled Robert to outflank irate citizens and municipal officials. (p. 130.)

Nelles' *The Politics of Development: Forest, Mines and Electric Power in Ontario, 1911–1941* (Toronto, 1974) is replete with similar illustrations. First-hand accounts of these practices can be found in the proceedings of the numerous inquiries commissioned by newly elected governments into the affairs of their predecessors (e.g. The Ontario Royal Commission to investigate Crown Timber returns (the Latchford-Riddell Commission whose proceedings are lodged at the Ontario Archives and whose *Report* was published in

1921–22 by the Ontario King's Printer) and the often doubtful reminiscences of political veterans (e.g. Doyle, *Front Benches and Back Rooms*).

The connection between corporate organization and government decision-making structures persists today. Christopher Leman suggests, for example, that 'one reason for the historic centralization of the provincial [natural resource] ministries was that the companies were themselves centralized, so that when a problem arose company executives would demand to speak to their ministry equivalent. Perhaps the pace of decentralization in the companies will continue to govern the extent to which the ministries will be able to truly decentralize [in the future].' C. Leman, 'The Canadian Forest Ranger: Bureaucratic Centralism and Private Powers in Three Provincial Natural Resource Agencies'. Paper, Canadian Political Science Association, 1981, 28.

[49] M.G. Lofquist to F.H. Keefer, 9 Feb. 1926, Ferguson Papers, Ontario Archives.

[50] See Kenneth M. Gibbons and Donald C. Rowat, *Political Corruption in Canada: Cases, Causes and Cures* (Ottawa, 1976). An incident in the life of the Conservative party in 1935 illustrated the pressures political leaders were under. At that time the interests controlling the Canadian Pacific Railway, lobbying for railroad unification, contributed $50,000 to the party's election fund and sought to control the Manion leadership. See J.L. Granatstein, *The Politics of Survival* (Toronto, 1967), 13, 16, 17, 20, 43-5.

[51] These comments are somewhat speculative, being based on the fragmentary evidence available in biographies, case studies and general histories. To some extent they fly in the face of accepted wisdom among sociologists, which tends to see businessmen's clubs as bastions of privilege; exclusive preserves where members of the economic élite maintain contact with one another and arrange deals that seal the fate of thousands. However, the data actually presented by the leading students of Canadian élites reinforces the argument presented here. Wallace Clements, using 1972 data, reports that 51.1 per cent of the Canadian corporate élite belongs to the six most important clubs. While this is a respectable percentage it is considerably less than one might expect of social institutions that are as important as Clements (*The Canadian Corporate Elite* (Toronto, 1975, 247-9) and John Porter (*The Vertical Mosaic* (Toronto, 1965), 304-5) suggest. Furthermore, it appears that these memberships do not include the international élite that controls many of Canada's most powerful corporations. (See Clements, *The Canadian Corporate Elite*, 117). In other words even the six most important clubs in the country must enjoy the support of far fewer key economic decision-makers than Clement's own figures indicate. Finally, it should be noted that the six clubs considered to be watering holes for the economic élite are all located in Ottawa, Toronto, and Montreal, a fact that reinforces the claim made here that clubs in regional centres no longer perform a significant socio-economic and political function.

[52] See, for example, Escott Reid, 'The Saskatchewan Liberal Machine Before 1929', *Canadian Journal of Economics and Political Science* 11 (1936), 27; Herbert Quinn, *The Union Nationale* (Toronto, 1963); Ernest Watkins, *R.B. Bennett* (London, 1963); Neil McKenty, *Mitch Hepburn* (Toronto, 1967) and Ramsey Cook (ed.), *Politics of Discontent* (Toronto, 1967).

[53] R.M. Dawson and N. Ward, *The Government of Canada* 5th. edn (Toronto, 1970), 473. Leon Epstein notes Dawson reporting as early as 1922 that 'few Canadian members of parliament have shown their independence of party.' Leon D. Epstein, 'A Comparative Study of Canadian Parties' *American Political Science Review* 58 (1964), 46-59. For an account of the role of constituency organizations in patronage politics see Norman Ward, 'The Bristol Papers: A Note of Patronage', *Canadian Journal of Economics and Political Science* 12 (1946), 1, 78-86. The local organization was concerned almost exclusively with civil service appointments and minor contracts. However, a letter from W.C. Cain, deputy minister of the Ontario Department of Lands and Forests, to several provincial MLAS illustrates both the effects of centralization and the efforts that were made to maintain the illusion of local influence: 'We are considering . . . making certain additions to our Provincial Forests and creating an occasional new one, and inasmuch as a part of a suggested Provincial Forest lies

within your constituency I am writing to you in order that you may understand it and take whatever credit is necessary for the addition if and when the occasion arises.' Cain to W.L. Miller, 9 Jan. 1939, Ontario Department of Lands and Forests, Central Files, #119191—Provincial Forests.

54 See S.D. Clark, *The Canadian Manufacturers' Association* (Toronto, 1939) and Forbes, *Maritime Rights*. O. Mary Hill credits the CMA with bringing about the creation of the Department of Trade and Commerce, a sure sign of sectoral influence. *Canada's Salesman to the World* (Montreal, 1977), 2.

55 Roger Gibbins, *Prairie Politics and Society* (Toronto, 1980), 84; O. Mary Hill, *Canada's Salesman to the World*. While the intervention of new groups was a sign of pressure-group development, the fact that the act was not passed until western farmers had protested on Parliament Hill underlines the decline of constituency influence in western politics. Similar pilgrimages to Ottawa characterized the Maritime Rights Movement; according to Forbes the failure of the traditional parties in the Maritimes to persuade Ottawa to accept Maritime claims reinforced a tendency to look to pressure groups to articulate the region's demands. (*Maritime Rights*, ch. 7, 'The Politics of Maritime Rights'; and 191-2.)

56 Forbes, *The Maritime Rights Movement*, 116, and Clark, *The Canadian Manufacturers' Association, passim.*

57 Ibid., 39.

58 Ibid., 15.

59 J.M. Beck, 'The Party System in Nova Scotia: Tradition and Conservatism' in Martin Robin (ed.), *Canadian Provincial Politics* (Scarborough, Ont., 1972), 168-98, 175.

60 See P.G. Johnson, 'The Nova Scotia Union of Municipalities as a Pressure Group'. Paper. Canadian Political Science Association, 1970, 21.

61 See J.E. Hodgetts, *The Canadian Public Service: A Physiology of Government, 1867-1970* (Toronto, 1973), particularly Part I, and Dwivedi, *The Administrative State in Canada* (Toronto, 1982), 61.

62 J.L. Granatstein, *The Ottawa Men: The Civil Service Mandarins, 1935-57* (Toronto, 1982), chs 2, 'The Early Civil Service', and 3, 'The Founders'.

63 See, for example, the complaint of Flora MacDonald in 'The Minister and the Mandarins', *Policy Options* (Sept./Oct. 1980), 29-32. It is our contention, however, that this fear is misplaced; that a great deal of power has indeed escaped the hands of the political executive, just as in an earlier period it escaped the legislature, but that rather than falling into the hands of a small group of mandarins it has been diffused throughout the administrative apparatus of government. The consequences of this are just as problematic as a shift of power to senior officials, but they are quite different.

64 This transition may be observed in most aspects of public administration in this country, but nowhere is it demonstrated more clearly than in the long struggle to remove the civil service, at the federal and provincial levels, from the influence of patronage. For the spoils system, which gave the victorious political party immense freedom in the firing and appointment of public servants, successive reforms have substituted formal procedures governing appointments, including publication of openings, competitive examinations, precise descriptions of duties, establishment of classification systems, and a host of other regulations intended to ensure that merit, rather than the intervention of political friends, governs appointment and advancement in the public service. The long story of reform may be traced in a number of studies, of which the most complete is J.E. Hodgetts, William McCloskey, Reginald Whitaker, and V. Seymour Wilson, *The Biography of an Institution: The Civil Service Commission of Canada, 1908-1967* (Montreal, 1972). Parallel experiences at the provincial level are analysed in J.E. Hodgetts and O.P. Dwivedi, *Provincial Governments as Employers* (Montreal, 1974).

65 See, for example, the effort involved in organizing the 1925 pilgrimage of some 600 Maritimers to Ottawa to protest the neglect of the region's interests in transportation policy. Forbes, *Maritime Rights*, 112-15. The size of the delegation and its members' resentment of

federal policy did much to give legitimacy to a cause the nation had chosen to ignore.

66 See Hodgetts, *The Canadian Public Service*, 108-9 and Dennis Guest, *The Emergence of Social Security in Canada* (Vancouver, 1980).

67 H.H. Hannam, 'The Interest Group and its Activities', Institute of Public Administration of Canada. *Proceedings of the Fifth Annual Conference* (1953), 173.

68 In many cases such organizations were sponsored and encouraged not by government but by the railways, which were anxious to sell off their vacant western lands. See David C. Corbett, *Canada's Immigration Policy* (Toronto, 1957), 11-15. Religious organizations were also active. See John H. Redekop, 'Mennonites and Politics in Canada and the United States,' *Journal of Mennonite Studies* I (1983), 1.

69 A. Holleaux, 'Le phénomène associatif', *Revue francaise d'administration publique* 8 (1978) 683-787, 689, and Vincent Lemieux, 'Administration et publics: leur problème de communication' *Recherches sociographiques* XVI (1973) 3, 299-307, 304.

70 For example, when the government of Angus L. MacDonald came to power in Nova Scotia in 1933 one of its first acts was to appoint a Director of Marketing in the provincial Department of Agriculture. The successful appointee put forward a proposal that included putting 'order into the marketing of primary products . . . We planned to achieve this order both through cooperatives and marketing boards.' (Quoted in A.A. MacDonald, *Policy Formation Process: Nova Scotia Dairy Marketing, 1933-1978* (Halifax, 1980), 35.) During the 1930s marketing legislation was seen as an important vehicle for organizing a diffused industry.

71 S.D. Clark, *Canadian Manufacturers' Association*, 72.

72 Hill, *Canada's Salesman to the World*, ms. 254.

73 N.J. Lawrie, *The Canadian Construction Association: An Interest Group Organization and its Environment* (Ph.D. thesis. University of Toronto, 1976), 219.

74 The origins of the Consumers' Association are reported in Helen Jones Dawson, 'The Consumers' Association of Canada', *Canadian Public Administration* 6 (1963), 92. Examples of the encouragement of citizen participation by those responsible for programs in regional economic expansion include the Prince Edward Island Development plan, which contained several provisions for citizen participation. See *Agricultural Rehabilitation and Development Act: Federal-Provincial Rural Development Agreement* (Ottawa, 1965) parts IV, VI and VIII; J.D. McNiven, 'Bureaucracy and Participation in Prince Edward Island'. Paper. Canadian Political Science Association. Annual Meeting. 1976; and a feasibility study for a combined high school and community centre at Port Hawkesbury, Nova Scotia, which was funded by DREE on condition that there be extensive citizen consultation. See Graham, Napier, Hebert and Associates, Ltd. *Project 3.9: Junior-Senior High School and Associated Community Facilities, Port Hawkesbury, Nova Scotia, Report 2,*(n.d.) vol. 1. The Ministry of State for Urban Affairs was seen by many citizens' groups as a source of material and moral support. It is not clear, however, whether very many were given significant support by the Ministry. The experience of the Movement for Citizens' Voice and Action (MOVE), a Halifax umbrella group, may have been typical. In March 1971 MOVE asked for a little less that $5,000 to support its efforts to co-ordinate some thirty citizens' groups interested in participating in the work of the Metro Area Planning Committee, a tri-level project supported by the Province of Nova Scotia and MSUA. By April 1972, after much correspondence and many telephone calls, neither the Province nor MSUA had approved the grant. (MOVE, 'Planning Meeting', 12 February 1973.)

75 *Lunenburg Progress-Enterprise*, 5 April, 1978, 16.

76 By 1981 Kayyam Paltiel was commenting that since the 1960s growing numbers of citizens' groups had discovered that start-up and maintenance funds were increasingly available from 'benevolent sympathizers, private foundations in search of an agenda, and most importantly, public agencies, bureaucrats and politicians in search of an expanded constituency, votes and political support. Whereas private-sector groups depend largely on their membership for support, external funding in the past twenty years has apparently played an ever-increasing role in the funding of citizen, non-profit and even the mixed-sector groups.' 'The Changing Environment and Role of Special Interest Groups', 206.

CHAPTER 3. 'TO HAVE A SAY, YOU NEED A VOICE'

[1] See Robert L. Heilbroner with Aaron Singer, *The Economic Transformation of America* (New York, 1977), J.K. Galbraith, *The New Industrial State* (New York, 1971), and *Economics and the Public Purpose* (Boston: 1973). A. Pizzorno perceives a transformation in 'the formal aspects of the political system and the system of representation in particular, in capitalist societies just before and immediately after World War I.' Universal suffrage, mass parties, the institutionalization of interest groups, and new types of legislation represented 'a gradual shift away from the universalistic laws of the age of classical liberalism toward both more specificity in the content of laws and delegation of power to administrative agencies.' A common theme among writers who addressed these phenomena—Gierke, Maitland, Laski, Cole, Durkheim, Bentley, Michels, Weber—was the recognition 'that the idea of a direct relationship between the state and the individual was unrealistic'. 'Interests and Parties in Pluralism' in S.D. Berger, *Organizing Interests in Western Europe* (Cambridge, 1981), 247-87, at 247-9.

[2] See J.W.B. Sisam, *Forestry Education at Toronto* (Toronto, 1961); R.S. Lambert with A. Paul Pross, *Renewing Nature's Wealth* (Toronto, 1967), 178; and Viv Nelles' *The Politics of Development: Forest, Mines and Electric Power in Ontario, 1911-1941* (Toronto, 1974).

[3] See, for example, William MacLeod, *Water Management in the Canadian North* (Ottawa, 1977); Thomas R. Berger, *Northern Frontier, Northern Homeland: Report of the Mackenzie Valley Pipeline Inquiry* (Ottawa, 1977), and Federal Environmental Assessment Review Office, *Beaufort Sea Hydrocarbon Production and Transportation* (Ottawa, 1984).

[4] The consequences of overly rapid development are traced in Raymond L. Foot, *The Case of Port Hawkesbury: Rapid Industrialization and Social Unrest in a Nova Scotia Community* (Toronto, 1979) and A. Paul Pross, *Planning and Development: A Case of Two Nova Scotia Communities* (Halifax, 1975). The problem of communities in decline is the subject of a large literature, of which Ralph Matthews, *The Creation of Regional Dependency* (Toronto, 1983) and Anthony Careless, *Initiative and Response: The Adaptation of Canadian Federalism to Regional Economic Development* (Montreal, 1977) are useful in the present context.

[5] Galbraith, *The New Industrial State.*

[6] Gerard Timsit et Celine Wiener, 'Administration et Politique', *Revue française de science politique* 30 (1980), 3, 506-33. For a review of bureaucratic influence in a number of countries see Ezra N. Suleiman, *Bureaucrats and Policy Making* (New York, 1984).

[7] A typical example of the technical nature of government regulation of industry was reported in the *Globe and Mail* on 11 December 1985 in a story on new controls governing the sale of table wines. The regulations limited permissible levels of ethyl carbamate—a chemical believed to be a carcinogen—to 30 parts per billion. A representative of the Canadian Wine Institute, which claims to represent 80 per cent of the country's wine producers, engaged in a vigorous debate with an official of the federal Department of Health and Welfare over highly technical issues, the industry representative maintaining that testing apparatus was not accurate to 30 parts per billion. He demanded to know how the Department intended testing for that level and stated that the Institute would 'question the results of those tests very aggressively.' The Department representative, while admitting that testing apparatus would have to be improved, maintained that a yeast-enriching agent, urea, produces ethyl carbamate and that the dangerous chemical could be virtually eliminated if urea were no longer used.

[8] The role of language in determining the power relations of policy actors is often commented on. See, for example, Guy Benveniste, *The Politics of Expertise* (Berkeley, Calif., 1972); Leo Panitch, 'The Development of Corporatism in Liberal Democracies,' *Comparative Political Studies* 10 (1977), 61-90; and J. Chevalier, 'Un nouveau sens de l'état et du service publique', in F. de Baecque and J.L. Quermonne (eds), *Administration et Politique sous la Cinquième République* (Paris, 1981), 188.

[9] The spread of forestry concepts into forest policy can be reviewed in Sisam, *Forestry Education at Toronto*; Lambert and Pross, *Renewing Nature's Wealth*; and Pross, 'The

Development of Professions in the Public Service: The Foresters in Ontario', *Canadian Public Administration* X (1967) 3, 376-404.

10 Jacques de Guise, 'Le colloque: une réflexion sur la relation Etat-citoyen', *Recherches sociographiques* XVI (1975) 3, 321-37.

11 David Hoffman, 'Liaison Officers and Ombudsmen: Canadian MPs and the Relations with the Federal Bureaucracy and Executive' in Thomas A. Hockin, *Apex of Power: The Prime Minister and Political Leadership in Canada'* (Scarborough, Ont., 1971), 146-62. Paul Thomas notes that a 1983 Gallup Poll found that 60 per cent of Canadians 'felt that constituency service ought to be the first priority of MPs.' 'Unfinished Reform', *Policy Options*, September 1984, 28-31, 31.

12 Kenneth M. Gibbons, and Donald C. Rowat, *Political Corruption in Canada: Cases, Causes and Cures* (Ottawa, 1976).

13 Norton Long expressed an influential American version of this sentiment when he wrote that 'important and vital interests in the U.S. are unrepresented, underrepresented, or malrepresented in Congress. These interests receive more effective and more responsible representation through administrative channels than through the legislature.' *The Polity* (Chicago, 1962), 68-9. Developments at the federal level in Canada are described in J.E. Hodgetts *et al.*, *Biography of an Institution* (Montreal, 1972) and V. Seymour Wilson, 'The Relationship between Scientific Management and Personnel Policy in North American Administrative Systems', *Public Administration Review* (London, 1973), 193-205.

14 J.E. Hodgetts and O.P. Dwivedi, *Provincial Governments as Employers: A Survey of Public Personnel Administration in Canada* (Montreal, 1974).

15 For the impact of professional development on forest policy see Sisam, *Forestry Education at Toronto*; K.G. Fensom, *Expanding Forestry Horizons: A History of the Canadian Institute of Forestry–Institut Forestier du Canada, 1908-1969* (MacDonald College, P.Q.: CIF, 1972); Pross, 'The Development of Professions' and 'Input versus Withinput: Pressure Group Demands and Administrative Survival' in Pross (ed.), *Pressure Group Behaviour in Canadian Politics* (Toronto, 1975), 148-72. The contribution of the Professional Institute of the Public Service of Canada to civil service reform is reported in John Swettenham and David Kealy, *Serving the State: A History of the Professional Institute of the Public Service of Canada, 1920-1970* (Ottawa, 1970).

16 H.H. Hannam, 'The Interest Group and its Activities', Institute of Public Administration of Canada. *Proceedings of the Fifth Annual Conference*, (Toronto, 1953), 173.

17 S. D. Clark, *The Canadian Manufacturers' Association* (Toronto, 1939), 71-2.

18 Robert Presthus, 'Interest Groups and the Canadian Parliament', *Canadian Journal of Political Science* IV (1971), 444-60, 445-6. See also Léon Dion, *Société et Politique* (Québec, 1971), vol. I, 290-303. Dion reviews attitudes to groups in several countries, pointing out that public suspicion of pressure-group influence is a common feature, though less prevalent in Germany and Italy than in France, for example.

19 See Grant McConnell, *Private Power and American Democracy* (New York, 1966) and Gibbons and Rowat, *Political Corruption in Canada*.

20 J.M. Beck, *The Evolution of Municipal Government in Nova Scotia, 1749 to 1973* (Halifax, 1973), 30, quoting the Halifax *Morning Chronicle*, 15 March 1911.

21 Helen Jones Dawson, 'The Consumers' Association of Canada', VI, *Canadian Public Administration* (1963) 92-118, 100, 102, 103. See also Jonah Goldstein, 'Public Interest Groups and Public Policy: The Case of the Consumers' Association of Canada', *Canadian Journal of Political Science* XII (1979) 1, 137-56, especially 142-6.

22 David Kwavnick, *Organized Labour and Pressure Politics: The Canadian Labour Congress, 1956-1968* (Montreal, 1972).

23 See Stephen Clarkson, 'The Defeat of the Government; the Decline of the Liberal Party, and the (Temporary) Fall of Pierre Trudeau' in Howard R. Penneman (ed.), *Canada at the Polls, 1979 and 1980: A Study of General Elections* (Washington, 1981), 152-89.

24 John Porter, *The Vertical Mosaic* (Toronto, 1965), 425-6. On the mandarins see J.L. Granatstein, *A Man of Influence: Norman A. Robertson and Canadian Statecraft, 1929-1968*

(Toronto, 1981) and *The Ottawa Men: The Civil Service Mandarins, 1935-57* (Toronto, 1982); Christina McCall Newman, *Grits* (Toronto, 1982); and V. Seymour Wilson, 'Mandarins and kibitzers: men in and around the trenches of power in Ottawa', *Canadian Public Administration* 26 (1983) 3, 446-61.

25 Mackintosh's comment is quoted by V.S. Wilson in 'Some Perspectives on Public Policy Analysis' in John H. Redekop, *Approaches to Canadian Politics* (Toronto, 1978), 247-79 at 251-3. Mackintosh, the archetypical 'mandarin', served for many years in senior positions and is considered by many economists to be the architect of Canada's post-war economic policy. Mitchell Sharp, who himself served as a senior civil servant and as a cabinet minister, gives an excellent illustration of the changing roles of elected and permanent officials: 'I recall Dr. Mackintosh's account of how he had been instructed to prepare a statement for [Prime Minister] King to use when announcing on the radio the overall price ceiling which came into effect towards the end of 1941. He showed his draft to the Prime Minister who, after reading the opening paragraphs, looked up and said: "This is important, isn't it, Mackintosh?" I couldn't imagine Mr. Pearson or Mr. Trudeau being so unaware of the momentous consequences of introducing overall price controls.' 'Decision-making in the federal cabinet', *Canadian Public Administration* 19 (1976), 1, 1-8, 3. On the other hand, though Mackenzie King's successors may have had a better grasp of economic policy, they were much less masters of the policy process.

26 In the provinces the civil service was slower to achieve a position of influence. In Québec, for example, Jean Meynaud, writing in the fifties, argued that the extreme weakness of the provincial civil service gave major interests a bargaining advantage. (Jean Meynaud, 'Groupes de pression et politique gouvernementale au Québec' in André Bernard (ed.), *Réflexions sur la Politique au Québec* (Montreal, 1968), 69-96, 83). Until the Quiet Revolution was well established, the political executive continued to be the focal point of lobbying activity. By the 1970s, however, civil-service influence was well established. J. Iain Gow commented in 1975 that the growing specialized expertise of public servants gave them a decided advantage over their political masters. Deputy ministers and assistant deputy ministers had even come to think of themselves as policy and program innovators, rather than as functionaries carrying out the wishes of the government of the day. (J. Iain Gow, 'L'histoire de l'administration publique québécoise', *Recherches sociographiques* XVI (1975) 3, 385-413, 404-5.) There is little doubt that senior federal servants had reached this stage by the end of the Second World War.

27 A.H. Cameron, Administrative Assistant (Health) B.C. Department of Health and Welfare, IPAC *Proceedings*, 1953, 204.

28 Wilfrid Eggleston, 'The Cabinet and Pressure Groups', Ibid., 157-67, at 160. McIlraith defined lobbying as 'interference or pressure by an organized group to influence government to serve the special interests of the group as opposed to the general interest'.

29 Ibid., 205.

30 See particularly the proceedings of the 1953 and 1957 IPAC meetings, which discussed, respectively, pressure groups and advisory committees. Properly representative advisory committees were seen by some as a more appropriate vehicle for presenting interest-group demands. They would, in effect, act as buffers between the administrator and pressure groups. In J.A. Corry's words, they were 'the democratic answer to the challenge of the corporate state.' (Quoted by T.K. Shoyama, 'Advisory Committees in Administration', IPAC, *Proceedings*, 1957, 145-53, at 147.) See Also D.C. Corbett, 'The Pressure Group and the Public Interest', IPAC, *Proceedings*, 1953, 185-95, and IPAC, *Proceedings*, 1957, where the utility of advisory committees is questioned.

31 See J.E. Hodgetts, 'The Civil Service and Policy Formation', *Canadian Journal of Economics and Political Science* 23 (1957) 4, 467-78, at 476.

32 G.W. Stead, Assistant Secretary to the Treasury Board, Ottawa, commented, for example, that 'when the bureaucrats in a department dream up some scheme for expanding their empire they use the advisory committee as a means of obtaining popular support.' IPAC, *Proceedings*, 1957, 156.

[33] IPAC, *Proceedings*, 1953, 205.

[34] H.J. Dawson, 'Relations between Farm Organizations and the Civil Service', *Canadian Public Administration* X (1967) 4, 450-71, 454.

[35] Quoted in Clive Baxter, 'Lobbying—Ottawa's Fastest Growing Business' in Paul Fox (ed.), *Politics Canada* (Toronto, 1966), 206-10.

[36] See Donald Barry's comments on the hesitation displayed by established Church groups in the debate over the Biafra issue. 'Interest Groups and the Foreign Policy Process: The Case of Biafra', in Pross, *Pressure Group Behaviour in Canadian Politics*, 115-48; 125 and 132. See also Kwavnick, *Organized Labour and Pressure Politics*, ch. 7.

[37] Fred Thompson and W.T. Stanbury, *The Political Economy of Interest Groups in the Legislative Process in Canada* (Montreal, Institute for Research in Public Policy, Occasional Paper No. 9, 1979), viii.

[38] Pross, 'Pressure Groups: Adaptive Instruments of Political Communication' in Pross (ed.), *Pressure Group Behaviour in Canadian Politics*, 1-27, 19-20.

[39] Robert Presthus, 'Interest Groups and the Canadian Parliament: Activities, Interaction, Legitimacy, and Influence', *Canadian Journal of Political Science* IV (1971) 4, 444-60. His Parliamentary respondents reported encountering group representatives primarily at Committee hearings (41 per cent); at informal meetings arranged by groups (33 per cent); and only rarely at social functions (20 per cent). See also Bruce MacNaughton and Allan Gregg, 'Interest Group Influence in the Canadian Parliament'. Paper. CPSA. June 1977.

[40] James Gillies and Jean Pigott, 'Participation in the Legislative Process', *Canadian Public Administration* 25 (1982) 2, 254-65, 256.

[41] Helen Jones Dawson, 'National Pressure Groups and the Federal Government' in Pross, *Pressure Group Behaviour in Canadian Politics* , 29-58, 39-45, *passim*. On this point see also Peter Aucoin, 'Pressure Groups and Recent Changes in the Policy-Making Process' in the same volume, 172-93.

[42] Dawson, 'National Pressure Groups', 41.

[43] A point first noted by J.E. Anderson, 'Pressure groups and Canadian Bureaucracy' in W.D.K. Kernaghan and A.M. Willms (eds), *Public Administration in Canada: Selected Readings* (Toronto, 1970), 370-9 and generally accepted in most subsequent studies.

[44] See successive editions of the *Canadian Almanac and Directory* and Brian Land, *Directory of Associations in Canada* (Toronto). The figures cited here are derived from a count of entries on randomly selected pages of the *Almanac and Directory*. They are not, therefore, accurate. However, they are consistent with the relative space accorded societies and associations in succeeding editions. The pattern of growth is also consistent with that recorded in Land's *Directory of Associations* since its establishment in the early 1970s. Discrepancies between these two sources (Land counted 11,000 in 1978; the *Almanac and Directory* 4,473) can be attributed to different presentation of listings (the *Almanac and Directory* lists Boards of Trade separately, for example, and they are not counted here) and to varying policies of inclusion (the *Directory of Associations*, for example, excludes regional and local groups after 1983).

[45] Hugh G. Thorburn, for example, draws attention to the increased number of interest group briefs (897) presented to the recent Royal Commission on the Economic Union and Development Prospects for Canada (Macdonald Commission), in comparison to the 331 presented to the 1937 Royal Commission on Dominion-Provincial Relations (Rowell-Sirois Commission) and the 297 presented to the 1957 Royal Commission on Canada's Economic Prospects (the Gordon Commission). *Interest Groups in the Canadian Federal System* (Toronto, 1985), 83-4.

[46] Hugh G. Thorburn, 'Pressure Groups in Canadian Politics: Recent Revisions of the Anti-Combines Legislation', *Canadian Journal of Economics and Political Science* XXX (1964) 2, 157-74.

[47] J. Hugh Faulkner, 'Pressuring the Executive', *Canadian Public Administration* 25 (1982) 2, 240-53, 251.

[48] The 1980-1 figures are presented in Faulkner, 'Pressuring the Executive', 251, those for

1966–7 in M. Rush, 'The Development of the Committee System in the Canadian House of Commons—Reassessment and Reform'. *The Parliamentarian*, LV (1974) 3, 149-59, 153.

[49] See Robert Bothwell, Ian Drummond, and John English, *Canada Since 1945: Power, Politics and Provincialism* (Toronto, 1981).

[50] The explosion of pressure group activity in this period is frequently commented on. A particularly vivid illustration is presented in the *Report* of the Royal Commission on the Economic Union and Development Prospects for Canada (Macdonald Commission) (Ottawa, 1985), Volume III, 58-9, in the form of a table prepared by William Coleman, showing the formation of business interest groups.

Period of Founding of Existing Associations Representing Business

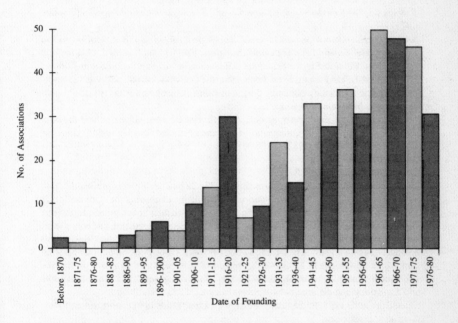

Source: William D. Coleman, 'Canadian Business and the State', in *The State and Economic Interests*, vol. 32, prepared for the Royal Commission on the Economic Union and Development Prospects for Canada (Toronto, 1985).

[51] *Financial Post*, 24 July 1976.

[52] *CAUT Bulletin*, February 1975.

[53] David B. Truman, *The Governmental Process* (New York, 1951), 66-108. A Canadian instance was the institutionalization of native and new-Canadian interest groups precipitated by the federal government's move towards a policy on bilingualism and biculturalism, cited in chapter 1.

[54] *Globe and Mail*, 14 June 1974.

[55] *Montreal Star*, 18 July 1970, and W.T. Stanbury, *Business Interests and the Reform of Canadian Competition Policy, 1971–1975* (Toronto, 1977).

[56] *Financial Post*, 1 July 1976.

[57] Halifax *Chronicle Herald*, 21 Dec. 1972, and R. John Arseneau, 'The Government–Small Business Relationship', Dalhousie University. Student Paper (1984).

[58] See *Financial Post*, 16 December 1972 and 9 June 1973.

[59] *Financial Post*, 16 December 1972.

[60] *CAUT Bulletin*, June 1974 and subsequent issues.

[61] See G. David Garson, *Group Theories of Politics* (Beverly Hills, Calif., 1978), ch. 4.

[62] Faulkner, 'Pressuring the Executive', 248-9. Khayyam Z. Paltiel considers this a major cause of group proliferation. See 'The changing environment and role of special interest groups', *Canadian Public Administration* 25 (1982) 2, 198-211, 205-6.

[63] Even after the reforms discussed below this remained a problem, as it has elsewhere. Radwanski, for example, describes Prime Minister Trudeau's practice of paying little attention to policy fields to which he attached a low priority. G. Radwanski, *Trudeau* (Toronto, 1978), 179.

[64] Described in G. Bruce Doern and Peter Aucoin (eds), *Public Policy in Canada* (Toronto, 1979), R. French, *How Ottawa Decides* (Ottawa, 1980), and Colin Campbell and George J. Szablowski, *The Superbureaucrats: Structure and Behaviour in Central Agencies* (Toronto, 1979).

[65] See French, *How Ottawa Decides*; James Gillies, *Where Business Fails: Business-Government Relations at the Federal Level in Canada* (Montreal, 1981); Colin Campbell, *Governments Under Stress: Political Executives and Key Bureaucrats in Washington, London and Ottawa* (Toronto, 1983), and Richard J. van Loon, 'Stop the music: the current policy and expenditure management system in Ottawa', *Canadian Public Administration* 24 (1981), 175-200.

[66] See French, *How Ottawa Decides*.

[67] On these points see particularly French, *How Ottawa Decides*; Gillies, *Where Business Fails*; Pross, 'Summary of Discussions—Fourteenth National Seminar, 1981', *Canadian Public Administration* 25 (1982) 2, 170-83; Richard J. Schultz, *Federalism and the Regulatory Process* (Montreal, 1979).

[68] Gillies, *Where Business Fails*.

[69] 'Comment,' in Neilson and MacPherson (eds), *The Legislative Process in Canada*, 214. Roman reports being told 'on more than one occasion by someone at the "private" level that they were amazed or frightened at the ease with which their policy proposals (often in important areas in which they had no specialized knowledge or expertise, had only a short time to prepare, and did very superficial research) sailed through to the Cabinet level virtually unaltered' (215). The diffusion of power was a major theme of the 14th National Seminar of the Institute of Public Administration of Canada, which addressed itself to the problem of 'governing under pressure—the special interest groups'. See Pross, 'Summary of Discussions' and the articles by Weaver, Faulkner, Gillies, and Pigott.

[70] Quoted in a review of J. Bruce-Gardyne and N. Lawson, *The Policy Game* (London, 1976).

[71] Confidential interview.

[72] Freda Hawkins, *Canada and Immigration: Public Policy and Public Concern* (Montreal, 1972), 312-13.

[73] Fensom, *Expanding Forestry Horizons*, 230-1.

[74] Canada. Department of the Environment. *Submission to the Management Committee: A Regularized Operational Program for Public Participation* (Mimeo. n.d. c.1975).

[75] By policy communities we mean the clustering of interest groups, associated agencies, and interested and/or informed individuals around the agencies generally considered to be the key policy actors in a specific field of government activity. The concept—which is discussed at length in chapter 5—is similar to, but more inclusive than, the American concept of the 'sub-government'. (See Randall B. Ripley and Grace A. Franklin, *Congress, The Bureaucracy and Public Policy* (Homewood, Ill., 1976).

[76] R.D.S. Macdonald, 'Inshore Fishing Interests on the Atlantic Coast: Their Response to Extended Jurisdiction by Canada', *Marine Policy* (July 1979), 171-89.

[77] Faulkner, 'Pressuring the Executive', 248.

78 See, for example, Marc Lalonde, Minister of National Health and Welfare, House of Commons, *Debates* (20 June 1975), 6954 (daily edition).

79 For example, Environment Canada provides grants to groups willing to prepare information projects for Environment Week, in order to 'further both [the Department's] objectives and the objectives of the environmentally concerned private citizen's action groups'. (Information Services. Environment Canada. Atlantic Region, 'Funding for . . . 1984 Environment Week Related Information Projects', (Halifax. mimeo., January 1984).) The majority of Canadian academic associations are supported by direct grants (See the annual *Reports* of the Social Sciences and Humanities Research Council of Canada), while others such as the Atlantic Provinces Economic Council receive both grants and contracts (APEC, Annual *Reports*). Faulkner, 'Pressuring the Executive', describes how the Canadian Arctic Resources Committee and other groups have been assisted to participate in regulatory hearings.

80 Thus the federal government required that local groups be accorded participation in regional development planning. See *Agricultural Rehabilitation and Development Act: Federal-Provincial Rural Development Agreement* (Ottawa, 1965), parts IV, VI and VIII.

81 Macdonald, 'Inshore Fishing Interests . . .' The *Policy for Canada's Atlantic Fisheries in the 1980s: A Discussion Paper* (Ottawa, 1981) took direct aim at the individualism of fishermen: 'Fishermen must continue the movement away from their historic pattern of individual voices to make their views known more effectively as a group. Greater unity has to come before fishermen can talk with any confidence about the future.' (See pp. 8-9.)

82 Brian Chapman remarks that 'it is . . . interesting to view the development of the Canadian police system as an exercise in the gradual emergence of new and continually changing administrative coalitions.' 'The Canadian Police: A Survey', *Government and Opposition* 12 (1977) 4, 496-516.

83 See Kwavnick, *Organized Labour and Pressure Politics.*

84 So, for example, Parks Canada maintains regular contact with conservation associations, various outdoor leisure groups, biologists, and geographers. The Canadian Forestry Service policy community includes members of the forestry profession and their associations, forest-industry groups and so on.

85 See Pross, 'Pressure Groups: Adaptive Instruments'.

86 Confidential letter.

87 This point, a major theme in Gillies, *Where Business Fails*, is illustrated in Sally M. Weaver, *Making Canadian Indian Policy* (Toronto, 1981). We should bear in mind, however, Schultz's argument (*Federalism and the Regulatory Process*) that by virtue of their responsibility for defining detailed regulation and interpreting policy issues to the centre, line departments retain considerable influence.

88 Faulkner, 'Pressuring the Executive', 252-3.

89 Quoted in Pross, 'Summary', 180.

90 The term 'legitimacy' as used in the following paragraphs refers to the extent to which the community at large acknowledges and supports the work of a particular institution. The terms 'legitimation' and 'legitimating capacity' refer to the ability of an institution to confer legitimacy on some other institution or on some claim or argument.

91 Some of the evidence supporting this position is referred to below and in the Gillies and French works cited above. For more detailed and fully documented discussions the reader is referred to the literature on accountability, particularly the *Reports* of the Auditor General of Canada during the mid-1970s, which repeatedly warned that government was not in control of the budgetary expenditure system, and the *Report* of the Royal Commission on Financial Management and Accountability (Lambert Commission, (Ottawa, 1979), which tended to confirm the Auditor General's criticism.

92 'I felt that the five years of minority government that we went through were a kind of situation where we weren't able to plan our legislation, we weren't able to bring in all the necessary reforms . . . and I was quite concerned about the machinery of government . . . One of the reasons why I wanted this job, when I was told that it might be there, is because I

felt it very important to have a strong central government, build up the executive, build up the Prime Minister's Office, strengthen Parliament.' Pierre Elliott Trudeau. Interview with J. Walz, *New York Times*, 22 Nov. 1968. PMO Transcript, quoted in George Radwanski, *Trudeau* (Toronto, 1978), 146.

93 Sandra Gwyn, 'Ottawa's incredible bureaucratic explosion', *Saturday Night*, August 1975.

94 Auditor General of Canada, *Report*, (Ottawa, 1976).

95 See Van Loon, 'Stop the Music', and the exchange of views it elicited between Douglas Hartle, Richard French and Van Loon in *Canadian Public Administration* 26 (1983) 1, 84-104; Paul G. Thomas, 'Public Administration and Expenditure Management', *Canadian Public Administration* 25 (1982) 4, 674-95; and Richard Van Loon, 'The Policy and Expenditure Management System in the Federal Government in the First Three Years', *Canadian Public Administration* 26 (1983) 2, 255-85.

96 Flora MacDonald, 'The Minister and the Mandarins', *Policy Options*, September/October 1980.

97 It is interesting to note, in a content analysis of the *Winnipeg Free Press*, that during the 1970s the paper shifted editorial concern from Cabinet and Parliament to the bureaucracy. See Allan Kornberg and Judith D. Wolfe, 'Parliament, the Media and the Polls' in Clarke *et al.*, *Parliament, Policy and Representation*, 35-58 at 46; *Globe and Mail*, 15 July 1982, 1; Marci MacDonald, *et al.*, 'The Money Wasters', *Maclean's*, 15 December 1975; Douglas Hartle, 'Refugees from Ottawa: five public servants and why they left', *Saturday Night*, March 1976; Gordon W. Stead, 'The Federal Bureaucracy and Canadian Disunity', in Elliot J. Feldman and Neil Nevitte (eds), *The Future of North America: Canada, the United States and Quebec Nationalism* (Cambridge/Montreal, 1979), 213-35, and MacDonald, 'The Minister and the Mandarins'.

98 As we have suggested, apart from the legitimacy they derive from subordination to the cabinet, Canadian federal agencies have very limited standing and credibility. Like their American counterparts they cannot avail themselves of the status of the state itself. Furthermore, despite their professional competence, public servants are not held in high esteem by the general public, which tends to look askance at experts and to applaud such sophisms as 'civil servants should be on tap, not on top'. This is not a topic discussed at length in the literature, though some useful insight is to be gained from the 1969 report of the Task Force on Government Information, *To Know and Be Known* (Ottawa, 1979), especially ch. 4, 'National Opinion Survey'. vol. II, 47-89, and David Zussman, 'The Image of the Public Service in Canada', *Canadian Public Administration* 25 (1982) 1, 63-80.

99 See Royal Commission on Government Organization, (Glassco Commission) *Report* (Ottawa, 1962) I, *Management of the Public Service*.

100 See Royal Commission on Bilingualism and Biculturalism, *Report* Book III, *The Work World*, vol. 3A, Part 2 'The Federal Administration; (Ottawa, 1969).

101 'Bureaucrat X', *Cover Your Ass: Or How to Survive in a Government Bureaucracy* (Edmonton, 1977). The titles of several chapters captured common perceptions of the bureaucracy, as in Delusions of Grandeur: Job Titles and Descriptions'; 'The Insignia of Rank: Office Space and Furniture'; 'Promotions: The Don't Make Waves Syndrome'; and 'The CYA Principle and Public Relations: or How to Abuse a Citizen Without Really Trying'.

102 V. Seymour Wilson, 'Representative Bureaucracy: linguistic/ethnic aspects in Canadian public policy', *Canadian Public Administration* 21 (1978) 4, 513-38.

103 See Rush, 'The Development of the Committee System . . .', 154. For discussions of committee impact on draft legislation see, among others, M.L. Friedland, 'Pressure Groups and the Development of the Criminal Law', in P.R. Glazebrook (ed.), *Reshaping the Criminal Law: Essays in Honour of Glanville Williams* (London, 1978); D.B. Butler, 'The Adequacy of Committee Consideration of Legislation: The Case of Bill C-183' in J.P. Satauri and J.R. Hurley, *The Canadian House of Commons Observed* (Ottawa, 1979); G.W.C. Hunter, *The Role of the Member of Parliament and the Standing Committees of the House of Commons* (M.A. thesis, Acadia University, 1982) and M. Rush, 'Committees in the Canadian House

of Commons' in John D. Lees and Malcolm Shaw, *Committees in Legislatures: A Comparative Perspective* (Durham, N.C., 1979), 191-241.

[104]John F. Bulloch, 'A View from a Special Interest Group' in Daniel L.Bon, *Lobbying: A Right? A Necessity? A Danger?* (Ottawa, 1981), 12.

[105]'The Committee Track Record: A limited Pay-off', *Parliamentary Government* 3 (1983) 4, 7-10, 9.

[106]Herb Breau, quoted in 'Commons Committee Witnesses: A Process of Enlightenment', *Parliamentary Government* 3 (1982), 4, 3-6, 6.

[107]Ibid.

[108]According to R.A. Weir, 'From 1965 to 1967, the period of intensive public debate over the medicaid (*sic*) programme, national officials of the CMA met physician-MPs informally only once and did not meet any larger group of MPs at all.' 'Federalism, Interest Groups and the Parliamentary Government: The Canadian Medical Association', *Journal of Comparative Political Studies*, XI (1973) 2, 159-75 at 165.

[109]'The Committee Track Record', 10.

[110]Ernest Steele, president of the Canadian Association of Broadcasters. Ibid.

[111]'A View from a Special Interest Group', 13.

[112]Canadian Bar Association, *Report of the Canadian Bar Association Committee on the Reform of Parliament* (Parliament as Lawmaker) (Ottawa, 1982), vii.

[113]On the other hand respondents were much less complimentary in their assessment of the work of parliamentarians, leading Kornberg *et al.* to conclude that the *institution* of Parliament rather than its then current membership and accomplishments had very broad public support. See Allan Kornberg, Harold D. Clarke, and Arthur Goddard, 'Parliament and the Representational Process in Contemporary Canada' in Harold D. Clarke *et al.* (eds), *Parliament, Policy and Representation* (Toronto, 1980), xxvi-25 at 9-10.

Out of a sample of 2,095 individuals over 18 interviewed in 1979 for the Canadian Gallup Polls, only 38 per cent reported that they had 'a great deal of respect' or 'quite a lot of respect' for the House of Commons. Thirty-six per cent had 'some' respect; 15 per cent very little; and 11 per cent had no opinion. Even so the House ranked fourth in a list of eight social institutions, behind the Church or organized religion, the Supreme Court, and public schools but ahead of newspapers, large corporations, political parties, and labour unions. (F. Kielty *et al.* *Canadians Speak Out: The Canadian Gallup Polls, 1980* (Toronto, 1980).

[114]A.H. Hanson, 'The Purpose of Parliament', *Parliamentary Affairs* XVII (1964) 3, 279-96, 295. Bertrand Badie and Pierre Birnbaum, *Sociologie de l'Etat* (Paris, 1982).

It may be objected that in Canada provincial regimes rival Ottawa's claim to legitimacy. It is acknowledged that in areas of shared or contested jurisdiction this rivalry would certainly affect public perceptions of legitimacy. On the other hand, where either one level of government or the other has clear jurisdiction over a specific policy field, one would expect the legislative to possess pre-eminent legitimacy in that field. Alan Cairns' 'The other crisis of Canadian federalism' (*Canadian Public Administration* 22 (1979), 175-95) is, in a sense, a discussion of the effect intergovernmental rivalry has on the legitimacy of both levels of government.

[115]Audrey Doerr, 'Public Administration: federalism and intergovernmental relations', *Canadian Public Administration* 25 (1982) 4, 564-79, 575.

[116]See Audrey Doerr, 'Parliamentary Accountability and Legislative Potential' in Clarke *et al.*, *Parliament, Policy and Representation*, 144-60.

[117]Douglas C. Nord, 'MPs and Senators as Middlemen: The special Joint Committee on Immigration Policy' in Clarke *et al.*, *Parliament, Policy and Representation*, 181-94.

[118]William D. Coleman, 'From Bill 22 to Bill 101: The Politics of Language under the Parti Québécois', *Canadian Journal of Political Science* XIV (1981) 3, 459-86.

[119]Rush, 'The Development of the Committee System' and 'Committees in the Canadian House of Commons'.

[120]Nord, 'MPs and Senators as Middlemen', 185.

¹²¹ Letter, John McDonough, Project Officer, Research Branch, Library of Parliament, to Dr P. Smith, 22 Feb. 1980, quoted in G.W.C. Hunter, *The Role of the Member of Parliament and the Standing Committees of the House of Commons*, M.A. thesis, Acadia University (1982), 82.

¹²² See ibid. and M. MacGuigan, 'The Role of the Standing Committee on Justice and Legal Affairs of the Canadian House of Commons: 1968–78' in J. Menezes (ed.), *Decade of Adjustment—Legal Perspectives on Contemporary Social Issues* (Toronto, 1980) and Butler, 'The Adequacy of Committee Consideration of Legislation'.

¹²³ See Kathryn Randle, 'Committees at the Cross-roads: Will Innovation Lead to Reform?', *Parliamentary Government* 2 (1981), 3.

¹²⁴ See Stanbury, *Business Interests and the Reform of Canadian Competition Policy*; MacGuigan, 'The Role of the Standing Committee on Justice and Legal Affairs'; Butler, 'The Adequacy of Committee Consideration of Legislation'; and Friedland, 'Pressure Groups and the Development of the Criminal Law', and Grace Skogstad, 'Interest Groups, Representation and Conflict Management in the Standing Committees of the House of Commons', *Canadian Journal of Political Science* XVIII (1985) 4, 739-78.

¹²⁵ M. Rush, 'Committees in the Canadian House of Commons', at 230 quoting Hockin, *CPA* (1970), 201.

¹²⁶ 'Commons Committee Witnesses'.

CHAPTER 4. FUNCTION: THE CONTEXT OF PRESSURE GROUP LIFE

¹ S.E. Finer, 'Interest Groups and the Policy Process in Great Britain' in Henry W. Ehrmann (ed.), *Interest Groups on Four Continents* (Pittsburgh, 1958), 117-44, 137.

² Robert Presthus, *Elite Accommodation in Canadian Politics* (Toronto, 1973) and *Elites in the Policy Process* (Toronto, 1974).

³ Ehrmann, *Interest Groups on Four Continents*, 1.

⁴ Ibid., 5.

⁵ Harry Eckstein, *Pressure Group Politics: The Case of the British Medical Association* (London, 1960).

⁶ Finer, *Anonymous Empire* (London, 1966), 98-100, and Graham K. Wilson, *Special Interests and Policy Making* (London, 1977), particularly ch. 9.

⁷ John T.S. Keeler, 'Corporatism and official union hegemony: the case of French agricultural syndicalism', in Suzanne D. Berger (ed.), *Organizing Interests in Western Europe: Pluralism, corporatism, and the transformation of politics* (Cambridge, 1981), 185-208. André Holleaux, 'La Phénomène associatif', *Revue française d'administration publique* 8 (1978), 683-727, estimates that 28 per cent of the French belong to one or more associations; 19.5 per cent to one only; 8 per cent to several. James Curtis, 'Voluntary Association Joining: A Cross-National Comparative Note', *American Sociological Review* 36 (1971), 872-80, estimates that in 1960 50 per cent of adult Americans were members of associations other than unions; in Britain (1959) 33 per cent; in Germany (1959) 34 per cent; in Italy (1959) 25 per cent; and in Mexico (1959) 15 per cent.

⁸ Curtis, 'Voluntary Association Joining', estimates that in 1968 51 per cent of adult Canadians were members of associations other than unions.

⁹ L.C. Bacchi, *Liberation Deferred: The Ideas of the English Canadian Suffragists: 1877-1918* (Toronto, University of Toronto Press, 1983), 34-5.

¹⁰ Ibid.

¹¹ Robert Presthus, 'Interest Groups and the Canadian Parliament: Activities, Interaction, Legitimacy and Influence', *Canadian Journal of Political Science* IV (1971) 4, 446-60, at 446.

[12] *Financial Post*, 10 Jan. 1972.

[13] Peter G. Johnson, 'The Union of Nova Scotia Municipalities as a Pressure Group', *Proceedings*, Canadian Political Science Association, Winnipeg, June 1970, 2, 5.

[14] C.E. Dalphond, 'L'information administrative: une analyse politique préliminaire', *Recherches sociographiques* XVI (1975) 3, 307-21, 311.

[15] Martin Robin, *The Rush for Spoils: The Company Province, 1871-1933* (Toronto, 1972), 55-6.

[16] See the *APEC Newsletter* and the organization's *Annual Reports*.

[17] See Peter Aucoin, 'Pressure Groups and Recent Changes in the Policy-Making Process' in A. Paul Pross (ed.), *Pressure Group Behaviour in Canadian Politics* (Toronto, 1975), 172-93, and ch. 3, *supra*.

[18] See Donald C. Savage, 'Freedom of Information Legislation and the University Community', *CAUT Bulletin*, Feb. 1983, 5-6.

[19] See Bacchi, *Liberation Deferred*.

[20] *Ottawa Citizen*, 24 June 1982.

[21] Romeo Leblanc, Speech, Rotary Club of Yarmouth, Nova Scotia, 28 November 1977.

[22] The pleas of federal officials for organization within the industry are found in many publications. See, for example, Environment Canada. Fisheries and Marine Service. *Policy for Canada's Commercial Fisheries* (Ottawa, May 1976); Lyndon Watkins, 'Fishermen Test Inshore Waters in Union Drive', *Globe and Mail* 13 Oct. 1979; R.D.S. Macdonald, 'Inshore fishing interests on the Atlantic coast: Their response to extended jurisdiction by Canada', *Marine Policy* (1979), 171-89; Department of Fisheries and Oceans' *Policy for Canada's Atlantic Fisheries in the 1980s: A Discussion Paper* (Ottawa, 1981), 8, 55, 59; the complaint of an MP that lack of 'direct input' by fishermen has caused many of the industry's ills, reported in the Halifax *Chronicle Herald*, 10 Dec. 1984; the November 1984 warning of Fisheries Minister John Fraser—echoing Romeo LeBlanc—that fishermen and fishing companies will only get support for the industry if they learn to speak with a united voice. (*Chronicle Herald*, 15 Nov. 1984).

[23] Kingston *Whig-Standard*, 21 June 1983.

[24] The classic exploration of the 'capture thesis' is Marver Bernstein, *Regulating Business by Independent Commission* (Princeton, 1955). Doern and Toner present a Canadian illustration in their discussion of Canadian energy policy. During the 1960s, they argue, the major oil companies, through their control of technical, geological, economic, and financial information, were able to manipulate federal and Alberta energy policy in their own interests. See G. Bruce Doern and Glen Toner, *The Politics of Energy* (Toronto, 1985), 131 ff.

[25] Kenneth Woodside, 'The Political Economy of Policy Instruments: Tax Expenditures and Subsidies in Canada', in M. Atkinson and Marsha Chandler, *The Politics of Canadian Public Policy* (Toronto, 1983), 173-99, 190-1.

[26] Peter Aucoin, *Public Accountability in the Governing of Professions: A Report on the Self-Governing Professions of Accounting, Architecture, Engineering and Law in Ontario* (The Professional Organizations Committee. Working Paper #4. 1978).

[27] Freda Hawkins, *Canada and Immigration: Public Policy and Public Concern* (Montreal, 1972), 301.

[28] See National Council of Welfare, *In the Best Interests of the Child: A Report by the National Council of Welfare on the Child Welfare System in Canada* (Ottawa, 1979) and L.F. Hurl, 'Privatized Social Service Systems: Lessons from Ontario Children's Services', *Canadian Public Policy* X (1984), 395-406.

[29] Reported in *Le Devoir*, 22 Sept. 1982.

[30] J.G. Nelson, 'Public participation in comprehensive resource and environmental management', *Science and Public Policy*, Oct. 1982, 204-50, 247.

[31] William D. Coleman, 'Canadian Business and the State' in Keith Banting (Research Coordinator), *The State and Economic Interests* (Toronto, Studies of the Royal Commission on the Economic Union and Development Prospects for Canada, vol. 32, 1985).

[32] Canada. Department of Fisheries and Oceans. *Policy for Canada's Atlantic Fisheries in the 1980s* (Ottawa, 1981), 8.

[33] John Kearney, 'The Transformation of the Bay of Fundy Herring Fisheries, 1976-78: An Experiment in Fishermen-Government Co-Management' in Cynthia Lamson and Arthur J. Hanson (eds), *Atlantic Fisheries and Coastal Communities: Fisheries Decision-Making Case Studies* (Halifax, 1984), 165-204.

[34] Canada. Task Force on Atlantic Fisheries, *Navigating Troubled Waters: A New Policy for the Atlantic Fisheries* (Ottawa, 1983) (Kirby Report), 344.

[35] Cheryl Ann Fraser, *Groundfish Management by Property Rights: The Southwest Nova Scotia Case* (Dalhousie University: MES thesis, 1985), 74.

[36] This view is most clearly expressed in Earl Latham, *The Group Basis of Politics* (New York, 1965), but see also David B. Truman, *The Governmental Process: Political Interests and Public Opinion* (New York, 1951). G. David Garson, *Group Theories of Politics* (Beverly Hills, Calif., 1978) presents a useful guide to the pluralist debate.

[37] See Philippe C. Schmitter and Gerhard Lehmbruch (eds), *Trends Toward Corporatist Intermediation* (Beverly Hills, Calif., 1979); Suzanne D. Berger (ed.), *Organizing Interests in Western Europe* (Cambridge, 1981); and Jeremy Richardson (ed.), *Policy Styles in Western Europe* (London, 1982).

[38] See Randall B. Ripley and Grace A. Franklin, *Congress, the Bureaucracy and Public Policy* (Homewood, Ill., 1976).

[39] Quoted in J.J. Richardson and A.G. Jordan, *Governing Under Pressure: The Policy Process in a Post-Parliamentary Democracy* (Oxford, 1979), 26. Bruce W. Heady, 'A Typology of Ministers: Implications for Minister-Civil Servant Relations in Britain' in Mattei Dogan (ed.), *The Mandarins of Western Europe: The Political Role of Top Civil Servants* (New York, 1975), 63-87 presents systematic documentation of this view. Wilson, considering Canadian cabinet structure, notes that the cabinet committee system may be creating policy pyramids that tend to find their peak in cabinet committees and sub-committees rather than in cabinet itself. (V. Seymour Wilson, *Canadian Public Administration and Public Policy* (Toronto, 1981, 300). Nor are the effects of specialization confined to massive, complex structures such as the federal government. An editorial in *Plan Canada* notes that at the local level fragmentation of government resulting from the practice of giving responsibility for a particular administrative or service function to some board, commission, or other authority separate from the elected council means that 'apart perhaps from street cleaning, there is hardly a single function of local government which, somewhere or other in this land of ours, is not in the care of its own exclusive band of single-minded, loyal protectors.' (*Plan Canada* 9 (1968) 2, 50). Peter Larkin, a prominent fisheries biologist, speaks similarly *vis-à-vis* fisheries policy and, in passing, makes a comment that illuminates our argument that those who do take part in policy discussions tend to opt for consensus rather than conflict: 'Characteristically, decision making in fisheries management involves, either directly or indirectly, consultation with representatives of all the groups that may be affected—industry, fishermen, experts, ethnic groups, social groups, and in a vague sort of way, the people at large . . . In these circumstances, the decisions are bound to have a certain character. "Why rock the boat?" is the usual theme of representatives. If disaster has not struck in the last three or four years, if things are more less the same, or only a little bit worse, why invite chaos or catastrophe?' Peter A. Larkin, 'A Confidential Memorandum on Fisheries Science' in Brian J. Rothschild, *World Fisheries Policy* (Seattle, 1972), 189-98 at 193-4.

[40] For a review of this nomenclature see Grant Jordan, 'Iron Triangles, Woolly Corporatism and Elastic Nets: Images of the Policy Process', *Journal of Public Policy* 1 (1981) Part 1. Our use of the term 'policy community' is a response to the need to adapt, not merely apply, concepts developed elsewhere. It diverges from conventional theory in that it moves away from a focus on the sub-government itself. In the United States, sub-governments generally include the responsible executive agency, the congressional committee that oversees its activities, and the most influential pressure groups concerned with the field. Each of these depends on the other for support of one kind or another, and out of their symbiotic relation-

ship grows an extremely powerful institution. Here we shall continue to use the term sub-government, but to describe only a part of the decision-making sub-structure that dominates each policy field in Canada. We do this to reflect the fact that the sub-government is less powerful here than in the United States and that other groups tend to be consulted more frequently. We treat the sub-government as only the central core of a broadly based policy community and we treat the policy community as our basic unit of analysis. We emphasize its dominance and draw attention to the inner circle/outer circle concept of the policy community.

[41] It is this aspect of the special public that particularly persuades this writer that it is more aptly described by the term 'community', rather than terms like 'special publics', 'sectors', 'networks', and so on, which suggest communication patterns and shared concerns and perspectives, but which exclude a social dimension. Observation of several special publics indicates that the social dimension is a fundamental lubricant and a key in maintaining the community's dominance in a policy field. The fishing industry provides particularly strong evidence of this. Anyone attending industry conventions is immediately aware of social stratification within the industry and of the development of codes of conduct, which are rigorously enforced. These are even more apparent in the workings of the advisory committees, which play an influential role in determining fish quotas and supervising harvesting arrangements. There the representatives of major companies, fishermen's organizations, and officials are clearly working within a framework of understanding that defines permissible behaviour and punishes unacceptable behaviour through lack of co-operation, chastisement, and so on. Nor do these patterns exhibit themselves only in the work environment. Funerals and marriages in the families of individuals prominent in the industry serve as occasions for industry leaders from across the Atlantic region to meet, renew ties, come to informal understandings, and otherwise reinforce the bonds that hold them together in an often fractious but communal relationship. Similar, though often less intense, patterns can be observed in other policy communities.

[42] Sally M. Weaver, *Making Canadian Indian Policy* (Toronto, 1981).

[43] J.D. Forbes, *Institutions and Influence Groups in Canadian Farm and Food Policy* (Toronto: Institute of Public Administration of Canada. Monographs on Canadian Public Administration. No. 10. 1985), 46.

[44] Coleman and Jacek, 'The Political Organization of the Chemical Industry in Canada'. Paper. Canadian Political Science Association, 1981, 58.

[45] Ibid., 32, 36. In another policy field Canadian minimum wage policy has been influenced by the experience of other countries and the work of international organizations. See Chris Parke, 'The Setting of Minimum Wage Policy in the Maritimes' (Halifax, 1980).

[46] J.B. Falls, 'Douglas H. Pimlott—Lessons for Action', *Nature Canada* 8 (Apr.-June 1979), 18-23.

[47] Committee documents. SSFC (then SSHRCC) *Bulletin* for the period. One of the reasons for the abatement of SSFC interest was that the environmental movement became institutionalized. Some commentators suggest that the environmental movement of the early 1970s had gone into eclipse by the end of the decade, but a more likely explanation—and one consistent with the argument we have just presented—is proposed by Diane Draper when she suggests that the rise and decline of environmental groups is associated not with 'fewer environmentally contentious issues' but with 'changes in institutional arrangements, some brought about in response to environmental group demands.' (Diane Draper, 'Environmental Interest Groups and Institutional Arrangements in British Columbia Water Management Issues' in Bruce Mitchel (ed.), *Institutional Arrangements for Water Management: Canadian Experiences* (Waterloo, 1975), 119-70.

[48] See Coleman and Jacek, 'The Chemical Industry in Canada'.

[49] Denis Stairs, 'Publics and Policy-Makers: The Domestic Environment of Canada's Foreign Policy Community'; Bruce Thorvaldson, *Trudeau and Foreign Policy*; and J.L. Granatstein, *A Man of Influence: Norman Robertson and Canadian Statecraft, 1929-1968* (Toronto, 1981), 379.

[50] M.L. Friedland comments, for example, that policy-making in the field of criminal law takes place in a more public forum than policy-making in many other fields, is more subject to intervention by issue-oriented groups, and is more likely to be characterized by heated debate. He suggests that this is because public policy in the field is declared in law rather than in regulation; that political parties prefer not to take a party line, but rather to invite public debate, and so on. 'Pressure Groups and the Development of the Criminal Law,' in P.R. Glazebrook (ed.), *Reshaping the Criminal Law: Essays in Honour of Glanville Williams* (London, 1978), 205.

[51] See Roderick Byers, *Canadian Foreign Policy and Selective Attentive Publics* (Ottawa, Department of External Affairs, mimeo. 1967) and Trevor Price, 'The Rise and Demise of the Ministry of State for Urban Affairs'. Paper. Canadian Political Science Association, 1981.

[52] This paragraph reflects the approach developed in E.E. Schattschneider, *The Semi-Sovereign People: A Realist's View of Democracy in America* (New York, 1960). The approach is examined more closely in ch. 10.

CHAPTER 5. TYPES OF GROUPS

[1] Robert Presthus, 'Interest Groups and the Canadian Parliament', *Canadian Journal of Political Science* IV (1971) 4, 444-60, 448.

[2] See, for example, W.A. Townsley, 'Pressure Groups in Australia' in Henry W. Ehrmann (ed.), *Interest Groups on Four Continents* (Pittsburgh, 1958), 9-32.

[3] Frederick C. Engelmann and Mildred A. Schwartz, *Canadian Political Parties: Origin, Character, Impact* (Scarborough, Ont., 1975), 96. For a more recent discussion of the role and behaviour of interest groups in federal politics see Hugh G. Thorburn, *Interest Groups and the Canadian Federal System* (Toronto, 1985).

[4] See, for example, J.D. Forbes' discussion of the role of producer interests in the policy community concerned with food production and distribution in *Institutions and Influence Groups in Canadian Farm and Food Policy* (Toronto: Institute of Public Administration of Canada. Monographs on Canadian Public Administration. No. 10. 1985), chs 3 and 7.

[5] The following paragraph draws on a large literature. See particularly Robert K. Merton, *Social Theory and Social Structure* (New York, 1968), chs 8, 9, and 10.

[6] See N.J. Lawrie, 'The Canadian Construction Association: An Interest Group and its Environment'. (Unpublished Ph. D. dissertation, University of Toronto, 1976); Ronald W. Lang, *The Politics of Drugs: The British and Canadian pharmaceutical industries and governments—A comparative study* (Farnborough, 1974); and Christopher Armstrong, *The Politics of Federalism: Ontario's Relations with the Federal Government* (Toronto, 1981), 100-13.

[7] Quoted in Brian J. Young, 'C. George McCullagh and the Leadership League' in Ramsay Cook, *The Politics of Discontent* (Toronto, 1967), 76-102, 82.

[8] Interview. J.Hugh Faulkner. 6 Oct. 1981.

[9] Forbes, *Food Policy System*, ch. 3.

[10] See the commentaries on successive annual conferences of the Canadian Library Association in the *Canadian Library Journal*.

[11] Phillip Selznick, *Leadership in Administration* (New York, 1957), 21.

[12] Ibid., 5.

[13] Ibid., 20.

[14] Ibid., 139.

[15] The concept of secondary inducements is developed in Mancur Olson, *The Logic of Collective Action* (Cambridge, Mass., 1971). Collective benefits may be enjoyed regardless of an

individual's participation in an organization, but secondary inducements, which are selective benefits, can be enjoyed only at the price of membership. R. Manzur presents a Canadian illustration in 'Selective Inducements and the Development of Pressure Groups: The Case of Canadian Teachers' Associations', *Canadian Journal of Economics and Political Science* II (1969) 1, 103-18.

16 David Kwavnick, *Organized Labour and Pressure Politics: The Canadian Labour Congress, 1956-1968* (Montreal, 1972), 2.

17 Forbes, *Food Policy System*, 117-18.

18 Ibid., 118.

19 Freda Hawkins' description of voluntary groups working in the immigration field could be applied to many other issue-oriented groups. They 'do not have an office, never keep records, and simply respond to the needs of the moment. Their program, objectives, and performance may change totally from year to year. Only a very few officials and experienced community workers in a particular city, who have been working with these agencies, committees and groups for some time can really assess the quality and usefulness of the work they do.' Freda Hawkins, *Canada and Immigration: Public Policy and Public Concern* (Montreal, 1972), 294. When we refer to the determination of the resource base, we recognize that the political activist in the group leadership will find the presence of selective inducements a mixed blessing. They attract members whose attitudes may impede resolute, unequivocal action. Furthermore, some forms of political action may have to be modified because they could threaten continuation of certain services.

20 Donald Barry, 'Interest Groups and the Foreign Policy Process: The Case of Biafra' in A. Paul Pross, (ed.), *Pressure Group Behaviour in Canadian Politics* (Toronto, 1975) 115-48.

21 For an early account of the Canadian Federation of Independent Business see Jonathan Manthorpe, 'Lobbyist who wins with any party', *Globe and Mail*, 14 June 1974. A later version is presented in John F. Bulloch, 'A View from a Special Interest Group' in Daniel L. Bon, *Lobbying: A Right? A Necessity? A Danger?* (Ottawa, 1981), 12.

22 Barry, 'Interest Groups and the Foreign Policy Process'.

23 B. and K. Devaux, 'The Enemies Within Citizen Participation' in Draper (ed.), *Citizen Participation: Canada*, (Toronto, 1971), 93-105.

24 Ian Hamilton, *The Children's Crusade: The Story of the Company of Young Canadians* (Toronto, 1970).

25 See Philip Lowe and Jane Goyder, *Environmental Groups in Politics* (London, 1983) and Jonathon Porritt, *Seeing Green* (Oxford, 1984). Two brief accounts of the attempt to establish the Greens in Canada are found in articles by Patricia Best, 'The Green Party pops up in Ontario', *Financial Post*, 31 Mar. 1984, and John Hay, 'The Struggling Greens', *MacLean's*, 14 May 1984.

26 Stanley Hoffmann, *Le Mouvement Poujade* (Paris, 1961).

27 Helen Jones Dawson, 'Relations Between Farm Organizations and the Civil Service in Canada and Great Britain', *Canadian Public Administration* 10 (1967) 4, 450-71, 456-7.

28 Ibid., 457n.

29 See Sally M. Weaver, 'The Joint Cabinet/National Indian Brotherhood Committee: A unique experiment in pressure group relations', *Canadian Public Administration* 25 (1982) 2, 211-40.

30 Larry Smith, 'Getting Your Way With a Bureaucrat', *Canadian Business*, Sept. 1980.

31 Sally M. Weaver, 'Towards a Comparison of National Political Organizations of Indigenous Peoples: Australia, Canada and Norway' (Mimeo, 1983), 57.

32 Ibid.

33 Ronald W. Lang, *The Politics of Drugs: The British and Canadian pharmaceutical industries and governments—A comparative study* (Farnborough, 1974), 134-6.

34 W.T. Stanbury, *Business Interests and the Reform of Canadian Competition Policy, 1971-75* (Toronto, 1977), ch. 8.

35 See Lowe and Goyder, *Environmental Groups in Politics*.

36 Weaver, 'Towards a Comparison of National Political Organizations', 59.

³⁷Ibid.

³⁸An interesting example is the Canadian Arctic Resources Committee, whose work and organization are described in Hugh J. Faulkner, 'Pressuring the Executive', *Canadian Public Administration* 25 (1982) 2, 240-54.

³⁹See Colin Languedoc, 'Success of lobby groups difficult to measure', *Financial Post*, 28 Feb. 1986.

⁴⁰H. Eckstein, *Pressure Group Politics: The Case of the British Medical Association* (London, 1960) and Allen Potter, *Organized Groups in British National Politics* (London, 1961). Space prohibits adequate discussion of these problems. Francis G. Castles illustrates them when he suggests that though the categories of 'interest' groups (which protect shared sectional interests) and 'attitude' groups (which promote shared attitudes about common causes or specific objectives) overlap considerably, 'one is able to assign a group to one or the other category quite easily.' *Pressure Groups and Political Culture* (London, 1967), 2. As one is content only to label groups, Castle's approach suffices. Once one attempts to describe relations between groups and their place in the political system, the typology is more hindrance than help because it is static and imprecise. Again Castle's study offers an illustration.

⁴¹Robert H. Salisbury, 'An Exchange Theory of Interest Groups' in Salisbury (ed.), *Interest Group Politics in America* (New York, 1970), 51.

⁴²S.E. Finer, *Anonymous Empire* (London, 1966).

⁴³See Peter H. Schuck, 'Public Interest Groups and the Policy Process', *Public Administration Review* (1977), 132-40.

⁴⁴Ibid.

⁴⁵See, for example, Lowe and Goyder, *Environmental Groups in Politics*, 10-15, for a brief discussion of the charge that environmental groups express class-based economic interests.

⁴⁶Olson, *The Logic of Collective Action*.

⁴⁷Roy C. Macridis, 'Interest Groups in Comparative Analysis', *The Journal of Politics* 23 (1961), 38, quoted in Alan C. Cairns, 'The Governments and Societies of Canadian Federalism', *Canadian Journal of Political Science* x (1977) 4, 695-725, 713.

⁴⁸William D. Coleman, 'Canadian Business and the State' in *The State and Economic Interests* (Toronto, Studies of the Royal Commission on the Economic Union and Development Prospects for Canada. Volume 32, 1985).

CHAPTER 6. GROUPS IN ACTION

¹Examples leap to mind. The films of Saul Alinsky. Songs such as 'We shall overcome'. The satiric theatre of Newfoundland's 'Cod Co'. Nor are they new inventions. At the end of the eighteenth century the Committee for the Abolition of the Slave Trade persuaded William Cowper to write 'The Negro's Complaint' and Josiah Wedgwood to issue a black and white medallion bearing a kneeling slave in chains and proclaiming 'Am I Not a Man and a Brother'. A more modest example is Haydn's 'Farewell' Symphony. In the last movement all but a few members of the orchestra rise, one after the other, and leave the stage, a re-enactment of the ruse used by Haydn and his colleagues to persuade their patron to leave his summer quarters and to let them return to their homes and families.

²J.D. Stewart, *British Pressure Groups: Their Role in Relation to the House of Commons* (Oxford, 1958), 2.

³See Kenneth M. Gibbons and Donald C. Rowat, *Political Corruption in Canada: Cases, Causes and Cures* (Ottawa, 1976). A recent survey of lobbying by a journalist is Paul Malvern, *Persuaders: Lobbying, Influence Peddling and Political Corruption in Canada*

(Toronto, 1985). A brief but tantalizing discussion of political violence in Canada is contained in R. Manzer, *Canada: A Socio-Political Report* (Toronto, 1974), 76-7.

[4] E.E. Schattschneider, *The Semi-Sovereign People* (New York, 1960), 71. An illustration of the tendency to confine issues to discussion by a special public is discovered by V.S. Wilson in a May 1977 *Presentation to the Prime Minister and Cabinet by the Canadian Federation of Agriculture*, which expresses concern about the threat 'of pressure, real or imagined, to further split and diversify the responsibility of matters related to food and agriculture policy within the structure of government.' *Canadian Public Policy and Administration* (Toronto, 1981), 392. J.D. McNiven, in a study of the Prince Edward Island development plan, found that the projects most likely to be terminated were those engendering public participation. The Rural Development Council, charged with fostering participation, found the chief planning agency, the Economic Improvement Corporation, difficult to deal with and unwilling 'to divulge but a few details of (its) participation proposals'. There was a tendency to shift funds originally earmarked for participation to programs in 'public education'. J.D. McNiven, *Evaluation of the Public Participation Programme Embodied in the Prince Edward Island Development Plan* (Halifax, 1974), 13, 31, 35.

[5] Charlotte Gray, 'Friendly Persuasion', *Saturday Night*, March 1983, 11-14, 11-12.

[6] J. Hugh Faulkner, 'Pressuring the Executive', *Canadian Public Administration* 25 (1982) 2, 241.

[7] Ibid., 241-2.

[8] Ibid., 243-4.

[9] For example, James Gillies, *Where Business Fails: Business-Government Relations at the Federal Level in Canada* (Montreal, 1981). A variant on this complaint is put forward by H.L. Laframboise, who argues that 'too many cooks spoil the broth' and suggests that extensive consultation leads officials to commit themselves too far in advance to interest groups. He holds that 'the most successful' policy-makers and managers have adhered to their own definitions of the appropriate level of consultation needed to promote the public interest. 'Conscience and Conformity: the uncomfortable bedfellows of accountability', *Canadian Public Administration* 26 (1983) 3, 325-44, 340-1.

[10] In 1980 said to be between $1,500 and $6,500 a month. Julianne La Breche, 'The Quiet Persuaders of Parliament Hill'. The firm's executives, headed for some years by Bill Lee, for several periods associated with Liberal cabinet ministers, and recently by Sam Hughes, for ten years president of the Canadian Chambers of Commerce. *Financial Post*, 2 February 1985.

[11] David Kwavnick, *Organized Labour and Pressure Politics: The Canadian Labour Congress, 1956-1968* (Montreal, 1972), ch. 7.

[12] Helen Jones Dawson, 'National Pressure Groups and the Federal Government' in A. Paul Pross (ed.), *Pressure Group Behaviour in Canadian Politics* (Toronto, 1975), 35-9.

[13] Forbes, 'Institutions and Interest Groups in the Canadian Food System Policy Process', 90-1.

[14] Halifax *Chronicle-Herald*, 13 Dec. 1974.

[15] Faulkner, 'Pressuring the Executive', 241-2.

[16] *Social Sciences in Canada* 13 (1985) 1, iii.

[17] The Canadian Chamber of Commerce was one of the first and most prominent of these. Originating in numerous boards of trade created by local business communities during the nineteenth century, it has grown into a national organization representing 165,000 businesses in 500 centres and operating offices in Ottawa and most of the provincial capitals. *Financial Post*, 2 Feb. 1985.

[18] See Richard Schultz, *Federalism, Bureaucracy and Public Policy: The Politics of Highway Transport Regulation* (Montreal, 1980).

[19] A. Paul Pross, 'Pressure Groups: Adaptive Instruments of Political Communication' in Pross (ed.) *Pressure Group Behaviour in Canadian Politics* (Toronto, 1975), 19.

[20] Larry Smith, 'Getting Your Way With a Bureaucrat', *Canadian Business*, September 1980. 104.

[21] Ibid., 104.

[22] Ibid.

[23] This and the following quotations are taken from ibid., 107.

[24] Many a proposal, for example, has slipped out of sight in the gaps between bureaucratic jurisdictions.

[25] 'In order to influence legislation and budgetary matters you must get into the system almost a year in advance, before the politicians begin thinking seriously about options. That is the time it takes the bureaucracy to study your proposal.' John Bulloch, 'A view from a special interest group' in Daniel L. Bon, *Lobbying: A Right? A Necessity? A Danger?* (Ottawa, 1981), 13.

[26] Jim Lotz, 'A citizen's guide to effective community action', *The Southender*, Dec. 1984.

[27] Lotz, 'A citizen's guide'.

[28] *Social Sciences in Canada* 13 (1985) 1, iv, and vii.

[29] La Breche, 'The Quiet Persuaders of Parliament Hill', 40.

[30] *Maclean's*, 14 May 1984.

[31] La Breche, 'The Quiet Persuaders of Parliament Hill', 40.

[32] John Cowan, 'Academic lobby aims to halt erosion of research funds', *CAUT Bulletin*, Feb. 1981, 5.

[33] Cowan, 'Academic lobby'.

[34] David Kwavnick, *Organized Labour and Pressure Politics*, 15-25 and Peter Aucoin, 'Pressure Groups and Recent Changes in the Policy-Making Process' in A. Paul Pross (ed.), *Pressure Group Behaviour in Canadian Politics* (Toronto, 1975), 172-93, 188-9.

[35] Forbes, 'The Canadian Food System Policy Process', 97-104.

[36] R. John Arseneau, 'The Government-Small Business Relationship'. Dalhousie University. Student Paper. 1984, 21; Charlotte Gray, 'Friendly Persuasion', *Saturday Night*, Mar. 1983 and *Maclean's*, 14 May 1984.

[37] In the words of one group leader, 'pressure groups have to resist government pressure to participate.' Quoted in A. Paul Pross, 'Governing Under Pressure: Summary of Discussions', *Canadian Public Administration* 25 (1982), 170-83, at 178.

[38] David Kwavnick, *Organized Labour and Pressure Politics*, 16.

[39] L.C. Bacchi, *Liberation Deferred: The Ideas of the English-Canadian Suffragists, 1877-1918* (Toronto, 1983), 73-85.

[40] Bacchi, *Liberation Deferred*, 85.

[41] Ibid.

[42] David Kwavnick, *Organized Labour and Pressure Politics*, 16.

[43] Ibid., 18.

[44] *The Institute*, Sept.–Oct., 1983.

[45] Donald Savage, 'Freedom of Information Legislation and the University Community', *CAUT Bulletin*, Feb. 1983, 5-6, 5.

[46] Ibid.

CHAPTER 7: BEYOND THE POLICY COMMUNITY

[1] Isaiah Litvak, 'The Lobbying Strategies of Business Interest Groups' in James D. Fleck and Isaiah A. Litvak (eds), *Business Can Succeed! Understanding the Political Environment* (Toronto, 1984) 65-75, 70.

[2] M.W. Bucovetsky, 'The Mining Industry and the Great Tax Reform Debate' in A.P. Pross (ed.), *Pressure Group Behaviour in Canadian Politics* (Toronto, 1975) 87-115, 107-8.

[3] Litvak, 'The Lobbying Strategies of Business Interest Groups', 70.

[4] Wanda Stephens, 'Canadian Pressure Groups and Elections: Is the Gag Law Necessary?' Student Paper. Dalhousie University. 1985.

[5] In the Spring of 1984 the Canadian Coalition on Acid Rain made a direct mailing to individuals aware of environmental issues. The mailing consisted of (1) a letter from Farley Mowat that began 'How long will your garden bloom if you water it with vinegar?' and requested financial support for lobbying the federal and American governments on the acid-rain issue; (2) a postcard to be sent to the Prime Minister that read, 'The recent Gallup Poll indicates that 75% of Canadians would be willing to donate one day's salary per year to beat acid rain. I'm one of them, and to show I'm serious I just sent a donation to the Canadian Coalition on Acid Rain. I'm sending this card to you to show my concern about our acid rain problem. Will you act too!' (the card's reverse showed a highway 'stop' sign with the words 'Stop Acid Rain'); (3) a flyer itemizing the dangers of acid rain; (4) two forms, one for donations to the Canadian Acid Precipitation Foundation, which would be eligible for the tax deductible receipts issued by charities, and one for donations to the Coalition, which would not. The latter began, 'Yes, Farley, I want to stop acid rain. I'm sending . . .' and would not be eligible for tax deductible receipts.

[6] *Globe and Mail*, 30 Aug. 1983.

[7] As a lobbyist put it during a campaign to ensure continuation of freight subsidies in the Maritimes: 'Politicians respond to what the media reveals.' Moncton *Times Transcript*, 3 June 1983.

[8] During the 1985 Ontario election a strong campaign was mounted against public support for Catholic secondary schools. Towards the end of the campaign, as the clamour reached a peak of intensity, the Anglican Archbishop of Toronto, Lewis Garnsworthy, 'forced [the issue] on the front pages by comparing Bill Davis' unilateral decree on funding to Adolf Hitler's method of operation.' Orland French, noting that 'this seemed like a crude comparison unworthy of the bishop and Mr. Davis', described it as 'the kind of jolt necessary to attract attention.' *Globe and Mail*, 1 May 1985.

[9] *Financial Post*, 10 December 1983. Thorburn attributes the paucity of these briefs to business conviction that the Trudeau government was unfriendly to business and uninterested in following its advice. Aware of the growing likelihood of a Liberal defeat in the next election, business preferred to direct its attention to influencing the likely winners. Hugh G. Thorburn, *Interest Groups in the Canadian Federal System* (Toronto, 1985), 114.

[10] James Gillies and Jean Pigott, 'Participation in the Legislative Process', *Canadian Public Administration* 25 (1982) 2, 254-64 and J. Hugh Faulkner, 'Pressuring the Executive', *Canadian Public Administration* 25 (1982) 2, 240-54.

[11] The Atlantic Provinces Economic Council first sponsored a meeting with Atlantic area MPs in 1975 (Halifax *Chronicle-Herald*, 7 March 1975). Other groups have brought specific issues to the separate party caucuses from the region. In 1983 business interests concerned about the possible elimination of transportation subsidies in the region organized meetings with the two regional caucuses. According to one group representative there was a good turnout at the PC's Atlantic region caucus, which was strongly supportive. The Liberal caucus turnout, on the other hand, was 'pretty poor, and we told them so. They didn't think it was worth turning up for.' (See A. Paul Pross, 'Mobilizing Regional Concern: An Historical Review of the Maritime Freight Rates Issue'. Paper. Conference on the Regional Organization of Business Interests and Public Policy. McMaster University. Hamilton, Ontario. 22-4 May 1985.) Faulkner credits the Québec caucus with particular influence during the Trudeau years. (See 'Pressuring the Executive', 244.) Forbes reports a particularly close liaison between the Canadian Dairy Commission and the Liberal caucus. (J.D. Forbes, 'Institutions and Interest Groups in the Canadian Food System Policy Process', *Report* (Ottawa, 1982), 63.

[12] See J. Pigott and G. Drewry, 'Parliament and hanging: further episodes in an undying saga', *Parliamentary Affairs* 27 (1974) 3, 251-61.

[13] Stewart, *British Pressure Groups*, 152-204.

[14] '. . . the Senate has had considerable impact upon the Investment Companies Act, the Income Tax Act, and the Foreign Investments Act . . . Salter Hayden, Chairman of the Senate's Banking and Commerce Committee, gives . . . a very simple explanation of how

senators successfully perform business review. These tactics comprise the essential components of lobbying from within. First, senators hear grievances from the business community members who feel that civil servants and Cabinet Ministers have ignored them. Then, senators astutely wield their corporate reputations through the powerful Banking Committee to persuade the department in charge of a bill that certain 'technical' changes must be made within it. If the department's Minister finds the case convincing, he will arrange for the government to sponsor amendments which would accomomodate the senators' concerns. Cumulatively "technical" changes often water down such bills, and this result is the aim of lobbying from within.' Colin Campbell, *The Canadian Senate: A Lobby from Within* (Toronto, 1978), 69.

[15] However, it is quite common for MPs to present the views of particular groups to the House. See, for example, the presentation of the case of the Canadian Aviation Fellowship during the dispute on bilingual air traffic control. *Hansard*, 12 July 1977, 7613.

[16] *Financial Post*, 8 October 1983. The Canadian House at times actively discourages 'lobbying' by Members. In 1983, it was reported that 'an outspoken group of antinuclear MP's and Senators' had been removed from the list of parliamentary associations eligible for travel and study funds. The chairman, a Conservative, and a Liberal member of the Canadian Parliamentarians for World Order charged that the government was punishing the group for taking 'unpopular stands with the government'. The Speaker, Madame Sauvé, would not allow the matter to be raised in the House, and a spokesperson for the Parliamentary Relations Secretariat told the press that a Commons-Senate committee had decided to withdraw funding because the association 'too strongly resembled a lobby group.' Kingston *Whig-Standard*, 16 March 1983.

[17] *Globe and Mail*, 30 August 1984.

[18] Thus 'Services and Subsidies to Business' topped the list of eleven priority areas identified by the Nielsen Task Force on Program Review. *Social Sciences in Canada* 13 (1985) 1.

[19] R. Lewis, 'The hidden persuaders', *Maclean's*, 13 June 1977, quoted in David MacDonald, 'The Art of the State: Resisting Pressure Group Demands in Canada'. Dalhousie University. Student Paper. 1985.

[20] Stephens, 'Canadian Pressure Groups and Elections'. See also Kristian S. Palda, 'The Election Act and Voter Information', *Canadian Public Policy* XI (1985) 3, 533-43.

[21] *Globe and Mail*, 17 July 1984.

[22] Ibid.

[23] *Globe and Mail*, 27 June 1984 and *Maclean's*, 9 July 1984.

[24] *Maclean's*, 9 July 1984.

[25] *Globe and Mail*, 27 and 28 June 1984.

[26] The *Globe and Mail* (28 June 1984) felt the government would be foolish to enforce the Act: 'The coming general election should be fought by all interested parties and not artificially restricted to the registered parties, the candidates and those voices which meet with their gracious approval.'

[27] Halifax *Mail-Star*, 19 July 1984.

[28] 'Political Action Committees', *Maclean's*, 14 May 1984. An academic account is found in M. Margaret Conway, 'PACs, the New Politics and Congressional Campaigns' in Allan J. Cigler and Burdett A. Loomis (eds), *Interest Group Politics* (Washington, 1983), 126-45.

[29] Richard Simeon, *Federal-Provincial Diplomacy: The Making of Recent Policy in Canada* (Toronto, 1973), 144-5. See also 280-3.

[30] Bucovetsky, 'The Mining Industry and the Great Tax Reform Debate'.

[31] Peter Foster, *The Blue-Eyed Sheiks: The Canadian Oil Establishment* (Don Mills, Ont., 1979) and *The Sorcerer's Apprentice* (Toronto, 1982); G. Bruce Doern and Glen Toner, *The Politics of Energy: The Development and Implementation of the NEP* (Toronto, 1985).

[32] See Roger Gibbins, *Prairie Politics and Society: Regionalism in Decline* (Toronto, 1980), 84-91, and Barry Wilson, *Beyond the Harvest: Canadian Grain at the Crossroads* (Saskatoon, 1981); on the 1982-83 dispute, *Globe and Mail*, 29 July 1983.

[33] E.R. Forbes, *Maritime Rights: The Maritime Rights Movement* (Montreal, 1979); Pross, 'Mobilizing Regional Concern'.

[34] Hugh G. Thorburn, *Interest Groups in the Canadian Federal System* (Toronto, 1985), 118.

[35] Ibid., 116. See also ibid., 53-4.

[36] Alan C. Cairns, 'The Governments and Societies of Canadian Federalism', *Canadian Journal of Political Science* x (1977) 4, 695-725, 706.

[37] Thorburn, *Interest Groups in the Canadian Federal System*, 116.

[38] See Faulkner, 'Pressuring the Executive', 243-4; Pross, 'Governing Under Pressure: Summary of Discussions', 175-6; Aucoin, 'Pressure Groups and Recent Changes in the Policy-Making Process', 175-7, 183, 185.

[39] See Pross, 'Mobilizing Regional Concern'.

[40] David Lies and James Lawrence, 'Red Tape and Fine Cheddar', *Harrowsmith* 3 (1978), 3.

[41] Pross, 'Mobilizing Regional Concern'.

[42] 'A Perspective on Canadian Mining: Interview with C. George Miller', *CRS Perspectives*, March 1985. In 1970, according to Gordon Robertson, there were nine meetings of the federal government and all the provinces that permitted, or involved, the attendance of outside groups. See 'The Changing Role of the Privy Council Office', *Canadian Public Administration* xiv (1971), 487-508 at 497. See also D.V. Smiley, *Canada in Question: Federalism in the Seventies*, 58.

[43] See for example Denis Stairs, 'Publics and Policy-Makers: The Domestic Environment of Canada's Foreign Policy Community', *International Journal*, Winter 1970-71; Donald Barry, 'Interest Groups and the Foreign Policy Process: The Case of Biafra' in Pross, *Pressure Group Behaviour in Canadian Politics*, 115-48; and Peter Willetts (ed.), *Pressure Groups in the Global System: The Transnational Relations of Issue-Orientated Non-Governmental Organizations* (London, 1982).

[44] Not all efforts to persuade the federal government to counteract the lobbying abroad of foreign pressure groups are successful. Provincial ministers of fisheries, for example, have complained that while the federal Department of Fisheries and Oceans prepared material countering the anti-sealing campaign, the Department of External Affairs refused to distribute it. (Interview with the Hon. John Leefe, Minister of Fisheries, Nova Scotia, 20 March 1984.) Some critics claim that Canadians do not spend enough on influencing the U.S. government in particular. A study undertaken at John's Hopkins University, for example, concluded that Britain, West Germany, Japan, and Israel spent more on registered U.S. lobbyists than Canada (*Globe and Mail*, 9 December 1983).

[45] *Financial Post*, 22 Sept. 1984.

[46] Kingston *Whig-Standard*, March 1983.

[47] For example, in October 1982 the President of the Canadian Export Association, warning that 'we are no longer living in a world of boy scouts', urged Canadian negotiators to follow closely the needs of exporters in order to take advantage of those opportunities that are available elsewhere. *Le Devoir*, 20 October 1982.

[48] Kingston *Whig-Standard*, March 1983.

[49] *Financial Post*, 3 December 1983. See also Alan Herscovici, *Second Nature: The Animal Rights Controversy* (Toronto, 1985).

[50] Halifax *Mail-Star*, 30 Dec. 1983.

[51] *MacLean's*, 11 March 1985. Perhaps one of the best known and most successful users of this approach is the Automobile Protection Association established by Phil Edmonston. For a brief outline of the association's goals and activities see its annual publication *Lemon-Aid Used Car Guide: 1985* (Toronto, 1984), 2-4, edited by Edmonston. Accounts of the group's campaign against the Ford Motor Company are found in *Maclean's*, 20 Sept. 1976, 8; *Time*, 20 Oct. 1975, 131ff.; *The 4th Estate*, 21 and 28 Jan. 1976; *Globe and Mail*, 25 Oct. 1976; and *Financial Post*, 9 Oct.1976, 11.

[52] For example, a major Halifax dispute over the destruction of an older building and modification of the city plan to permit construction of a high-rise condominium. See 'Halifax

Condo Battle Heads for the Courts', *Globe and Mail*, 8 May 1984, and 'NS Court Ruling Bolsters Opponents of Halifax Project', *Globe and Mail*, 8 Oct. 1984, and 'To Build or Not to Build? High Rise Splits Citizens', *Globe and Mail*, 27 July 1985.

[53]John Swaigen, *How to Fight for What's Right: The citizen's guide to public interest law* (Toronto, James Lorimer & Company Ltd., 1981), 131-2.

[54]See Peter Cumming, *Nova Scotia's Herbicide Case: A Court Diary* (Gabarus, N.S., 1983); *Between the Issues: The Newsletter of the Ecology Action Centre*, various issues, 1983; the Halifax *Chronicle-Herald*, 16 Sept. 1983, 3 Oct. 1983, 8 Oct. 1983, 10 Dec. 1983, and the *Globe and Mail*, 17 Sept. 1983. A film of the case, *Herbicide Trials*, has been issued by the National Film Board.

[55]Swaigen, *How to Fight for What's Right*, 3.

[56]Ibid., 12-17.

[57]H. Patrick Glenn, 'Class Actions in Ontario and Quebec', *Canadian Bar Review* 62 (1984) 3, 247-77, 277.

[58]Swaigen, *How to Fight for What's Right*, 133.

CHAPTER 8. THE INTERIOR LIFE OF GROUPS

[1]David Truman, *The Process of Government* (New York, 1964) *passim*, but particularly 56-62.

[2]V.O. Key, *Parties, Pressure Groups and Politics* (New York, 1958).

[3]Mancur Olson, *The Logic of Collective Action* (Cambridge, Mass., 1971), 132-41.

[4]Ibid., 14.

[5]Terry M. Moe, *The Organization of Interests* (Chicago, 1980), 28.

[6]W.D. Coleman and H.J. Jacek, 'The Political Organization of the Chemical Industry in Canada', Paper. CPSA. 1981, 62. It is interesting to note that the Canadian Manufacturers' Association was offering additional incentives to members in the 1920s and 1930s. See S.D. Clark, *The Canadian Manufacturers' Association* (Toronto, 1939), 40-63.

[7]Olson, *The Logic of Collective Action*, 133.

[8]Ibid., ch. 1 and 133-4.

[9]Helen Jones Dawson, 'The Consumers' Association of Canada', *Canadian Public Administration* VI (1963) 1, 92-118, 96.

[10]For example, in December 1982 the Consumers' Association, contesting higher postal rates, strongly criticized the Canada Post Corporation for its failure to keep a general ledger and records of assets, liabilities, and inventory. The association was told of these deficiencies when it asked for information in order to prepare a submission on postal-rate increases to the Government of Canada (Kingston *Whig Standard*, 21 Dec. 1982). The CAC is also a frequent participant in media coverage of budget speeches and similar events in the annual cycle of economic news.

[11]See *TransAction*, Transport 2000's quarterly publication.

[12]See Moe, *The Organization of Interests*, 16-19, 30-4 (on the effect of imperfect information), and 119-21 on non-economic incentives to participate.

[13]Ibid., 32.

[14]J.A. Corry, remarks to a conference on 'Citizen Involvement in Government: The Art of the Possible', sponsored by the Institute for Research on Public Policy and the Government Studies Programme, Dalhousie University, 1979. The remarks are elaborated in the published version of Dr Corry's talk, entitled 'Sovereign People or Sovereign Governments' in H.V. Kroeker (ed.), *Sovereign People or Sovereign Governments* (Montreal, 1981), 3-13, especially 10-13.

[15]Léon Dion, 'Participating in the Political Process', *Queen's Quarterly* LXXV (1968) 3, 433.

[16] A. Holleaux, 'Le phénomène associatif', *Revue française d'administration publique* 8 (1978), 683-727, 701-2.

[17] J. Meynaud, *Nouvelles études sur les groupes de pression en France* (Paris, 1962), 24-6.

[18] For a fascinating discussion of the use of substantive and process knowledge see Guy Benveniste, *The Politics of Expertise* (Berkeley, Calif., 1972).

[19] Ian Helliwell, 'The National Energy Board's 1974–75 Natural Gas Supply Hearings', *Canadian Public Policy* 1 (1973), 2, 415-25.

[20] Coleman and Jacek, 'Chemical Industry in Canada', 37.

[21] Larry Smith, 'Getting Your Way With a Bureaucrat', *Canadian Business*, Sept. 1980, 104.

[22] John F. Bulloch, 'A View From a Special Interest Group' in Daniel L. Bon, *Lobbying: A Right? A Necessity? A Danger?* (Ottawa, 1981), 8.

[23] Ibid., 12.

[24] Smith, 'Getting Your Way . . .'

[25] Bulloch, 'A View . . .', 13.

[26] D.A. Chant, 'Pollution Probe: Fighting Polluters With Their Own Weapons' in A.P. Pross, *Pressure Group Behaviour in Canadian Politics* (Toronto, 1975), 61-8.

[27] Ibid., 64.

[28] David Hoffman, 'Interacting With Government: The General Public and Interest Groups' in Donald MacDonald (ed.), *Politics in Ontario* (Toronto, 1975), 275-92, at 288-9.

[29] Quoted in A.P. Pross, 'Governing Under Pressure: The Special Interest Groups—Summary of Discussion', in Pross (ed.), *Governing Under Pressure: The Special Interest Groups— 14th National Seminar, Institute of Public Administration of Canada* (Toronto, 1982), 171-83, at 180.

[30] Coleman and Jacek, 'The Chemical Industry in Canada . . .' 27, 31, and 37.

[31] Ibid.

[32] For an excellent discussion of the two concepts as they relate to pressure groups see D. Kwavnick, *Organized Labour and Pressure Politics* (Montreal, 1972), 3-25.

[33] David Kwavnick, 'Pressure Group Demands and the Struggle for Organizational Status: The Case of Organized Labour in Canada', *Canadian Journal of Political Science* III (1970) 1, 56-72, 58.

[34] N.J. Lawrie, *The Canadian Construction Association* (Toronto, University of Toronto Ph.D. thesis., 1976), 58. See also Mayer N. Zald and Michael A. Berger, 'Social Movements in Organizations: Coup d'Etat, Insurgency, and Mass Movements', *American Journal of Sociology* 83 (1978) 4, 823-61.

[35] Ibid., 113.

[36] Sally M. Weaver, 'The Joint Cabinet Committee/National Indian Brotherhood Committee: A Unique Experiment in Pressure Group Relations', *Canadian Public Administration* 25 (1982) 2, 211-39, at 227-9.

[37] Kwavnick, *Organized Labour and Pressure Politics*, 73-4.

[38] Kell Antoft, 'The Role of Non-Governmental Agencies in the Provincial-Municipal Relationship in Nova Scotia', Typescript. n.d.

[39] The 1979 budgets of the chemical professional groups surveyed by Coleman and Jacek averaged $141,200. (Coleman and Jacek, 'The Chemical Industry in Canada . . .', 36.) In 1978-9 the National Anti-Poverty Organization received $108,750 in grants alone from the federal government. House of Commons *Debates*, 23 Jan. 1979, Question No. 588.

[40] According to the 1985 edition of Brian Land (ed.), *Directory of Associations in Canada* (Toronto, 1985) a selection of public-interest groups counted memberships as follows: Against Drunk Driving, 16,000; Canadian Wolf Defenders, 455; Greenpeace Foundation, 35,000; Canadian Abortion Rights Action League, 8,700; Non-Smoker's Rights Association, 3,000; Consumer's Association of Canada, 150,000; and the Canadian Wildlife Association, 450,000.

[41] See Donald Barry, 'Interest Groups in the Foreign Policy Process', in Pross, *Pressure Group Behaviour . . .* , 117-47, at 125-32.

[42] See Cathy Munroe and Jim Stewart, *Fishermen's Organizations in Nova Scotia: The Potential for Unification* (Halifax, 1981), 131.

[43] Holleaux, 'Le phénomène associatif', 696; *Le Monde*, 28 January and 12 Dec. 1982.

[44] House of Commons. *Debates*, 20 June 1975, 6954. (Daily edition.)

[45] House of Commons. *Debates*, 23 Jan. 1979. Question No. 558.

[46] During the Berger inquiry into the feasibility of the Mackenzie Valley Pipeline, $1.2 million was awarded to Indian organizations to help them prepare briefs, and another $540,000 to other organizations. J. Hugh Faulkner, 'Pressuring the Executive', *Canadian Public Administration* 25 (1982) 2, 240-54, at 248.

[47] In 1983, for example, the Executive Director of the Social Science and Humanities Research Council of Canada noted that the Council had supported the two principal learned societies in the humanities (Canadian Federation for the Humanities) and the social sciences (Social Science Federation of Canada) at a rate varying between 62.7 per cent and 80.9 per cent of budget. (*Council Update*, Summer 1983, 8). SSHRCC support for learned societies reached $1.8 million in 1983-4, but declined to $1.5 million in 1984-5. (*Five-year Plan for Financing Research in the Social Sciences and the Humanities, 1985-1990* (Ottawa, 1985), 10.)

[48] Munroe and Stewart, *Fishermen's Organizations in Nova Scotia*, 82 and John Kearney, 'The Transformation of the Bay of Fundy Herring Fisheries, 1976-1978: An Experiment in Fishermen-Government Co-Management' in Cynthia Lamson and Arthur J. Hanson, *Atlantic Fisheries and Coastal Communities* (Halifax, 1984), 165-205.

[49] Coleman and Jacek, 'The Chemical Industry in Canada . . .', 42.

[50] Quoted in Bon, *Lobbying: A Right? . . .* , 14.

[51] The experience of the Nova Scotia Fishermen's Association is a case in point. The NSFA, which espoused a philosophy of independence quite different from the collective-bargaining approach adopted by its chief rival, the Maritime Fishermen's Union, set out to organize the inshore fishermen. A start-up grant of $50,000 from the government of Nova Scotia became an embarrassment. On the one hand it earned the Association the stigma of being 'government controlled'; on the other, government recognition entailed an obligation to participate extensively in fisheries policy discussions. The association's resources could not sustain such a level of participation; members came to feel that the leadership was losing touch with the rank and file. Despite their criticism of government support, members resisted a reorganization and revised fee structure designed to ensure independence from government, so that ultimately the association was forced to abandon its attempt to speak for all Nova Scotia's inshore fishermen. Munroe and Stewart, *Fishermen's Organizations in Nova Scotia*, 81-92.

[52] Interviews: K. Antoft, D. Rigby.

[53] Dominique Clift argues, for example, that Montreal's English language community was unable to evolve a credible independent response to the Parti Québécois's referendum position because its interest associations were heavily subsidized by the federal Privy Council Office and Secretary of State. 'L'Etat et les groupes d'intérêts', *Canadian Public Administration* 25 (1982) 2, 265-77, 268.

[54] Thomas R. Berger, *Northern Frontier, Northern Homeland. Report of the Mackenzie Valley Pipeline Inquiry* Vol. 2 (Ottawa, 1977), 225-6. Quoted by D. Gamble in Bon, *Lobbying: A Right? . . . .*

[55] Their tax status is a central concern of public-interest groups. Under the Income Tax Act charitable organizations are not required to pay income tax and are entitled to issue donors tax deductible receipts. A charitable organization has been defined by the courts as 'a trust for the relief of poverty, a trust for the advancement of education, a trust for the advancement of religion or a trust for other purposes beneficial to the community.' (John Swaigen, *How to Fight for What's Right* (Toronto, 1981), 126.) The great majority of public-interest groups claim charitable status under the latter section of the definition, but are constrained by the view of the courts that trusts established for political objectives are not valid charities. (Ibid.) At first glance this would appear to rule out a great deal of public-interest group activity, but as the term 'political' has not been authoritatively defined in this context it puts

a great deal of discretion in the hands of the officials responsible for determining whether or not an organization is entitled to charitable status. A 1977 circular issued by Revenue Canada defined the appropriate activity of charitable groups so narrowly that many groups complained of harassment. (See ibid., and House of Commons, *Debates*, 1 May 1978.) Such complaints reached a peak prior to the 1984 election. In April 1984, for example, the National Coalition of Voluntary Organizations, representing 126 associations, complained that a number of its members had received form letters from Revenue Canada warning that attempts to influence municipal, provincial, or federal policies or legislation could lead to loss of charitable status. The group cited the experience of the Quebec Social Rehabilitation Association, a prisoner rehabilitation organization that was denied charitable status because it had publicly argued against the building of more prisons. (Halifax *Chronicle-Herald*, 4 April 1984) In response, the 1985 federal budget provided that organizations would be entitled to participate in political activities if the activities were 'ancillary and incidental to their charitable purposes'. The greatest part of their resources would have to be devoted to their charitable work. They would not be permitted to support a particular party or candidate. (*Financial Post*, 8 June 1985). Although this clarifies the position of many groups providing services directly to the community (e.g., social welfare groups, prisoners' aid societies, and so on), the status of many other groups formed to promote the public interest must be still in doubt.

[56] The Canadian Library Association, for example, derives approximately half of its revenue from the sale of publications. (Canadian Library Association. *The 1979-80 Revised Members' Handbook and Directory* (Ottawa, 1979), 11.

[57] See Dawson, 'The Consumers' Association of Canada', 99.

[58] N.J. Lawrie, *The Canadian Construction Association*, 165. A similar problem of distance between the Canadian Federation of Agriculture and its individual members led to the creation of the National Farmers' Union in the 1930s. See Helen Jones Dawson, 'An Interest Group: The Canadian Federation of Agriculture', *Canadian Public Administration* III (1960) 2, 134-49 and 'Relations Between Farm Organizations and the Civil Service in Canada and Great Britain', *Canadian Public Administration* X (1967) 4, 450-71.

[59] The Atlantic Provinces Economic Council, by no means a wealthy organization, for many years maintained offices in New Brunswick and Newfoundland in order to encourage region-wide support and to maintain its legitimacy as a regional organization.

[60] The Canadian Library Association's *1979–80 Revised Members' Handbook and Directory* lists 25 standing committees, 3 co-ordinating groups, and 2 special-interest groups concerned with matters as diverse as the promotion of literacy, the law of copyright, association publications, professional education, and the bringing of library services to special groups.

[61] See, for example, 'The Nuts and Bolts of Association Management' in *Canadian Associations*, March 1985, 19-34, and Moe's discussion of the influence of staff on group goals, *The Organization of Interests*, 98-9.

[62] See, for example, David Kwavnick, 'Pressure Group Demands and Organizational Objectives: The CNTU, the Lapalme Affair, and National Bargaining Units', *Canadian Journal of Political Science* VI (1973) 4, 582-601.

[63] Land, *Directory of Associations*; *Canadian Associations*.

CHAPTER 9. MODELS OF INTEREST PARTICIPATION: CORPORATISM

[1] The Maritime Rights debate illustrates the fact that interest groups, even sub-government members, are not always the first to organize issues out of politics; they are often forced out of politics by party leaders. At the turn of the century the Prairies and the Maritimes were equally concerned about the effects of federal transportation policy on their regional econo-

mies. Unfortunately the remedies they proposed and the claims they made on the policy system brought the two regions into conflict with one another so much so that the fledgeling Progressive Party was unable to hold Maritime support. The Conservatives and Liberals were no more effective in dealing with the conflict internally. They, however, could count on the inertia of the traditional vote. Certain that ultimately Maritimers would remain loyal to the established parties, the Liberals, in particular, set aside demands from that region in favour of appeasing the more volatile West and eliminating the rival Progressives. Maritimers found themselves in a paradoxical situation. Unable to articulate their demands through the party system, they turned to interest groups and successfully established several that were effective in bringing the issue to national attention. The Maritime business community had sought to achieve reform of transportation policy—rolling back of freight rate increases, restoration of regionally sensitive management to the Intercolonial Railway—by raising the level of conflict surrounding it. This goal was achieved through broadening the base of discussion—instead of being simply a matter of business economics, the issue was associated with the Confederation settlement (a standard Canadian ploy for raising the level of conflict). Once that association was accepted by public opinion a host of issues that were not part of the original debate became relevant and lured a widening circle of interests into the fray. To this point, then, pressure groups were more successful than parties in championing the Maritime Rights cause. Conversely, however, once Mackenzie King succeeded in convincing the public that Ottawa had satisfactorily addressed the major Maritime demands, he was able to confine further debate to these same groups and a few officials. In this small policy community the issue has remained, with some minor excursions, ever since. See E.R. Forbes, *Maritime Rights: The Maritime Rights Movement* (Montreal, 1979) and A. Paul Pross, 'Mobilizing Regional Concern: An Historical Review of the Maritime Freight Rates Issue' Paper. Conference on the Regional Organization of Business Interests and Public Policy. McMaster University. Hamilton, Ontario. 22-4 May 1985.

[2] John Meisel, 'The Decline of Party in Canada' in Hugh Thorburn (ed.), *Party Politics in Canada* 4th edn (Scarborough, Ont., 1979), 119-35; Peter McCormick, 'Is the Liberal Party Declining? Liberals, Conservatives and Provincial Politics, 1967-1980', *Journal of Canadian Studies* 18 (1983-4) 4, 88-107; Vaughan Lyon, 'The Future of Parties . . . Inevitable . . . Obsolete', *Journal of Canadian Studies* 18 (1983-4) 4, 108-31; and Stephen Clarkson, 'The Defeat of the Government, the Decline of the Liberal Party, and the (Temporary) Fall of Pierre Trudeau' in Howard Penniman (ed.), *Canada at the Polls, 1979 and 1980: A Study of General Elections* (Washington, 1981) 152-89.

[3] J.Hugh Faulkner, 'Pressuring the Executive', *Canadian Public Administration* 25 (1982) 2, 240-54.

[4] See Law Reform Commission. *Parliament and Administrative Agencies* (Ottawa, 1982) and Paul G. Thomas, 'Administrative law reform: legal versus political controls on administrative discretion', *Canadian Public Administration* 27 (1984) 1, 120-8, a review article that takes as its point of departure a working paper of the Law Reform Commission on *Independent Administrative Agencies* (Ottawa, 1980. Working Paper No. 25). A 1975 study of the Commission catalogues 14,885 discretionary powers accorded administrative officials by the 1970 Revised Statutes of Canada. The compiler of the catalogue claims only that the list 'probably provides a reasonable sample of the discretionary powers subordinate to Parliament, of their nature and of the authorities who exercise them.' He suggests, however, that these are only the 'tip of the iceberg'. The list excludes a number of powers specified in the statutes, as well as discretionary powers accorded by the regulations and 'most important, no attempt was made to discover the number of implicit powers capable of exercise or actually exercised.' Philip Anisman, *A Catalogue of Discretionary Powers in the Revised Statutes of Canada, 1970* (Ottawa, 1975), 33-4.

[5] Richardson, J.J. and A.G. Jordan, *Governing Under Pressure: The Policy Process in a Post-Parliamentary Democracy* (Oxford, 1979).

[6] For Britain see Richardson and *Governing Under Pressure*; the U.S.: E.E. Schattschneider, *The Semi-Sovereign People* (New York, 1960); Europe: Suzanne Berger (ed.), *Organizing*

Interests in Western Europe (Cambridge, 1981); J.J. Richardson (ed.), *Policy Styles in Western Europe* (London, 1982); generally: Philippe C. Schmitter and Gerhard Lehmbruch, (eds), *Trends Toward Corporatist Intermediation* (Beverly Hills, Calif., 1979).

[7] For example, J.Cheverny, 'Le mode autoritaire de l'anarchie', *Esprit*, janvier, 1970; F. Bloch-Lainie, 'Les associations comme contre-pouvoirs', *Pouvoirs* 7 (1978), 65.

[8] For example, Dominique Clift, 'L'Etat et les groupes d'intérêts: perspectives d'avenir', *Canadian Public Administration* 25 (1982) 2, 265-78.

[9] Grant Jordan, 'Pluralistic Corporatisms and Corporate Pluralism', *Scandinavian Political Studies* 7(New Series) (1983) 3, 137-53.

[10] See Linn A. Hammergran, 'Corporatism in Latin American Politics: A Re-examination of the Unique Tradition', *Comparative Politics* 9 (1977) 4, 443-63; Les Metcalfe and Will McQuillan, 'Corporatism or Industrial Democracy?', *Political Studies* XXVII (1979) 2, 266-82; and Leo Panitch, 'Corporatism in Canada?' in Richard Schultz, Orest M. Kruhlak, John C. Terry, *The Canadian Political Process* (Toronto, 1979) 53-72. Leo Panitch, 'Recent Theorizations of Corporatism', *British Journal of Sociology* XXXI (1980) 2, 159-88; Jordan, 'Pluralistic Corporatisms and Corporate Pluralism'; Schmitter and Lehmbruch, *Trends Toward Corporatist Intermediation*; G. David Garson, *Group Theories of Politics* (Beverly Hills, 1978).

[11] Philippe C. Schmitter, 'Still the Century of Corporatism?' in Philippe C. Schmitter and Gerhard Lehmbruch (eds), *Trends Toward Corporatist Intermediation* (Beverly Hills, 1979), 7-52, 13.

[12] Philippe C. Schmitter, 'Interest intermediation and regime governability' in Berger, *Organizing Interests in Western Europe*, 287-331, at 292.

[13] Léon Dion, *Société et Politique* (Québec, 1971) vol. 1, 198. See also Garson, *Group Theories of Politics*, ch. 2, 'Pluralists, Statists and Corporatists: Elements in the Emergence of Group Theories'.

[14] Schmitter, 'Interest intermediation and regime governability', 213, 292.

[15] I am grateful to Bill Coleman for drawing this point to my attention.

[16] Ibid.

[17] Ibid., 174. See also his article, 'The Role and Nature of the State' in Panitch (ed.), *The Canadian State* (Toronto, 1977), 10, where he expresses concern about the extent to which labour organizations are invited to act as 'agencies of control over their members'.

[18] It is this tendency in corporatist writing that leads Robert E. Goodin to write that 'corporatism fits into the broad tradition (of sub-government theory) but focuses too narrowly on the incorporation of economic interests, ignoring other issue-specific sub-governments organized along rather different lines.' ('Banana Time in British Politics', *Political Studies* XXX (1982) 1, 42-58, at 48. Although Schmitter's work is subject to this criticism, it is arguable that his definition is not.

[19] See Gerhard Lehmbruch, 'Liberal Corporatism and Party Government', *Comparative Political Studies* 10 (1973) 1, 3.

[20] For example in agriculture. (See Metcalfe and McQuillan, 'Corporatism or Industrial Democracy?')

[21] Quoted in Panitch, 'Corporatism in Canada?', 55. Several recent publications dealing with corporatist tendencies in Canada and/or with government relations with business-interest associations appeared as this manuscript reached the final stages of editing. It is regrettable that I have been able to draw only in a limited way on the papers prepared under Keith Banting's direction for the Macdonald Royal Commission (*The State and Economic Interests*. The Collected research studies/Royal Commission on the Economic Union and Development Prospects for Canada. Toronto, 1986). In preparing the discussion in this section I have had access to manuscript material that will have a considerable impact on future discussions of corporatism in Canada. These are William Coleman's *Business and Politics: A Study of Collective Action* and Herman Bakvis's 'Alternative Models of Governance: Federalism, Consociationalism and Corporatism' in H. Bakvis and W. Chandler, *Federalism and the Role of the State*. However, since neither of these works had been published at the

time of writing, I do not draw upon them, though I have been guided away from several assumptions that have been accepted in earlier discussions. I find that there are several difference between my approach and that presented by Bakvis and Coleman, of which the most important is a tendency on my part to place greater emphasis on the role of the state in organizing corporatist activity. I accept the view that corporatism can be a decentralizing phenomenon—even that it can be use to shield economic interests from state intervention—but I am also aware that government agencies frequently find it useful to encourage the formation of groups and the creation of associations that might ultimately be considered peak associations. Throughout this book a number of illustrations of this process are given and some reasons are suggested for it (e.g., the need to establish the legitimacy of groups; to establish order within the policy community; to balance the influence of rival interests; to generate support for policies advocated by agencies, and so on.) In other words, I am inclined to agree with Eric A. Nordlinger that one should 'look at least as much to the state as to civil society to understand what the democratic state does in the making of public policy and why it does so'. (*On the Autonomy of the Democratic State* (Cambridge, Mass., 1981) 203). Systems of interest representation can be used by state bureaucracies to facilitate their autonomy.

22 Robert Presthus, *Elite Accommodations in Canadian Politics* (Toronto, 1973), 25. See Garson, ch. 5, for useful comments on Presthus. Panitch's riposte is in 'Corporatism in Canada'.

23 J.M. McLeod, 'The Corporatist Strain in Canadian Politics: The Invisible Fist', Paper. The Conference on Canadian Political Ideas, York University, 1978. Quoted in Panitch, 'Corporatism in Canada?'

24 Panitch, 'Corporatism in Canada?', 55.

25 Ibid., 56.

26 Ibid.

27 See also J.I. Gow, 'L'histoire de l'administration publique québécoise', *Recherches sociographiques* XVI (1975) 3, 385ff. Gow points out that these unions soon moved away from church domination and presumably from the concepts associated with church sponsorship.

28 Panitch, 'Corporatism in Canada?', 57.

29 It might also be argued that on attaining power the proponents of corporatism found that they could achieve their ends by creating (informal) limited arrangements that were not explicitly corporatist. Thus Duplessis was able to co-opt union leaders by appointing them to boards, commissions, and so on. See Herbert F. Quinn, 'Quebec: Corruption under Duplessis' in K. M. Gibbon and D. C. Rowat, *Political Corruption in Canada* (Ottawa, 1976), 67-81. Similarly, the structure of provincial support of education and municipal government permitted a good deal of central control.

30 Panitch, 'Corporatism in Canada?' 63-4.

31 Ibid., 64.

32 Ibid. This notwithstanding, there are latent tendencies in unionism that relate to tripartism. One could argue that the wish of the Canadian Labour Congress to broaden its mandate would have this effect. See David Kwavnick, *Organized Labour and Pressure Politics: The Canadian Labour Congress, 1956-1968* (Montreal, 1972).

33 William D. Coleman and Henry J. Jacek, 'The Political Organization of the Chemical Industry in Canada'. Paper. Canadian Political Science Association (1981), 60.

34 Panitch, 'Corporatism in Canada', 61.

35 Douglas Brown, Julia Eastman, with Ian Robinson, *The Limits of Consultation: A Debate Among Ottawa, the Provinces and the Private Sector on an Industrial Strategy'* (Kingston and Ottawa, 1981), 176.

36 Brown *et al.*, *The Limits of Consultation*, 176.

37 Ibid.

38 Ibid., 178.

39 Ibid., 179.

40 Ibid., 188.

41 See 'Bad News, Bad Marks: Tory Summit', *Vancouver Sun*, 22 March 1985; 'Conference on Economy Called Waste', *Globe and Mail*, 22 March 1985; 'Deep Rift Between Business and Labour Revealed as Economic Talks Begin', *Globe and Mail*, 23 March 1985; 'Agreement Eludes Ottawa', Winnipeg *Free Press*, 24 March 1985.

42 G. Majone, 'Choice among policy instruments for pollution control', *Policy Analysis* 2 (1976) 589-613, quoted in Metcalfe and McQuillan, 'Corporatism or Industrial Democracy?', 267. An institutional interpretation helps explain the quiescence of corporatist trends between the late 1930s and the 1970s: it could be argued that early interest in corporatism reflected sectoral dissatisfaction with the partisanship of the executive-dominated system of policy-making then in place. (See ch. 2.) With the development of a sectorally oriented bureaucracy in the 1940s and 1950s this dissatisfaction receded as sectoral interests found adequate means of representation through the public service. In the late 1960s, with the growing diffusion of power that then emerged, problems of representation again became important and corporatism reappeared on the public agenda.

43 Government of Canada. *The Way Ahead: A Framework for Discussion* (Ottawa, 1976); Robert K. Logan (ed.), *The Way Ahead for Canada: A Paperback Referendum* (Toronto, 1977); Québec. La conférence au sommet Québec, 1982, *Rapport* (Québec, Editeur officiel du Québec, 1982).

44 Schmitter, 'Interest intermediation and regime governability', 313.

45 Ibid., 312.

46 See David Halberstam, *The Best and the Brightest* (New York, 1972); Colin Campbell and George Szablowski, *The Superbureaucrats: Structures and Behaviour in Central Agencies* (Toronto, 1979); and Colin Campbell, *Governments Under Stress: Political Executives and Key Bureaucrats in Washington, London and Ottawa* (Toronto, 1983).

47 As an official of the Department of Fisheries and Oceans said of the 1982 Kirby Task Force review of fisheries policy, 'It's hell! Pure hell!'

48 See Richard French, *How Ottawa Decides: Planning and Industrial Policy-Making, 1968–1980* (Toronto, 1980).

49 SCITEC, *Conference Proceedings: Research for survival—The critical points and the decision making process* (Ottawa, 1977).

50 Schmitter, 'Interest intermediation and regime governability', 313.

51 These remarks are based on the annual reports, newsletters, and press releases of the Social Sciences and Humanities Research Council, the Social Sciences Federation of Canada, the Canadian Political Science Association, SCITEC. Another scientifically oriented 'consortium' was established in 1978 when the CAUT and the Canadian Federation of Biological Sciences built on 'impressive lobbying activities' *vis-à-vis* government funding. Twelve groups were involved by May 1978 and others, like the Canadian Manufacturers' Association, had shown interest in joining. (*CAUT Bulletin*, May 1978.) The existence of inter-group relations of the type we have mentioned here contrast strongly with Panitch's assertion that 'one-to-one relationships between interest groups and the state (are) normally constitutive of pressure group politics' outside the limited sphere that he recognizes as corporatist. See 'Recent theorizations . . .', 173.

52 See Helen Jones Dawson, 'An Interest Group: The Canadian Federation of Agriculture', *Canadian Public Administration* III (1960) 2, 134-49, and 'Relations Between Farm Organizations and the Civil Service in Canada and Great Britain', *Canadian Public Administration* X (1967) 4, 450-71.

53 See Cathy Munroe and Jim Stewart, *Fishermen's Organizations in Nova Scotia—the Potential for Unification* (Halifax, 1981).

54 Léon Dion. Talk. 10th Anniversary Conference. L'Ecole Nationale d'Administration Publique. 28 May 1979.

55 A. Paul Pross, *The statutory basis of planning in the Maritime provinces* (Halifax, 1974). Some observers suggest that the advisory group developed by Premier Davis of Ontario constitutes a form of tripartite corporatism. (See A. Paul Pross, 'Governing Under Pressure:

Summary of Discussions', *Canadian Public Administration* 25 (1982) 2, 170-83.) However, since the group was informally selected by the Premier himself and had neither authority nor representative capacity, it cannot be treated as a corporatist body.

[56] Coleman and Jacek, 'The Chemical Industries in Canada', 57. Coleman and Jacek suggest that the chemical industry élite is compact enough to make formation of a true peak association unnecessary.

[57] *Le Devoir*, 22 Oct. 1982.

[58] Brown, *et al.*, *The Limits of Consultation*, 178.

CHAPTER 10. MODELS OF REPRESENTATION: PLURALISM AND POST-PLURALISM

[1] Philippe C. Schmitter, 'Still the Century of Corporatism?' in Philippe C. Schmitter and Gerhard Lehmbruch, *Trends Toward Corporatist Intermediation* (Beverly Hills, 1979), 7-52, 15.

[2] Robert Benewick, 'Politics without ideology: the Perimeters of Pluralism' in R. Benewick *et al.* (eds), *Knowledge and Belief in Politics* (London, 1973), 130-50; Grant Jordan, 'Pluralistic Corporatisms and Corporate Pluralism', *Scandinavian Political Studies* 7 (New Series) (1983) 3, 137-53.

[3] As, for example, in the editor's introduction to a special issue of the *Political Quarterly* devoted to pressure groups: '. . . pressure groups give us today a genuinely pluralist society in all spheres and levels of government. And without pluralism we should indeed be helpless before the Great Leviathan.' *Political Quarterly* 29 (1958) 1, 4.

[4] See, for example, G. David Garson, *Group Theories of Politics* (Beverly Hills, 1978). Robert A. Dahl, *Dilemmas of Pluralist Democracy* (New Haven, 1982) and Schmitter and Lehmbruch *Trends Toward Corporatist Intermediation*.

[5] Jordan, 'Pluralistic Corporatisms and Corporate Pluralism'.

[6] Arthur F. Bentley, *The Process of Government* (Evanston, Ill., 1935), 222. For an extensive review of American interest-group theory see Garson, *Group Theories of Politics*.

[7] Bentley, *The Process of Government*, 208.

[8] Mancur Olson, Jr, 'Orthodox Theories of Pressure Groups' in Robert H. Salisbury (ed.), *Interest Group Politics in America* (New York, 1970), 10.

[9] Bentley, *The Process of Government*, 429.

[10] Ibid.

[11] As Eckstein puts it in his analysis of the British Medical Association:

When we have stated the groups involved in the British medical politics have we stated everything there is to state about the subject? We can, of course, use the concept 'group' in such a way that it becomes impossible to answer no, and most of the more audacious group theorists do precisely that when asked to account for any specific policy. . . .

So interpreted, the group approach undoubtedly tells us all there is to know about British medical politics or any other kind of politics, but only by allowing us to state in group language what otherwise we would state in different terms. As used by its more extravagant exponents, group theory tends indeed to become nothing more than a language, based on the plausible, but arbitrary metaphysic that in politics the ultimately 'real', the component alike of individuals and institutions, the unit which really 'acts' and underlies ideas, is the group—not individuals, interactions, institutions, or larger political systems. Nothing can escape the clutches of this metaphysics if only one stretches it far enough, but precisely because of this nothing is illuminated by it either.

(*Pressure Group Politics* London, 152-3.)

[12]Garson, *Group Theories of Politics*, 30.

[13]J. A. Corry, *My Life and Work: A Happy Partnership* (Kingston, 1981), 231-2 quoted in V. Seymour Wilson, 'Mandarins and Kibitzers'. . . .

[14]Theodore Lowi, *The End of Liberalism* (New York, 1969).

[15]David B. Truman, *The Governmental Process: Political Interests and Public Opinion* (New York, 1964).

[16]For two recent and more appreciative assessments of the mainstream pluralist literature see Jordan, 'Pluralistic Corporatisms and Corporate Pluralism', and Garson, *Group Theories of Politics*, ch. 2, 'Pluralist, Statist and Corporatist Elements'. Jordan argues that the pluralists were much aware of the inequities in pressure group representation, and concerned to establish remedies for it. Garson, in a sweeping analysis, locates the pluralist in the context of the development of modern political thought, arguing that 'group theory served the intellectual purpose of aiding in the redefinition of democracy to avoid the seemingly unrealistic assumptions about individual rationality and motivation. It served the ideological purpose of defending contemporary democratic practice against the surge of fascist and communist philosophy. And it served the cultural purpose of revitalizing the values of decentralism and consensus. But group theory was not intended to be a theory of coordination of state, or even a theory in the predictive sense at all . . .' (71).

[17]E.E. Schattschneider, *The Semi-Sovereign People* (New York, 1960) 23, 21.

[18]Pressure group politics was seen to be ancillary to party politics. This is explicitly stated in the facile argument, popular in the 1960s, that political parties aggregate demands while pressure groups present unaggregated, or special, demands. See, for example, Henry W. Ehrmann's statement in an otherwise authoritative discussion that the function of pressure groups is to 'transmit the unaggregated demands present in a given society to the centres of authoritative decision-making' ('The Comparative Study of Interest Groups' in Erhmann (ed.), *Interest Groups on Four Continents* (Pittsburgh, 1958), 1-8, 3. The argument is made more subtly in the following extract from V. O. Key's leading text, *Politics, Parties and Pressure Groups* (New York, 1958), 171:

> Among those functions most clearly assigned to parties is the nomination of candidates and the assumption of responsibility for the conduct of the government once an election is won. . . . Parties, too, make commitments on broad questions of public policy. So do some pressure groups, but parties do not, and need not, take positions as parties on wide ranges of public policy and administration. To private organization falls the task of formulation of recommendations and their advocacy in this sphere of government action that includes matters important to limited numbers of persons, quite technical matters, and the minutiae of government policy and operation as they affect particular interests.

> Thus pressure group politics complements party politics. The one is the great product of the spatial organization of electoral units, and has the capacity to conduct debates on the general public interest. The other fills the lacunae left by the party system. It expresses the needs of the functionally organized economy by asking for technical adjustments to broad public policy.

[19]John F. Manley, 'Neo-Pluralism: A Class Analysis of Pluralism I and Pluralism II', *American Political Science Review* 77 (1983) 368-83, at 370.

[20]See, for example, L.C. Bacchi, *Liberation Deferred: The Ideas of the English Canadian Suffragists: 1877-1918* (Toronto, 1983), 120-1, for a description of the different approaches to organizing of middle-class and working women. R. Manzer, *Canada: A Socio-Political Report* (Toronto, 1974), 321-3 comments on contemporary trends. Frances Fox Piven and Richard A. Cloward, *Poor People's Movements: Why they succeed, how they fail* (New York, 1979) is an extensive analysis of a series of case studies; it concludes that methods of interest articulation used by the middle and upper classes are counterproductive for the poor.

[21]R.M. MacIver, *The Web of Government* (New York, 1947), 220-1.

[22]Mancur Olson, *The Logic of Collective Action* (Cambridge, Mass., 1971), 14.

[23]M. Crenson, 'Non-issues in City Politics: The case of air pollution' in M. Surkin and A. Wolfe, *An End to Political Science* (New York: 1970), 144-66, 149.

[24] Theodore Lowi, *The End of Liberalism*.

[25] Ibid., 295-6.

[26] Robert H. Salisbury, 'An Exchange Theory of Interest Groups' in Salisbury (ed.), *Interest Group Politics in America*, 32-6. In a more recent publication, however, Salisbury notes that a new understanding of American interest groups will 'systematically distinguish institution-based interest activity from that deriving support from individual citizens, and it will note the former's greater staying power and long-term effectiveness in Washington.' ('Interest Groups: Toward a New Understanding' in Allan J. Cigler and Burdett A. Loomis (eds), *Interest Group Politics* (Washington, 1983), 354-69, 365.

[27] See his *The Logic of Collective Action*.

[28] Salisbury, 'An Exchange Theory of Interest Groups'', 33-4.

[29] E.E. Schattschneider, *The Semi-Sovereign People*, 70.

[30] Ibid., 68.

[31] E.E. Schattschneider, *Party Government* (New York, 1962) 33.

[32] Schattschneider, *The Semi-Sovereign People*, 31.

[33] For example, Salisbury, Olson, Crenson, cited above.

[34] Thus an effort is made to ensure that conflict remains 'private'. It is 'taken into the public arena precisely because someone wants to make certain that the power ratio among the private interest most immediately involved shall not prevail.' (*The Semi-Sovereign People*, 38.) In other words, the resort to politics is a resort to extreme measures.

[35] Garson, *Group Theories of Politics*, 126-7. See also P. Bachrach and M. Baratz, 'Two Faces of Power', *American Political Science Review* 56 (1962) 4, 947-52 and 'Decisions and Non-decisions: An analytical framework', *American Political Science Review* 57 (1963) 3, 632-42. David Kwavnick, after presenting several striking Canadian illustrations, concludes that 'once the views of the interest groups are known the proverbial timidity inherent in bureaucratic organization is their most trustworthy ally. The anticipated representation is among the most powerful tools available to interest groups in influencing the policy advice that a minister will receive from his officials.' *Organized Labour and Pressure Politics* (Montreal, 1972), 182.

[36] Randall B. Ripley, and Grace A. Franklin, *Congress, the Bureaucracy and Public Policy* (Homewood, Ill., 1976), 5-6.

[37] Ibid.

[38] Schattschneider, *The Semi-Sovereign People*.

[39] See Garson, 'Group Theories of Politics'; Salisbury, 'Interest Groups: Toward a New Understanding' and Michael T. Hayes, 'Interest Groups: Pluralism or Mass Society', both in Allan J. Cigler and Burdett A. Loomis (eds), *Interest Group Politics* (Washington, 1983). Eric A. Nordlinger, *On the Autonomy of the Democratic State* (Cambridge, Mass., 1981).

[40] Robert L. Heilbroner with Aaron Singer, *The Economic Transformation of America* (New York, 1977) and J.K.Galbraith, *The New Industrial State* (New York, 1971).

[41] Richardson and Jordan, *Governing Under Pressure*, 190. See also J.J. Richardson (ed.), *Policy Styles in Western Europe* (London, 1982).

[42] Ibid., 191.

[43] Robert E. Goodin, 'Banana Time in British Politics', *Political Studies* xxx (1982) 1, 42-58.

[44] Ibid., 48-9.

[45] Ibid., 48.

[46] The appreciation of a less cohesive inner core in British policy-making leads Jordan to adopt Heclo's network 'image' as a vehicle for conceptualizing the policy process in the United Kingdom. See Grant Jordan, 'Iron Triangles, Woolly Corporatism and Elastic Nets: Images of the Policy Process', *Journal of Public Policy* 1 (1981) Part 1. See also H. Heclo, 'Issue networks and the executive establishment' in Antony King (ed.), *The New American Political System* (Washington, 1978).

[47] William D. Coleman, 'Canadian Business and the State' in Keith Banting (Research Coordinator), *The State and Economic Interests* (The Collected research studies/Royal Commission on the Economic Union and Development Prospects for Canada. Toronto, 1986), 245-90, 275.

[48] Ibid., 276.

[49] Pierre Fournier, 'Consensus Building in Canada: Case Studies and Prospects' in Banting, *The State and Economic Interests*, 291-336, 327.

[50] A policy community approach is not explicit in Canadian pressure group studies. However, there are close parallels between it and the sectoral approach adopted by Julien Bauer in *Administration consultatif: La commission du textile et du vêtement* (Montreal: Note de recherche No. 11. Département de science politique. Université de Québec à Montréal, 1978). See also J.D. Forbes, 'Institutions and Interest Groups in the Canadian Food System Policy Process', *Report* (Ottawa, 1982) and A. Paul Pross, Susan McCorquodale with Sheilagh Dunn, *Economic Resurgence and the Constitutional Debate: The Case of the East Coast Fishing Industry* (forthcoming).

[51] An illustration is found in timber-cutting policy applied in Ontario parks. In the late 1960s conventional wisdom endorsed the traditional practice of cutting in the parks; by then, however, environmentalists concerned with preserving wilderness areas had begun to bitterly attack the practice. Ontario parks policy has been suspect ever since. See 'National concern over fate of Algonquin Park', *Canadian Audubon* 30 (Nov.-Dec. 1968), 153, and D.H. Pimlott, 'Struggle to Save a Park', *Canadian Audubon* 31 (May-June 1969), 72-81.

[52] The Applebaum-Hébert Committee noted, for example, that the non-departmental agencies administering cultural policy found in the late 1970s that their traditional arm's-length relationship with ministers was being called increasingly into question and that they, and their policy communities, were having to adapt to more direct ministerial involvement in policy formation and in their internal affairs. (Canada. Department of the Communications. *Report of the Federal Cultural Policy Review Committee* (Ottawa, 1982), 20-6.

[53] Douglas Brown, Julia Eastman with Ian Robinson, *The Limits of Consultation: A Debate Among Ottawa, the Provinces and the Private Sector on an Industrial Strategy* (Kingston and Ottawa, 1981).

[54] William Coleman and Henry J. Jacek, 'The Political Organization of the Chemical Industry in Canada' Paper. Canadian Political Science Association (Halifax, 1981), 41.

[55] On the 'On-to-Ottawa' trek see Walter D. Young, *Democracy and Discontent: Progressivism, Socialism and Social Credit in the Canadian West* (Toronto, 1978) and Michiel Horn (ed.), *The Dirty Thirties* (Toronto, 1972). The issue of charitable society status is reviewed in John Swaigen, *How to Fight for What's Right: The citizen's guide to public interest law* (Toronto, 1981). The issue was a part of Progressive Conservative criticism of Liberal administration of the Department of National Revenue and played a minor role in the 1984 election. See Halifax *Chronicle Herald*, 4 April 1984, reporting group complaints that they were 'being threatened by Revenue Canada with loss of their ability to accept tax deductible donations if they take stands on public policy issues', and the *Globe and Mail*, 12 March 1985, quoting Revenue Minister Perrin Beatty, who indicated that he was prepared to allow registered charities to become involved in non-partisan political activity. This approach was confirmed in the 1985 budget.

[56] 'The poor', according to Marjorie Hartling, executive director of the National Anti-Poverty Organization, 'are out. They're not of everything.' (Quoted in H.V. Kroeker (ed.), *Sovereign People or Sovereign Government* (Montreal, 1981), 91). See, more extensively, Piven and Cloward, *Poor People's Movements*.

CHAPTER 11. SPACE, SECTOR AND LEGITIMACY:
ADDRESSING THE DILEMMAS OF REPRESENTATION

[1] A particularly comprehensive review of European ideas about parliamentary forms of sectoral representation is found in J.-P. Parrot, *La représentation des intérêts dans le mouvement des idées politiques* (Paris, 1974).

[2] See, for example, the experience of residents of Port Hawkesbury reported in Raymond Foote, *The Case of Port Hawkesbury: Rapid Industrialization and Local Unrest in a Nova Scotia Community* (Toronto, 1979) and A. Paul Pross, *Planning and Development: A Case of Two Nova Scotia Communities* (Halifax, 1975).

[3] Pendleton Herring, *The Politics of Democracy* (New York, 1940), 331, quoting M.L. Wilson in *Democracy Has Roots* (New York, 1939), 113-14.

[4] For example, W.E. Lyons remarks that 'the impact of space in Canadian legislative representation is especially prominent in the early debates over the principles and formulae to be used in reapportionment, particularly in the concern of the Maritimes provinces that they would lose representation as the population of the rest of the country increased. This became an important issue between 1892 and 1914 when the region did lose representation.' (*One Man—One Vote* (Toronto, 1970), 3. We would argue that the impact of space is still fundamental to Canadian politics.

[5] ' "Group of 10" MPs Urge Economic Boost for Montreal', Montreal *Gazette*, 17 May 1982 and 'Liberal Seals are Showing Some Bite', *Globe and Mail*, 15 Feb. 1983.

[6] See Kingston *Whig-Standard*, 16-25 May 1983, *Globe and Mail*, 29 July and 15 Nov. 1983.

[7] R. MacGregor Dawson and Norman Ward, *The Government of Canada* 4th edn (Toronto, 1963), 361.

[8] Roy Romanow, John White, and Howard Lesson, *Canada...Notwithstanding: The Making of the Constitution, 1976-82* (Toronto, 1984), 108-11 and 'Four Western NDP MPs Break Ranks on Patriation', *Globe and Mail*, 19 Feb. 1981.

[9] Confidential interview.

[10] Halifax *Chronicle Herald*, 7 March 1975.

[11] J. Meynaud, *Nouvelles études sur les groupes de pression en France* (Paris, 1962). 251 See also Philippe Schmitter, 'Interest intermediation and regime governability' in Suzanne D. Berger (ed.), *Organizing Interests in Western Europe* (Cambridge, 1981), 287-331.

[12] Colin Campbell, *The Canadian Senate: A Lobby from Within* (Toronto, 1978).

[13] Ibid., 69.

[14] Helen Jones Dawson, 'National Pressure Groups and the Federal Government' in A. Paul Pross (ed.), *Pressure Group Behaviour in Canadian Politics* (Toronto, 1975).

[15] See the Law Reform Commission reports cited in footnote 8, ch. 9.

[16] W.D. Baker, (MP) and G.W. Baldwin (MP), 'Government Institutions' Position Paper. PC Annual Meeting, 4-6 November 1977.

[17] James Gillies and Jean Pigott, 'Participation in the Legislative Process', *Canadian Public Administration* 25 (1982) 2, 254-65, 256.

[18] J.I. Gow, 'L'histoire de l'administration publique québécoise', *Recherches sociographiques* XVI (1975) 3, 385-413.

[19] A.H. Hanson, 'The Purpose of Parliament', *Parliamentary Affairs* XVIII (1964) 3, 279-96, 295.

[20] Ibid.

[21] See ch. 3, 76.

[22] We see policy formulation as part of the culminating stage of policy determination. It involves the bringing about of compromises between rival interests and the ultimate selection of alternatives. Because both are functions that engage the political responsibility of the executive, they properly belong to the Prime Minister and the Cabinet. Policy formulation also involves the precise delineation of policy, a task that is best left to the bureaucracy, duly supervised by the executive.

[23] An argument very close to the 'level of conflict' argument presented by E.E. Schattschneider in *The Semi-Sovereign People* (New York, 1960) and the 'search for consensus' argument presented by J.J. Richardson and A.G. Jordan, *Governing Under Pressure: The Policy Process in a Post-Parliamentary Democracy* (Oxford, 1977).

[24] John F. Bulloch, 'A View from a Special Interest Group' in Daniel L. Bon, *Lobbying: A Right? A Necessity? A Danger?* (Ottawa, 1981), 13.

25 As our earlier comments have implied, the bureaucracy's search for legitimating support by no means focused exclusively on Parliament. Massive public-relations campaigns directed at the public at large; experimentation with representative bureaucracy; efforts to reconstitute traditional patterns of accountability; and a greater part of the work undertaken to create and/or enlarge policy communities impinge on Parliament's role but appear to have been designed to influence public opinion in general. Some of these ventures, in fact, may eventually challenge Parliament. Corporatist arrangements or even policy communities fully representative of policy sectors could fall into that category.

26 A.H. Hanson, 'The Purpose of Parliament'.

27 See, for example, Gillies and Pigott, 'Participation in the Legislative Process', Faulkner, 'Pressuring the Executive', and Kathryn Randle, 'Committees at the Crossroads: Will Innovation Lead to Reform?', *Parliamentary Government*, 2 (1981) 3, 3.

28 The Canadian Bar Association, *Report of the Canadian Bar Association Committee on the Reform of Parliament* (Parliament as Lawmaker) (Ottawa, 1982) 29-30. The CBA committee pointed out that not all the task forces had had as much success with their recommendations.

29 This is consistent with John Stewart's observation that further reform of the committee system would not see the committees make more decisions but would provide that 'the governors and members would meet on the issues of the times and do so before the governors had decided what they, under the full weight of their responsibility, must recommend to the House.' *The Canadian House of Commons* (Montreal, 1977), 283.

30 It is tempting to speculate on the further evolution of both Parliament and interest groups under the Mulroney regime, which came to power after most of these comments were written. Despite Mr Mulroney's attempts to constrain public servants' communications with the media in the weeks immediately following his election, the norms of behaviour developed in the public service during the Liberal years tended to reassert themselves once his government had settled into office. Mr Mulroney's frank recognition of interest-group participation in policy discussions will, if anything, encourage the further development of more open relations between groups, agencies, and Parliament. Much will depend on whether his government will continue the use of task forces and on whether it will be able to halt or reverse the diffusion of power.

31 See, for example, R. Manzer, *Canada: A Social and Political Report* (Toronto, 1974), 321 and Mildred A. Schwartz, *Politics and Territory: The Sociology of Regional Persistence in Canada* (Montreal, 1974), ch. 9.

32 These are listed in ch. 1, note 5.

33 Consumer and Corporate Affairs Canada. *Lobbying and the Registration of Paid Lobbyists: A Discussion Paper* (Ottawa, 1985), 2-3.

34 *Globe and Mail*, 20 December 1985.

35 There is less agreement about that activities that lobbying regulation should cover. The U.S. Federal Regulation of Lobbying Act, for example, seems to be concerned only with lobbying directed at influencing the passage of legislation (Title III. Legislative Reorganization Act of 1946. Public Law 601, 79th Congress. 2d. Session. 2 USC 261-270). Efforts to influence the bureaucratic interpretation of legislation or its implementation do not appear to be covered. Most Canadian bills have taken a broader approach, seeking to regulate those who work to influence the introduction and passage of legislation and who work to affect policy decisions at the ministerial and bureaucratic level. The Consumer and Corporate Affairs discussion paper suggests a broad definition that would cover attempts '(i) to make or amend federal legislation or regulation; (ii) to make or change federal policies or programs; (iii) to influence federal decisions on the awarding of contracts, grants, and contributions; or (iv) to influence federal appointments to public office' (*Lobbying and the Registration of Paid Lobbyists*, 20). The discussion paper suggests that it might be extended to include as well individuals who gather and sell information to clients lobbying on their own behalf, and individuals who arrange meetings between clients and public officials. (Ibid.)

36 *Lobbying and the Registration of Paid Lobbyists*, 21.

320 | Notes

37 Julianne La Breche, 'The Quiet Persuaders of Parliament Hill', *Financial Post Magazine*, 29 November 1980.

38 'Environmentalists Await Airlift to Wolf Hunt Area', Vancouver *Sun*, 29 Feb. 1984.

39 'Activist No Longer Welcome in Rotary', Halifax *Chronicle Herald*, 24 Sept. 1985.

40 See, for example, the reports of the McCruer, MacDonald, and Keable commissions. Respectively: Ontario. Royal Commission into Civil Rights *Report* (Toronto, 1968); Canada. Privy Council Office. Commission of Inquiry Concerning Certain Acts of the Royal Canadian Mounted Police *Report* (Ottawa, 1981); and Québec. Commission d'enquête sur des opérations policières en territoires québécois. *Rapport* (Québec, 1981).

41 Consumer and Corporate Affairs Canada, *Lobbying and the Registration of Paid Lobbyists*, 21-4.

42 See Norman J. Ornstein and Shirley Elder, *Interest Groups, Lobbying and Policymaking* (Washington, 1978) ch. 4.

43 'Policy capacity' is defined as 'the properties that a system possesses which move associations into it and encourage their fruitful participation in policy formation and implementation.' William Coleman, 'Canadian Business and the State' in Keith Banting (Research Coordinator), *The State and Economic Interests* (The Collected research studies/Royal Commission on the Economic Union and Development Prospects for Canada. No. 32. Toronto, 1986) 243-90, 262. Associations considered to have policy capacity 'will be able to order and coordinate the complex activity in which they are involved as a result of demands by members and other organizations, particularly by the State. Secondly, they will be independent of both members and the State.' (Ibid.)

44 Secretary of State. *People in Action: Report of the National Advisory Council on Voluntary Action to the Government of Canada* (Ottawa, 1977), 162.

45 Ibid., 165.

46 The 1977 study noted with approval the criteria for awarding five-year sustaining grants established by the Department of National Health and Welfare. (Ibid., 179-84.) They called for the development of five-year plans by recipient organizations, including evaluation procedures; they required that the organizations be national in scope and possess a network of affiliated agencies at the provincial and municipal levels; and insisted that target populations be represented in group governing bodies, except where physical and mental handicaps made that impracticable. The study recommendation that similar criteria be adopted by the federal government in general appears to have gone unheeded.

47 See Peter H. Schuck, 'Public Interest Groups and the Policy Process', *Public Administration Review* 37 (1977) 2, 132-40.

48 For a discussion of American approaches to litigation by groups see Stephen L. Wasby, 'Interest Groups in Court: Race Relations Litigation' in Allan J. Cigler and Burdett A. Loomis (eds), *Interest Group Politics* (Washington, 1983). See also ch. 7, above.

49 See Samuel A. Martin, *An Essential Grace: Funding Canada's Health Care, Education, Welfare, Religion and Culture* (Toronto, 1985), particularly chs. 7 and 10.

50 Again, see Secretary of State, *People in Action*.

51 In May, 1985, for example, the Nova Scotia Municipal Board delivered an interpretation of revisions to the provincial Planning Act that greatly distressed local citizens' groups. The Board concluded that the revisions barred individuals who were not immediately affected from appealing re-zoning decisions of municipal authorities. Citizens' groups had argued that such an interpretation would inhibit attempts to bring a broader public interest to bear on such decisions. See Halifax *Chronicle Herald*, 23 May 1985.

52 J.C. Nelson, 'Public participation in comprehensive resource and environmental management', *Science and Public Policy*, Oct. 1982, 240-50.

53 Gregory Pyrcz, 'Pressure Groups' in T.C. Pocklington (ed.), *Liberal Democracy in Canada and the United States* (Toronto, 1985), 340-73, 372.

54 John William Kafka, *The Fisheries Policy Process: A Case Study of the Atlantic Bluefin Tuna* (Dalhousie University. Unpublished M.A. thesis. Halifax, 1981), 116-17.

A Select Bibliography

ON CANADIAN PRESSURE GROUPS

Anderson, J.E. 'Pressure groups and Canadian Bureaucracy' in W.D.K. Kernaghan and A.M. Willms, eds, *Public Administration in Canada: Selected Readings.* Toronto: Methuen, 1970 (370-9).

Angus, Margaret. 'Health, Emigration and Welfare in Kingston, 1820-1840' in Donald Swainson, ed., *Oliver Mowat's Ontario.* Toronto: Macmillan, 1972 (120-35).

Armstrong, Christopher and H.V. Nelles. 'Getting Your Way in Nova Scotia: Tweaking Halifax, 1909-1917'. *Acadiensis* V, 1976, 2, (105-31).

Armstrong, R. 'Pressure Group Activity and Policy Formation: Collective Bargaining in the Federal Public Service' in W.D.K. Kernaghan, ed., *Bureaucracy in Canadian Government.* Toronto: Methuen, 1969 (120-8).

Andrew, Caroline. 'Women and the Welfare State'. *Canadian Journal of Political Science* XVII, 1984, 4, (667-83).

Archbold, William D. 'The Business Council on National Issues: A New Factor in Business Communication'. *Canadian Business Review* 4, 1977, 2, (13-15).

Archibald, Clinton. 'Corporatist Tendencies in Quebec' in Alain G. Gagnon, *Quebec: State and Society.* Toronto: Methuen, 1984 (353-64).

Arnopoulos, Sheila McLeod and Dominique Clift. *The English Fact in Quebec.* Montreal: McGill-Queen's, 1984.

Atkinson, M.M. and W. Coleman. 'Bureaucrats and Politicians in Canada: An Examination of the Political Administrative Model'. *Comparative Political Studies* 18, 1985 1, (66).

Aucoin, Peter. 'Pressure Groups and Recent Changes in the Policy-Making Process' in A. Paul Pross, ed., *Pressure Group Behaviour in Canadian Politics.* Toronto: McGraw-Hill, 1975 (172-93).

————. *Public Accountability in the Governing of Professions: A Report on the Self-Governing Professions of Accounting, Architecture, Engineering and Law in Ontario.* Toronto: The Professional Organizations Committee, 1978.

Ba, Tran Quang. 'Les études canadiennes sur les groupes de pression: un travail pré-théorique à faire?' *Communications.* Montréal: Société canadienne de Science politique, 1976.

Bacchi, L.C. *Liberation Deferred: The Ideas of the English-Canadian Suffragists, 1877-1918.* Toronto: University of Toronto Press, 1983.

Badgley, R.F. and Samuel Wolfe. *Doctor's Strike: Medical Care and Conflict in Saskatchewan.* Toronto: Macmillan, 1967.

Baetz, Mark. 'Sector Strategy'. *Policy Options*, January 1985, (14-16).

Baird, R. 'Interest Groups and Departments in Alberta'. *Proceedings* Canadian Political Science Association. Winnipeg: June 1970.

Bakvis, Herman. 'Alternative Models of Governance: Federalism, Consociationalism and Corporatism' in H. Bakvis and W. Chandler, eds, *Federalism and the Role of the State*. Toronto: forthcoming.

Banting, Keith. Research Coordinator, *The State and Economic Interests*. Toronto: University of Toronto Press. The Collected Research Studies/ Royal Commission on Economic Union and Development Prospects for Canada. No. 32, 1986.

Barry, Donald. *Interest Groups and the Canadian Foreign Policy Formulation Process: The Case of Biafra*. Halifax: Dalhousie University, MA thesis, 1971.

_____. 'Interest Groups and the Foreign Policy Process: The Case of Biafra' in A. Paul Pross, ed., *Pressure Group Behaviour in Canadian Politics*. Toronto: McGraw-Hill, 1975 (115-48).

Bartha, Peter F. 'Managing Corporate External Issues: An Analytical Framework' in James D. Fleck and Isaiah A. Litvak, eds, *Business Can Succeed! Understanding the Political Environment*. Toronto: Gage, 1984 (9-27).

_____. 'Organizational competence in business-government relations: A managerial perspective'. *Canadian Public Administration* 28, 1985, 2 (202-20).

Bauer, Julien. *Administration consultative: La Commission du Textile et du Vêtement*. Montréal: Département de Science politique. Université de Québec à Montreal. Note de recherche n°. 11, 1978.

_____. 'Patrons et patronat au Québec'. *Canadian Journal of Political Science*, IX, 1976 (473-91).

Baxter, Clive. 'Lobbying—Ottawa's Fastest Growing Business' in Paul Fox, ed. *Politics Canada*. Toronto: McGraw-Hill, 1966 (206-10).

Belanger, M. *L'Association volontaire: le cas des Chambres de Commerce*. Québec: Laval University, Ph.D. thesis, 1969.

Bercuson, David J. 'Western Labour Radicalism and the One Big Union: Myths and Realities' in S. Trofimenkoff, ed. *The Twenties in Western Canada*. Ottawa: National Museum of Man, 1972 (32-49).

Berry, Glyn R. *Bureaucratic Politics and Canadian Economic Policies Affecting the Developing Countries—the Case of the 'Strategy for International Development Cooperation 1975-1980*. Halifax: Dalhousie University. Ph.D. thesis, 1981.

_____. 'The Oil Lobby and the Energy Crisis'. *Canadian Public Administration* 17, 1974, 4 (600-35).

Bliss, Michael. 'The Protective Impulse: An Approach to the Social History of Oliver Mowat's Ontario' in Donald Swainson, ed., *Oliver Mowat's Ontario*. Toronto: Macmillan, 1972 (174-88, 174-5).

Bon, Daniel L. *Lobbying: A Right? A Necessity? A Danger?* Ottawa: The Conference Board of Canada, 1981.

Braden, George. *The Emergence of Interest Groups in the North West Territories*. Halifax: Dalhousie University. MA Thesis, 1976.

Brown, Douglas and Julia Eastman with Ian Robinson. *The Limits of Consultation: A Debate Among Ottawa, the Provinces and the Private Sector on an Industrial Strategy*. Kingston and Ottawa: Queen's University Institute of Intergovernmental Relations and the Science Council of Canada, 1981 (176).

Brown-John, Lloyd. 'Comprehensive regulatory consultation in Canada's food processing industry'. *Canadian Public Administration* 28, 1985, 1 (70-98).

Bucovetsky, M.W. 'The Mining Industry and the Great Tax Reform Debate' in A.P. Pross, ed., *Pressure Group Behaviour in Canadian Politics*. Toronto: McGraw-Hill, 1975 (87-115).

Burke, Mike, Harold D. Clarke, Lawrence LeDuc. 'Federal and Provincial Political Participation in Canada: Some Methodological and Substantive Considerations'. *Canadian Review of Sociology and Anthropology* 15, 1978, 1 (61-75).

Byers, Roddick. 'Executive Leadership and Influence: Parliamentary Perceptions of Canadian Defence Policy' in Thomas A. Hockin, ed., *Apex of Power*. Scarborough: Prentice-Hall, 1971.

Bulloch, John F. 'A View from a Special Interest Group' in Daniel L. Bon, *Lobbying: A Right? A Necessity? A Danger?* Ottawa: Conference Board, 1981 (12).

Cairns, Alan C. 'The Governments and Societies of Canadian Federalism'. *Canadian Journal of Political Science* X, 1977, 4 (695-725).

Campbell, Colin. *The Canadian Senate: A Lobby from Within*. Toronto: Macmillan, 1978.

Canada. Consumer and Corporate Affairs. *Lobbying and the Registration of Paid Lobbyists: A Discussion Paper*. Ottawa: Consumer and Corporate Affairs, 1985.

Canada. Environment Canada. *Environmentally Interested Citizen's Groups in Canada*. Ottawa: Canada DOE Information Branch, 1974.

Canada. Library of Parliament. Research Branch. 'Pressure Groups in Canada'. *The Parliamentarian* LI, 1970, 1 (11-20).

Canada. Government of Canada. *The Way Ahead: A Framework for Discussion*. Ottawa: Privy Council Office, 1976.

Canadian Associations. Journal of the Institute of Association Executives.

Canadian Manufacturers' Association. *Inside Government*. Toronto: The Association, 1981.

Chant, D.A. 'Pollution Probe: Fighting Polluters with Their Own Weapons' in A. Paul Pross, ed., *Pressure Group Behaviour in Canadian Politics*. Toronto: McGraw-Hill, 1975 (59-68).

Clague, Michael. 'Citizen Participation in the Legislative Process' in James A. Draper, ed., *Citizen Participation: Canada*. Toronto: New Press, 1971 (30-44).

Clark, S.D. 'The Canadian Manufacturers' Association: A Political Pressure Group'. *Canadian Journal of Economics and Political Science* V, 1938, 4.

_____. *The Canadian Manufacturers' Association*. Toronto: University of Toronto Press, 1939.

Clark, S.D., J. Paul Grayson, and Linda M. Grayson, eds. *Prophecy and Protest: Social Movements in Twentieth-Century Canada*. Toronto: Gage, 1975.

Clift, Dominique. 'L'Etat et les groupes d'intérêts: perspectives d'avenir'. *Canadian Public Administration* 25, 1982, 2 (265-78).

Coleman, William D. 'Analysing the associative action of business: policy advocacy and policy participation'. *Canadian Public Administration* 28, 1985, 3 (413-33).

_____. *Business and Politics: A Study of Collective Action*. (forthcoming)

_____. 'Canadian Business and the State' in Keith Banting, Research Coordinator *The State and Economic Interests*. Toronto: University of Toronto Press. The Collected research studies/Royal Commission on the Economic Union and Development Prospects for Canada. No. 32. 1986 (245-90).

_____. 'Federalism and Interest Group Organization' in H. Bakvis and W. Chandler, eds. *Federalism and the Role of the State*. Toronto: forthcoming.

_____. 'From Bill 22 to Bill 101: The Politics of Language under the Parti Québécois'. *Canadian Journal of Political Science* XIV, 1981, 3 (459-86).

_____. *The Independence Movement in Quebec, 1945-1980*. Toronto: University of Toronto Press, 1984.

_____ and Wyn P. Grant. 'Regional Differentiation of Business Interest Associations: A Comparison of Canada and the United Kingdom'. *Canadian Journal of Political Science* XVIII, 1985, 1 (3-30).

_____ and H.J. Jacek. 'The Roles and Activities of Business Interest Associations in Canada'. *Canadian Journal of Political Science* XVI, 1983, 2 (257-280).

Corbett, D.C. 'The Pressure Group and the Public Interest' in J.E. Hodgetts and D.C. Corbett. *Canadian Public Administration*. Toronto: Macmillan, 1960 (452-62).

Corry, J.A. 'Sovereign People or Sovereign Governments' in H.V. Kroeker, ed., *Sovereign People or Sovereign Governments*. Montreal: Institute for Research on Public Policy, 1981 (3-12).

Cumming, Peter. *Nova Scotia's Herbicide Case. A Court Diary*. Garbarus, Nova Scotia: Herbicide Fund Society, 1983.

Curtis, James. 'Voluntary Association Joining: A Cross-National Comparative Note'. *American Sociological Review* 36, 1971 (872-80).

Dalhousie Institute of Public Affairs and Richard H. Leach. *Interprovincial Relations in the Maritime Provinces*. Fredericton: Maritime Union Study, 1970 (81).

Dawson, Helen Jones. *Agricultural Interest Groups in Canada and Great Britain*. Oxford University, unpublished thesis, 1966.

_____. 'The Consumers Association of Canada'. *Canadian Public Administration* VI, 1963, 1 (92-188).

_____. 'An Interest Group: The Canadian Federation of Agriculture'. *Canadian Public Administration* III, 1960, 2 (134-49).

_____. 'Relations Between Farm Organizations and the Civil Service in Canada and Great Britain'. *Canadian Public Administration* X, 1967, 4 (450-71).

_____. 'National Pressure Groups and the Federal Government' in A. Paul Pross, ed., *Pressure Group Behaviour in Canadian Politics*. Toronto: McGraw-Hill, 1975 (27-58).

Decarie, Graeme. 'Something Old, Something New . . . Aspects of Prohibitionism in Ontario in the 1890's' in Donald Swainson, ed., *Oliver Mowat's Ontario*. Toronto: Macmillan, 1972 (154-71).

Delbridge, Pat. 'David vs. Goliath: Voluntary Sector Interest Groups in Canada Today' in James D. Fleck and Isaiah Litvak, eds, *Business Can Succeed! Understanding the Political Environment*. Toronto: Gage, 1984 (46-64).

Deveaux, Bert and Kaye. 'The Enemies Within Community Development' in James A. Draper, ed. *Citizen Participation: Canada*. Toronto: New Press, 1971 (93-105).

Dion, Léon. 'Anti-politics and marginals'. *Government and Opposition* 9, 1974, 1 (28-41).

_____. *Le bill 60 et la société québécoise*. Montréal: Editions HMH, 1967.

_____. 'Participation in the Political Process'. *Queen's Quarterly* 75, 1968 (3).

_____. 'Politique consultative et système politique'. *Canadian Journal of Political Science* II, 1969, 2 (226-44).

_____. 'Quebec Interest Groups and the Search for an Alternative Political System'. *The Annals of the American Academy of Political and Social Science* 413, 1974 (124-44).

_____. 'A la recherche d'une méthode d'analyse des partis et des groups d'intérêt'. *Canadian Journal of Political Science* II, 1969, 1 (45-63).

_____. *Société et Politique: la vie des groupes*. Québec: Laval, 1971.

Doern, G. Bruce. 'The National Research Council: The Causes of Goal Displacement'. *Canadian Public Administration* XIII, 1970, 2 (140-85).

_____. 'Pressure Groups and the Canadian Bureaucracy: Scientists and Science Policy Machinery' in W.D.K. Kernaghan, ed., *Bureaucracy in Canadian Government*. Toronto: Methuen, 1969 (112-19).

_____, and Glen Toner. *The Politics of Energy: The Development and Implementation of the NEP*. Toronto: Methuen, 1985.

_____. *Science and Politics in Canada*. Montreal: McGill-Queen's University Press, 1972.

Donovan, S.J. and R.B. Winmill. 'The Beauharnois Power Scandal' in Kenneth M. Gibbons and Donald C. Rowat, *Political Corruption in Canada: Cases, Causes and Cures*. Ottawa: Carleton, 1976 (57-66).

Draper, Dianne. 'Environmental Interest Groups and Institutional Arrangements in British Columbia Water Management Issues' in Bruce Mitchell, ed., *Institutional Arrangements for Water Management: Canadian Experiences*. Waterloo, Ontario: University of Waterloo, 1975 (119-70).

Dussault, René. 'L'Evolution du professionalisme au Québec'. *Canadian Public Administration* 20, 1977, 2 (275-91).

Edwards, Gordon. 'Nuclear Power: A New Dimension in Politics'. *Alternatives* 5, 1976, 2 (26-32).

Eggleston, Wilfrid. 'The Cabinet and Pressure Groups'. *Proceedings of the Fifth Annual Conference, The Institute of Public Administration of Canada*. Toronto: IPAC, 1953 (156-7).

Emmerson, D.W. 'Legislation for Professionals in Quebec—Government Moves for Tighter Controls'. *Chemistry in Canada*. December 1972 (28-9).

Engelmann, F.C. and Mildred A. Schwartz. *Canadian Political Parties: Origin, Character, Impact*. Scarborough: Prentice-Hall, 1975.

Faulkner, J. Hugh. 'Pressuring the Executive'. *Canadian Public Administration* 25, 1982, 2 (240-54).

Fensom, K.G. *Expanding Forestry Horizons: A History of the Canadian Institute of Forestry-Institut Forestier du Canada, 1908–1969*. MacDonald College, P.Q.: CIF, 1972.

Fleck, James D. and Isaiah A. Litvak, eds, *Business Can Succeed! Understanding the Political Environment*. Toronto: Gage, 1984.

Forbes, E.R. *Maritime Rights: The Maritime Rights Movement*. Montreal: McGill Queen's University Press, 1979.

Forbes, J.D. *Institutions and Influence Groups in Canadian Farm and Food Policy*. Toronto: Institute of Public Administration of Canada. Monographs on Canadian Public Administration. No. 10, 1985.

_____. 'Institutions and Interest Groups in the Canadian Food System Policy Process'. *Report*. Ottawa: Economic Council of Canada. Regulation Reference. 1982.

Foster, Peter. *The Blue-Eyed Sheiks: The Canadian Oil Establishment*. Don Mills, Ontario: Collins, 1979.

_____. *The Sorcerer's Apprentice*. Toronto: Collins, 1982.

Fournier, Pierre. 'Consensus Building in Canada: Cases Studies and Prospects' in Keith Banting, Research Coordinator, *The State and Economic Interests*. Toronto: University of Toronto Press. The Collected research studies/Royal Commission on the Economic Union and Development Prospects for Canada. No. 32, 1986 (291-336).

Fox, David. *Public Participation in the Administrative Process*. Ottawa: Law Reform Commission. Administrative Law Series. 1979.

Frank, J.A. 'La dynamique des manifestations violentes'. *Canadian Journal of Political Science* XVII, 1984, 2 (324-49).

Frechette, W.D.H. 'The CMA—Spokesman for Industry' in Paul Fox, ed., *Politics Canada*. Toronto: McGraw-Hill, 1970 (172-5).

Friedland, M.L. 'Pressure Groups and the Development of the Criminal Law' in P.R. Glazebrook, ed., *Reshaping the Criminal Law: Essays in Honour of Glanville Williams*. London: Stevens and Sons, 1978.

Fulton, M. Jane and W.T. Stanbury. 'Comparative lobbying strategies in influencing health care policy'. *Canadian Public Administration* 28, 1985, 2 (269-300).

Gibbons, Kenneth M. and Donald C. Rowat. *Political Corruption in Canada: Cases, Causes and Cures*. Ottawa: Carleton, 1976.

Gifford, C.G. 'Grey is Strong'. *Policy Options*, October 1985 (16-17).

Gillies, James. *Where Business Fails: Business-Government Relations at the Federal Level in Canada*. Montreal: Institute for Research on Public Policy, 1981.

_____ and Jean Pigott. 'Participation in the Legislative Process'. *Canadian Public Administration* 25, 1982, 2 (254-64).

Glenn, H. Patrick. 'Class Actions in Ontario and Quebec'. *Canadian Bar Review* 62, 1984, 3 (247-77).

Goldstein, Jonah. 'Public Interest Groups and Public Policy: The Case of the Consumers' Association of Canada'. *Canadian Journal of Political Science* 16, 1979, (1).

Granatstein, G. *Marlborough Marathon: One Street Against a Developer*. Toronto: James Lewis and Samuel, 1971.

Gray, Charlotte. 'Friendly Persuasion'. *Saturday Night*, March 1983.

_____. 'How to be a Lobbyist'. *Chatelaine*, Nov. 1985 (104-6).

Grayson, L.M. and J. Paul Grayson. 'Interest Aggregation and Canadian Politics: The Case of the Central Bank'. *Canadian Public Administration* 16, 1973, 4 (557-72).

Groulx, L.H.J. 'L'action communautaire: diversité et ambiguité', *Canadian Journal of Political Science* VIII (1975) 510-19.

Guindon, Hubert. 'Social Unrest, Social Class and Quebec's Bureaucratic Revolution'. *Queen's Quarterly* 71, 1964, 2 (150-62).

de Guise, Jacques. 'Le colloque: une réflexion sur la relation Etat-citoyen'. *Recherches sociographiques* XVI, 1975, 3 (321-37).

Gunther, Peter E. 'The Atlantic Provinces Economic Council: Structure and Prospects'. *Canadian Business Review* 4, 1977, 4 (17-19).

Hagy, James William. 'Quebec Separatists: The First Twelve Years' in W.E. Mann, ed., *Social and Cultural Change in Canada*. Toronto: Copp Clark, 1970 (288-95).

Hamilton, Ian. *The Children's Crusade: The Story of the Company of Young Canadians*. Toronto: Peter Martin Associates, 1970.

Hannam, H.H. 'The Interest Group and its Activities'. *Proceedings of the Fifth Annual Conference, the Institute of Public Administration of Canada*. Toronto: IPAC, 1953 (171-81).

Hawkins, Freda. *Canada and Immigration: Public Policy and Public Concern*. Montreal: McGill-Queen's University Press, 1972.

Herscovici, Alan. *Second Nature: The Animal Rights Controversy*. Montreal: CBC Enterprises, 1985.

Hodgetts, J.E. 'Bureaucratic Initiative, Citizen Involvement and Administrative Accountability'. *Transactions of the Royal Society of Canada* Series IV, vol. XII, 1974 (227-36).

_____. 'The Civil Service and Policy Formation'. *Canadian Journal of Economics and Political Science* XXIII, 1957, 4 (467-79).

Hoffman, David. 'Interacting With Government: The General Public and Interest Groups' in Donald MacDonald, ed., *Politics in Ontario*. Toronto: Macmillan, 1975 (275-92).

Horowitz, Gad. *Canadian Labour in Politics*. Toronto: University of Toronto Press, 1968.

Hosek, Chaviva. 'Women and the Constitutional Process' in Keith Banting and Richard Simeon, *And No One Cheered: Federalism, Democracy and The Constitution Act*. Toronto: Methuen, 1983 (280-300).

Hudon, Raymond. 'Polarization and Depolarization of Quebec Political Parties' in Alain G. Gagnon, *Quebec: State and Society*. Toronto: Methuen, 1984 (314-30).

_____. 'La poursuite des fins organisationnelles par un groupe de pression: la CSN et les unités nationales de négociation dans l'affaire Lapalme (deux versions contradictoires)'. *Canadian Journal of Political Science* VII, 1974, 2 (328-33).

Hurl, L.F. 'Privatized Social Service Systems: Lessons from Ontario Children's Services'. *Canadian Public Policy* X, 1984 (395-406).

Ilgen, Thomas L. 'Between Europe and America, Ottawa and the Provinces: Regulating Toxic Substances in Canada'. *Canadian Public Policy* XI, 1985, 3 (578-90).

Isbister, Fraser. 'The CNTU Comes of Age' in W.E. Mann, ed., *Social and Cultural Change in Canada*. Toronto: Copp Clark, 1970 (261-74).

Islam, Nasir and Sadrudin A. Ahmed. 'Business influence on government: a comparison of public and private sector perceptions'. *Canadian Public Administration* 27, 1984, 1 (87-102).

Jacobs, Dorene E. 'The Annex Ratepayers' Association: Citizen's Efforts to Exercise Social Choice in Their Urban Environment' in James A. Draper, ed., *Citizen Participation: Canada*. Toronto: Copp Clark, 1970 (261-74).

Johnson, P.G. *The Union of Nova Scotia Municipalities*. Halifax: Dalhousie University. MA thesis. 1969.

_____. 'The Union of Nova Scotia Municipalities'. *Proceedings* Canadian Political Science Association. Winnipeg: June 1970.

Kealey, Linda, ed., *A Not Unreasonable Claim*. Toronto: The Women's Press, 1979.

Kearney, John. 'The Transformation of the Bay of Fundy Herring Fisheries, 1976-78: An Experiment in Fishermen-Government Co-Management' in Cynthia Lamson and Arthur J. Hanson, eds, *Atlantic Fisheries and Coastal Communities: Fisheries Decision-Making Case Studies*. Halifax: Dalhousie Ocean Studies Programme, 1984.

Kome, Penney. *Women of Influence: Canadian Women and Politics*. Toronto: Doubleday, 1985.

Kroeker, H.V., ed., *Sovereign People or Sovereign Governments*. Montreal: Institute for Research on Public Policy, 1981.

Kwavnick, David. 'Interest Group Demands and the Federal Political System: Two Canadian Case Studies' in A. Paul Pross, ed., *Pressure Group Behaviour in Canadian Politics*. Toronto: McGraw-Hill, 1975 (69-86).

_____. *Organized Labour and Pressure Politics: The Canadian Labour Congress, 1956-1968*. Montreal: McGill-Queen's University Press, 1972.

_____. 'Pressure Group Demands and Organizational Objectives: The CNTU, the Lapalme Affair, and National Bargaining Units'. *Canadian Journal of Political Science* VI, 1973, 4 (582-601).

_____. 'Pressure Group Demands and the Struggle for Organizational Status:

The Case of Organized Labour in Canada'. *Canadian Journal of Political Science* III, 1970, 1 (56-72).

Kyba, Patrick. 'Ballots and Burning Crosses: The Election of 1929' in Norman Ward and Duff Spafford, *Politics in Saskatchewan*. Don Mills: Longmans, 1968 (105-24).

La Breche, Julianne. 'The Quiet Persuaders of Parliament Hill'. *Financial Post Magazine* November 29, 1980.

Lamande, Yves. 'Le Membership d'une Association du 19ième siècle: Le cas de Longueuil (1857-1860)'. *Recherches sociographiques* XVI, 1975, 2 (219-41).

Lamson, Cynthia. *'Bloody Decks and a Bumper Crop': The Rhetoric of Sealing Counter-Protest*. St John's: Memorial University of Newfoundland. Institute for Social and Economic Research. 1979.

Land, Brian. *Directory of Associations in Canada*. Toronto: University of Toronto Press.

Lang, Ronald W. *The Politics of Drugs: The British and Canadian pharmaceutical industries and governments—A comparative study*. Farnborough: Saxon House, 1974.

Lawrie, N.J. 'The Canadian Construction Association: An Interest Group and its Environment'. Unpublished Ph.D. dissertation, University of Toronto, 1976.

Lemieux, F. 'Lobbying Plus . . . The CMA' in Paul Fox, ed., *Politics: Canada*. Toronto: McGraw-Hill, 1970.

Lemieux, V. 'Administration et publics: leur problème de communication'. *Recherches sociographiques* XVI, 1973, 3 (299-307).

Lenoski, J. Gerard. *Interest Groups and the Canadian Legislative Process: A Case Study of the Canada Water Act*. Ottawa: Carleton University, MA thesis, 1972.

Lipsig-Mumme, Carla. 'The Web of Dependence: Quebec Unions in Politics Before 1976' in Alain G. Gagnon, *Quebec: State and Society*. Toronto: Methuen, 1984 (286-313).

Litvak, Isaiah. 'The Lobbying Strategies of Business Interest Groups' in James D. Fleck, and Isaiah A. Litvak, eds, *Business Can Succeed! Understanding the Political Environment*. Toronto: Gage, 1984 (65-75).

————, and Christopher J. Maule. 'Interest-Group Tactics and the Politics of Foreign Investment: The Time-Reader's Digest Case Study'. *Canadian Journal of Political Science* VII, 1974, 4 (616-29).

Logan, Robert K., ed. *The Way Ahead for Canada: A Paperback Referendum*. Toronto: Lester and Orpen Dennys, 1977.

Loney, Martin. 'A political economy of citizen participation' in Leo Panitch, ed., *The Canadian State: Political Economy and Political Power*. Toronto: University of Toronto Press, 1977 (446-72).

Long, Anthony and Menno Boldt. 'Conformity Trap'. *Policy Options*, September 1984 (5-8).

McCalla, Douglas. 'The Commercial Policies of the Toronto Board of Trade, 1850-1860'. *The Canadian Historical Review*, 50, 1969 (51-67, 55).

MacDonald, A.A. *Policy Formation Process: Nova Scotia Dairy Marketing, 1933–1978*. Halifax: Dalhousie University Institute of Public Affairs, 1980.

Macdonald, Leslie T. *Taxing Comprehensive Income: Power and Participation in Canadian Politics, 1962-1972*. Ottawa: Carleton University. Ph.D. thesis. 1985.

Macdonald, R.D.S. 'Inshore Fishing Interests on the Atlantic Coast: Their Response to Extended Jurisdiction by Canada'. *Marine Policy*, July 1979 (171-89).

McGillivray, Don. 'Lobbying at Ottawa' in Paul Fox, ed., *Politics: Canada*. Toronto: McGraw-Hill, 1970 (163-72).

McKie, Craig. 'Some Views on Canadian Corporatism' in Christopher Beattie and Stewart Crysdale, eds, *Sociology Canada: Readings*, 2nd edition. Toronto: Butterworth, 1977 (226-40).

McLeod, J.M. 'The Corporatist Strain in Canadian Politics: The Invisible Fist'. Paper. The Conference on Canadian Political Ideas. York University, 1978.

MacNaughton, Bruce and Allan Gregg. 'Interest Group Influence in the Canadian Parliament'. Paper. CPSA. June 1977.

McNiven, J.D. *Evaluation of the Public Participation Programme Embodied in the Prince Edward Island Development Plan*. Halifax: Dalhousie University Institute of Public Affairs, 1974.

Mahon, Rianne. 'Canadian public policy: the unequal structure of representation' in Leo Panitch, ed., *The Canadian State: Political Economy and Political Power*. Toronto: University of Toronto Press, 1977 (164-98).

Malvern, Paul. *Persuaders: Lobbying, Influence Peddling and Political Corruption in Canada*. Toronto: Methuen, 1985.

Manzer, Ronald. 'Selective Inducements and the Development of Pressure Groups: The Case of Canadian Teachers' Associations'. *Canadian Journal of Economics and Political Science* II, 1969, 1 (103-18).

Martin, Andrew. 'The Politics of Employment and Welfare: National Policies and International Interdependence' in Keith Banting, Research Coordinator, *The State and Economic Interests*. Toronto: University of Toronto Press. The Collected Research Studies/Royal Commission on Economic Union and Development Prospects for Canada. No. 32, 1986 (157-241).

May, Elizabeth. 'Canada's Moth War: Cape Breton Islanders Break a Multi-National'. *New Ecologist*, July-August 1978 (115-20).

_____. *Budworm Battles*. Halifax: Four East Publications, 1982.

Meisel, John. 'Recent Changes in Canadian Parties' in Hugh G. Thorburn, ed., *Party Politics in Canada*. Scarborough: Prentice-Hall, 1967 (33-54).

Menard, Johanne. 'L'Institut des Artisans du Comté de Drummond, 1856-1890'. *Recherches sociographiques* XVI, 1975, 2 (207-19).

Meynaud, Jean. 'Groupes de pression et politique gouvernementale au Quebec' in André Bernard, ed., *Réflexions sur la politique au Quebec*. Montréal: Sainte Marie, 1968 (69-96).

Milner, Henry. 'Quebec Educational Reform and the Protestant School Establishment' in Alain G. Gagnon, *Quebec: State and Society*. Toronto: Methuen, 1984 (410-26).

Mooney, George S. 'The Canadian Federation of Mayors and Municipalities: Its Role and Function'. *Canadian Public Administration* 3, 1960 (82-92).

Munroe, Cathy and Jim Stewart. *Fishermen's Organizations in Nova Scotia—the Potential for Unification*. Halifax: School of Public Administration, 1981.

Munton, Don. *Groups and Governments in Canadian Foreign Policy. Proceedings of a Conference. Ottawa. 1982*. Toronto: Canadian Institute for International Affairs, 1985.

Nelson, J.G. 'Public participation in comprehensive resource and environmental management'. *Science and Public Policy*, Oct. 1982 (240-50).

Niosi, Jorge. *Canadian Capitalism: A Study of Power in the Canadian Business Establishment*. Toronto: James Lorimer, 1981.

Nord, Douglas C. 'MPs and Senators as Middlemen: The special Joint Committee on Immigration Policy' in Clarke *et al.*, *Parliament, Policy and Representation*. Toronto: Methuen, 1980 (181-94).

Olley, Robert E. 'The Canadian Consumer Movement: Basis and Objectives'. *Canadian Business Review* 4, 1977, 4 (26-9).

O'Neill, T.J. *Educator, Advocate and Critic: APEC's 25 Years*. Halifax: Atlantic Provinces Economic Council, 1979.

Ouellet, F. *Histoire de la Chambre de Commerce de Québec, 1809–1959*. Québec: Université Laval, 1959.

Palda, Kristian S. 'Does Canada's Election Act Impede Voters' Access to Information'. *Canadian Public Policy* XI, 1985, 3 (533-42).

Paltiel, Khayyam Z. 'The changing environment and role of special interest groups'. *Canadian Public Administration* 25, 1982, 2 (198-210).

Panitch, Leo. 'The Development of Corporatism in Liberal Democracies'. *Comparative Political Studies* XI, 1977, 1 (61-90).

_____. 'Corporatism in Canada?' in Richard Schultz, Orest M. Kruhlak, John C. Terry, *The Canadian Political Process*. Toronto: Holt, Rinehart and Winston, 1979 (53-72).

_____. 'Recent Theorizations of Corporatism'. *British Journal of Sociology* XXXI, 1980, 2 (159-88).

_____. 'The Tripartite Experience' in Keith Banting, Research Coordinator, *The State and Economic Interests*. Toronto: University of Toronto Press. The Collected Research Studies/Royal Commission on Economic Union and Development Prospects for Canada. No. 32, 1986 (35-120).

Pappert, Anne. 'A New Life on Lease: The Tenant Fight for Rental Rights is Paying Off'. *Financial Post Magazine*, June 1985 (25).

Parke, Chris. 'The Setting of Minimum Wage Policy in the Maritimes'. Halifax: Dalhousie Institute of Public Affairs, 1980.

Parliamentary Government. 'Committees, MPs and Witnesses'. *Parliamentary Government* 3, 1982 (4).

_____. 'The Committee Track Record: A limited Pay-off'. *Parliamentary Government* 3, 1983 (4 ,7-10, 9).

Pigott, Jean and G. Drewry. 'Parliament and hanging: further episodes in an undying saga'. *Parliamentary Affairs* 27, 1974, 3 (251-61).

Pinard, Yolande and Marie Lavigne, eds. *Travailleuses et féministes*. Montréal: Boreal Express, 1983.

Ponting, J.R. and R. Gibbins. *Out of Irrelevance: A socio-political introduction to Indian Affairs in Canada*. Toronto: Butterworth, 1980.

Presthus, Robert. *Elite Accommodations in Canadian Politics*. Toronto: Macmillan, 1973.

_____. *Elites in the Policy Process*. Toronto: MacMillan, 1974.

_____. 'Interest Groups and the Canadian Parliament: Activities, Interaction, Legitimacy, and Influence'. *Canadian Journal of Political Science* IV, 1971, 4 (444-60).

_____. 'Interest Groups and Lobbying: Canada and the United States'. *The Annals of the American Academy of Political and Social Science* 413, 1974 (44-57).

Pross, A. Paul. 'The Development of Professions in the Public Service: The Foresters in Ontario'. *Canadian Public Administration* X, 1967, 3 (376-404).

_____. 'Governing Under Pressure: Summary of Discussions'. *Canadian Public Administration* 25, 1982 (170-83).

_____. 'Parliamentary Influence and the Diffusion of Power'. *Canadian Journal of Political Science* XVIII, 1985, 2 (235-66).

_____, ed. *Pressure Group Behaviour in Canadian Politics*. Toronto: McGraw-Hill, 1975.

_____. 'Pressure Groups: Talking Chameleons' in Michael S. Whittington and Glenn Williams, *Canada in the 1980s*. Toronto: Methuen, 1984.

_____. 'Space, Function and Interest in the Canadian State' in O.P. Dwivedi, ed., *The Administrative State in Canada*. Toronto: University of Toronto Press, 1982 (107-29).

_____. 'From System to Serendipity: The Practice and Study of Public Policy in the Trudeau Years'. *Canadian Public Administration* 25, 1982, (4).

Pyrcz, Greg. 'Pressure Groups' in T.C. Pocklington, *Liberal Democracy in Canada and the United States: An Introduction to Politics and Government*. Toronto: Holt, Rinehart, 1985.

Quebec. La conférence au sommet Québec, 1982, *Rapport*. Québec: Editeur officiel de Quebec, 1982.

Redekop, John H. 'Mennonites and Politics in Canada and the United States'. *Journal of Mennonite Studies* I, 1983 (1).

Salter, Liora. 'Observations on the Politics of Assessment: The Captan Case'. *Canadian Public Policy* XI, 1985, 1 (64-76).

Sanders, Douglas. 'The Indian Lobby' in Keith Banting and Richard Simeon, *And No One Cheered: Federalism, Democracy and The Constitution Act*. Toronto: Methuen, 1983 (301-33).

Savage, Donald C. 'Freedom of Information Legislation and the University Community'. *CAUT Bulletin*. (Canadian Association of University Teachers) February 1985 (5-6).

Schwartz, Mildred A. *The Environment for Policy-Making in Canada and the United States*. Montreal: C.D. Howe Institute, 1981.

_____. 'Politics and Moral Causes in Canada and the United States'. *Comparative Social Research* 4, 1981 (65-90).

Schwartz, Mildred A. 'Group Basis of Politics' in John H. Redekop, ed., *Approaches to Canadian Politics*. Scarborough: Prentice-Hall, 1978.

Senior, Hereward. 'Orangeism in Ontario Politics, 1872–1896' in Donald Swainson, ed., *Oliver Mowat's Ontario*. Toronto: Macmillan, 1972 (136-53).

Sewell, John. *Up Against City Hall*. Toronto: James Lewis and Samuel, 1972.

Sharp, P.F. *Agrarian Revolt in Western Canada*. Minneapolis: University of Minnesota Press, 1948.

Simeon, Richard. *Federal-Provincial Diplomacy: The Making of Recent Policy in Canada*. Toronto: University of Toronto Press, 1973 (144-5; see also 280-3).

Skogstad, Grace. 'Interest Groups, Representation and Conflict Management in the Standing Committees of the House of Commons'. *Canadian Journal of Political Science* XVIII, 1985, 4 (739-73).

Slayton, M. and Michael Trebilcock. *The Professions and Public Policy*. Toronto: University of Toronto Press, 1978.

Smith, Larry. 'Getting Your Way With a Bureaucrat'. *Canadian Business*, September 1980.

Splane, Richard B. *Social Welfare in Ontario, 1791–1893*. Toronto: University of Toronto Press, 1965.

Sproule-Jones, Mark and Patricia L. Richards. 'Toward a Theory of the Regulated Environment'. *Canadian Public Policy* x, 1984, 3 (305-16).

Stairs, Denis. 'Public and Policy-Makers: The Domestic Environment of Canada's Foreign Policy Community'. *International Journal*, 1970–71, (221-48).

Stanbury, W.T. *Business-Government Relations in Canada*. Toronto: Methuen, 1986.

_____. *Business Interests and the Reform of Canadian Competition Policy, 1971–75*. Toronto: Methuen, 1977.

_____. 'Lobbying and Interest Group Representation in the Legislative Process' in W.A.W. Neilson and J.C. Macpherson, eds, *The Legislative Process in Canada*. Montreal: Institute for Research in Public Policy, 1978 (167-226).

_____. 'Regulation and the Redistribution of Wealth'. *Canadian Public Administration* 26, 1983, 3 (378-401).

Stanfield, Robert L. 'The Fifth George C. Nowlan Lecture', Acadia University, 7 Feb. 1977 (mimeo.).

Swettenham, John and David Kealy. *Serving the State: A History of the Professional Institute of the Public Service of Canada, 1920–1970*. Ottawa: The Institute, 1970.

Tanguay, Brian. 'Concerted Action in Quebec, 1976–1983: Dialogue of the Deaf' in Alain G. Gagnon, *Quebec: State and Society*. Toronto: Methuen, 1984 (365-86).

Tanner, Adrian, ed., *The Politics of Indianness: Case Studies of Native Ethnopolitics in Canada*. St John's: Memorial University of Newfoundland. Institute of Social and Economic Research. 1983.

Taylor, Malcolm G. 'Quebec medicare: policy formulation in conflict and crisis'. *Canadian Public Administration* 15, 1972, 2 (211-50).

_____. 'The Role of the Medical Profession in the Formulation of Public Policy'. *Canadian Journal of Economics and Political Science* xxvi, 1960, 1 (108-27).

Teichman, Judith. 'Businessmen and Politics in the Process of Economic Development: Argentina and Canada'. *Canadian Journal of Political Science* xv, 1982, 1 (47-66).

Thompson, Fred and W.T. Stanbury. 'Looking Out for No. 1: Incumbency and Interest Group Politics'. *Canadian Public Policy* x, 1984, 2 (239-45).

_____. *The Political Economy of Interest Groups in the Legislative Process in Canada*. Montreal: Institute for Research on Public Policy, 1979 (vii).

Thorburn, Hugh G. *Interest Groups and the Canadian Federal System*. Toronto: University of Toronto Press. Collected research studies/Royal Commission on the Economic Union and Development Prospects for Canada. No. 69. 1985.

_____. *Planning and the Economy: Building Federal-Provincial Consensus*. Ottawa: Canadian Institute for Economic Policy, 1984.

_____. 'Pressure Groups in Canadian Politics: Recent Revisions of the Anti-Combines Legislation'. *Canadian Journal of Economics and Political Science* xxx, 1964, 2 (157-74).

Torrance, Judy. 'The Response of Canadian Governments to Violence'. *Canadian Journal of Political Science* x, 1977, 3 (473-96).

_____. *Public Violence in Canada, 1867–1982*. Montreal: McGill-Queen's University Press, 1986.

Trebilcock, M.J., R.S. Pritchard, D.G. Hartle, and D.N. Dewees. *The Choice of Governing Instrument*. Ottawa: Economic Council in Canada, 1982.

Townson, Frank W. 'The Labour Federations as Pressure Groups' in Donald C. Rowat, ed., *Provincial Government and Politics: Comparative Essays*. Ottawa: Department of Political Science, 1972 (495-520).

Trofimenkoff, Susan Mann and Alison Prentice, eds. *The Neglected Majority*. Toronto: McClelland and Stewart, 1977.

Tuohy, Carolyn J. 'Pluralism and Corporatism in Ontario Medical Politics' in K.J. Rea and J.T. McLeod, eds, *Business and Government in Canada: Selected Readings* 2nd edition. Toronto: Methuen, 1976 (395-413).

_____. 'Private Government, Property and Professionalism'. *Canadian Journal of Political Science* IX, 1976, 4 (668-81).

Verney, Douglas V. 'The Role of the Private Social Research Council of Canada in the Formation of Public Science Policy, 1968–1974'. *Canadian Public Policy* I, 1975, 1.

Waterman, A.M.C. 'The Catholic Bishops and Canadian Public Policy'. *Canadian Public Policy* IX, 1983, 3 (374-82).

Waterman, A.M.C. 'The Catholic Bishops and Canadian Public Policy: A Reply'. *Canadian Public Policy* X, 1984, 3 (338-9).

Weaver, Sally M. 'The Joint Cabinet/National Indian Brotherhood Committee: a unique experiment in pressure group relations'. *Canadian Public Administration* 25, 1982, 2 (211-39).

_____. *Making Canadian Indian Policy*. Toronto: University of Toronto Press, 1981.

_____. 'Federal Policy-Making for Métis and Non-status Indians in the Context of Native Policy'. *Canadian Ethnic Studies* XVII, 1985, 2 (80-102).

Weir, R.A. 'Federalism, Interest Groups and Parliamentary Government: The Canadian Medical Association'. *Journal of Comparative Political Studies* XI, 1973, 2 (159-75).

Welch, Susan. 'Dimensions of Political Participation in a Canadian Sample'. *Canadian Journal of Political Science* VIII, 1975, 4 (553-9).

West, James V. *Public Interest Groups and the Judicial Process in Canada: The Need for a More Realistic Jurisprudence*. Ottawa: Carleton University. Department of Political Science. Occasional Papers. No. 5, 1979.

White, Terrence H. 'Canadian Labour and International Unions in the Seventies' in S.D. Clark, J. Paul Grayson, and Linda M. Grayson, eds, *Prophecy and Protest: Social Movements in Twentieth-Century Canada*. Toronto: Gage, 1975 (288-305).

Wilkinson, B.W. 'The Catholic Bishops and Canadian Public Policy: A Comment'. *Canadian Public Policy* X, 1981, 1 (88-92).

Young, Brian J. 'C. George McCullagh and the Leadership League' in Ramsay Cook, ed., *The Politics of Discontent*. Toronto: University of Toronto Press, 1967.

Young, R.A. 'Planning for Power: The New Brunswick Electric Power Commission in the 1950's'. *Acadiensis* XII, 1982, 1 (73-100).

Yudelman, David. *Canadian Mineral Policy Formulation: A Case Study of the Adversarial Process*. Kingston, Ontario. Queen's University. Centre for Resource Studies. Working Paper No. 30, 1984.

Index

abortion issue, 162–3
academic associations, 223, 139, 144–5, 197
ACCESS (A Citizen's Committee for the Right to Public Information) 90, 153
access, to policy-makers, 61, 109, 129, 131, 134, 165, 167, 208, 256, 261, 270
action-oriented messages: *see* pressure group communications, content
adaptive capacity of groups: *see* pressure groups, adaptiveness
advertising, by pressure groups, 9, 156–7, 162–4
advisory boards, 3, 9, 52, 69, 103, 116, 134, 146, 152, 198, 267
agency-group relations: *see* pressure group-agency relations
aggregation of interests, 11, 43, 87, 107, 214, 231, 244
agriculture, as policy field, 101–2, 112–13, 116
Agriculture, federal Department of, 56, 67, 102, 223
Alberta Environment Trust, 94
alliances between groups, 90, 118, 144, 145–9 *passim*, 153, 167, 222–3, 224
Amnesty International, 170
analysis of pressure groups, 13, 14, 16, 108, 114, 127, 128, 129, 229, 245, 272–4
animal rights groups, 126
Anti-Inflation Program, 3, 218
anti-pluralists, 228, 231–4
anti-poverty groups, 200–1
Arctic International Wildlife Range, 65
articulation of interests, 11, 13, 87, 107, 114–15, 123
Assembly of First Nations, 7
Atlantic Provinces Economic Council, 89, 252
attentive public, 98, 104, 105, 113, 132, 134, 149–54, 245, 246, 272; defined, 99
attitude groups, 127
Auditor-General, 73
Australia, pressure groups, 124, 126
Automotive Parts Manufacturers' Association of Canada, 152, 156

Bacchi, Laura, 85
Bachrach, P., 235
Baldwin, Ged, 153
Baratz, M., 235
Bay of Fundy Herring Co-op, 197
Beaufort Environmental Assessment Panel, 65
Beck, J.M., 39, 53
Bégin, Monique, 197, 251
benevolent associations, 81
Bennett, R.B., 38, 169
Bentley, A., 13, 228–9, 231–2, 234
Biafra, 117, 118, 119, 196
bilingualism and biculturalism, 7
boards of trade, 28, 29, 38, 81; Halifax, colonial commercial interests, 20, 25; Toronto Board of Trade, 28, 29, 30; Vancouver Board of Trade, 35
boycott, 157
Britain, lobbying by Canadian groups, 170
Britain, pressure groups, 20, 25, 60, 76, 84, 85, 86, 110, 127, 130, 211, 212, 238, 241, 255; influence on Canadian groups, 31
British Columbia, government of, 3
British Columbia Employers' Council, 224
British North America Act, 102
Brown, Douglas, 219, 224
Bryce, R.B., 55
Bucovetsky, M.W., 165
budgetary process, impact of reform on distribution of power, 66, 111; impact on pressure groups, 90, 143
Bulloch, John, 64, 75, 186, 187, 257
bureaucracy: decline in legitimacy, 71, 72, 73–4, 221–2, 243, 257–8; policy role, 16, 21, 24, 39, 40, 41, 46, 56, 133–4, 165, 166, 184, 209, 213, 248, 254, 255, 257
bureaucratic methods, impact on pressure groups, 37, 41–2, 45, 52, 60, 134
bureaucratic mores, 56–7, 140, 143, 146–7, 151–2, 174
bureaucratic organization, impact on pressure groups, 30, 40–1, 42, 80, 108, 110, 111, 112, 113–14, 137, 138–9, 140, 146, 174

bureaucratic pluralism, 70
business community, 26, 64, 81, 125, 161, 167
Business Council on National Issues, 92, 127, 144, 145, 161, 224
business-interest associations, 26, 28, 29, 34, 47, 92, 116, 125, 130, 159, 166, 178, 191, 195, 197, 235, 240
businessmen's clubs, 37

Cabinet, 1, 3, 9, 21, 35, 51–2, 54, 66, 72–3, 81, 97, 107, 110, 132, 133, 134, 135, 136, 137, 155, 241, 248; decline in legitimacy of, 71–4, 221, 257
Cairns, A.C., 166
calculus of participation, 128, 181, 182
'Canada Committees' (federal Department of Agriculture), 102
Canadian Agricultural Chemicals Association, 102
Canadian Agricultural Services Co-ordinating Committee, 102
Canadian Almanac and Directory, 62
Canadian Arctic Resources Committee, 65, 198
Canadian Association of Broadcasters, 75
Canadian Association of Equipment Distributors, 64
Canadian Association of University Teachers, 64, 90, 153, 178
Canadian Automobile Association, 122
Canadian Bankers' Association, 145
Canadian Bar Association, 76, 90, 153, 184, 259
Canadian Brotherhood of Railway Transport and General Workers, 214
Canadian Business, 124, 140
Canadian Cancer Institute, 181
Canadian Cattlemen's Association, 116
Canadian Citizenship Council, 68
Canadian Civil Liberties Association, 87, 122
Canadian Club (Toronto), 137
Canadian Confederation of Mayors and Municipalities, 106
Canadian Construction Association, 20, 44, 111, 192, 202
Canadian Council for Urban and Regional Research, 199
Canadian Daily Newspaper Publishers' Association, 162
Canadian Egg and Poultry Council, 113
Canadian Egg Marketing Agency, 113
Canadian Egg Producers' Council, 113

Canadian Environmental Law Association, 94
Canadian Environmental Law Research Foundation, 171
Canadian Federation of Agriculture, 42, 44, 61, 113, 116, 123, 132, 136, 223
Canadian Federation of Independent Business, 64, 75, 118, 127, 145, 161, 186, 224
Canadian Fertilizer Institute, 185
Canadian Hatchery Association, 113
Canadian Holocaust Remembrance Association, 171
Canadian Home Builders' Association, 94
Canadian Importers' Association, 64
Canadian Institute of International Affairs, 105, 152
Canadian Institute of Public Opinion, 76
Canadian Institute of Real Estate Companies, 64
Canadian institutes, 26, 27
Canadian International Development Agency, 124
Canadian Labour Congress, 136, 193, 214, 218, 225
Canadian Library Association, 90, 113, 153, 203
Canadian Life Insurance Officers' Association, 111
Canadian Manufacturers' Association, 20, 38–9, 43, 52, 92, 125, 127, 128, 136, 161, 167, 169, 224
Canadian Masonry Contractors' Association, 94
Canadian Medical Association, 75, 128
Canadian Nature Federation, 65
Canadian Parents for French, 12
Canadian Petroleum Association, 156
Canadian Pharmaceutical Manufacturers' Association, 111, 190, 195
Canadian Political Science Association, 139, 203, 223
Canadian Poultry and Egg Producers' Council, 113
Canadian Real Estate Association, 125
Canadian Soap and Detergent Association, 195
Canadian Suffrage Association, 86
Canadian Tax Foundation, 145
Canadian Transport Commission, 181
Canadian Trucking Association, 139
Canadian University Service Overseas, 124
Canadian Wildlife Federation, 7, 177–8
caucus, 136, 160, 251–2, 259

Central Mortgage and Housing Corporation, 106

central policy institutions, 9, 35–6, 45, 46, 66, 150, 220–3, 244, 273–4; access to, 66–7; lobbying of, 66, 134–7; problems of reform in, 66, 72

Chamber of Commerce, 38, 92, 126, 136, 161, 162

Chant, Donald, 124, 188, 189

charitable associations, 26, 28, 30, 94

charitable foundations, 196

charitable society, tax status, 246, 269

chemical industry associations, 185, 190, 224

Children's Aid Societies, 28, 94

Citizenship Branch, 68

civil rights movement, 232

Civil Service Act (Canada, 1912, 1918), 51

Clark, Clifford, 40, 42, 52

Clark, S.D., 39, 43, 52

Clarke, Harold D., 76

class actions, 173

class struggle, 215, 218, 231–2

coercion, 130, 184

Coleman, William D., 14, 102, 103, 129, 185, 190, 195, 219, 224

collective action, 128, 182

collective benefits, 128, 177–9, 180, 182, 184

collectivism, 227

Columbia University, Canadian Studies Program, 152

Combines Investigation Branch, 125

committees of inquiry, 62

Communications, Department of, 139

Company of Young Canadians, 122

competition policy, 79, 92

concertation, 212

conferences, function of, 105, 152, 158

conflict, level of, 107, 135, 147, 155, 168, 235–6, 237, 242, 244, 256

confrontation, 140, 143, 149, 189, 240

Conseil d'hygiène publique (Québec), 33

Conseil de l'agriculture (Québec), 33

Conseil du Patronat (Québec), 224–5

consensus management, 236–7, 238–9, 240, 245, 246

consensus-seeking activity, 61, 74, 105, 147, 150, 215, 235, 239–40, 241, 242

Constitution Act (1982), including references to Charter of Rights, 20, 79, 163, 172

Consumer and Corporate Affairs, Department of, 125, 262, 265

consumer groups, 5, 64, 125

consumer interests, 92, 102–3

consumer movement, 7, 21, 64, 182

Consumer's Association of Canada, 7, 44, 54, 144, 180, 181, 202

continuum framework: see institutional continuum

coon dog issue, 90

corporatism, 12, 14, 97, 211, Chapter 9, 227, 238, 244, 248; defined, 213–14, Marxist approach, 215

corruption, 51, 53, 130, 131, 211

Corry, J.A., 2, 183, 230

Cotret, Robert de, 219

Council of Maritime Premiers, 89, 166, 167

courts, 165, 170–3

Cover Your Ass, 74

Crenson, M., 235

Criminal Code, 78, 171

Crossman, Richard, 97

Crow rate, 79, 166, 251

Dahl, Robert, 232

Dairy Commission, 102

Dairy Farmers of Canada, 116

Dawson, Helen Jones, 54, 56, 60–1, 123, 180, 202, 225

Dawson, R. MacGregor, 1

Defence, Department of National, policy community associated with, 106

delegated legislation, 210, 254–5

demonstrations, 156

Deutsch, John, 40

Devaux, B., 122

Devaux, K., 122

Devoir, Le, 224

Diefenbaker, John, 66

diffusion of power, 17, 24, 40, 45, 46, 63, 66, 67, 71, 73, 75, 76, 81, 110, 132, 157, 159, 165, 171, 188, 211, 221, 241, 243–4, 245, 257, 260, 271, 272

Dion, Léon, 183, 223

Directory of Associations in Canada, 62

Duplessis, Maurice, 38, 217

Eastern Fishermen's Federation, 196, 197, 223

Eastman, J., 219, 224

Eckstein, Harry, 85, 127

Economic Council of Canada, 9, 10, 11, 138, 218, 223

economic development: impact on pressure groups, 33–5, 39, 44, 45, 80; role of state, 21, 30, 40, 46, 47, 48–50, 94, 166, 215, 243, 249–50

efficacy, 182

Eggleston, Wilfrid, 55
Ehrmann, Henry W., 84
Elections Act (Canada), 161-5, 171
élite accommodation, 1, 5, 13, 25, 37, 40,
    84, 229, 232; comparison between
    Canada and the United States, 13, 84; in
    colonial period, 25
Elizabeth Fry Society, 181-2
End of Liberalism, The, 233
Energy and Chemical Workers' Union, 191
Energy Mines and Resources, Department
    of, 98, 185
Energy Probe, 65
Engelmann, Frederick, 13, 110
'Enterprise 77', 218
Environment, Department of, 65, 69, 139;
    encouragement of pressure groups, 68
environmental groups, 86-7, 103, 119, 128,
    169, 171, 264
environmental movement, 7, 64, 104, 126,
    188
environmental policy, 104, 126, 155
ethnic groups, 7, 21, 115
Europe: pressure group activity, 170; state-
    group relations, 97, 197, 214-15, 228,
    238
executive, communication with the, 134-7
Executive Consultants Limited, 135-6
Expert Committee on Pesticide Use in
    Agriculture, 102
Expert Committee on Weeds, 102
'Expert Committees', federal Department of
    Agriculture, 102
expressive groups, 128
External Affairs, Department of, 103, 105,
    117, 119, 196; foreign policy review, 105
external influence on Canadian domestic
    policy, 169-170

farm groups, 102
Faulkner, J. Hugh, 62, 65, 68, 71
federalism, impact on pressure groups, 110,
    139, 165, 225, 241
Ferguson, G. Howard, 36, 37
Finance, Department of, 67, 135, 145, 222
Financial Post, 159
financial resources of groups, 194-201,
    266-70; see also pressure group resources
Finer, S.E., 84, 85, 86, 127
Fingard, Judith, 32
First Ministers' Conference, 107, 165, 244
Fisheries and Oceans, Department of, 95
Fisheries Council of Canada, 88, 91
Fisheries, Department of, 67, 91
fisheries policy, 103

fishermen's associations, 90, 95
fishery, pressure group communications, 91
fishing interests, 69, 88, 95, 130, 136, 223
fledgeling groups, 64, 116, 120-1 (Table
    5-1), 122, 246
food policy process, 102, 116
Forbes, J.D., 102, 116
forest interests, 32-3
forest policy, 47, 48, 104
Forestry Chronicle, 68
Forestry Development Board, 68
forestry movement, 31, 170
forestry profession, support for Forestry
    Branch, 68
France, pressure groups, 20, 76, 85, 86,
    110, 122, 183-4, 212, 257
Franklin, Grace A., 236
fraternal associations, 27, 28, 30, 81
freedom of information, 153
fruit growers' associations, 32; Guelph
    Agricultural College, 32
functional constituency, 43, 133, 210, 211
functions of pressure groups, 4, 15-16,
    17, 25-6, 27, 42, 43, 79-80, 81, 84, 87,
    88, 95-6, 107, 176; administration, 14,
    42, 84, 87, 88, 93-5, 96, 176;
    communication, 4, 9, 14, 27, 52, 84, 87,
    88-92, 96, 107, 113, 114, Chapters 6 and
    7, 208, 240, 256; communication between
    governments, 89, 165-6; communication
    between groups, 90, 151; communication
    within government, 89; communication
    with special publics, 88, 146; interest
    promotion, 3, 9, 15, 27, 28, 84, 87, 88,
    96, 109, 128-9, 145; legitimation, 14, 43,
    69, 70, 78, 84, 87, 88, 92-3, 96, 105,
    107, 132, 140, 142, 146, 148, 153, 156,
    158, 165, 176, 241, 244, 256; regulation,
    14, 84, 87, 88, 93-5, 96, 176; systemic
    functions, 88-95, 129

Galbraith, John Kenneth, 49, 238
Gamble, Don, 198
Germany, pressure groups, 122
Gillies, James, 255
Glenn, H. Patrick, 173
Goddard, Arthur, 76
Golden, Aubrey, 162
Goodin, Robert E., 238-9
Gotlieb, Allan, 169
Gourley, Robert, 25
governability, 220
government, expansion of activities, 40, 63,
    139
government, growth of, 63, 71, 73

government agencies, policy role of line
agencies, 3, 66, 67, 133, 211; problems
of co-ordination, 66; vested interest in
programs and jurisdiction, 165
Governmental Process, The, 13, 231
government encouragement of pressure
groups, 9, 16, 20, 42, 44, 45, 52, 65, 68,
74, 91-2, 93, 119, 133, 212, 244,
266-70, 273; consultation processes, 65;
core funding, 65, 196-7; funding, 9, 12,
69, 196-201, 266-70; positional policies,
12, 44-5, 69, 119, 137, 146, 191-2, 193,
267; regulatory policies, 44, 65, 69;
rhetorical encouragement, 65; secondment
of personnel, 196-7, 270
government liaison officers, 65
Government of Canada, The, 1
Gow, J. Iain, 255
Grain Act (Canada, 1912), 38
Green Paper on Immigration, 77, 78
Green Party, 122
Greenpeace, 103, 126, 170, 181
Guise, Jacques de, 50
gun control issue, 77, 161

Hamel, Jean-Marc, (Chief Electoral
Officer), 162-5 *passim*
Hannam, H.H., 42, 52
Hanson, A.H., 255-6, 258
Hawkins, Freda, 94
Health and Welfare, Department of, 98,
139, 197
Heeney, A.D.P., 55
Heilbroner, R., 238
Hepburn, Mitchell, 38, 112
Herring, Pendleton, 231
Hockin, Tom, 79
Hoffman, David, 189
Holleaux, André, 43, 183
House of Commons, Committee on Justice
and Legal Affairs, 78
Howe, C.D., 55
How to Fight for What's Right, 170

ideology, 118, 190, 216, 217, 225, 227
Indian and Northern Affairs, Department of,
98
Indian-Eskimo Association, 122
Indian groups, 3, 7, 69, 122, 126, 170
Industry and Humanity, 217
Industry, Trade and Commerce, Department
of, 10, 44, 67, 218
information flow, 56, 134, 146, 148, 160,
204, 261, 267
information monopolies, 186

Inspector of Prisons and Asylums (Ontario),
28, 44
Institute for Research on Public Policy, 152
Institute of Association Executives, 62, 205
Institute of Canadian Advertising, 125
Institute of Public Administration of
Canada, 55, 56, 95
institutional continuum, 108, 114, 120-1,
125, 127, 129, 188, 213
institutional incentives to join pressure
groups, 184
institutionalization of groups, 38, 42, 62,
64, 80, 114, 117-27, 138, 190, 225, 229
institutionalized pressure groups, 1, 8, 21,
26, 38, 41, 62, 64, 98, 104, 107, 112,
114-16, 118, 119, 120-1 (Diagram 5-1),
122, 124, 126, 184, 188, 190, 192, 194,
199, 204, 213, 225, 240, 246, 258
interdepartmental committees, 132
intergovernmental conferences, 155, 168,
248
intergovernmental relations, 76, 165-8,
243, 244-5
International Fund for Animal Welfare, 126,
170
International Labour Organization, 103
international organizations, participation in
policy communities, 31, 103, 168
Investment Dealers' Association, 161
'iron triangles', 97, 236, 239-240
issue-oriented groups, 25, 64, 104, 105,
107, 111-12, 114, 117-19, 120-1 (Table
5-1), 122, 126, 127, 129, 178, 184, 185,
189, 190, 194, 213, 246, 265, 266

Jacek, Henry J., 14, 102, 103, 185, 190,
195, 219, 224
Japan Automobile Manufacturers'
Association, 152
John Howard Society, 181
Joint Cabinet-National Indian Brotherhood
committee, 126, 192
Jordan, G., 238, 239
journals, specialized, function in policy
community, 105
journals, trade, 196
junior officials, 133, 187

Key, V.O., 177, 231
King, Mackenzie, 37, 217
Kirk, David, 132
knowledge: as a resource of groups,
185-91; substantive policy, 134, 145,
185-7, 235; *see also* policy process
knowledge

Kornberg, Allan, 76
Kwavnick, David C., 147, 191, 225

Labour, Department of, 56, 69
labour movement, 39, 42, 116, 170, 188,
    195, 217, 218, 235
La Breche, Julianne, 144–5
Lalonde, Marc, 197
latent interests, 8, 30, 65, 68, 113, 176,
    228, 230; concern to policy-makers, 6;
    defined, 5–6
Laurier, Sir Wilfred, 35
Lawrie, N.J., 202
lead agency, 99, 103, 105, 131, 134, 136,
    137–45, 152, 241
leadership, in pressure groups, 7, 10, 13,
    109, 115, 119, 146, 150, 180, 186, 190,
    191, 193, 198, 199, 201–5, 235
LeBlanc, Romeo, 44, 91
legislative spokesmen, 160–1
legislatures, private members, 34–5, 43–4,
    50, 145, 160, 187–8, 250–1, 262; role in
    policy process, 16, 24, 50, 53, 60, 72,
    110, 211, 218–19
legitimating institutions, search for, 46,
    71–9, 140, 142, 250, 257
legitimating messages: see pressure group
    communications, content
Lemieux, Vincent, 43
liberal ideology, 231, 238
liberal individualism, 227, 231
line agencies, resistance to co-ordinative
    role of central policy agencies, 67
litigation, 132, 170–3, 269; costs of, 131,
    171–2
Litvak, Isaiah, 156
lobbying, 3, 34–5, 53, 55, 65, 80, 125, 131,
    132, 134–5, 143, 178, 187, 194; see also
    pressure group tactics.
Lobbying: A Right? A Necessity? A
    Danger?, 2
Lobbying and the Registration of Paid
    Lobbyists, 262
lobbyists, 2, 14, 56, 131, 133, 135, 140–5,
    160, 198, 255; regulation of, 2, 14,
    262–6, 273
local influence, 35–8, 41, 111
local pressure groups, 30, 31–2, 38, 41, 45,
    171, 225; direct communication with
    public, 157
Logic of Collective Action, The, 177
Lowi, Theodore, 230, 233, 234, 245

McCullagh, George, 111
MacDonald, Flora, 73

Machinery and Equipment Manufacturers'
    Association, 94
McIlraith, George, 55
MacIver, R.M., 232
Mackenzie Valley Pipeline (Berger) Inquiry,
    65, 128, 156, 197, 200
Mackintosh, W.A., 40, 55
MacLean, A.K., 44
Maclean's, 161
McLeod, Jack, 216–17
Macridis, Roy C., 129
management of groups, 119, 201–5
mandarins, 40, 53, 55, 56, 60, 61, 70, 72,
    110, 118, 141, 241, 256
mandate, of pressure groups, 149, 191–4,
    208, 246–7
Manzer, Ronald, 7
marketing boards, 102, 240
Marxist critique of Bentley, 231–2
material benefit groups, 128, 270
Mather, Barry, 262
mature groups, 116, 120 (Diagram 5–1),
    122
mechanics' institutes, 26–7, 29
media, 56, 62, 64, 78, 105, 118, 122–3,
    131, 135, 143, 151, 154, 155, 156, 157,
    158, 159, 168, 174, 219, 235, 246
Medical Research Council of Canada, 144
Meisel, John, 1
membership of groups, 9, 10, 11, 12, 15,
    109, 115, 117, 119, 122–3, 126, 146,
    176–81, 189–90, 191, 193, 195–6, 199,
    201, 263, 265
Métis Federation, 3, 7, 21, 65, 122
Meynaud, Jean, 184
middle class, 7, 31
Mines and Technical Surveys, Department
    of, 189
ministers, 3, 9, 38, 41, 60, 133, 136–7, 160,
    187; preoccupation with departmental
    issues, 66
Ministries of State, 99
mobilization, funnel of, 6 (Figure 1–1)
Moe, Terry M., 179–85
Monroe, Denis, 88
Montreal Suffrage Association, 86
movements, trans-national, 85
Mowat, Sir Oliver, 35
multinational corporations, 103

National Aboriginal Conference (Australia),
    124, 126
National Anti-Poverty Association, 197
National Assembly (Québec), 50, 255
National Cancer Institute, 94

National Citizens' Coalition, 157, 162–5
passim, 171, 173
National Economic Conference (1985), 219
National Energy Board, interventions
before, 65, 185
National Energy Policy, 76, 103, 156
National Farmers' Union, 113, 123, 145,
223
National Indian Brotherhood, 7, 124, 126,
192
National Science and Engineering Research
Council, 138
native peoples' groups, 7, 21, 65, 98, 124,
128, 170, 197
Neilson, W.A., 124
networks, 97, 239
Nigeria, 117, 118, 119
non-decision making, 232, 233, 235
non-material rewards of pressure group
participation, 181, 182, 185
Nord, Douglas C., 77, 78
northern development policy, 104
Nova Scotia Fishermen's Association, 197
Nova Scotia Voluntary Planning, 224

oil lobby, 185–6
Oil Producers' Association of Canada, 185
Olson, Mancur, 128, 177–85 *passim*, 229,
232, 234
Ontario Federation of Hunters and Anglers,
90
Ontario Trappers' Association, 90
Ontario Waste Management Corporation,
124
On-to-Ottawa Trek, 246
organizational characteristics of pressure
groups, 11, 108, 110, 112–13, 114–16,
117, 122, 129, 139, 140, 157, 181, 201–5
Organization for Economic Co-operation
and Development, 103
Oxfam, 170

Paltiel, Kayyam Z., 21
Panitch, Leo, 216, 217, 218, 219, 220, 224
Parliament, 1, 3, 14, 16, 21, 25, 38, 46,
62, 71, 74, 75, 76, 81, 102, 103, 125,
155, 159–161, 165, 188, 210, 212, 248,
Chapter 11; committees, 60, 61, 62,
74–5, 77, 78–9, 160, 210, 253, 257–8,
268; free votes, 160; joint Committee on
Regulations and other Statutory
Instruments, 153; legitimacy, 210; private
members: *see* legislatures, private

members; role in policy process, 34, 50,
51, 70, 75–9, 208, 211, 212, 218, 222,
248, 253–5, 256–61, 272; task forces, 62,
78, 160, 259
patronage, 30, 111, 260
peace movement, 169, 264
peak associations, 64, 103, 214, 220, 221,
223, 244
Pearson, Lester, 66
pension revolt (1985 budget), 3
Petroleum Association for the Conservation
of the Environment, 104, 195
pharmaceutical industry, 125
Pharmaceutical Manufacturers' Association,
195
Piggot, Jean, 60, 255
Pimlott, Douglas H., 104
Planned Parenthood, 181
Plumptre, Beryl, 124, 182
pluralism, 70, 96, 211, 212, 216; Chapter
10, particularly 227–31; defined, 227,
246
pluralists, 13, 65, 213
policy, as product of successive
administrative decisions, 56
policy committees, 9, 12, 17, 42, 68, 69,
70, 74, 77, 78, 93, 96–107 (100–1,
Figures 4–1 and 4–2), 112, 113, 118,
125–6, Chapter 6, 155, 165, 167, 173,
187, 189, 199, 208–10, 221, 222, 226,
234–5, 239, 241–7, 248, 271, 272;
defined, 98–9; provincial, 167; supporting
line agencies, 69, 74, 133
policy community, food policy, 101 (Figure
4–2), 102, 112–13, 116, 145, 167
policy environment, 16, 109–10, 129,
149–50, 155, 173–5, 201, 242
policy field, 106, 131
policy institutions, changing roles, 21, 51,
62
policy language, 49, 50, 151, 256
policy-makers: *see* Cabinet, ministers,
political leaders, senior officials
policy-making institutions, 21, 22–3 (Table
2–1); problem of overload, 66
policy process: changes in, 41, 54, 62,
70–1, 165, 174–5; group intervention in,
2, 13, 15, 17, 45, 54, 58–9 (Table 3–2),
60, 70, 98, 114, 131, 168, 173–5, 267,
271; impact of changes on pressure
groups, 21, 33–5, 63; in colonial period,
24–5, 30, 50; knowledge, 115, 142,
187–91; lengthiness, 70; more dynamic,

70, 243, 259; public involvement in, 49, 70, 271, 272; sensitivity to local needs, 29, 31–7, 41; structure, 156

political communication, 87, 107, 114, 119, 123, 213

political culture, impact on group behaviour, 53, 85–6, 166, 182

political leaders, 34, 60, 112, 146, 155, 161, 167

political parties, 1, 4, 8, 9, 13, 16, 21, 24, 30, 34–8, 39, 46, 49, 50, 51, 52, 53, 55, 111, 122, 161–5, 184, 208–9, 210, 212, 235, 260, 274

political system, impact on pressure group behaviour and structure, 16, 33–5, 61, 84, 128–9

politicians, 50, 131, 146, 148, 160

Pollution Probe, 124, 188–90, 192

positional politics, 146, 149, 151

post-pluralism, 227, 234–47

Potter, Allen, 127

poultry marketing groups, 116

pressure group-agency dependence, 69, 70

pressure group-agency relations, 14, 40, 41, 44–5, 56, 60, 61, 68, 69–70, 77, 79, 98, 110–11, 123, 124, 132, 133, 134–5, 137–45, 149, 186, 189, 209, 240, 243–4

pressure group communications, content, 90, 136, Chapters 6 and 7 *passim*

pressure group legitimacy, 9, 10, 12, 25, 38, 41, 53–4, 55, 56, 147, 153, 158, 176, 180, 191, 208, 214, 235

pressure group objectives, 115, 116, 117, 122, 127, 130, 131, 135–6, 176, 180, 201, 203

pressure group studies, 1, 13, 14, 16, 84, 96, 108; American, 84, 96, 211, 228, 232, 238, 251; comparative studies, 84, 85, 129, 238, 240; Europe, 96–7, 228, 249; *see also* pluralism, corporatism

pressure group tactics, 9, 60, 61, 67, 78, 80, 85–6, 105, 109, 110, 115, 116–17, 118, 123, 125, 126, 127, 135, 136, 138, 140–3, 144, 145, 153, 156, 166, 174–5, 187, 189, 193, 194–5

pressure groups: adaptiveness, 21, 46, 60, 81, 84, 85, 109, 110, 111, 126, 129, 138, 165, 246; and elections, 160–5; and Parliament, 60, 75, 79, 188, 209–10, 254; and privatization, 95; as index of political power, 2, 108, 109–10; changes in form and behaviour, 33–5, 80; cross-system variations, 85, 86–7; defined,

3–12; defining characteristics, 3–4; distinguished from government, 8–11; distinguished from interest groups, 4–8; impact of public attitudes to development, 54; impact on democratic government, 1, 2, 3, 4, 15, 16, 17, 18, 21, 27, 109, 198, 199, Chapters 9–11 *passim*; in colonial period, Chapter 2; inequalities among, 144, 145, 171–2, 208, 211, 234, 235, 246, 261, 267, 269, 274; influence in policy process, 1, 3, 4, 13, 15, 20, 21, 24, 45, 53, 54, 60–1, 68, 72, 95, 117, 173–5, 184, 208, 255; influence on foreign governments, 168–70; internal capacity, 128, 148, 150, 157, 267; internal operations, 176; international influences on, 29–30, 31; non-partisanship, 39, 53; non-political activities, 5, 115, 178; proliferation, 40, 61, 62, 63–4, 80, 136, 205, 261; relationship to political system, 12, 13, 32–3, 40, 88, 97, 105, 108, 111–12, 129, 149, 164–5, 174–5, 198, 199, 208, 211, 266; resources, 10, 11, 38, 98, 109, 116, 122–3, 127, 130, 131, 136, 144, 152–3, 156, 157, 170, 172, 174–5, 176, 181, 185–200, 201, 203, 246, 266–70; role in economic management, 95, 155, 215; seen as new political force, 64

Presthus, Robert, 13, 14, 25, 53, 60, 84, 87, 109, 216, 217

Prime Minister, 1, 55, 167, 251; overview role, 66, 274

Prime Minister's Office, 135, 167

prisoners' aid associations, 28, 30, 33, 94

Privy Council Office, 67, 99, 135, 220, 222

Process of Government, The, 13

professional associations, 4, 29, 49, 51, 52, 111, 115, 195, 197, 235

professionalism, in interest representation, 143

professions, impact on policy role of politicians, 50–1

provincial governments, 1, 47–8, 103, 135, 136, 193

public agenda, 166, 175, 235

public debate, 62, 118, 126, 130, 135, 149, 155, 161, 166, 198, 208, 270

public hearings, 158–9, 271

public interest, 12, 56, 65, 87, 93, 140, 161, 179, 200, 210, 212, 230, 232, 273, 274

public-interest groups, 128, 171–3, 174–5, 183, 194, 195, 196, 197, 267, 268, 270

publicity, avoidance of, 62, 140
public opinion: as means of influencing
  policy-makers, 3, 67, 110, 118, 123, 132,
  147, 154, 156–65, 170, 172, 208; attitude
  to pressure groups, 53, 54, 55, 64
public service: neutral competence, 55, 66,
  73–5; role in policy process, 1, 112, 125,
  132, 208
Pyrcz, Gregory, 273

Québec, anglophones, 8; language
  legislation, 77; nationalist groups, 21;
  'Summit', 220, 223–4

Rankin, T. Murray, 153
ratepayers associations, 8
Red Cross, 170
Regional Economic Expansion, Department
  of, 10, 44,
regionalism, impact on pressure groups, 86,
  167, 180, 202–3, 240
regulatory boards, 62, 93, 94, 116, 127,
  137, 171, 200, 241, 268, 271
religious groups, 32, 123, 196, 246
responsibility to participate, 182–3
Revenue Canada, 246
Richardson, J., 238, 239
Ripley, Randall B., 236
Robertson, Norman, 40, 55, 169
Robinson, Ian, 219, 224
Robinson, Svend, 161
Roman, Andrew, 67
routinization of policy, 105, 107, 236–7,
  242
Rowat, Donald C., 153
Royal Commission on Bilingualism and
  Biculturalism, 7
Royal Commission on Financial
  Management and Accountability
  (Lambert), 73
Royal Commission on the Economic Union
  and Canada's Development Prospects
  (Macdonald Commission), 158–9
Rush, Michael, 77, 79
Rusty Ford Owners' Association, 8

Salisbury, Robert H., 127, 234
Saskatchewan Grain Growers' Association,
  147
Saskatchewan Wheat Pool, 116
Schattschneider, E.E., 231, 233–7, 244
Schmitter, Philippe, 213, 214, 215, 216,
  222, 223, 224, 227
Schwartz, Mildred C., 13, 110

Science and Technology, Ministry of State
  for, 223
Science Council of Canada, 138, 222
SCITEC, 222–3
sealing, campaign against, 103, 157, 170,
  194, 264
sectoral representation, 17–18, 24, 33,
  37–8, 40, 43–4, 51, 53, 54, 111, 161,
  184, 209, 211, 231, 245, 248, 248–56,
  261, 273
sectoral tensions within groups, 202
selective benefits (selective inducements),
  115, 117, 118, 128, 177–9, 180, 181,
  184, 185, 193, 195, 205
Selznick, Philip, 114
Senate, 160
senior officials, policy role, 1, 3, 9, 15, 35,
  40, 41, 55, 56, 60, 72–3, 125, 131,
  132–3, 188, 221
Shortt, Adam, 40
Simeon, Richard, 165–6
Small Business, Minister of State for, 64
Smith, Larry, 140
socialization, 182, 183
Social Science Federation of Canada, 90,
  104, 138, 139, 144, 223
Social Sciences and Humanities Research
  Council of Canada, 138, 139, 223
societal corporatism, 215–15
Solicitor-General, 139
solidary groups, 5, 8, 32, 37, 68, 176
solidary interests, 5, 6, 30, 52, 65, 113,
  229; defined, 5
Sons of Temperance, 32
spatial representation, 16–17, 18, 24, 34,
  40, 51, 53, 54, 161, 209, 211, 231, 245,
  248, 249–56, 261, 272
special interest state, 2, 54, 233, 234, 273
specialization, 42, 97, 98, 111, 112, 113,
  209, 210, 234, 240, 250, 272
staff, 10, 30, 32, 38, 41, 45, 62, 116, 119,
  122, 123, 124, 127, 135, 138, 139, 146,
  186, 190–1, 201–5
Stanbury, Robert, 161
Stanfield, Robert, 1, 2, 3, 13, 16, 21,
  248–9, 261
state, relationship to pressure group system,
  4, 12, 40, 45, 88, 97, 105, 108, 109,
  111–12, 213, 214, 215, 225, 227, 228,
  238
State, Secretary of, 138–9, 268
state corporatism, 214–15, 238
Statistics Canada, 185
Steele, Ernest, 75

student groups, 21
sub-governments, 97, 98, 99, 103, 105, 107, 113, 131, 145-9, 150, 175, 209, 236, 237, 238, 239-42, 245, 246, 272
Sulphur Development Institute of Canada, 197-8
Supply and Services, Department of, 113
Swaigen, John, 170-3 *passim.*
system-specific pressure group behaviour and structure, 84, 85, 86, 95, 96, 109, 116

Task Force on the Atlantic Fishery, 95
tax policy, 165
Taylor, K.W., 55, 56
technostructure, 46-7, 50-3, 61, 81, 91, 102, 110, 111, 134, 209; defined, 48-9
temperance movement, 31, 90, 147-8, 170
Thorburn, H.G., 62, 166
Tier I and Tier II, 219, 224, 243
Timsit, Gerard, 49
Towers, Graham, 40
trade associations, 87, 90
Transport, Canada Department of, 67, 102
Transport 2000, 181
Treasury Board, 67, 99, 135, 222
tripartism, 215, 216, 217, 218, 220, 222, 223, 238, 240
Trudeau, Pierre Elliott, 72, 218, 224
Truman, David, 13, 64, 176, 228, 230-1, 232, 234
typologies of groups, 15, 17, 84, 108, 114, 127-9, 176

Union of Nova Scotia Municipalities, 53, 88, 193
United Auto Workers of Canada, 213-14
United Farmers of Alberta, 37, 217
United Grain Growers, 116
United Nations Human Rights Committee, 170

United States: and public policy in Canada, 103; Canadian lobbying in, 168-70; congressional committees, 97, 236, 240; political action committees, 163; pressure groups, 2, 13, 51, 54, 60, 76, 84, 97, 127, 156, 157, 160, 162, 163, 173, 212, 216, 228-34, 235, 238, 241, 266; U.S. pressure groups' influence on Canadian groups, 15, 31, 171
upper class influence in pressure groups, 235
Urban Affairs, Ministry of State for, 44, 106, 199

Vancouver business community, lobbying for transcontinental railroad, 89
Veterans' Affairs, Department of, 56
voluntarism, 45, 85, 270
voluntary associations, 9, 30, 31-2, 33, 34, 94, 195, 235

water policy, 189
Way Ahead, The, 220
wealth of groups: *see* financial resources of groups
Weaver, Sally M., 124, 126
Wheat Board, 102
Whitaker, R., 216
White Paper on Employment and Incomes (Government of Canada), 55
Wiener, Celine, 49
Women's Christian Temperance Union, 32, 86
women's movement, 7, 21, 31-2, 63, 148, 160, 170
women's suffrage movement, 31, 85, 86, 90, 147-8, 170
World University Service, 124

Yukon Conservation Authority, 65